Money and Schools

For both aspiring and experienced education leaders in school budgeting, finance, and resource management courses, *Money and Schools* explains and demonstrates the relationship between money and equality of educational opportunity. Grounded in research and best practices, this book provides a broad overview of school finance, budgeting, and resource allocation, as well as a detailed examination of day-to-day funding operations. Full of rich pedagogical features—such as chapter-by-chapter case studies, point/counterpoint discussions, and portfolio exercises—this accessible and engaging book offers strong connections to real-world experiences and detailed information on pre-K–12 funding history, concepts, and current operations.

New to this edition:

- Cutting edge research on the relationship of money and student learning outcomes, alterations to state aid distribution formulas, new federal education initiatives, and a changing landscape in school finance litigation.
- New concepts that have gained traction since the last edition of the book, including school choice and privatization, Common Core State Standards, value-added teacher evaluation, and growth of online options at the K–12 level.
- Updated and enhanced web resources and recommended reading lists that are aligned with the key concepts and content of each chapter, in addition to online instructor resources.

Faith E. Crampton is President and CEO of Crampton & Associates, an education consulting firm, who retired as Associate Professor of Education Finance and Policy at the University of Wisconsin-Milwaukee.

R. Craig Wood is Professor of Educational Administration and Policy at the University of Florida and Chair of the National Education Finance Conference.

David C. Thompson is Professor and Chair of the Department of Educational Leadership at Kansas State University where he holds the Elvon G. Skeen Endowed Chair for Education.

Money and Schools

Sixth Edition

Faith E. Crampton, R. Craig Wood and David C. Thompson

R Routledge
Taylor & Francis Group

NEW YORK AND LONDON

Sixth edition published 2015
by Routledge
711 Third Avenue, New York, NY 10017

and by Routledge
2 Park Square, Milton Park, Abingdon, Oxon, OX14 4RN

Routledge is an imprint of the Taylor & Francis Group, an informa business

© 2015 Taylor & Francis

First edition published by Eye On Education 1998
Fifth edition published by Eye On Education 2012

Library of Congress Cataloging in Publication Data
Money and schools/by Faith E. Crampton, R. Craig Wood, and
    David C. Thompson. — Sixth edition.
    pages cm
    David C. Thompson is listed as the first author on the title page of the
    previous edition.
    Includes bibliographical references and index.
    1. School budgets—United States—Handbooks, manuals, etc.
    2. Schools—United States—Accounting—Handbooks, manuals, etc.
    3. Education—United States—Finance—Handbooks, manuals, etc.
    I. Wood, R. Craig. II. Thompson, David C., 1951- III. Title.
    LB2830.2.T56 2015
    371.2'06—dc23
    2014031068

ISBN: 978-1-138-02505-9 (hbk)
ISBN: 978-1-138-02506-6 (pbk)
ISBN: 978-1-315-77539-5 (ebk)

Typeset in Sabon and Helvetica Neue
by Florence Production Ltd, Stoodleigh, Devon, UK

Brief Contents

Contents

PART II

Operationalizing School Money   **107**

4   School Funds: Accountability and Professionalism   109

Figures

Tables

About the Authors

Dr. Faith E. Crampton's professional career has spanned public education, senior administrative positions in state government, senior research and policy positions in national education and legislative organizations, and graduate faculty positions in public and private research universities. She is past President of the Fiscal Issues, Policy, and Education Finance Special Interest Group of the American Educational Research Association and a past member of the Board of Directors of the American Education Finance Association and the Board of Directors for the University Council for Educational Administration's Center for the Study of Education Finance. She currently serves on the Board of Advisors for the National Education Finance Conference where she is a Distinguished Fellow of Research and Practice. She has published widely in leading academic as well as practitioner-oriented journals, such as the *Journal of Education Finance*, West's *Education Law Reporter*, *Journal of Educational Administration*, *Educational Considerations*, *National Association of Secondary School Principals Journal*, *NASSP Bulletin*, *Journal of School Business Management*, *Journal of the Council of Education Facilities Planners International*, *Multicultural Learning and Teaching*, and *School Business Affairs*, in addition to authoring numerous monographs, reports, book chapters, and policy briefs. She is Executive Editor of *Educational Considerations* and a Legislative Editor for the *Journal of Education Finance*. She coauthored the groundbreaking book, *Saving America's School Infrastructure*, with a foreword by the Honorable Senator Edward M. Kennedy. Dr. Crampton has presented scholarly papers and given invited presentations to national and international research and policy organizations, such as the American Education Finance Association, American Educational Research Association, British Educational Management and Administration Society, Center for Budget Policy and Priorities, Council of Education Facilities Planners International, Council of State Governments, Education Commission of the States, Education Writers Association, NAACP, National Conference of Professors of Educational Administration, National Conference of State Legislatures, National Education Association, University Council for Educational Administration, and U.S. Department of Education. Currently, Dr. Crampton is an education consultant serving as President and CEO of Crampton & Associates, a firm specializing in rigorous, results-oriented education finance research and policy analysis. She holds a Ph.D. in Educational Policy and Leadership from The Ohio State University and an M.B.A. from Marquette University. She began her career as a public school teacher.

Dr. R. Craig Wood is one of the leading scholars in the field of financing public education in America. He is currently Professor of Educational Administration and Policy at the University of Florida. His career has spanned public school classroom teacher, school district business manager, and assistant superintendent for finance for school districts across the nation. Prior to his present position he was a professor of educational administration at Purdue University. He is one of the most prolific authors in America regarding the funding of public education. His publications record includes more than 250 book chapters, monographs, and scholarly journal articles including the American Education Finance Association's *Annual Yearbooks* and the Education Law Association's *Handbook of School Law* series. His books include *Education Finance Law*, *Fiscal Leadership for Schools*, and *Principles of School Business Management*. He serves on the editorial boards of *Education Law Reporter*, *Journal of Education Finance*, *Education Law and Policy Review*, and *Educational Considerations*. He has published his research in such journals as the *Journal of Education Finance*, the *Kentucky Law Review*, the *Saint Louis University Public Law Review*, the *University of Arkansas Law Review*, the *Brigham Young University Education and Law Journal*, and *Education Law and Policy Review*. He has conducted education finance litigation workshops for the National Conference on State Legislatures and the National Association of Attorneys General. He has served as the lead expert involving state constitutional challenges to financing public education in many states over the years. He has consulted with over two dozen state legislatures regarding the financing of public education. He is a past President of the American Education Finance Association as well as its Executive Director. He is currently the Vice President of the Education Law Association housed at Cleveland Marshall College of Law, Cleveland, Ohio. He serves as the Chair of the National Education Finance Conference. He holds an Ed.D. and M.A. Ed. in Educational Administration from the Virginia Polytechnic Institute and State University and a B.S. *cum laude* from Campbell University in North Carolina.

Dr. David C. Thompson's 40-year professional career has spanned school teacher, principal, superintendent, and the professoriate. His chapters and journal articles appear in prestigious venues including the *Journal of Education Finance*, West's *Education Law Reporter*, and more. He has authored fifteen books including six editions of *Money and Schools*, along with coauthoring *Saving America's School Infrastructure* (2003) with the foreword by the late Honorable Senator Edward M. Kennedy. Dr. Thompson's scholarly reputation has led to service as advisor or expert witness for various state departments of education, state legislatures, attorneys general, and attorneys and litigants in school finance totaling thousands of school districts in more than 26 states. His research in public school finance and litigation has been presented by him to many national organizations including the American Education Finance Association, Education Law Association, American Educational Research Association, National Conference of State Legislatures, National Center for Education Statistics, National Education Association, American Federation of Teachers, and more. His work has also been presented to groups such as the National Association of Attorneys General. He is cited in nearly 500 instances in national law journals, including such influential locations as the *Columbia Journal of Law and Social Problems*, *Cornell*

Journal of Law and Public Policy, Harvard Journal of Law and Public Policy, Stanford Law Review, and *Yale Law and Policy Review,* and he was footnoted in the United States Supreme Court ruling in *BOE of Oklahoma City Public Schools.* He has received numerous national awards, including the University Council for Educational Administration's *Award of Appreciation for Sustained and Meritorious Service,* the *Outstanding Education Research Award* at Kansas State University, the *Distinguished Fellow of Research and Practice* award from the National Education Finance Conference, and the *Lifetime Achievement Award* also from NEFC. Dr. Thompson holds an Ed.D. in educational administration from Oklahoma State University and post-doctoral work in education law from Harvard. He has been at Kansas State University since 1987, serving from 1989 to 2006 as Founding Co-Director of the UCEA Center for Education Finance, and serving continuously as Professor and Chair of the Department of Educational Leadership since 1993, for which he was named the University Presidential Outstanding Department Head (2012). In 2013, he was appointed to the Kansas State University Academy of Fellows. He also holds the Elvon G. Skeen Endowed Chair for Education.

Preface

Welcome to the sixth edition of *Money and Schools*! To those who used the earlier editions, we welcome you back. To new users, we offer a special welcome and hope you will be able to satisfy your interest in school finance and resource management through this book. As was true with each of the previous five editions, we have again attempted to shed new light on the critical needs of the field in a way that is clear, precise, and engaging. Our reasoning for this approach is simple—we believe that how schools are funded is of critical importance in today's world of high stakes accountability, and we believe that effective educational leaders must understand the relationship between money and the aims of education and be responsive to public perceptions about how fiscal resources are utilized. In our view, the topic is vibrant, and the need for clarity and precision cannot be overstated.

Our approach in this book is due in meaningful part to who we are as authors. Our professional histories as practitioners and university professors permeate the book by reflecting on how we believe new generations of school leaders should be prepared. Who we are therefore says a great deal about what readers should expect from this sixth edition of *Money and Schools*. Plainly put, we are experienced scholars, researchers, and public school practitioners, and we believe the impact of our collective history is important to readers' willingness to accept what we say in this book. We are scholars because we work in major research universities, carrying out scholarly agendas and teaching courses in educational leadership, specifically in school finance-related issues. We are researchers, within and outside our university affiliations, engaging in the search for new knowledge and best practices in educational leadership and school finance. It is equally important that we have deep and extensive practitioner roots. Collectively, we have served as superintendents, assistant superintendents, school business managers, grant managers, principals, and classroom teachers in public school systems across the United States. We have also provided extensive consulting work on behalf of school districts, and for more than two decades we have been involved in court cases in numerous states as expert witnesses on behalf of plaintiffs or defendants seeking objective analysis of funding for schools. The especially critical aspect of our professional histories is that we have not written this book solely from a theory base, nor have we used the book as a bully pulpit to advance any political views. Instead, who we are relates to this book by virtue of the fact that we are practitioners who have done what readers are most interested in—built budgets, cut budgets, raised taxes, faced angry constituents, hired and fired staff, and experienced the accountability of high stakes student testing. As a result, we believe readers' experience with this book will be enhanced by knowing us for who we are—we are school people like most of our readers.

THE CURRENT CONTEXT

The context of schooling and its funding remains in a state of flux. Although the federal No Child Left Behind (NCLB) law was enacted in 2001 with high hopes for raising academic achievement, particularly among students historically considered at risk, forty-two states have now received waivers for more flexibility in meeting its goals. While the reauthorization of NCLB languishes in the U.S. Congress, the U.S. Department of Education introduced a competitive grant program for states in 2009, called Race to the Top (RTTT), whose major goal is also to improve student achievement. RTTT differs substantially from NCLB in that it is voluntary and provides funding for approximately half of states. However, of late, much more attention has been given to the Common Core Standards (CCS) initiative, a joint effort of the Council of Chief State School Officers and the National Governors Association. In 2007, they introduced this initiative to encourage states to apply consistent, high standards for student achievement. Although the standards have been adopted by many states, their implementation remains rocky. At the same time, there has developed a broader backlash against what is viewed as excessive student testing and the accompanying use of instructional time for test preparation at the expense of other learning activities. Still, many states are pressing forward with mandates for greater school and district accountability, including tying teacher evaluation to student test scores. School leaders face additional challenges as many states continue to reduce education funding or provide minimal increases in response to a slow economic recovery from the 2007–2009 economic recession. Together, these conditions require schools and districts to do more with fewer resources. Although our profession has always believed that education is a high stakes enterprise in which all children deserve equal educational opportunity, the result of new demands and uncertain funding drives home the need for school leaders to understand how critical effective leadership is to student success.

The current context demands that school leaders must be highly effective, and, to that end, a critically important skill is understanding the relationship between not only opportunity and money but also outcomes and money. The widely adopted Interstate School Leaders Licensure Consortium's (ISLLC) standards for school leadership preparation, authored by the Council of Chief State School Officers (CCSSO), state that all leaders should be competent in six standards, wherein fiscal resources play a critical role in the achievement of acceptable student outcomes. Although CCSSO is in the process of reviewing and refreshing the standards, many states still work from the original version, as follows:

- Standard 1: A school administrator is an educational leader who promotes the success of all students by facilitating the development, articulation, implementation, and stewardship of a vision of learning that is shared and supported by the school community.

- Standard 2: A school administrator is an educational leader who promotes the success of all students by advocating, nurturing, and sustaining a school culture and instructional program conducive to student learning and staff professional growth.
- Standard 3: A school administrator is an educational leader who promotes the success of all students by ensuring management of the organization, operations, and resources for a safe, efficient, and effective learning environment.
- Standard 4: A school administrator is an educational leader who promotes the success of all students by collaborating with families and community members, responding to diverse community interests and needs, and mobilizing community resources.
- Standard 5: A school administrator is an educational leader who promotes the success of all students by acting with integrity, fairness, and in an ethical manner.
- Standard 6: A school administrator is an educational leader who promotes the success of all students by understanding, responding to, and influencing the larger political, social, economic, legal, and cultural context.

Effective school leaders, then, are key to meeting state and federal mandates for the academic success of all students. The ISLLC standards clearly support the same end, and in equally clear fashion the standards call for school leaders to understand the current economic and fiscal context of schools and its connection to the outcomes of teaching and learning. As a result, the context of this sixth edition of *Money and Schools* is that federal law demands equality of educational opportunity and outcomes for all students; that school performance accountability expectations at the state level continue to increase even while fiscal resources may not; and that the education profession must embrace rigorous performance accountability.

FEATURES OF THE NEW EDITION

Based upon feedback from reviewers and textbook adopters, the content of sixth edition is organized via the same overarching structure as the previous edition. The volume is divided into three parts:

- Part I: Overview of Broad Concepts
- Part II: Operationalizing School Money
- Part III: A View of the Future

Part I consists of three chapters:

- Chapter 1. Schools, Values, and Money
- Chapter 2. Funding Schools: A Policy Perspective
- Chapter 3. Basic Funding Structures

Part II consists of eight chapters:

- Chapter 4. School Funds: Accountability and Professionalism
- Chapter 5. Budget Planning
- Chapter 6. Budgeting for Personnel
- Chapter 7. Budgeting for Instruction
- Chapter 8. Budgeting for Student Activities
- Chapter 9. Budgeting for School Infrastructure
- Chapter 10. Budgeting for Transportation and Food Service
- Chapter 11. Legal Liability and Risk Management

Part III consists of two chapters:

- Chapter 12. Site-Based Leadership
- Chapter 13. The Future of School Funding

Together, these three major sections resemble an inverted pyramid, starting with the broad social context of schools and continuing into specialized examinations of various elements of school budgeting in individual chapters.

At the broadest level, it is important for school leaders to understand that money and student achievement are related (Chapter 1). It is also critical to know that education's current condition is a product of a long history that involves the interplay of complex aspects of our cultural and governmental heritage (Chapter 2). The next logical step is to review sources of revenue and expenditure (Chapter 3), in that frustrations with and misunderstanding of school budgets often can be traced back to these areas.

After this broad overview, Part II offers a detailed view of daily funding operations. Chapter 4 explains how accountability, ethical behavior, and professionalism are essential qualities of effective school leaders, and that understanding the flow of money into schools and its proper handling is the basis for all sound decision making. School budget planning (Chapter 5) is next addressed from the perspective of how budgets are built, with subsequent chapters exploring in greater detail the major elements of budget construction. Specifically, issues of budgeting for personnel (Chapter 6), budgeting for instruction (Chapter 7), and budgeting for student activities (Chapter 8) are elements that cut across sound budgeting behaviors at both district and school levels. The same can be said about budgeting for school infrastructure (Chapter 9), budgeting for transportation and food service (Chapter 10), and the need to budget for liability and risk management (Chapter 11).

The third section looks to the future. Clearly, site-based leadership will continue to offer schools districts an effective structure to meet the continuing and increasing demands surrounding accountability and student outcomes, both of which have strong budget implications (Chapter 12). Finally, a look to the future of school funding is essential (Chapter 13) because schools and society continue to face radical change.

Each chapter opens with a challenge and chapter drivers. The challenge is a provocative quote on the subject of the chapter that is designed to pique student interest and curiosity. The chapter drivers consist of a series of questions related to the content of the chapter. Students are asked to reflect upon these as they read the chapter. Chapters end with a point/counterpoint discussion, a case study, portfolio exercises, web resources, and a recommended reading list to further engage students:

- The challenge, chapter drivers, and content of the chapter prepare students for the Point–Counterpoint exercise. This exercise represents a debate on a major issue in the chapter. As such, it is a stimulating student activity that can be conducted in a face-to-face class or in an online setting.
- Each case study presents a situation that school leaders actually experience in their day-to-day work, and it is centered on one or more resource-related issues presented in the chapter. Students are asked to answer a series of questions about the case that offer opportunities for reflection, analysis, and critical thinking. These can be answered individually or in groups. Like the Point–Counterpoint exercise, discussion of the case study, guided by the questions, can be conducted in a face-to-face setting or online course.
- A number of school leadership preparation programs ask students to assemble a portfolio of their work as a capstone project. The portfolio exercises were developed with that requirement in mind. In addition, individual instructors will find that the portfolio exercises lend themselves to course projects that can be engaged in individually or in small groups.
- Web resources and the recommended reading list provide students with options to advance and broaden the knowledge base they have gained through the chapter. These resources can also be useful to students as they prepare for Point–Counterpoint debates, answer case study questions, and complete portfolio exercises. The recommended reading list also provides instructors with suggestions for additional assigned readings on one or more topics in the chapter.

WHAT'S NEW IN THIS EDITION?

Changes to this new sixth edition center on critically reviewing and revising all content on the basis of absolute currency, analyzing continuing and emerging trends, and explicating the nearly unprecedented uncertainty of schools' political, economic, and social environment. More specifically, the sixth edition contains:

- Current and cutting edge research on the relationship between money on student outcomes.
- Elimination of some text, tables, and figures that either no longer fit current economic trends or which tend to become dated too quickly—notwithstanding, the text is still heavily data-driven since a deep grasp of school funding requires familiarity and comfort with fiscal data.
- Addition of new comprehensive tables, along with expanded and updated tables carried forward from the previous edition. Where appropriate, 50-state tables are provided for easy cross-state comparisons.

- Addition of new, visually appealing graphs and charts that distill complex information into an easy-to-understand format.
- New concepts that have gained traction since the last edition of this book.
- Updated and enhanced web resources and recommended reading lists that are aligned with the key concepts and content of each chapter. A number of the recommended readings are available online.
- Online instructor resources.

WHO SHOULD READ THIS BOOK

From its title, it is clear that this book is intended for both broad and specialized audiences. Choosing this book indicates that readers have a connection to schools that causes them to demonstrate a high level of interest in education's costs. Specifically, this book reaches out to school administrators, classroom teachers, school boards, and laypersons in the broader public. Although that sounds like everyone, each of these audiences has a different value for the book. Administrators will find that the material confirms their existing knowledge, reminds them of things not considered recently, and extends their knowledge by engaging recent federal and state education reform movements. We have long advocated that the first group of people who should know more about school funding is classroom teachers. We also believe school board members will benefit from this book. Finally, laypeople can benefit from this book, in that we are all taxpayers. So, in the end, this book represents a practical resource anyone for who wants a better understanding of school finance, budgeting, and resource management.

HOW CAN YOU LEARN MORE?

If you find your interest piqued by issues in this new sixth edition, there are many ways to learn more about money and schools. Obvious ways are reading other books and taking classes relating to school funding. Several excellent textbooks are available that go more deeply into the issues introduced here—we've authored several such books. Higher education courses can be helpful in refreshing your knowledge or extending your grasp of these issues. Depending on your current employment and career goals, internships with practicing administrators can be a great learning aid. Other ways to learn more include attending state department of education budget workshops, as well as seminars conducted by state professional groups such as administrator organizations and school boards associations. A number of such seminars are offered online as "webinars." Valuable resource people also exist right at home, such as your school district's chief financial officer or business manager, who is required to carry out budgeting as a daily activity. Finally, you can contact us.

Acknowledgments

As with previous editions, the authors acknowledge that no book is ever written without the valuable assistance of others. Much credit for all that is good about this sixth edition goes not only to each of us as coauthors, but also to manuscript reviewers and resource people whose ability to discern and clarify a variety of issues proved invaluable.

The authors wish to thank the following people who contributed to the sixth edition of *Money and Schools* in important ways. To begin, the authors are grateful to reviewers of the previous five editions: William Andrekopoulos, Cardinal Stritch University; Eric Bartleson, Mankato State University; Michael Boone, Southwest Texas State University; Dennis Brennan, University of the Pacific; Kathleen Brown, University of Missouri–St. Louis; William E. Camp, University of North Texas; Carlos Cruz, Texas A&M University–Kingsville; Leonard Etlinger, Chicago State University; Joe Flora, University of South Carolina; Gerald Fowler, Shippensburg University; John Freeman, University of Alabama; Frank Gallant, University of Idaho; Catherine Glascock, Ohio University; W. B. Haselton, University of Louisville; Jack Herlihy, Eastern Kentucky University; Seth Hirshorn, University of Michigan; Albert Jurenas, Florida Atlantic University; Larry K. Kelly, Arizona School Administrators Association; Dennis Lauro, Assistant Superintendent, Pelham, NY; T. C. Mattocks, Idaho State University; Joseph Natale, Superintendent, Warwick Valley, NY; Doug Nelson, Washington State University; William Owings, Old Dominion University; Ray Proulx, University of Vermont; Augustina Reyes, University of Houston; R. Anthony Rolle, University of South Florida; Ross Rubenstein, Georgia State University; William Salwaechter, Oklahoma State University; Catherine Sielke, University of Georgia; Carlee Escue Simon, University of Cincinnati; David Steele, Seattle Pacific University; Ed Stehno, Fort Hays State University; Donald Tetreault, University of South Carolina; Bill Thornton, University of Nevada, Reno; Herb Torres, Las Cruces Public Schools, New Mexico; Gary C. Wenzel, State University of West Georgia; P. Allen Whitlatch, South Dakota State University; and Richard Wiggall, Illinois State University.

The authors are also grateful for thoughtful book reviews and other extended commentary on prior editions from Carla Edlefson, Professor of Educational Administration at Ashland University, Richard King, Professor of Educational Leadership at the University of South Florida, Jeffrey Maiden, Professor of Educational Administration at University of Oklahoma, and Randall Vesely, Assistant Professor of Educational Leadership at University of Toledo.

Gratitude is especially expressed to the reviewers of this sixth edition: Jeffrey Maiden, University of Oklahoma; Maureen McClure, University of Pittsburgh; Lenford C. Sutton, Illinois State University; and Randall Vesely, University of Toledo.

Finally, we continue to be humbly grateful for the longstanding acceptance of our work by the field, whose opinions we value most of all.

PART

I

Overview of Broad Concepts

CHAPTER 1

Schools, Values, and Money

THE CHALLENGE

The principal expresses the philosophy of his school this way: "We don't focus on what we can't do at this school; we focus on what we can do. And we do whatever it takes to get kids across the finish line." See, this principal is challenging the soft bigotry of low expectations. And that is the spirit of our education reform and the commitment of our country: *No dejaremos a ningún niño atrás.* We will leave no child behind.

George W. Bush (2004)[1]

CHAPTER DRIVERS

Please reflect upon the following questions as you read this chapter:

- What is the context of public education today?
- What is the emerging nature of schools?
- Where did schools come from?
- What should schools be doing?
- What are schools capable of doing?
- What is the effect of money on schools?
- Does money make a difference in student achievement?
- What happens when schools get more (or less) money?
- Where might public schools be headed?

---

1 *Washington Post*, "Text: President Bush's Acceptance Speech to the Republican National Convention," September 4, 2004, www.washingtonpost.com/wp-dyn/articles/A57466–2004Sep2.html.

THE CONTEXT OF PUBLIC EDUCATION TODAY

In previous editions of this textbook we have begun with the statement that the context of public education is undergoing dramatic change. We have argued that education—indeed all of global society—is being relentlessly restructured on a massive scale equal to many events from our past that history books now record as having reshaped the fate of entire nations. That statement continues to be true, and the pace of change has not only failed to slow, but instead gives every appearance of accelerating. As a result of such a seemingly eternal truth, we should consider the context of such change as we begin our study of money and schools—i.e., schools are not immune to today's economic, political, and social upheaval, and many observers would assert that our public education system is at risk.

The assertion that public schools might be endangered is rooted in issues that have been raised at all levels of society over the past several decades. Although the past is often subject to a romanticism that fails to objectively ask whether the world was ever rational and gentle, the past few decades have fomented a new tendency toward hostile challenges over a wide range of real and imaginary injustices—an adversarial approach that has led to a national culture that no longer seems to value civility, tolerance, social justice, or the common good. Recent national and state elections provide evidence of these "culture wars" where extremist candidates and commentators from both the political left and right accuse one another of being guilty of singlehandedly destroying the America they know and love. The breakdown of civility is evident in election results so tightly drawn as to divide the nation along bitter ideological lines such that challenging the outcomes of national, state—and even local—elections through the courts has become the norm. At its most fundamental level, this rift in society is based upon diametrically opposed views of the role of government, which includes the funding of public education.

School leaders are not spared this turmoil. As an integral part of modern society, public schools transmit culture and win approval (or scorn) for their perceived success in preparing future generations for living and working in a global context. Because the splinterings in society are increasingly irreconcilable, education today is caught more than ever among competing demands that propound the mission of schools from opposite ends of the political and social continuum. The questions arising from such a context are profound. For example, what are public schools becoming? For that matter, where did schools come from, and what does that say about what schools are today? Of profound importance are the contentious questions: What should schools be doing? What are schools capable of doing? These questions do not exist in a vacuum; often, the answers are the subject of partisan debates that encompass both conservative and liberal political agendas. Far too often, these debates end in gridlock rather than compromise, much less consensus, and it is the children who attend our public schools and dedicated educators who are the losers.

The struggle is grandly illustrated in contemporary terms by recent federal initiatives, such as the sweeping No Child Left Behind Act of 2001[2] (NCLB) and the

---

2 P.L. 107–110, No Child Left Behind Act of 2001.

selective, competitive Race to the Top (RTTT) grant program of 2009,[3] both of which have asserted confident answers to critical education policy questions like: What is the impact of money on schools? Do schools need more money? What actually happens when schools get more money? Yet, in the current dissonant social and political context, NCLB has come under attack, with 42 states now receiving waivers from its rigorous (or some might say burdensome and unreasonable) student achievement benchmarks,[4] while RTTT has been criticized, in part, because school children in fewer than half of the states have received funding.[5] More recently, a new set of academic standards, national in scope and referred to as the "Common Core,"[6] has emerged to equal parts of praise and criticism by education and legislative/political constituencies as well as the popular media. All of these challenges raise the ultimate question: Where is public education headed?

These are worrisome issues as we face an unpredictable future—issues that school leaders must be prepared to address. As a result, the rest of this chapter, along with Chapter 13, sets the stage for the critical importance of schools and money in challenging times. As we launch that discussion, it is important to acknowledge that adequate and equitable support of public schools is essential to the future of our nation, if for no other reason than the individual and collective wellbeing of the nation and world depend on preparing each new generation to take the economic, political, and social reins of leadership in a democratic society. As a result, this book sets forth a view of schools and money grounded in research and best practices. With that said, our journey begins with the context of public education because it is within that setting where school moneys are obtained and spent.

WHAT ARE SCHOOLS BECOMING?

A burning question on the minds of many people across the political spectrum is: What is the emerging nature of schools? Although the question is too complex to fully answer here, it is useful to raise the issue because speculating about the answer is fundamental to understanding schools and money as far into the future as we can see.

Where Did Schools Come From?

The battle for control of education is by no means new, although it has shown recent signs of escalation as the stakes for winners and losers have shifted over time in an

---

3 American Recovery and Reinvestment Act of 2009 (ARRA), Section 14005–6, Title XIV, P.L. 111–5; The White House, "Fact Sheet: The Race to the Top," News Release, November 4, 2009, Office of the Press Secretary, www.whitehouse.gov/the-press-office/fact-sheet-race-top; U.S. Department of Education, "Race to the Top Fund," http://www2.ed.gov/programs/racetothetop/index.html.

4 Michele McNeil, "NCLB Waivers: A State-by-State Breakdown," *Education Week*, February 25, 2014, www.edweek.org/ew/section/infographics/nclbwaivers.html.

5 Elaine Weiss, "Mismatches in Race to the Top Limit Educational Improvement" (Washington, DC: Economic Policy Institute, September 2013), www.epi.org/publication/race-to-the-top-goals.

6 For further information, see "Common Core State Standards Initiative," www.corestandards.org. Note that the Common Core State Standards were developed jointly by the National Governors Association and the Council of Chief State School Officers.

increasingly knowledge-based society. But it is important to recognize at the outset that part of the current struggle for control of schools stems from our national history in that people as a rule are resistant to change, particularly when change is perceived as threatening to their way of life. It is therefore an important insight to know that nothing, including resistance to change, exists without historical roots, and the past gives many clues into a vast array of otherwise loosely connected realities.[7]

The unique history of the United States has contributed much to current struggles over schools in that the structure of education today is the product of a long and tense evolutionary process. The history of American education began with the establishment of schools in the original colonies nearly 400 years ago. The first law formally requiring schools came into existence in 1642 with adoption of a law in Massachusetts requiring the town fathers to determine if children were being given adequate religious and occupational training. Similar action followed in several other colonies so that by 1720 laws mandating some amount of schooling were in place in Connecticut, Maine, New Hampshire, and Vermont.[8] These laws were destined to be broadened as the idea of enlightened self-government was added to the defense for requiring public education, giving birth to the now familiar democratic principles as argued by Thomas Jefferson, William Penn, and others who wielded great influence on the emerging nature of schooling in the new nation.

In addition to the practical reasons for encouraging public education, the intense isolation of the colonies and the later westward expansion were powerful contributors to the evolving structure of public schools. The original colonies were fiercely independent, even to the point of deciding separately whether they each would give financial support to the American Revolution. In the post-war era, the early Congress struggled with its lack of funds to pay war debts, much of which stemmed from intense resistance to any centralized government, and it was a harbinger of a politically mistrustful future that the early nation witnessed a bitter war of contrasting ideologies such as those of Hamilton and Jefferson regarding establishment of a strong federal government. Westward expansion, with its geographic isolationism, only exacerbated the independent streak of early Americans, leading to strong local views on how schools should be organized. Yet at the same time the nation's make-up was shifting dramatically in other ways with soaring immigration, establishment of great cities, and growing sentiment against child-labor abuse. Through a long series of complex events, the Common Schools Movement arose under early advocates like Horace Mann, so that public education somewhat resembling the structure of schools today began to emerge by 1840.

---

7 For a more detailed discussion, see David C. Thompson, R. Craig Wood, and David S. Honeyman, "Financing Public Schools in America: Federal, State, and Local Responses," in *Fiscal Leadership for Schools: Concepts and Practices*, 76–87 (New York: Longman, 1994).

8 Although innovative for their time, it is important to remember that early colonial schools bore little resemblance to the public schools of today. For instance, girls, African Americans, and Native Americans were generally excluded. The curriculum was decidedly religion-based, and tuition was charged limiting education to those who could afford it. See, Carl F. Kaestle, "Victory of the Common School Movement," *Historians on America* (Washington, DC: U.S. Embassy, 2008), http://iipdigital. usembassy.gov/st/english/publication/2008/04/20080423212501eaifas0.8516133.html#axzz30gqNday5.

Probably the most striking features of public schools in the growing nation were the frequency with which they were established and the localism which characterized them. The empty vastness of the nation led to the creation of thousands of tiny "one-room" schools. Although no one knows how many schools existed across the nation before a trend toward consolidation began, the number had to be at least equal to the number of towns in the states and territories at any given time. The only meaningful way to understand the staggering proliferation of schools is to look to the first formal attempts to tally public schools, with U.S. Department of Education data showing that in 1929 there were 238,306 elementary schools, of which 148,712 were one-teacher schools; and 23,930 secondary schools—a total of 248,117 schools—compared to 98,817 schools in 2010! These statistics go far in explaining the fiercely local nature of schooling, and speak loudly to why we still today find schools only two or three blocks apart with low enrollments across the United States. After all, if there were almost 250,000 schools, it stands to reason that there was a multitude of preferences for how schooling should be carried out, especially because states did not seek to regulate schools until well into the 20th century.

The evolution of public schools in the United States is, of course, far more complex than is presented here, but historic roots illustrate current realities. Just as children predictably internalize some of the same values taught to them during their own upbringing, the customs and culture of local communities are deeply held values that affect the nature of schools, and the stubborn pride of Americans in creating and preserving local traditions for schools is legendary. The desire for local control is well expressed by the continual fear of many modern rural school districts, as citizens hasten to charge, "as the school goes, so goes the town." Indeed, we have served as senior administrators in communities where countless school district patrons repeatedly told us with great anxiety, "If the school goes, the post office and the churches will follow close behind"—in other words, schools are the heart of the community in many people's minds, so much so that the strongest pillar of a community is perceived lost if schools close. Consequently, a strong sense of local tradition produces a fierce struggle at any cost to save schools, and the entirety of the struggle over education—be it racial integration, local taxes, curriculum, or school budgets—is rooted in the American tradition of local control and resistance to outside interference.

What Should Schools Be Doing?

Where schools came from is part of the answer to what schools are becoming, but another aspect of the question about what schools are becoming is wrapped up in the sub-question: What should schools be doing?

Although we have come a long way from the political and social isolation of the past, the insular nature of schools in the United States continues to stand as a reminder of the great difficulty of trying to reach consensus on what schools should be about. Almost any news report today chronicles some new dispute about schools, ranging from threats to withdraw fiscal support to impassioned calls for reforms because of some perceived breakdown in schools' effectiveness. Almost daily, administrators lose their jobs due to arguments over what schools should be doing. Teacher unions and professional negotiations become deeply mired in either restricting educational activities or in promoting programs of special interest. School board candidates often run on platforms of educational reform, and legislators are subjected to tremendous pressures from groups specifically organized to force (or prevent) changes in what schools are doing. No one is immune to such pressure, in large part because people believe that schools are critical to the nation's future—so much so that control of schools is tantamount to control of the future.

Historic opinions on what schools should do have centered mostly on issues relating to morality, democracy, and equality. Intense interest among the early colonies in preparing children for a morally upright life through religious teachings was noted previously. Leaders like Thomas Jefferson, Horace Mann, and many others weighed in, broadening the scope of education and arguing that an enlightened citizenry is the most effective curb against tyranny. More recently, concerns for equality of educational opportunity and social justice have been added to the aims of schooling. The landmark *Brown v. Board of Education* decision in 1954,[9] overturning the race-based doctrine of "separate but equal," was clear evidence of expanded concern about equality in education and all other aspects of the human condition. The Civil Rights Act of 1964 and the expansive civil rights laws that followed have had enormous educational implications, giving rise to a massive body of federal and state case law and statutes controlling expansive and far-reaching concepts, including gender equity, rights of students with disabilities, and rights of citizens under equal access provisions.

The ever-increasing likelihood for ideological conflict provides a window on current views regarding what schools should be doing, especially in context of the nature of equality of educational opportunity and social justice. Little disagreement exists about education as an engine for economic productivity, although ensuring equal access to educational opportunity provides fertile ground for disputes relating to equity. Critics charge that many students do not have access to economic-enhancing opportunities such as technology or higher education, which is then posited to ensure the perpetuation of disadvantaged populations far into the future—a position immediately attacked by philosophical and political opponents who forcefully invoke local choice to exceed or offer only a minimally adequate educational program. Even greater disagreement exists today about the role of education with regard to morality, particularly when issues infringe on parents' personal or religious beliefs related to topics such as human sexuality, or evolution vs. creationism and intelligent design. But it is still the broader issue of attempts to force uniformity on schools in social and academic equality that produces the greatest conflict regarding what schools should be about. Is it the role of schools to provide only a "minimum" level of educational opportunity, or is it education's role to provide exactly the same educational opportunities to all students? Or, is it the role of education to provide equal educational outcomes? There are no simple answers because the long-held tradition of local control of schools bumps up against more modern, expansive, and nuanced conceptions of social justice. Those who

---

9 374 U.S. 483 (1954).

argue for full enforcement of equal opportunity often assert that localism led to racially and economically segregated schools in the first place. This debate is carried out on multiple levels—courts struggle with lawsuits over school funding; legislatures receive intense pressure from political advocates of all stripes; and taxpayers revolt, while school boards, teachers, administrators, and children are caught in a tug-of-war ultimately resulting in diminished resources due to expensive litigation and lack of cooperation. In the end, there is no one voice speaking for what education should be doing because the many voices seek different and often conflicting ends.

What Are Schools Capable of Doing?

A critical, although oft overlooked, component of the current debate is consideration of what schools are actually capable of doing. Depending upon whom one asks, answers range from "nothing" to "everything." Those whose views fall to the extreme right on the political continuum see public schools as a failed social experiment, a wasteful government monopoly that should be dismantled through vouchers and privatization. At the opposite end of the continuum are those whose faith in the virtues of expanding social justice measures and equality of educational opportunity is just as unshakable. Others, somewhere between the two extremes, look back with nostalgia (and perhaps through rose-tinted glasses) to a time when schools reflected their own "traditional" values, however those might be defined. Still others, who felt excluded or even bullied as students, recall those times less fondly and hope their children will have a better educational experience in a more inclusive school environment. With such a diversity of voices, it is difficult to find common ground, except that all fervently believe schools are the major vehicle to some essential outcome. Yet the question must be asked as to what schools are actually capable of doing; that is, can school achieve the aims of all, and, importantly, at what price? This generates subquestions, to which data offer some insight. For example: What is the effect of money on schools? What happens when schools get more money? Do schools really need more money? What will happen if schools receive less money? These questions envelop the larger question of what schools should be doing by raising the stakes as partisan factions simultaneously compete to increase or decrease spending on schools. Although the questions are painfully clear, the answers are unsatisfying, especially relating to what schools are capable of doing.

What Is the Effect of Money on Schools?

An ongoing and often heated debate centers on whether money has a measurable effect on student achievement. Because public education is increasingly driven by the results of high stakes testing, the question of the relationship between expenditures and educational outcomes has become central in funding debates at the local, state, and national levels. However, after nearly half a century of research, a definitive answer to this question remains elusive. Because teaching and learning are complex human endeavors affected by many factors within and outside the classroom, it is not surprising that it is difficult to isolate the effect of a single variable, i.e., spending levels, on student achievement. Nonetheless, researchers in the U.S. (and, more recently, internationally)[10] have grappled with this question for decades, and, given the intensity of current policy debates about raising student achievement while holding down costs, it is likely that this line of inquiry will endure. As such, it is helpful to chronicle the history of this line of research and the accompanying controversy around its application to schools.

The history of this type of research, referred to as "production-function studies," constitutes a fascinating journey. To begin, the methodology itself is controversial. The production-function methodology is based upon the application of a private sector manufacturing model that equates education to a factory assembly line, whereby the components of education are reduced to three: inputs; throughputs or process; and a single output.[11] (see Figure 1.1.) However, because of the difficulty of quantifying educational processes, e.g., pedagogy, production-function studies have focused on inputs, many of which are directly or indirectly related to money, and the outcome of a single student achievement test score on a standardized instrument.[12] Therefore, from its earliest applications in the 1960s, the production function has been attacked for not only the inappropriateness of the application of a manufacturing model to education, but also for its failure to include variables that reflect what educators would consider an essential component—the educational process.

Production-function studies are often traced back to the Coleman Report,[13] a study which was funded by the federal government as part of the Civil Rights Act of 1964. The research focused on questions of racial inequality in schools, using indicators of quality such as curriculum, teacher qualifications, resources, and standardized test scores. The central findings affirmed that, a decade after the *Brown* decision, there still existed significant racial segregation of schools and race-based disparities in educational offerings and opportunities. However, it was a more general set of findings that engendered the controversy that still surrounds this research approach today; that is, the impact of a child's home environment, e.g., parental education and parental attitudes toward education, dwarfed the effects of school-related factors and resource levels.

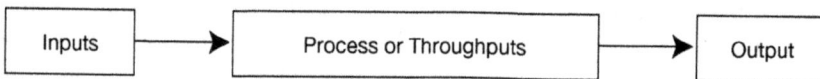

| Inputs | → | Process or Throughputs | → | Output |

FIGURE 1.1 Model of the Production Function

---

10 See, e.g., Jaap Scheerens, "Review of School and Instructional Effectiveness Research," Paper commissioned for the *EFA Global Monitoring Report 2005: The Quality Imperative.*

11 See, Faith E. Crampton, "Spending on School Infrastructure: Does Money Matter?" *Journal of Educational Administration* 47 (Spring 2009): 305–322.

12 Another outcome that has been used is high school graduation.

13 James S. Coleman, Ernst Campbell, Carol Hobson, James McPartland, Alexander Mood, Frederic Weinfeld, and Robert York, *Equality of Educational Opportunity* (Washington, DC: U.S. Government Printing Office, 1966).

Response to the Coleman Report in the research community was swift and dramatic. Many critiques of the study's methods and interpretation of results ensued and have endured up to the present.[14] A spate of counter-studies sprang up after the Coleman Report, typified by the Summers and Wolf study,[15] which examined 627 sixth-grade students in the Philadelphia schools, finding that certain variables such as better teacher preparation, presence of high achievers, and smaller class size did have a positive effect on achievement. Another approach is found in research emanating from the Effective Schools Movement, which has been characterized by some as an ideological protest against the Coleman Report. This body of research sought to identify traits of effective schools that could be emulated to boost student achievement; however, it relied more upon qualitative research methods which are difficult to replicate and generalize.

Of greatest importance to this discussion, is that a narrower application of the production function ensued that focused more sharply upon the relationship of money (either direct expenditure or indirect expenditure, e.g., through teacher salaries), to student achievement. For better or worse, this approach has endured from the 1970s up to the present and continues to yield results that are inconsistent, conflicting, and counter-intuitive. This is largely due to methodological problems, poorly conducted studies, researcher bias, and failure to include or quantify "process variables" that are essential if one claims to be using a production-function approach.[16] Even overarching studies of production-function research results referred to as meta-analyses, conducted mainly from the late 1980s into the 1990s, have yielded similar conflicting results.[17]

More recent research has emerged that is radical in its critique of the production-function model itself as an appropriate and practical application for measuring the impact of fiscal-related resources on educational outcomes. Although student achievement scores remain the focus, this new approach addresses one of the key shortcomings of the statistical technique, referred to as multiple regression, commonly used for production-function research; that is, multiple regression analysis allows for only one educational output, e.g., a test score, to be analyzed at a time. This, of course, is

---

14 Chief among criticisms have been nonresponse and stratification of variables resulting in non-comparable data, errors in data entry, and misinterpretation of interaction effects. Simply put, nonresponse refers to the misleading impression of a very large data set when in fact the number of respondents was far smaller than intended, raising questions of generalizability. Stratification refers to data being examined in separate sets, perhaps wrongly constructed, so that effects of variables such as race, religion, and so forth might have been exaggerated or misleading. Errors in data entry plague all large data sets and may make the results suspect. Finally, misinterpretation of interaction effects refers to a lack of sophistication in research design, in which causal relationships are inferred that were not really verified by the data.

15 Anita Summers and Barbara Wolfe, "Do Schools Make a Difference?" *American Economic Review* 67 (September 1977): 639–652.

16 Throughput or process variables are sometimes referred to as the "black box" in the production-function model. See, e.g., Jennifer King, "Illuminating the Black Box: The Evolving Role of Education Productivity Research," in *Education Finance in the New Millennium*, edited by Stephen Chaikind and William J. Fowler, Jr., 121–138 (Larchmont, NY: Eye on Education, 2001).

17 See, e.g., Eric A. Hanushek, "The Impact of Differential Expenditures on School Performance," *Educational Researcher* 18 (May 1989): 45–51, 62; and Larry Hedges, Richard Laine, and Rob Greenwald, "Does Money Does Matter: A Meta-Analysis of Studies of the Effect of Differential School Inputs on Student Incomes," *Educational Researcher* 23 (April 1994): 5–14.

unrealistic. In the real world of educational testing, students are generally tested at a minimum in two subjects, reading and mathematics, and more frequently in a range of subjects, including, for example, science and social studies. A small number of researchers have begun to use a more sophisticated statistical technique, referred to as canonical analysis, which allows for the inclusion of multiple education outcomes in the research.[18] In addition, to open the "black box," other researchers are engaging in theory building that provides a foundation for evaluating the impact of investments in education.[19] These represent emergent bodies of research, but the results have generally been promising, and, as such, they may prove more useful approaches to answering not only the question as to whether or not money matters, but also when and how does it matter?

What Happens When Schools Get More (or Less) Money?

Unfortunately, no longitudinal, systematic studies of these two questions have been conducted. Furthermore, it is generally considered unethical to conduct experimental studies whereby resources are intentionally withheld from one school in order to compare it to another school. As a result, we are left in large part with anecdotal information and case studies; although these are informative, they cannot be generalized to all schools. A third and related question is also of great importance to school leaders: What should schools do when they receive more, or less, money?

Turning to the first question, it is important to note that rarely in the history of taxpayer funding have schools received windfalls of new money. The more common scenario is incremental funding of a few percentage points. Although every new dollar is important, it is difficult for schools to make dramatic changes or undertake significant reforms without substantial new funds. As such, school boards often decide in the process of approving an annual budget where to allocate the new funds using their best judgment. Budget hearings are open to the public in most states, so hypothetically anyone can provide input. Some districts may engage staff and community in more formal mechanisms, such as listening sessions or focus groups. However, most districts do not have formal plans for how to allocate new funding; and so they risk allocating these moneys haphazardly, often in response to internal and external political pressures. Ideally, such decisions should flow from district and school strategic plans which have prioritized how new funds will be allocated should they become available. In addition, as we will see in Chapter 5 on budget planning, districts can prepare themselves for this scenario by using an approach like PPBES (Planning, Programming, Budgeting, and Evaluation Systems), a comprehensive approach that prioritizes the district's educational goals and objectives and accompanying expenditures. Thus, when new funds become available, the school board has a blueprint to follow.

---

18 See, e.g., Robert C. Knoeppel and James S. Rinehart, "Explaining the Relationship between Resources and Student Achievement: A Methodological Comparison of Production Functions and Canonical Analysis," *Educational Considerations* 35 (Spring 2008): 29–40.

19 See, e.g., Faith E. Crampton, "Spending on School Infrastructure: Does Money Matter?" *Journal of Educational Administration* 47 (Spring 2009): 305–322.

An equally interesting question is raised by asking what would happen if schools were to receive less money. Although here too there is not a body of research literature upon which to draw, there tend to be more case studies that can be instructive. In a recent five-state study of school districts that suffered significant reductions in state aid, researchers found that school districts tended to reduce funding in four areas:[20]

- Personnel and instruction resulting in increases in class size
- Early childhood education (pre-K and kindergarten)
- Elective courses, such as art, music, physical education, science, technology, foreign languages, and advanced courses
- Extracurricular activities, like athletics and drama

In some cases, courses and programs were eliminated entirely. Or, in the case of extracurricular activities, schools charged hefty fees for student participation. In many states, schools have limited or no ability to charge fees for the required academic program or transportation.[21] Also, under federal law, they cannot reduce or eliminate services to students with disabilities. However, faced with reductions in aid, districts in states that are more permissive face the temptation to increase revenues by adding fees to even core academics, e.g., charging for "consumables," like workbooks.

School districts face difficult and unpleasant decisions when they receive less money. No matter what they cut or eliminate, someone in the community will be angered. Nonetheless, districts should consider the same approach to receiving less money as they would with the opposite scenario; that is, the use of strategic education and fiscal planning found in approaches like PPBES to guide them in setting priorities for budget reductions. Granted, nothing will make budget cuts less wrenching for schools and communities, but a rational, thoughtful approach may minimize the pain.

On balance, few schools are faced with excess funds, and most schools are not faced with financial ruin, although money has become more difficult to secure and its distribution increasingly more contentious. In addition, it is a stark reality that accountability, both achievement-based and fiscal efficiency-driven, has become a powerful weapon in the hands of state legislatures and governors, as states have demanded sweeping reforms while courts have ruled on a wide array of issues under the aegis of equality of educational opportunity. All these events serve to underscore fierce competition for fiscal resources and an increasingly fragmented society that is unwilling to support increased funding for education without evidence of greater cost-effectiveness and higher student achievement.

---

20 Jeff Bryant, *Starving America's Public Schools* (Washington, DC: Campaign for America's Future, 2011) www.ourfuture.org/report/2011104111/starving-america-s-public-schools.

21 See, "Before Charging School Bus Fees, Districts Must Know State Law," by Ryan Gray, *School Transportation News*, August 13, 2010, www.stnonline.com/resources/operations/related-regular-transportation-articles/2601-charging-school-bus-fees.

WHERE PUBLIC SCHOOLS MAY BE HEADED

In large part, this chapter has set the context for topics to be discussed in the remaining chapters by providing a history of public education in this country along with an assessment of the current and complex social, economic, and political environment in which pre K–12 education finds itself today. A free, common public school system has been part of the fabric of this nation for more than 150 years as an essential building block of the foundation for a democratic society. To remain a vibrant part of that democracy, it is essential to adequately and equitably fund public schools so that they can continue to deliver upon the promise of equality of educational opportunity and upward mobility which serve as centerpieces of the American dream. The chapters that follow delve into the many facets of schools and money, from budgeting for their central function of instruction to the supporting role of student activities, infrastructure, and auxiliary services, to name just a few.

As we prepare to look more specifically at the operational elements of schools and money in upcoming chapters, we are convinced that schools—through their leaders—must communicate strategic plans and clear budget goals and processes to stakeholders or risk losing their support. In other words, schools must promote their virtues, take the lead in performance accountability, and engage their constituents. If educational leaders fail to do so, then it is clear where education is headed—into a world that includes ever-expanding alternatives to public schools, and a concomitant loss in support for public education.

POINT–COUNTERPOINT

POINT

The lack of adequate funding for public schools has long hampered progress in student achievement. Everyone knows that money matters in schools. If elected officials and private citizens are frustrated by declining test scores, the right answer is to step up to the plate and spend for education—in other words, to remain the world's leader will require spending for schools at the level of other advanced nations.

COUNTERPOINT

Money doesn't matter. What matters is parental involvement. Parents of failing students inevitably blame everyone but themselves. These are the same parents who expect schools and the government to take over their responsibilities—like providing breakfast, lunch, and afterschool snacks. Because these irresponsible parents do not teach their children respect for teachers and other authority figures, they disrupt the learning environment for children who want to learn. Spending more money on education won't buy good parenting. It's time for schools to refocus their attention away from money to holding parents accountable.

- Which of these views is closest to your own? Explain.
- What has happened to both funding and achievement levels in your state and school district in recent years? Is there a relationship between them? Explain.
- Could existing funding in your school or district be used more effectively? If yes, provide some examples.

CASE STUDY

As a newly hired high school principal, you were surprised when the superintendent asked to speak with you about the upcoming tax referendum. As the conversation progressed, you learned that two previously supportive school board members had raised concerns at a recent board meeting about the referendum in which local voters would be asked to approve an increase in property taxes to maintain education programs, such as PK–12 gifted education, Advanced Placement (AP) courses, and a staff of guidance/career counselors for students at all grade levels. The rationale behind the tax increase request was to maintain the district's history of education excellence as demonstrated by the following: The district's scores on state-mandated standardized achievement tests were consistently among the state's best; the district's mean ACT scores were well above the national average; and more than 80% of the district's graduates pursued postsecondary education.

The superintendent explained that the two board members had been contacted by members of a local taxpayer organization who presented them with data that showed local district spending had outpaced inflation (per the Consumer Price Index) for the last decade and that the district's property taxes were the highest in a ten-county area and sixth highest in the state. In addition, the taxpayer association members maintained that the education programs that would benefit from the tax increase served only a small percentage of the student body. Furthermore, they asserted that over the past few years, district residents had been hit hard by the sluggish economy. There had been layoffs with a local plant closing, and those with jobs were not seeing much in the way of wage increases. Given these conditions, they asserted that residents could ill afford even a small increase in property taxes.

The bottom line, the superintendent confessed, was how to protect the district's education goals in the face of these data. Not only might the district lose the referendum and have to reduce the scope of these programs, but a defeat might embolden the taxpayer organization to recall those board members who had supported it, leading to the election of fiscal conservatives whose main goal would be to reduce taxes at the expense of education quality and opportunity.

The superintendent then explained your role in passage of the referendum. Given these new developments, the superintendent was charging each principal with developing a specific, outcome-oriented plan for his or her school that would justify the tax increase and—importantly—identify the potential damage resulting from a failed referendum. Although the vote was still four months away, moving ahead now was important because significant time would be needed to carry the message to the board and the community.

Below is a set of questions. As you respond, consider the content of this chapter and apply your new knowledge to the situation.

- What observations about the community can you draw from this case study?
- What questions or concerns about the referendum are likely to be raised by the community?
- What data will be needed to justify a tax increase in a community like this one?
- How will you go about carrying out your charge?
- How does this school district and community compare to yours?

PORTFOLIO EXERCISES

- Write a brief reflection paper in which you identify your beliefs and values about what schools are capable of doing. Present your reflection in class; and then compare and contrast your views with those of other students.
- Interview five educational stakeholders in your community on their views about the relationship between money and student achievement. Select persons from various walks of life, e.g., a school board member, a business owner, a teacher, a member of the clergy, an administrator, a retired person, a student, a local elected official, a parent. Compare and contrast their views.
- Talk to the person(s) in your school district who are responsible for assessing school performance. These might include central office and school site personnel, such as directors of assessment or curriculum, principals, and counselors. Ask about district and school performance profiles and trends, and determine how the district and individual schools go about raising student achievement where needed. Ask if any formal attempt is made to link money and achievement, and, if so, how.
- In small groups, develop a list of the 25 most influential or powerful persons in your community. Profile these influencers, identifying why you included them on your list. Describe their beliefs about money and schools. Present your list to the class and reach consensus with other groups on your community's power structure.

> • Research the news media in your community for the last year, recording attitudes toward schools. Look specifically for reporting on school funding and school performance data. Identify general attitudes, issues deemed newsworthy, and community opinions. Analyze your findings to determine your community's support level for education.

WEB RESOURCES

American Association of School Administrators, www.aasa.org

American Federation of Teachers, www.aft.org

Council of Chief State School Officers, www.ccsso.org

National Association for Elementary School Principals, www.naesp.org

National Association of Secondary School Principals, www.nassp.org

National Education Association, www.nea.org

National School Boards Association, www.nsba.org

ONLINE VIDEO RESOURCE

Campaign for America's Future."School Cuts Hurt Kids." http://ourfuture.org/report/starving-america-s-public-schools

RECOMMENDED READING

Common Core State Standards Initiative.n.d. "Preparing America's Students for Success." www.corestandards.org.

Crampton, Faith E. "Spending on School Infrastructure: Does Money Matter?" *Journal of Educational Administration* 47 (Spring 2009): 305–322.

Gray, Ryan. "Before Charging School Bus Fees, Districts Must Know State Law." *School Transportation News*, August 13, 2010, www.stnonline.com/resources/operations/related-regular-transportation-articles/2601-charging-school-bus-fees.

Hanushek, Eric A. "The Impact of Differential Expenditures on School Performance." *Educational Researcher* 18 (May 1989): 45–51. http://hanushek.stanford.edu/publications/impact-differential-expenditures-school-performance.

Hedges, Larry, Richard Laine, and Rob Greenwald. "Does Money Does Matter: A Meta-Analysis of Studies of the Effect of Differential School Inputs on Student Incomes." *Educational Researcher* 23 (April 1994): 5–14.

Kaestle, Carl F. "Victory of the Common School Movement." *Historians on America.* Washington, DC: U.S. Department of State, 2008. http://iipdigital.usembassy.gov/st/english/publication/2008/04/20080423212501eaifas0.8516133.html#axzz30gqNday5.

Knoeppel, Robert C., and James S. Rinehart. "Explaining the Relationship between Resources and Student Achievement: A Methodological Comparison of Production Functions and Canonical Analysis." *Educational Considerations* 35 (Spring 2008): 29–40.

Lu, Adrienne. "Q&A: Common Questions about the Common Core." *Stateline.* Washington, DC: The Pew Charitable Trusts, December 2013. www.pewstates.org/projects/stateline/headlines/qa-common-questions-about-the-common-core-85899523670.

Ravitch, Dianne. *Reign of Error.* New York: Alfred A. Knopf, 2013.

Thompson, David C., R. Craig Wood, and David S. Honeyman. *Fiscal Leadership for Schools: Concepts and Practices.* New York: Longman, 1994.

U.S. Department of Education."Race to the Top Fund." http://www2.ed.gov/programs/racetothetop/index.html.

Weiss, Elaine."Mismatches in Race to the Top Limit Educational Improvement."Washington, DC: Economic Policy Institute, September 2013.http://www.epi.org/publication/race-to-the-top-goals.

Zimmerman, Jonathan. *Whose America? Culture Wars in the Public Schools.* Cambridge, MA: Harvard University Press, 2005.

CHAPTER 2

Funding Schools:
A Policy Perspective

THE CHALLENGE

The fear of economic and social decline is so great that education reform has become a national agenda wherein critics link America's preeminence in world markets, gainful employment, and the survival and stability of democracy to the education system. As school leaders, it is important to understand that school finance is at the heart of schooling because it requires much money to pay for either the successes or failures of education.

Thompson, Wood, and Honeyman (1994)[1]

CHAPTER DRIVERS

Please reflect upon the following questions as you read this chapter:

- What is the scope of education finance in America?
- How are education and economics related?
- What is the structure of school governance in America?
- From where do schools derive financial support?
- What constitutes adequate and equitable funding for schools?
- Can schools at once serve economics, equality, productivity, and liberty?

---

1 David C. Thompson, R. Craig Wood, and David S. Honeyman, *Fiscal Leadership for Schools: Concepts and Practices* (New York: Longman, 1994).

A MORE EXPANSIVE VIEW

The previous chapter ended with a warning that there is a growing belief in the United States that public education's performance is at least lackluster, if not suffering a crisis of confidence. Clearly, research on linkages between student achievement and school funding levels is mixed, but there is more to the issue than pure economics. At the same time, it is never as simple as a "bottom line," because the whole discussion revolves around fiscal considerations in tandem with other important social and political principles that cannot be ignored if society is to sustain a civil democracy.

There are additional social, political, and economic issues that complicate and drive how educational leaders should act (and react) in today's intensely sociopolitical climate. The benefits and costs of education are never as easy as looking only at growth in revenue and spending for schools—society must also examine the broader scope of funding education from a *policy* perspective. The concept of *investment* in education, versus an attitude of *expenditure control*, is important too because spending for education should take into account the value of education to the economy and to society itself. Certainly, a key part of spending on children's educational needs is affected by whether federal, state, and local governments are appropriately sharing the duty to fund schools. Issues of adequate and equitable funding of schools are of major concern for educators, politicians, and taxpayers. The debate concerning money for schools is more than just thinking about strong test scores: it also includes considering the ethics of civic responsibility, at least as long as society wishes to pursue opportunity, equality, and liberty for everyone.

WHAT IS THE SCOPE OF EDUCATION FINANCE IN AMERICA?

Every text regarding the financing of education in the last 50 years has remarked that education is "big business." Although individuals are accustomed to hearing about enormous costs relating to every aspect of society, the enormous demands of modern life on human and fiscal resources are still mammoth (see Figures 2.1 and 2.2). Most Americans know that the nation is deeply in debt, but the sum of approaching $20 trillion is unfathomable.[2] This abstract number takes on more meaning if restated as *each* American citizen's share of the national debt, which translated to a staggering amount of nearly $50,000 per person in 2014[3] (see Figure 2.3). An examination of Figure 2.1 clearly reflects that federal expenditures are largely social programs representing a transfer of wealth. In contrast to the national debt, however, funding for schools is mostly paid on a current basis, meaning that revenues must cover expenditures. Inasmuch as most government spending goes to domestic and international programs, including schools, the scope of public finance in the United States is sizable. Under these conditions, it is not surprising that Chapter 1 is titled "Schools, Values, and Money."

---

2 Note that the federal fiscal year begins October 1 and ends September 30.
3 For a current overview of spending see, U.S. Debt Clock, www.usdebtclock.org.

AGENCY

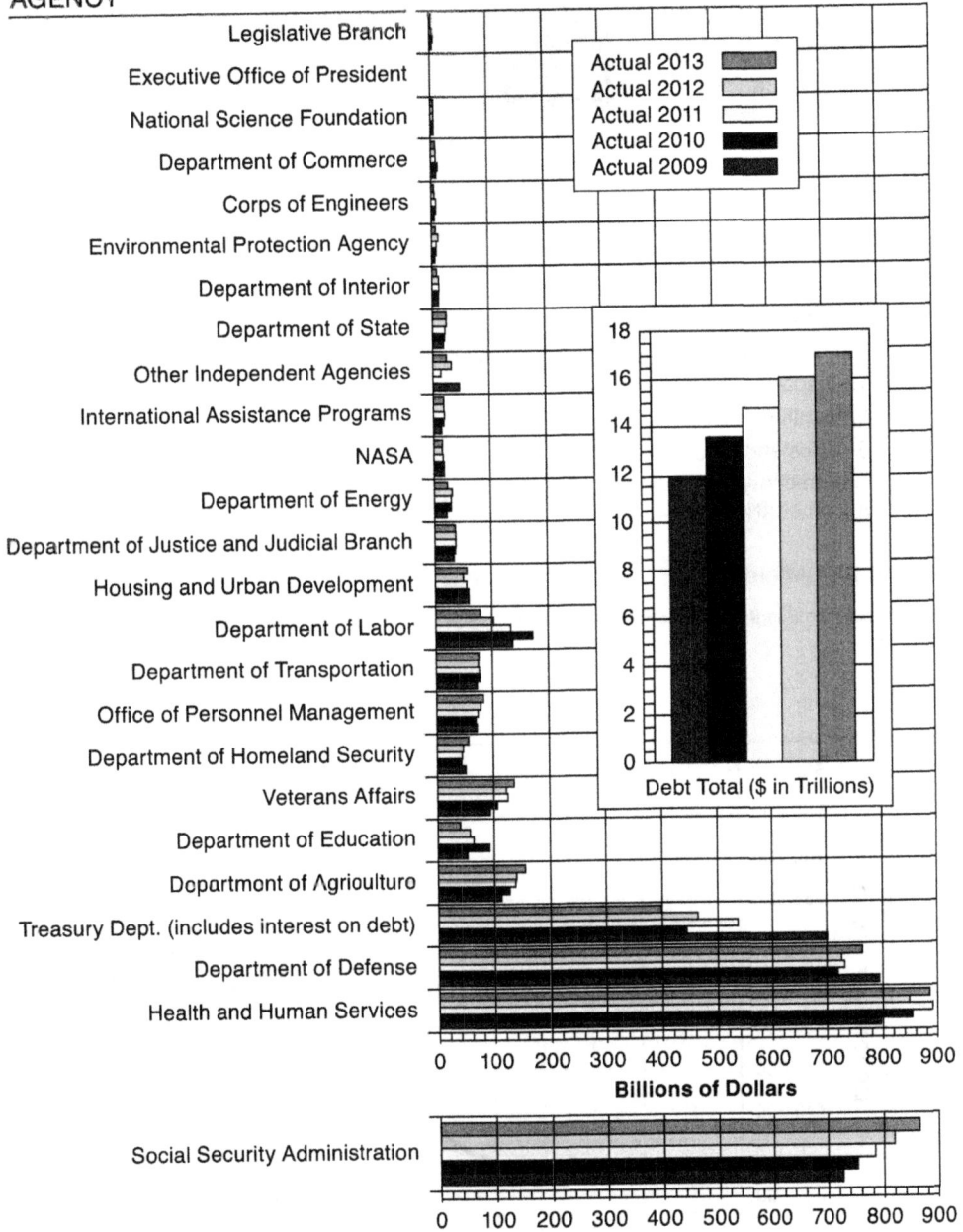

FIGURE 2.1 Federal Expenditures: 2009–2013

Source: National Debt Awareness Center. "How Congress Spends Your Money." www.federalbudget.com.

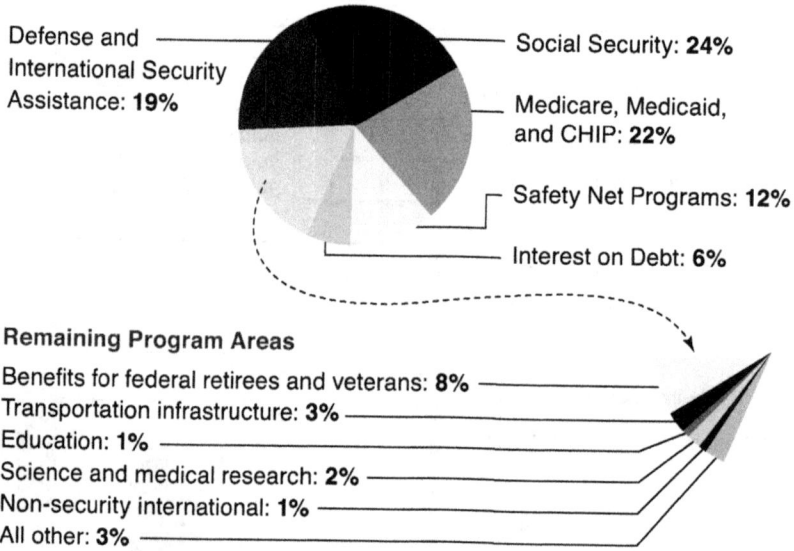

Defense and — International Security Assistance: **19%**

Social Security: **24%**

Medicare, Medicaid, and CHIP: **22%**

Safety Net Programs: **12%**

Interest on Debt: **6%**

Remaining Program Areas

Benefits for federal retirees and veterans: **8%** ———
Transportation infrastructure: **3%** ———
Education: **1%** ———
Science and medical research: **2%** ———
Non-security international: **1%** ———
All other: **3%** ———

FIGURE 2.2 Where Do Our Federal Tax Dollars Go?

Source: Center on Budget and Policy Priorities. Federal Fiscal Year 2013 data. www.cbpp.org/cms/?fa=view &id=1258.

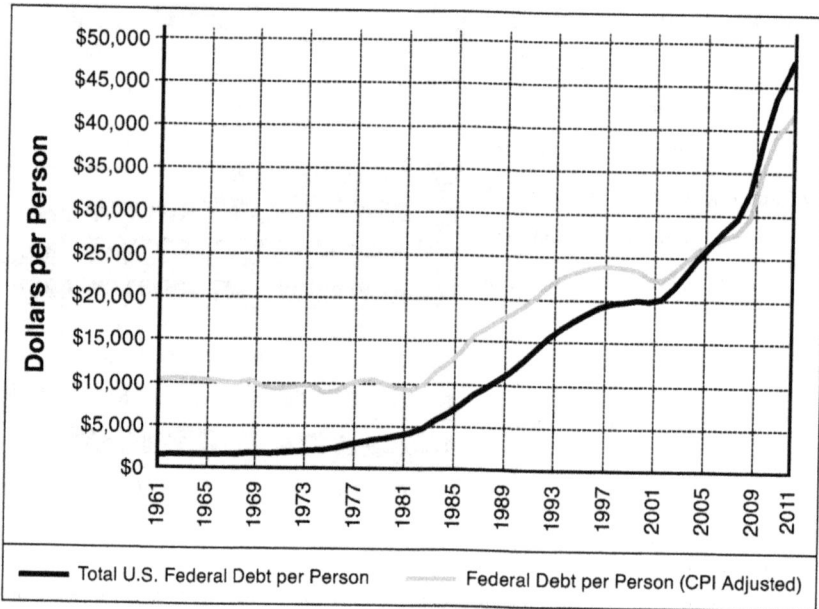

FIGURE 2.3 Federal Government Debt Per Person: 1981–2011

Source: Data 360. "Federal Debt Per Person US." www.data360.org/dsg.aspx?Data_Set_Group_Id=273.

Revenue Growth for Schools

Skyrocketing growth in school revenue has been longstanding, even in earlier times when needs were simpler. Although consistent data collection did not begin until the early 20th century, revenues from 1920 to 2011 reflect the increasing importance of education to our nation (see Table 2.1). In 1920, total revenues for K–12 schools were $970 million. By 1930, revenues had increased to $2.09 billion. An important observation is that despite the huge costs of World War I, school revenue rose steadily, due partly to the need for training a fighting force and partly to postwar prosperity. It is important to note that the revenues referenced in this section are expressed in current dollars; that is, they have not been adjusted for inflation.

Growth in school revenue experienced only brief lags over the ensuing years. The first 30 years of the last century saw rapid growth, with only the Great Depression forcing visible slowing of revenues. From 1930 to 1940, school revenue grew only slightly from $2.09 to $2.26 billion; yet the increase was remarkable in light of the economic horrors facing the nation.

The surge in money for schools resumed with the recovery spurred by World War II. Between 1940 and 1950, revenue more than doubled to $5.4 billion. The pattern continued from 1950 to 1960, aided by the space race, triggered by the launch of the Soviet satellite *Sputnik I* and giving rise to a national education agenda under the National Defense Education Act (NDEA) in 1958.[4] NDEA led to unequaled growth in both K–12 and higher education funding; new federal funding directed at instruction in mathematics, science, and foreign languages fueled an era in which an information economy would replace a fading industrial economy.

National awareness of global competition brought about by the launch of *Sputnik* was accompanied by rapid change in the social order of the United States, especially between 1950 and 1970. The nation's population, toughened by economic depression and war, moved out of rural America to the cities. Two events forever changed education and its fiscal patterns. The first was the 1954 landmark court case *Brown v. Board of Education*,[5] in which the United States Supreme Court ruled that racial segregation of schools in which African-American students were ostensibly offered a "separate but equal" education was unconstitutional. The second event was the profound social change of the 1960s, including the War on Poverty proposed by President Lyndon Johnson in 1964. *Brown* reshaped the fundamental nature of public schools via desegregation, with massive costs to taxpayers, while the War on Poverty marked the beginning of an extensive list of federal entitlements to schools through the initial Elementary and Secondary Education Act of 1965,[6] whereby the federal share of education revenues nearly doubled by 1968. Although the federal government had long tried to aid schools, these two events sparked a revolution that would alter the face of education in the United States. Although these events did not account for all growth in school funding during that time, the era from 1950 to 1970 remains

---

4 20 U.S.C. 401 et seq.
5 374 U.S. 483 at 493 (1954).
6 PL 89–10, 20 U.S.C. 2701 et seq.

TABLE 2.1 Revenues for Public Elementary and Secondary Schools by Source of Funds for Selected Years: 1920–2011

School Year	Total ($000s)	Federal %	State %	Local %
1919–20	970,121	0.3	16.5	83.2
1929–30	2,088,557	0.4	16.9	82.7
1939–40	2,260,527	1.8	30.3	68.0
1949–50	5,437,044	2.9	39.8	57.3
1959–60	14,746,618	4.4	39.1	56.5
1969–70	40,266,922	8.0	39.9	52.1
1979–80	96,881,164	9.8	46.8	43.4
1989–90	208,547,573	6.1	47.1	46.8
1990–91	223,340,537	6.2	47.2	46.7
1991–92	234,581,384	6.6	46.4	47.0
1992–93	247,626,168	7.0	45.8	47.2
1993–94	260,159,468	7.1	45.2	47.8
1994–95	273,149,449	6.8	46.8	46.4
1995–96	287,702,844	6.6	47.5	45.9
1996–97	305,065,192	6.6	48.0	45.4
1997–98	325,925,708	6.8	48.4	44.8
1998–99	347,377,993	7.1	48.7	44.2
1999–2000	372,943,802	7.3	49.5	43.2
2000–01	401,356,120	7.3	49.7	49.7
2001–02	419,501,976	7.9	49.2	49.2
2002–03	440,111,653	8.5	48.7	48.7
2003–04	462,026,099	9.1	47.1	47.1
2004–05	487,753,525	9.2	46.9	46.9
2005–06	520,621,788	9.1	46.5	46.5
2006–07	555,710,762	8.5	47.4	47.4
2007–08	584,683,686	8.2	48.3	48.3
2008–09	592,422,033	9.6	46.7	46.7
2009–10	596,390,664	12.7	43.4	43.4
2010–11	604,293,209	12.5	44.1	44.1

Source: *Digest of Education Statistics 2013*. Table 235.10. Washington, DC: NCES, Institute for Education Sciences, U.S. Department of Education, 2014, 260.

Note: The revenues in this table are expressed in current (unadjusted) dollars.

unmatched as revenues grew to $14.7 billion by 1960 and to $44.5 billion by 1970. Although inflation and the enormous enrollment growth of the postwar baby boom must be taken into consideration, revenue grew at historic rates during these years of social progress and economic prosperity.

The era from 1970 to 1980 was marked by continued education and social reform such as the passage of a groundbreaking federal law, *The Education for All Handicapped Act* of 1975,[7] which ensured that all children with disabilities, some of whom had been previously excluded from public schools, would receive an appropriate education in the least restrictive environment. In addition, many states' systems for funding schools were deemed inequitable and ruled unconstitutional by state courts, and education costs soared, as did those in all other economic sectors, due to inflation. By 1980, education revenues totaled nearly $106 billion. Although public education's share of the gross domestic product (GDP) began wavering in 1980, revenue growth continued because redistribution of wealth and funding increases followed the court-ordered restructuring of many state school finance systems. The resiliency of school revenues was also apparent in the economic slump of the 1980s, more than doubling to $223 billion in 1990, continuing throughout the roaring economy of the 1990s to more than $401 billion in 2001, and over $600 billion for the 2010–2011 school year.

Although these data suggest that education has prospered, another view is worth considering because there are at least three factors that help to explain the growth in school revenues over time. First, these data speak only to national totals, with each state facing different social and economic situations tied to its fiscal ability and voter preferences. Second, some data suggest that schools' ability to serve may have been weakened despite fiscal growth, particularly during the economic downturns of the new millennium such that test scores have lagged despite more resources. Third, schools underwent vast demographic changes during the last half of the 20th century alone: A school district that provided inferior facilities and funding for many minority students and excluded many students with disabilities was transformed into one that provides a public education to all students regardless of the cost in order to ensure equality of educational opportunity. Over time public schools have been transformed with the accompanying costs.

While some may disagree that these historic changes adequately account for the scope of increases in revenues, two points emerge that are key to an accurate view of the social and economic context of money and schools. First, since Americans have long regarded education as the key to economic and social mobility, they have fought hard for good schools under strong local control. Second, Americans have historically directed vast resources to schools, a fact that underscores how much they value education because people resist paying for what does not have personal meaning. But as critics have noted, the United States, which once touted its educational system as the best in the world, now sees its students falling behind a number of nations in academic achievement while spending across the nation on education continues to

---

7 PL 94–142, 20 U.S.C. 1499 et seq.

increase. These critics ask whether the public will continue funding a school system that it sees as losing ground to global competitors. However, a more constructive approach takes the long view by considering education as an investment in the future of this nation and its citizens, rather than as a failing business enterprise.

EDUCATION AND ECONOMICS

Debate over the value of education has not been limited to recent fears concerning student test scores. For many years, education finance researchers have held that education makes a positive contribution to national economic and social well-being as well as global competitiveness, and so there have been attempts to quantify the value of schooling.

Economics Defined

It is hard to reduce the complex field of education finance to a simplistic economic discussion. However, it is useful to think of economics as the production, allocation, and consumption of goods and services for the satisfaction of human needs and wants. Economics is therefore interested in goods and services in relation to supply and demand. Rogers and Ruchlin captured it well: "Economics is concerned with two primary phenomena, desires and resources," which lead to a "confrontation . . . because desires are infinite, whereas resources are finite."[8] Economics in a society where commodities must be bought thus means that some goods and services will be scarce or unequally available, while others are plentiful and less valued.

This definition presents a challenge for a capitalist democracy like the United States. Capitalism needs markets while democracy requires equal access to essential commodities that aid freedom and promote economic productivity and social mobility. A conflict arises because public education in a capitalist democracy must be purchased with tax dollars, raising issues regarding the funding and distribution of education fairly to people in different circumstances.

Education as an Economic and Social Good

Because economics deals with goods and services and the supply of commodities to individuals and society, it has a direct relationship to the financing of elementary and secondary education. Among the most important relationships is that education produces human capital, contributes to economic health, and drives the economic and social welfare of entire nations. These benefits accrue to individuals and to society as a whole; therefore, they are central to understanding whether education is an investment or an expense.

---

8 Daniel C. Rogers and Hirsch S. Ruchlin, *Economics and Education* (New York: Free Press, 1971), 5.

Education and Human Capital

Starting in the 1980s, a series of national reports on the condition of education has served as a reminder of enduring beliefs that education produces human capital. Education finance researchers have explored the link between economic prosperity and education, holding that while linkages are not fully explained, education and economics are highly interdependent. Renowned economists including John Kenneth Galbraith, Milton Friedman, and Theodore Schultz have all found a positive relationship, arguing that the historic elements of land, capital, and labor must be expanded to include human capital. According to Schultz, "Human capital has the fundamental attributes of the basic economic concept of capital; namely, it is a source of future satisfactions, or of future earnings, or both of them. What makes it human capital is the fact that it becomes an integral part of the person."[9]

By this view, education takes on real worth. Whereas ownership of land, growth in capital assets, and costs of unskilled labor were the old bases of economic analysis, the addition of human capital views the costs of unskilled labor as a true *cost*, while the expense of creating skilled workers becomes an *investment*. Because capital is used to create new wealth, human capital is an important step in knowing whether education is an expense or an investment because creating highly skilled workers is thereby key to stimulating economic growth.

Education and National Economic Health

The justification for capitalist society is freedom to create private wealth by competing in a free market. The justification for democratic society is based partly on the limitations of a survival-of-the-fittest economy. Thus a capitalist market in a democratic society demands fundamental opportunities. Applied to education, schooling in a private market would favor only those able to buy it. The ultimate test of the concept of education as enhancing human capital has played out in the United States, where one of the most powerful generators has been universal access to public education so that more people can create a greater store of private wealth (education), and—in turn—sell their skills in an open market at higher prices. This floor of opportunity reflects a belief that education results in important individual and societal benefits. Rather than the negative effects of competition and high labor costs hurting production, distribution of education at public expense has been seen to create a stronger economy, a higher quality of life for individuals and families, and a more stable society.

Belief in a link between economics and education has been strong in our nation's history, especially over the last century. In 1918, the Commission on Reorganization of Secondary Education declared the need to prepare students for work as one of its "seven cardinal principles."[10] In 1951, the "Ten Imperative Needs of Youth," issued

---

9 Theodore Schultz, "The Human Capital Approach to Education," in *Economic Factors Affecting the Financing of Education*, edited by Roe L. Johns, Irving J. Goffman, Kern Alexander, and Dewey H. Stollar (Gainesville, FL: National Educational Finance Project, 1970), 31.

10 U.S. Bureau of Education, "Cardinal Principles of Secondary Education," A Report of the Commission on Reorganization of Secondary Education, Bulletin, no. 35 (Washington, DC: Department of the Interior, U.S. Government Printing Office, 1918).

by the National Association of Secondary School Principals, gave emphasis to job training.[11] In 1955, the White House Conference on Education promoted various goals for schools, among which good work habits were prominent.[12] Also in 1955, the United States Chamber of Commerce said, "People who have a good education produce more goods, earn more money, buy and consume more goods, read more magazines and newspapers, are more active in civic and national affairs, enjoy a higher standard of living, and in general, contribute more to the economy."[13] More recently, the many national reports on education have confirmed a deep belief in the direct link between economic and social productivity and schools.

Whether there is proof of a link between education and national economic health seems less arguable when comparing developed and developing nations. Few would argue that education widely dispersed does not aid economic and social goals. As the World Bank noted long ago,

> The emphasis in low-income countries is on development of low-cost basic education.... In middle-income countries, where first-level education is already widely available, educational quality is emphasized and with it the expansion of facilities to meet the needs of an increasingly sophisticated economy.... As absorptive capacity ... grows, the priority shifts toward providing higher level technical skills, as well as developing skills in science, technology, information processing, and research.[14]

In sum, education is an economic engine that not only creates jobs in local communities but also provides employers with skilled workers who, in turn, stimulate the local economy as consumers.

Education and Individual Benefits

Another way of knowing whether education is an investment or an expense rests in examining the individual benefits of education. Individuals are prime beneficiaries of schooling because others are excluded from direct and equal use of each person's unique skills. Individuals benefit by enjoying greater social mobility, better pay, higher status, and more cultural opportunities. Benefits spill over to society too because salaries are returned to the economy as affluence leads to more consumerism. Better-educated individuals are also healthier, have less unemployment, are more open to change, and work more efficiently.

---

11 National Contest Committee of the National Association of Secondary School Principals, "National Contests for Schools 1951–52," *NASSP Bulletin* 35 (October 1951): 5–10.

12 White House Conference on Education, Remarks, November 28, 1955.

13 Chamber of Commerce of the United States of America, *Education as an Investment in America* (Washington, DC: 1955), 31.

14 Habte Aklilum, *Education and Development: Views from the World Bank* (Washington, DC: World Bank, 1983), 8.

Unemployment Rate in 2013 (%)   **Median Weekly Earnings in 2013 ($)**

Unemployment Rate	Education Level	Median Weekly Earnings
2.2	Doctoral degree	1,623
2.3	Professional degree	1,714
3.4	Master's degree	1,329
4.0	Bachelor's degree	1,108
5.4	Associate's degree	777
7.0	Some college, no degree	727
7.5	High school diploma	651
11.0	Less than a high school diploma	472

All Workers: 6.1%   **All Workers: $827**

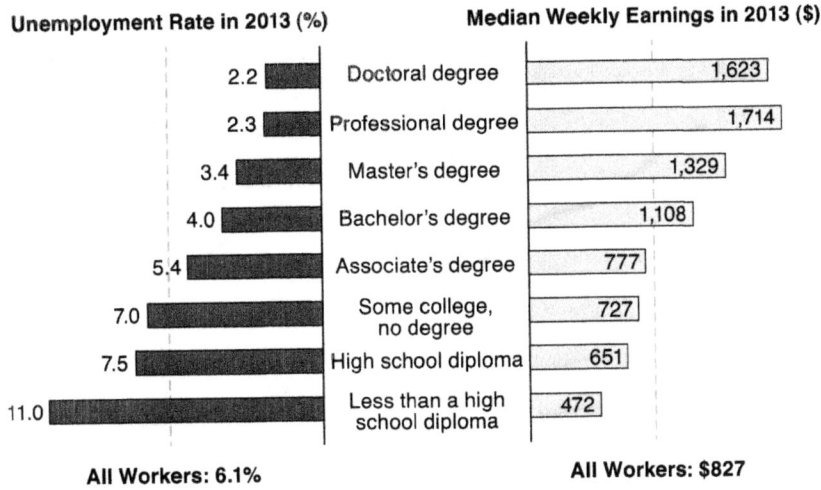

FIGURE 2.4 Education Pays: Earnings and Unemployment Rates by Educational Attainment

Note: Data are for persons age 25 and over. Earnings are for full-time salary and wage workers.

Source: U.S. Department of Labor. Bureau of Labor Statistics. "Employment Projections." Current Population Survey. www.bls.gov/emp/ep_chart_001.htm.

Individual benefits are dramatic. Figure 2.4 compares weekly earnings of workers by level of education, ranging from high-school dropout to doctoral degree. Figure 2.4 reflects that workers with higher levels of education consistently earn higher wages. Projecting such differences onto a lifetime of work, one can see that education clearly has a powerful impact on individuals' finances and quality of life. In addition to higher wages, those with higher levels of education are less likely to be unemployed. Figure 2.5 compares levels of adult unemployment by education level between 1992 and 2009. The historical trend is stark. For example, an adult who did not complete high school is three times more likely to be unemployed than a college graduate.

Social and Economic Efficiencies of Education

It is illogical to claim that the *spillover* effects of educational opportunity do not benefit all of society. To argue that schooling is merely a commodity is to claim that education does not merit equal access because its benefits are solely individual. To argue that only a minimum level of education is needed is to miss a fourth step in evaluating whether education is an investment or an expense by not observing that society and the economy would suffer far greater costs were it not for efficiencies inherent to public education.

The *exclusion principle* is the basis for arguing against broad social services in favor of the view that high spending for schools is inefficient. The issue is one of whether social spending (including for schools) yields a positive return or whether it drains money in return for low achievement scores. This view ignores that social services are intended to prevent even greater social misfortune and that spending for public aims is

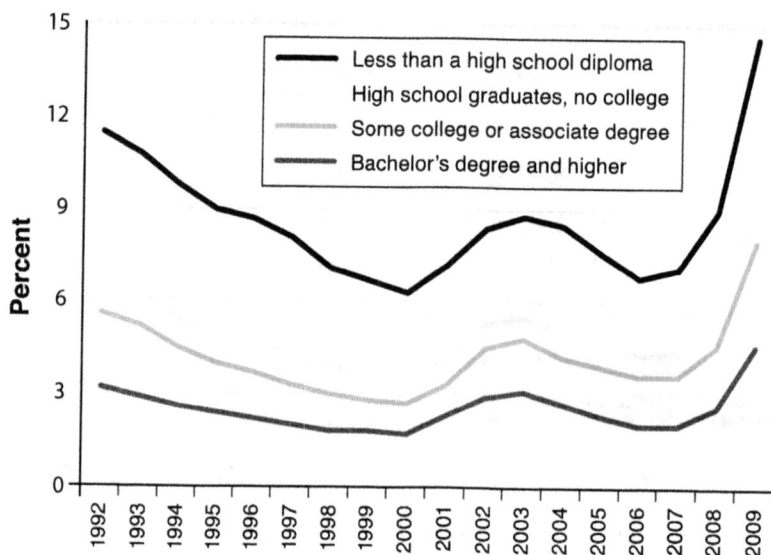

FIGURE 2.5 Unemployment Rates for People 25 Years and Over by Educational Attainment: 1992–2009

Source: U.S. Department of Labor. Bureau of Labor Statistics. "USA Unemployment Rate: Various Levels of Education."

actually more efficient because it would fall to charity to pay such costs absent taxation, but that it is inefficient (even impossible) to provide all such services on a charitable basis.

The exclusion principle sees individuals as the sole beneficiaries of an expenditure or a good or service. Implicit is the belief that exclusion is at least neutral in its impact on others and—importantly—economically efficient for the recipient. In other words, for the exclusion principle to work, depriving others of a benefit cannot result in great harm, and the cost should be attractive to the beneficiary. However, highway taxes are a good example of the illogic arising from strict application of the exclusion principle. It might be argued that failure to provide public roads would not cause unreasonable harm to others. But even if one were to accept that doubtful premise, applying the exclusion principle to roads leads to economic *inefficiencies* because most people could not provide their own roads due to prohibitive cost. Analogously, depending on charity to provide critical social services is automatically inefficient and introduces the risk that society would stop providing services if the force of taxation were absent. In other words, many critical services are more efficiently produced in the public sector at a relatively minimal individual cost, so that small sacrifices by many make up a collective benefit that otherwise would be very difficult to provide and would be seriously missed.

Like many tax-funded services, education's efficiencies compete against other concepts in a capitalist democracy. For example, arguments to privatize schools to improve performance and enhance individual choice weigh against the concept that education does not neatly fit the exclusion principle. Critics falter when they claim that students are the sole beneficiaries of schooling because spillover in social mobility, higher pay, socioeconomic status, more employment, cultural opportunities, and other benefits show that taxing and spending for schools improves the well-being of society as a whole. Likewise, democracy requires an informed citizenry; that is, most people could not privately pay for education, so inequalities among individuals would be exacerbated. For many reasons, the benefit of investing in public schools, and the various forms thereof, cannot be efficiently gained by any exclusionary mechanism.

Returns on Educational Investment

Chapter 1 examined a more skeptical view of spending for education, allowing that critics have had much to say when attacking school productivity. Achievement is a formidable challenge, and it is sensible for taxpayers to ask if spending more money on schools is efficient when potentially higher-performing alternatives exist.

This chapter has noted that school revenues and expenditures are vast and there is an investment return that test scores alone do not fully capture. The discussion has focused on broad concepts. Many studies have examined the cost–benefit question. The field has provided studies of returns regarding educational investment that can be grouped into at least two kinds. The first group examined the relationships between education and economic growth whereas the second group examined the return on investment to individuals and society. Generally, the latter group is referred to as rate-of-return studies.

Education and Economic Growth

As stated earlier, Americans have long believed in education's impact on personal economic prosperity. It is appropriate and desirable to also look more broadly at education's contribution to national economic prosperity. These studies generally have examined changes in gross domestic product (GDP) to estimate the impact of education; that is, the added value of human capital.

As a public policy, examining returns on investment in a society that currently provides approximately half a trillion dollars annually for public K–12 schools is reasonable. Answering such public policy questions is more difficult. Although educational finance researchers always prefer to work with exact quantification, researchers are sometimes forced to settle for estimates. Presently, no way exists by which to measure exact output of educational investment relative to dollar inputs so education finance researchers have estimated residual effects in the economy.

A *residual* effect can be likened to the analogy of a sum and its parts, where several values are added to reach the conclusion that the whole is greater than the sum of its parts. Although application of that analogy to education finance is not exactly correct, it illustrates the approach taken by some researchers in assessing the dynamic contribution of education to the economy. Economics has usually considered growth a function of changes in land, labor, and volume of physical capital. If one variable changes, production will change in response; that is, changes in gross national product (GNP) depend on changes in land, capital, and labor. Where the equation fails is in relation to changes in the "educational stock" of employees (i.e., human capital) because labor traditionally has not included a value for workers' qualifications. Failure to account for human capital has resulted in an unexplained residual effect. In other words, solving the equation results in the analogy of the sum and its parts, as land, labor, and capital sum to *less* than 100% of dynamic increase in GNP—with the unexplained residual being human capital.

Recognized studies have supported the concept of residual effect. Schultz argued that people acquire a stock of knowledge and skills that is useless until put to work. As worker knowledge grows, productivity increases. Examining data regarding the labor force, Schultz looked at the distribution of education by years of schooling and the cost at each level after adjusting for increases in length of the school year over time.[15] He found that the "stock of education" as measured by the cost of producing that same education had increased from $180 billion (adjusted to 1956 prices) in 1929 to $535 billion in 1957. He also found that only $69 billion in costs could be tied to the 38% growth in the size of the labor force. From this, it was imputed that the remaining $286 billion represented a net increase in the stock of education. At the same time, labor income grew $71 billion beyond where it would be if earnings had stayed constant at 1929 levels. The $71 billion was termed residual. After annualizing returns, Schultz held that the increase in education per person from 1929 to 1957 explained 36% to 70% of residual economic growth—in essence, he concluded that the economy improved by 36% to 70% as a consequence of investing in schools.

A second approach is seen in Denison's classic works as he studied the impact of 20 variables in the United States from 1909 to 1957. Using changes in worker age, gender, hours, and so on, he calculated increases in labor productivity and found a residual of 0.93%, with 0.67% of that amount attributable to education—a net effect attributing 23% of increased productivity to schooling. In a later study, Denison showed that increases in education explained 33% of growth in GNP from 1973 to 1981. Another Denison study, in which he examined the economies of nine Western nations and concluded that the value of education was highest for the United States, was even more positive.[16]

Rate-of-Return Studies

The impact of education can also be seen at smaller levels by considering the relative value of schooling at elementary, secondary, and postsecondary levels. These studies have followed two models: calculating the present discounted value of education and calculating individual rates of return for added schooling. Both methods imply

---

15 Theodore Schultz, "Education and Economic Growth," in *Social Forces Influencing American Education*, 16th Yearbook of the National Society of Education, edited by Nelson B. Henry and Paul A. Witty (Chicago: University of Chicago Press, 1961), 63.

16 Edward F. Denison published a series of studies examining these concepts. See, *The Sources of Economic Growth in the United States and the Alternatives Before Us* (New York: Committee for Economic Development, 1962); *Why Growth Rates Differ* (Washington, DC: Brookings Institution, 1967); *Why Growth Rates Differ: Postwar Experience In Nine Western Countries* (Washington, DC: Brookings Institution, George Allen & Unwin Ltd, 1968); *Accounting for United States' Economic Growth, 1929–1969* (Washington, DC: Brookings Institution, 1974); *Accounting for Slower Economic Growth: The United Sates in the 1970s* (Washington, DC: Brookings Institution, 1979).

that consumers' decisions concerning how much education to buy have an effect on personal income.

The *present-discounted-value* (PDV) method takes actual present value of schooling and multiplies by a discount rate to estimate its future value. PDV is similar to a price deflator that holds dollars constant for purchasing power over time. For example, the average teacher salary in 1970 in current dollars was $8,626. By 2012, the figure had risen to $56,643.[17] Although factors such as seniority and advanced degrees account for some of the increase, a large part of the change is due to inflation.[18] Holding prices constant and deflating salaries to the same year permits comparison of true gains or losses. The price deflator analogy helps in understanding the PDV method of assessing the worth of education to an individual.

The *individual rate-of-return* (IRR) method also has been used. Its advantage lies in not having to predict an accurate discount rate by using a zero interest rate; that is, what is education worth in *today's* market? The IRR method examines the cost of each level of education compared to benefits at each level. The principle is that the higher the expected income and the lower the cost, the higher the rate of return will be. Figure 2.5, discussed earlier, shows weekly earnings based on dropping out, completing high school, completing some college or an associate degree, and completing college. The differential is significant at each level of educational attainment; according to such data, the rate of return is highly favorable.

Of course, the cost varies for different levels of education. Elementary schooling costs least, if for no other reason than that facility costs are lower than for the specialized program needs in high schools. But there are other costs for different levels of education that affect profitability of extra units of schooling. For instance, in advanced nations child labor is nonexistent. Yet as children grow, the cost of education should include loss of earnings from their being in school instead of in the workforce. Similarly, at postsecondary levels, costs are increased by tuition and living costs. Additionally, more years of postsecondary education do not yield uncapped earnings because career choice affects income. For example, the income of a teacher with a doctoral degree will not match that of a physician although they both have the same number of years of formal education. Also, some societies value some professions more than others, though they require the same amount of education, and hence pay one profession more than another.

Some recent studies have tested returns on elementary schooling, but these studies are largely confined to developing nations that are beginning to develop educational systems. In such nations, even a few years of schooling offer substantial returns on investment. Far more studies have examined returns on secondary schooling. Becker studied returns in the 20th century, finding an IRR for high school graduates of

---

17 U.S. Department of Education, *Digest of Education Statistics 2012*, "Estimated Average Annual Salary of Teachers in Public Elementary and Secondary Schools, by State: Selected Years, 1969–70 through 2011–12," Table 91 (Washington, DC: Institute of Education Sciences, National Center for Education Statistics), nces.ed.gov/programs/digest/d12/tables/dt12_091.asp.

18 Edwyna Synar and Jeffrey Maiden, "A Comprehensive Model for Estimating the Financial Impact of Teacher Turnover," *Journal of Education Finance* 38, 2 (2012): 130–144.

16% in 1939, 20% in 1949, and 28% in 1958.[19] His estimates were close to Schultz's, who estimated the return on high school at 25%. Other studies have agreed, with the added note that human capital has grown at the same time.

Returns on postsecondary education are murkier. Career choice has a strong bearing on earnings, and higher levels of education reach a point of diminishing returns where more school does not yield more income. There is an argument that the United States is overinvested in higher education, creating a glut of overqualified people because the nation's job market cannot keep up with the supply of college graduates. Postsecondary studies show returns on undergraduate degrees varying by career field, with graduate degrees even more dependent on field. Yet despite variation, all returns on education are sizable because when all options are weighed, evidence shows that poorly educated people are left behind in a nation that has steadily escalated its social and economic standards at a dizzying pace.

Education and Socioeconomic Investment

Arguments that many services are best provided at public expense are well founded, especially from an efficiency perspective. Other benefits accrue too, including freedom, lower crime, less need for other types of public support, and socioeconomic mobility. These benefits have led scholars to claim that society pays many such costs as a way to stem an adverse tide, while the cost of education actually reverses the tide and pays long-term dividends.

At the most basic level, the greatest return on education is survival of democracy itself. Democracy may be described as government by consent, with the freedom to decide to be led and to decide for oneself the leaders to be chosen. These decisions are not made lightly because they require defenses against abuse, namely, a level of thinking and literacy to prevent class-based, class warfare, greed and to foster informed voter behavior. Liberals and conservatives alike have embraced this view—long ago, Adam Smith noted in *The Wealth of Nations* that education is necessary to prevent people from becoming incapable of self-enlightenment and devoid of all charity.[20] Thomas Jefferson, a champion of public schools, argued eloquently that "if a nation expects to be ignorant & free, in a state of civilization, it expects what never was & never will be."[21]

The relationship between education, democracy, and self-reliance thus cannot be overestimated, and from these roots flow other benefits as people are empowered to lead productive lives. Much research, for example, points to reduced crime and reduced need for welfare assistance due to education. If the cost of schools is high, the cost of crime is higher because that money could have better uses. Economists and criminologists alike take a dim view of how society might misspend its resources, arguing that

---

19 Gary Becker, *Human Capital: A Theoretical and Empirical Analysis, with Special Reference to Education* (New York: National Bureau of Economic Research, 1964).

20 Adam Smith, *An Inquiry into the Nature and Causes of the Wealth of Nations* (New York: Modern Library, 1937), 734–735.

21 Thomas Jefferson, letter to Charles Yancey, January 6, 1816, page 7.

locking up millions of Americans misses the investment mark when comparing the United States to other developed countries; that is, those nations most inclined to incarcerate residents typically engage in the lowest welfare spending, while those nations most inclined to support welfare spending typically have the lowest incarceration rates.[22] And it has long been widely known that far too many prison inmates are juveniles and therefore prime candidates for education, so that when the cost of education is compared to the cost of incarcerating young offenders the loss to society is enormous. The proposition is irrefutable—even the harshest critic should agree that money is better spent on education and job training than incarceration. Perhaps the greatest accolade for investing in education was given by Alfred Marshall:

> We may then conclude that the wisdom of expending public and private funds on education is not to be measured by its direct fruits alone. [O]ne new idea, such as Bessemer's chief invention, adds as much to England's productive power as the labour of a hundred thousand men. All this spent during many years in opening the means of . . . education to the masses would be well paid for if it called out one more Newton or Darwin, Shakespeare or Beethoven.[23]

Whether society will continue to embrace such grand expressions seems highly questionable. Today's populace is less willing to invest uncritically in schools, and the latest trends in education legislation seem focused on a market model with immediate results. NCLB and the Race to the Top are the most current examples of models that pay close homage to consumer preferences, with huge implications for how investment in schools occurs. The net sum is that all things change, and the ebb and flow of economic thought and the purposes of schooling are meaningfully swayed by the times. Our society has been undergoing a decades-long radical change in how it sees money and schools, thereby raising the question of how schools have historically been financed and where public education may be headed—a question that requires some basic understanding of school governance structures.

THE STRUCTURE OF SCHOOL GOVERNANCE IN AMERICA

Americans accustomed to the vast educational system of our time may be surprised to learn that formal public education is a recent event in this nation. Yet even ancient civilizations often had good education systems for their day. The ancient Greeks saw education as the cornerstone of democracy, holding that the mark of a free man was the ability to read, write, think, and speak. Americans today are likely to argue that

---

22 See, for example, David Downes and Kirstine Hanson, "Welfare and Punishment in Comparative Perspective," in *Perspectives on Punishment: The Contours of Control*, edited by Sara Armstrong and Lesley McAra, 133–154 (Oxford, UK: Oxford University Press, 2006).

23 Alfred Marshall, "Education and Invention," in *Perspectives on the Economics of Education*, edited by Charles S. Benson (Boston: Houghton Mifflin, 1961), 83.

the nation's founders foresaw an entitlement to education when they declared that the right to life, liberty, and the pursuit of happiness are secure only in a republic governed by consent of an intelligent people. Surely, today's American would say, the nation's most precious documents have—since the founding of the nation—promised everyone the educational wherewithal for self-governance. Whether that guarantee was actually intended is not clear, but it is true that education resembling what schools are like today did *not* exist prior to the 19th century. This is not to say that there were no schools, but that the current nature of educational systems is in vivid contrast to the historic structure of schools in America.

Brief Historical Roots of American Education

Only a cursory understanding of American history is needed to picture the struggles of settlers in a vast, hostile wilderness. Simply surviving and creating a new way of life was hard enough without the problems of setting up broad government services. In the earliest days of the nation, little in the way of schooling occurred because settlers were too busy feeding themselves and ensuring their personal safety. And there was little motivation for schooling because the skills needed to survive under these conditions had little to do with books.

Whenever schooling did occur in early America, it was the exclusive province of the home or church. But concern for education was evident early on: The first school law was enacted in Massachusetts in 1642, requiring towns to see if children were being taught to read in order to understand religion and to learn a vocation. Formal interest began to grow, and in 1647 Massachusetts passed Ye Old Deluder Satan Act to strengthen the teaching of morality to children by reading the Bible. As the colonies grew, compulsory education for morality gained popularity, and Connecticut, Maine, New Hampshire, and Vermont all passed similar laws by 1720.

As nations move beyond survival mode, they seek higher-order forms such as formal education systems. Toward the end of the 18th century, interest in formal education had taken shape in most colonies. Although education for morality had been the aim of early school laws, the War of Independence in 1776 raised new concern for education in a young nation that had chafed under British rule. The war inspired a call for enlightened government to secure the freedoms that had first led to war. Thomas Jefferson, the great champion of liberty, was among the loudest voices calling for an end to ignorance through education for the common people. In a radical shift from centuries of elitist political control, Jefferson argued that ordinary citizens must be taught to elect good leaders and to keep guard on government. These skills, he said, could only be developed by education for the commoner—a new idea in a world inexperienced in self-determination.

Despite a need to foster morality and self-rule, government-sponsored education progressed slowly for many years after the Revolutionary War. Caught up in westward expansion, Americans found no time for luxuries like schooling. Nor was there much desire, as liberal education had left a distaste with colonists whose experiences had associated education with aristocracy. Moral and economic education could be taught at home, and in the mind of the colonist morally literate and politically wise voters were a luxury that must wait.

Survivalism and expansionism, however, did not last forever. Not everyone wanted to go west, and some were too poor to leave. Great cities sprang up in the early 1800s, populated by droves of immigrants. These groups were both the beginning and the result of industrialization in the new nation because they provided the labor by which great industries could be built. As cities grew, more industry arose, fueling a need for more labor, which in turn caused cities to grow again. As the cycle fed itself, industry began to recognize that not all growth was good because the vast throngs of workers lacked skills. The solution was to call for a new role for education by demanding vocational schooling. Although industrialists argued about whether education solved a need or whether it increased labor costs, the effect was to add economics to education's emerging role.

Rapid growth, especially in great cities, had the effect of increasing the demand for formal education systems. Although the nation had opened its doors to rapid growth in order to aid settlement and expansion, the dizzying speed was unexpected. Immigration skyrocketed—from 1820 to 1840 the nation grew by only 751,000, while from 1840 to 1850 more than 1.7 million people entered the country; more than 16 million immigrants came to the United States between 1840 and 1900. The nation was unprepared to deal with the influx, and social problems became severe as unskilled immigrants clustered into cities. Rural Americans migrated to industrial centers too, because they either had tired of frontier life or were driven from the land. From 1820 to 1900, the U.S. population grew from 10 million to 76 million, resulting in cities beset with problems of poverty and illiteracy.

Solutions had to be found. Educating for morality and self-government were still important, but leaders such as Horace Mann and Henry Barnard argued that education for economic productivity was needed too. Under their leadership, the roots of a uniform public school system emerged in the common school movement. Spurred by immigration, the common school movement reached its peak between 1840 and 1880. Although driven by the need for education for economic productivity, the movement held a fourth thread that would imbed itself in the mind of America. Because it had its roots in people who had fled injustice in search of the American dream, the movement embraced not only a commitment to morality, self-determination, and economics, but also loyalty to justice and equality.

The common schools movement was nothing short of miraculous. It laid the basis for refinements that would profoundly shape the nature and scope of American schools. One refinement forever altered the face of education. Although much of the nation's prosperity was brought about by a favorable political climate for commerce, an unsavory aspect of industry before 1900 was the presence of child labor. The United States had followed the European model of exploiting children, but with industrialization came labor unions, which in the last half of the 19th century worked to improve wages of adults with the side effect of advocating for child labor laws. The common schools movement was jointly benefited because child labor laws had the effect of removing children from the workforce, making schools an obvious caretaker.

By the dawn of the 20th century, public education only faintly resembled colonial schools. But though the resemblance was small, the roots were deep. Education for morality had moved from religion to humanism based on the views of social reformers, but the expectation that schools would build character remained. Likewise, as the nation won its freedom, education for self-governance held strong to preserve democracy. As industry and commerce grew, education for economics was spurred by massive immigration, setting the stage for calls for reform that critics would issue throughout the 20th century. In sum, schools had been given a key role in a nation that had become vast and diverse—a role reformers struggle with today as wars over morality, democracy, economics, and equality still rage.

Development of School Organization in America

Not surprisingly, the history of schooling in the United States has had a powerful influence on modern educational governance. Within the broad picture of growth there were other distinct trends spanning more than 200 years. For instance, the tendency of people to cluster on the basis of religious, political, or ethnic heritage led to strong views concerning education and how it should be governed. Early New England developed as a religious state with strong regulation and taxation for schools. Religious groups disfavoring state control also settled the middle colonies, including Maryland, New Jersey, and Pennsylvania. Following still another model, other middle and southern colonies leaned toward the view that public schools were charity schools for paupers, thereby eschewing state control or tax support. Such attitudes were deeply rooted and are still evident today in geographic regions notable for the prevalence or absence of private schools and where state school-funding approaches may show sympathy for those same views.

It is equally unsurprising that westward settlement led to school governance designs having little commonality. Scholars have long decried the problems of tracing educational history due to settlers' fierce resistance to any government control. Katz captures the tension well:

> The conflicts between the democratic localists and the bureaucrats often assumed the atmosphere of an undeclared guerrilla war of sabotage and resistance, as local school districts refused to comply with state regulation and parents refused to comply with the state's representative, the teacher. Insofar as most of the resistance came from inarticulate people, it is the hardest and most maddening aspect of nineteenth century educational history to document. That it existed is, however, beyond doubt, as the frustrated testimony of local and state reformers testifies in almost every document they wrote.[24]

---

24 Michael B. Katz, "From Voluntarism to Bureaucracy in American Education," in *Power and Ideology in Education*, edited by Jeremy Karabel and A. H. Halsey (New York: Oxford University Press, 1977), 394.

Although reformers long tried to impose a standardized educational system, many years passed before the design emerged that is seen today. As the population center of the nation shifted westward, political preferences formed as people settled in and built schools. Intolerant attitudes led dissidents to move on when local traditions did not satisfy their will. Aided by long distances due to sparsely settled lands, the result was creation of thousands of tiny schools serving equally tiny settlements.

Table 2.2, which shows the number of school districts from 1870 to 2010, makes several points. First, citizens today can find schools in their communities that seem inordinately close together, but which hark back to times when travel was difficult, making neighborhood schools a necessity. Second, in earlier times each small town had its own school, a truly vast number given all the towns that lived and died. Third, the number of school districts has been far greater than for any other duplicate units of government because school district boundaries in many states are not coterminous with other governments such as counties. Fourth, while no one knows the highest number of school districts that existed before the turn of the 20th century, the number far exceeded the 117,108 districts found in 1940. Finally, the relationship between growing state control and the number of districts is clear, as the more than 117,000 districts in 1940 fell to less than 14,000 in 2010.

Although thousands of school districts have closed over the years, a high degree of organizational uniformity has not followed. The U.S. Constitution permits wide variation by leaving control of schools to individual states subject to the controlling state constitutional language. States have responded by creating school systems differing greatly in structure, operation, control, and fiscal support. The effect has been to create a system rooted in strong local control, although earlier discussion accurately suggested that local control is weakening as states have adopted an education reform agenda over recent decades. The total picture is best described as a patchwork quilt, as education is highly state-specific in many ways, with vast organizational differences among and within states (see Table 2.3), which reflects the diversity in school organization in the 50 states as late as 2012, when the number of school districts by state ranged from one in Hawaii to over a thousand in California, Illinois, Ohio, and Texas. But most importantly, the struggle over the purpose of schools has endured—a struggle not only regarding the aims of education and who is in control, but also about who is responsible for education's costs and at what level they should be funded. Figure 2.6 shows recent trends in student enrollments by state.

Charter schools exist in 42 states and are allowed under various state laws. Generally, a charter school is publicly funded via tax revenues equal to that of a traditional public school. Charter schools, pursuant to state statutes, are exempt from some, or nearly all, state statutes, rules, and regulations. Charter schools are not exempt from federal laws, rules, or regulations. Typically, charter schools must meet all accountability standards imposed by states. Dependent upon state statute, charter schools may, or may not, be eligible for facility funding and auxiliary programs. In most states, charter schools receive approximately the same funding for the general fund as traditional schools. They may or may not be eligible for state start-up funds or grants.

TABLE 2.2 Number of Public School Districts in Selected Years: 1870–2010

School Year	Regular Public School Districts	Total, All Schools	Total Schools, with Reported Grade Span	Schools with Elementary Grades		Schools with Secondary Grades
				Total	One Teacher	
1869–70	n.a.	116,312	n.a.	n.a.	n.a.	n.a.
1879–80	n.a.	178,122	n.a.	n.a.	n.a.	n.a.
1889–90	n.a.	224,526	n.a.	n.a.	n.a.	n.a.
1899–1900	n.a.	248,279	n.a.	n.a.	n.a.	n.a.
1909–10	n.a.	265,474	n.a.	n.a.	212,448	n.a.
1919–20	n.a.	271,319	n.a.	n.a.	187,948	n.a.
1929–30	n.a.	248,117	n.a.	238,306	148,712	23,930
1939–40	117,108	226,762	n.a.	n.a.	113,600	n.a.
1949–50	83,718	n.a.	n.a.	128,225	59,652	24,542
1959–60	40,520	n.a.	n.a.	91,853	20,213	25,784
1970–71	17,995	n.a.	89,372	65,800	1,815	25,352
1979–80	15,944	87,004	n.a.	n.a.	n.a.	n.a.
1989–90	15,367	83,425	81,880	60,699	630	23,461
1999–2000	14,928	92,012	90,538	68,173	423	26,407
2000–01	14,859	93,273	91,691	69,697	411	27,090
2001–02	14,559	94,112	92,696	70,516	408	27,468
2002–03	14,465	95,615	93,869	71,270	366	28,151
2003–04	14,383	95,726	93,977	71,195	376	28,219
2004–05	14,205	96,513	95,001	71,556	338	29,017
2005–06	14,166	97,382	95,731	71,733	326	29,705
2006–07	13,856	98,793	96,362	72,442	313	29,904
2007–08	13,838	98,916	97,654	73,011	288	30,542
2008–09	13,809	98,706	97,119	72,771	237	29,971
2009–10	13,629	98,817	97,521	72,870	217	30,381

Note: n.a. = not available.

Source: Digest of Education Statistics 2010. Table 91. Washington, DC: NCES, Institute for Education Sciences, U.S. Department of Education, 2011.

TABLE 2.3 Number of Operating Public Schools and Districts, State Enrollments, Teachers, and Pupil/Teacher Ratio by State: School Year 2011–2012

	Operational Schools	Operational Districts	Membership	Teachers	Pupil/ Teacher Ratio
United States	98,328	17,992	49,521,669	3,103,263	16.0
Alabama	1,618	170	744,621	47,723	15.6
Alaska	511	54	131,167	8,088	16.2
Arizona	2,252	662	1,080,319	50,800	21.3
Arkansas	1,108	289	483,114	33,983	14.2
California	10,170	1,187	6,287,834	268,689	23.4
Colorado	1,813	259	854,265	48,078	17.8
Connecticut	1,150	200	554,437	43,805	12.7
Delaware	221	44	128,946	8,587	15.0
District of Columbia	228	56	73,911	6,278	11.8
Florida	4,212	76	2,668,156	175,006	15.2
Georgia	2,388	216	1,685,016	111,133	15.2
Hawaii	287	1	182,706	11,458	15.9
Idaho	762	149	279,873	15,990	17.5
Illinois	4,336	1,075	2,083,097	131,777	15.8
Indiana	1,933	394	1,040,765	62,339	16.7
Iowa	1,411	361	495,870	34,658	14.3
Kansas	1,359	321	486,108	37,407	13.0
Kentucky	1,565	194	681,987	41,860	16.3
Louisiana	1,437	132	703,390	48,657	14.5
Maine	621	260	188,969	14,888	12.7
Maryland	1,451	25	854,086	57,589	14.8
Massachusetts	1,835	401	953,369	69,342	13.7
Michigan	3,550	869	1,573,537	86,997	18.1
Minnesota	2,392	555	839,738	52,832	15.9
Mississippi	1,069	163	490,619	32,007	15.3
Missouri	2,408	572	916,584	66,252	13.8
Montana	826	500	142,349	10,153	14.0
Nebraska	1,090	288	301,296	22,182	13.6
Nevada	649	18	439,634	21,132	20.8
New Hampshire	477	281	191,900	15,049	12.8
New Jersey	2,596	700	1,356,431	109,719	12.4
New Mexico	866	135	337,225	21,957	15.4
New York	4,752	923	2,704,718	209,527	12.9
North Carolina	2,577	236	1,507,864	97,308	15.5
North Dakota	513	223	97,646	8,525	11.5

TABLE 2.3 *continued*

	Operational Schools	Operational Districts	Membership	Teachers	Pupil/ Teacher Ratio
Ohio	3,714	1,079	1,740,030	107,972	16.1
Oklahoma	1,774	575	666,120	41,349	16.1
Oregon	1,261	221	568,208	26,791	21.2
Pennsylvania	3,181	784	1,771,395	124,646	14.2
Rhode Island	308	54	142,854	11,414	12.5
South Carolina	1,223	105	727,186	46,782	15.5
South Dakota	704	171	128,016	9,247	13.8
Tennessee	1,802	140	999,693	66,382	15.1
Texas	8,697	1,262	5,000,470	324,282	15.4
Utah	1,020	126	598,832	25,970	23.1
Vermont	320	369	89,908	8,364	10.7
Virginia	2,170	221	1,257,883	90,832	13.8
Washington	2,365	316	1,045,453	53,119	19.7
West Virginia	759	57	282,870	20,247	14.0
Wisconsin	2,243	462	871,105	56,245	15.5
Wyoming	354	61	90,099	7,847	11.5

Source: Patrick Keaton. *Selected Statistics from the Common Core of Data: School Year 2011–12.* Table 2. Washington, DC: U.S. Department of Education 2013. nces.ed.gov/pubs2013/2013441.pdf.

Typically charter schools receive approval to operate for a specific period of time. A review by the local school board and/or state agency is normally required for the charter school to receive renewal for a specified period of time. Most evaluations of charter schools focus on financial management, curricular offerings, and state achievement standards. State and local regulations vary among the states that allow charter schools. Current data specific to charter schools are changing as charter schools are being created every year in most states while some are being denied continuance for failure to meet standards. States have widely varying models regarding the number, funding, and governance of charter schools, including the manner of accounting. In some states, a charter is for only a single campus, while in others, states have created regulations that allow for a charter for multiple campuses in multiple locations. Table 2.4 reflects the growth of charter schools across the nation, in terms of the number of charters, as well as the enrollment in the last several years.

In recent years, a number of states have seen a growing movement toward virtual education. Forty-eight states have some form of distance education for students at the elementary and secondary level. In 2010, 55% of public school districts had students who took at least one course in a virtual format, with approximately 1.8 million students

25 Barbara Queen and Laurie Lewis, *Distance Education Courses for Public Elementary and Secondary School Students: 2009–10* (U.S. Department of Education, National Center for Education Statistics, Washington, DC), 7–8.

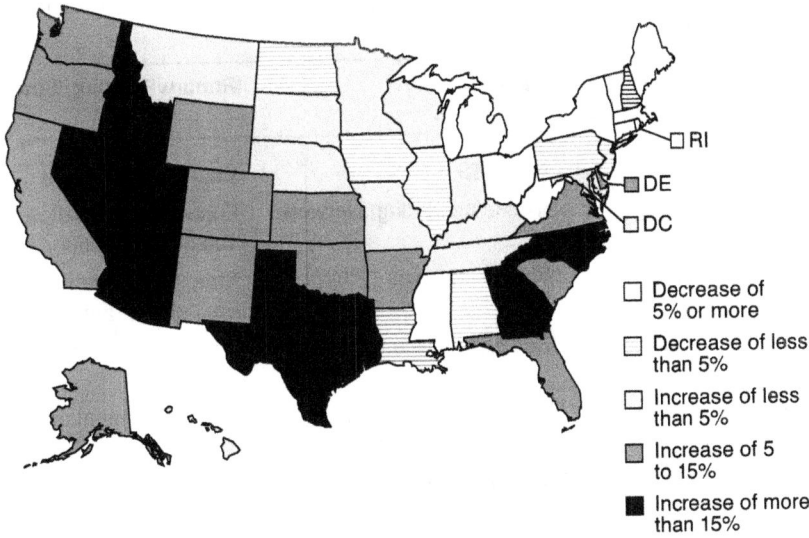

FIGURE 2.6 Projected Percentage Change in Enrollment in Public Elementary and Secondary Schools by State: Fall 2007–2019

Source: William J. Hussar and Tabitha M. Bailey. "Projected Percentage Change in Enrollment in Public Elementary and Secondary Schools by State: Fall 2007–Fall 2019." Figure 4. *Projections of Education Statistics to 2019*, 6. http://nces.ed.gov/pubs2011/2011017.pdf.

enrolled.[25] Nearly every state has some manner of funding distance education. In education finance distribution formulas that are enrollment driven, the funds typically follow the student. In many instances it operates much like a block grant to the virtual school. Some states have a statewide virtual school while others allow students to enroll with any approved virtual course provider. The creation and elimination of virtual schools and course providers reflects the ever-changing nature of this type of elementary and secondary education. Additionally, many school districts offer virtual courses independent of the state. Table 2.5 provides an overview of the different types and models of statewide public virtual education at the elementary and secondary level.

TABLE 2.4 Number and Enrollment of Charter Schools for Selected Years: 2001–2011

	2001	2006	2007	2008	2009	2010	2011
Charter Schools	1,993	3,780	4,132	4,388	4,694	4,952	5,274
Enrollment	448,343	1,012,906	1,157,359	1,276,731	1,433,116	1,610,285	1,787,091

Source: Digest of Educational Statistics 2012. Table 108. National Center for Educational Statistics. nces.ed.gov/programs/digest/d12/table/dt12_108.asp.

TABLE 2.5 Overview of State Public Elementary and Secondary Education Virtual Schools

State	Year Established	Name	Primary Funding Source*
Alabama	2005	ACCESS	State Appropriation
Alaska	2011	Alaska's Learning Network	Enhancing Education through Technology Fund
Arkansas	2012	Virtual Arkansas	State Department of Education Grant
Colorado*	1998	Colorado Online Learning	State Department of Education
Connecticut*	2012	Connecticut Distance Learning Consortium	State Appropriation
Florida	1997	Florida Virtual School	State Department of Education
Georgia	2005	Georgia Virtual School	State Department of Education
Hawaii*	1996	Hawaii Virtual Learning Network	State Department of Education
Idaho	2002	Idaho Digital Learning Academy	State Appropriation
Illinois	2009	Illinois Virtual School	State Appropriation
Iowa*	2012	Iowa Connections Academy and Iowa Virtual Academy	State Department of Education
Kentucky	2012	Kentucky Virtual Campus	State Department of Education
Louisiana	2000	Louisiana Virtual School	State Board of Elementary and Secondary Education
Maryland*	2002	Maryland Virtual Learning Opportunities	State Department of Education
Massachusetts*	2013	Massachusetts Virtual Academy	State Department of Education
Michigan	2000	Michigan Virtual School	State Appropriation
Mississippi	2006	Mississippi Virtual Public School	State Appropriation
Missouri	2007	Missouri Virtual Instruction Program	State Appropriation
Montana	2010	Montana Digital Academy	State Appropriation
New Mexico*	2001	IDEAL-NM (Innovative Digital Education and Learning New Mexico)	State Department of Education
North Carolina	2002	North Carolina Virtual Public School	State Board of Education

TABLE 2.5 *continued*

State	Year Established	Name	Primary Funding Source*
North Dakota*	2000	North Dakota Center for Distance Education	State Appropriation and Course Fees
Oklahoma*	2000	Oklahoma Virtual High School and Oklahoma Connections Academy	State Board of Education
Oregon*	2005	Oregon Virtual School District	State Virtual School District Fund
South Carolina	2007	South Carolina Virtual School Program	State Appropriation
South Dakota	2006	South Dakota Virtual School	State Department of Education
Tennessee*	2011	Tennessee Virtual Academy	State Department of Education
Texas*	2007	Texas Virtual School Network	State Appropriation
Utah*	1994	Utah Electronic High School	State Office of Education Funds
Vermont*	2009	Vermont Virtual Learning Cooperative	State Board of Education
Virginia*	2005	Virtual Virginia	State Appropriation
Washington*	2009	Office of the Supt. of Public Instruction's Digital Learning Department	State Board of Education
West Virginia*	2000	West Virginia Virtual School	State Department of Education
Wisconsin*	2008	Wisconsin Virtual School	State Department of Public Instruction and CESA's (Cooperative Education and Service Agencies)
Wyoming	2008	Wyoming Switchboard Network	State Department of Education

*State virtual schools with an asterisk are privately/publicly funded while those without are entirely publicly funded.

Sources: Justin C. Ortagus, Luke J. Stedrak, and R. Craig Wood."The Funding of Virtual Schools in Public Elementary and Secondary Education." *Educational Considerations* 39 (Spring 2012): 44–54. Updates provided by Luke J. Stedrak.

SOURCES OF FISCAL SUPPORT FOR SCHOOLS

This chapter has briefly examined the links between economics and education and the development of school organizations. Fiscal support for schools has faced a difficult path marked by uncertainty about who should bear the costs. Although education has long interested federal, state, and local policymakers, the types and amounts of support from each level of government have varied. In fact, how schools are funded today is a direct function of how federal, state, and local policymakers have accepted (or denied) responsibility for education.

Federal Support for Schools

Most Americans today are likely to be unsure about the extent of federal involvement in funding public schools. But most people would say that even if the amount of support were questionable, the federal government has had a profound impact on schools. That answer would correctly reflect the federal government's role in education, as it indeed has exercised influence in many ways.

Beginning with the Northwest Ordinance of 1787, which surveyed lands and granted the sixteenth section of each township for educational uses, the federal government embarked on a threefold mission of aiding schools in the name of national interest. One goal was to enhance national defense. A second was meant to aid higher education, and the third sought to influence economic and social issues via education. An additional, but indirect, goal has been by appointments to federal judgeships, which have impacted rulings on lawsuits involving education. At times these goals overlapped, so that the federal role has been greater than otherwise would have been true.

Although scholars often advocate a stronger federal hand in education, they agree on why the federal role has been limited. Many of the nation's founders opposed a strong national government, and even Alexander Hamilton, virtually the lone sympathizer with federalism at the Constitutional Convention in 1787, did not argue for a strong federal role in education. Resistance to central government was so high that only two years after the Constitution was ratified, Congress passed a set of amendments, known as the Bill of Rights, which had profound impacts on education. The Tenth Amendment was important to education because its curbs on federalism spoke to the framers' intent by stating, "The powers not delegated to the United States by the Constitution, nor prohibited by it to the States, are reserved to the States respectively, or to the people."[26] With these words, the doctrine of sovereign limits was formed such that the federal government was *forbidden* a direct role in education because the Constitution is silent on schools; that is, education by default is a state responsibility.

Though education was thus made a state function, Congress has managed a long history of federal influence on education through other direct and indirect avenues. Direct authority has been derived in two ways. The first has been through the powers

26 U.S. Const. Amend. X.

of Congress in Article 1 of the Constitution, which requires Congress to provide a strong national defense—a duty that Congress has used to send large sums of money to schools. The second way has been by creative interpretation of Article 1, Section 8, wherein lies the general welfare clause, which reads that Congress shall have power to "lay and collect taxes, duties, imposts and excises, [and] to pay the debts and provide for the common defense and general welfare of the United States." National defense has been a simple way for Congress to be involved in education, but—more importantly—Congress and the courts have construed the general welfare clause to allow broad federal interest in schools, particularly in the arenas of social and economic issues. Aiding that path has been Congress's indirect influence, as it has used persuasive ways such as withholding federal funds from programs unrelated to schools unless states embrace federal education goals.

Federalism and Defense Education

Education for defense has a long history, with its beginnings generally marked by establishment of the U.S. Military Academy in 1802. Designed to train military leaders, the academy gave rise to other defense colleges: the Naval Academy in 1845, the Coast Guard Academy in 1876, and the Air Force Academy in 1954. The Reserve Officer Training Corps (ROTC) also was created at universities so that future leaders could link civilian education with military training. Other education aid followed, some of which was meant to enhance defense or to help veterans re-enter civilian life.

Although a full list of federal interests in defense education is too lengthy to include here, a sample gives the flavor and breadth. In 1918, the Vocational Rehabilitation Act provided disabled veterans with job training, and similar aid to World War II veterans was given in 1943.[27] In 1944, Congress created the Serviceman's Readjustment Act, known as the GI bill[28] providing educational benefits to millions of returning veterans. In 1941, a change to the Lanham Act granted federal aid to construct and operate schools in areas impacted by federal facilities. In 1950, Congress passed legislation which enhanced this aid, a program that sent millions of dollars to local school districts that lost tax base to military installations.[29] Immediately after World War II, the military established American schools overseas for the children of soldiers in foreign lands. These schools continue today as Department of Defense Schools (DODS).

Some of the largest outlays for defense education were sparked by cold wars and the technology race. In 1950, Congress created the National Science Foundation, which first served defense by training mathematics and science teachers. In 1958, the National Defense Education Act (NDEA) was passed to further improve education in mathematics, science, and foreign languages in response to the launch of the Soviet satellite *Sputnik I*.[30] The NDEA also provided higher education loans and job training for defense occupations. More recently, Congress extended the GI bill to persons

---

27 PL 78–16.
28 PL 78–346.
29 PL 81–815 and PL 81–874.
30 PL 85–865.

entering the military after 1985.[31] Many other programs followed: the Education for Economic Security Act of 1984 reflecting new thinking on defense in the modern world;[32] a continuing interest as typified by the National Defense Authorization Act of 2000;[33] the Higher Education Relief Opportunities for Students Act of 2001 which provided financial waivers to deal with student and family situations resulting from the September 11, 2001, terrorist attacks;[34] and the Higher Education Relief Opportunities for Students Act of 2003 which dealt with student financial aid to address student and family situations resulting from wars and national emergencies.[35]

Federalism and Higher Education

A corollary of federal defense has been aid to higher education. Generally, there is an attempt to separate federal interest in general higher education with the debut of the federal government in nonmilitary higher education affairs marked by the Morrill Act of 1862,[36] which established agricultural and mechanical colleges through land grants or direct payments to all states. A second Morrill Act followed in 1890.[37] In some instances these schools became the land grant universities, with missions of research, teaching, and service in a practical tradition.

Federal interest in higher education did not end with the Morrill Acts. The 1935 Bankhead Jones Act made grants to states for agricultural experiment stations,[38] a program that spilled over to public schools as the Agricultural Adjustment Act of 1938 authorizing farm commodity supports, which later developed into school lunch and milk programs.[39] The 1950 Housing Act authorized loans to construct college housing.[40] Likewise, the Higher Education Facilities Act of 1963 granted aid for classrooms, libraries, laboratories, and other facilities.[41]

With the vast social reforms of the 1960s, the federal government plunged headlong into various aids and entitlements under the Civil Rights Act of 1964,[42] some of which aided higher education. The Civil Rights Act granted funds for in-service training in higher education, especially dealing with desegregation. Other grants such as the Health Professional Educational Assistance Amendments provided scholarships for needy students;[43] likewise, the Higher Education Act of 1965 funded community service and teacher training programs and created the National Teacher Corps and

---

31 PL 95–525.
32 PL 98–377.
33 PL 106–398.
34 PL 107–122.
35 PL 108–76.
36 7 U.S.C. 301 et seq.
37 7 U.S.C. 301 et seq.
38 PL 74–182, 7 U.S.C. 17
39 PL 75–430, 35 U.S.C. 1281.
40 PL 81–475.
41 PL 88–204.
42 PL 88–352.
43 PL 89–290.

graduate fellowships aimed at aiding disadvantaged groups.[44] A long list of government involvements in education over the last several decades similarly reflects contemporary concerns: The Taxpayer-Teacher Protection Act of 2004, which increases the amount of loans that may be forgiven for highly qualified math, science, and special education teachers who agree to serve in high-poverty schools for five years;[45] the Student Grant Hurricane and Disaster Relief Act of 2005, which waived repayments for students receiving federal grant assistance if they were residing in, employed in, or attending an institution of higher education located in a major disaster area;[46] and the Hurricane Education Recovery Act of 2005, which provided funds for states affected by Hurricane Katrina to restart school operations, provide emergency aid for displaced students, and assist homeless youth.[47] By 2013 federal investment in higher education, counting loans, grants, work-study programs, and direct tax benefits exceeded $176 billion.[48] Although K–12 education has been left to the states, the federal government has supported higher education aggressively.

Federalist Interest in Justice and Education

Federal interest in economic and social issues has not been neatly severable from other federal aims, but it has been the most pervasive and sustained of all federal goals for education. Particularly for K–12 schools due to the Tenth Amendment's silence on education, overlap between federal programs has been most apparent, as Congress has had to be creative in order to exert influence. The legal basis for federal intervention rests in the general welfare clause, which has been held to grant broad powers up to the point of congressional free will unless overturned by a court. In *United States v. Butler*, the U.S. Supreme Court ruled that the general welfare clause could be broadly construed unless Congress acted arbitrarily—a difficult judgment made on a case-by-case basis.[49] A further test came in *Helvering v. Davis*, in which the court held that the general welfare clause need not be confined to the constitutional framers' intent, but could shift with the needs of the nation.[50]

Brown v. Board of Education changed the entire nature of schools by ruling that segregation of students denies equal opportunity.[51] But it was not until the Civil Rights Act of 1964 that the federal government seriously entered into the field of education.[52] The events that followed would have a lasting effect by sparking a massive influx of federal aid into a variety of programs aimed at fundamental fairness in the nation's schools.

---

44 PL 89–239.
45 PL 108–409.
46 PL 109–67.
47 PL 109–148.
48 See, *Budget Views and Estimates for Fiscal Year 2014*, Committee on Education and the Workforce, 113th Congress, First Session, February, 2013, 1.
49 56 S. Ct. 312 (1936).
50 57 S. Ct. 904 (1937).
51 347 U.S. at 493.
52 PL 88–352.

Although the list of federal interests is vast, two congressional acts especially accounted for changing the federal relationship to schools—the Elementary and Secondary Education Act (ESEA) of 1965[53] and the Education of the Handicapped Act in 1975.[54] One of Congress's most dramatic policy changes to education came via the ESEA. Much of the ESEA was aimed toward disadvantaged children because the law was a direct outgrowth of the Civil Rights Act. ESEA made grants to elementary and secondary school programs for low income children and provided for libraries, textbooks, and other materials. ESEA also aided educational centers, strengthened state education agencies, and provided funds for research and training. The original ESEA had more than 40 entitlements, each addressing specific interests of Congress.

With regard to fiscal outlays, the most far-reaching provisions of ESEA lay with Title I's provision of supplementary services to low income and culturally disadvantaged children. Children qualified if they met certain criteria, such as the $2,000 family income limit. Entire schools could qualify for Title I status if they met threshold numbers of qualifying children in a single school. Schools qualified on three criteria: number of low-income families; number of children receiving Aid to Families with Dependent Children (AFDC); and a formula taking into account the statewide expenditure per pupil. Title I grew rapidly from $746.9 million in 1965 to its peak of $3 billion in 1980. In 1981, Congress repealed the ESEA in response to President Reagan's efforts to streamline the bureaucracy and to reverse erosion of state control that was said to have occurred under an activist Congress. In 1982, Congress passed the Education Consolidation and Improvement Act (ECIA), which continued ESEA but restructured federal involvement. Title I continued as Chapter 1, but many other programs were collapsed. Chapter 1 changed too, as more local discretion came via block grants. More than 40 other programs were collapsed into Chapter 2 while new provisions relating to administration were made under Chapter 3, reducing the role of the federal government and returning many powers to the states. ECIA did allow several other programs to remain freestanding, including Vocational Education, Education of the Handicapped, National School Lunch, Higher Education, Impact Aid, Title VII Bilingual Education, and Title IX Women's Educational Equity.

Congress also broadened its involvement in education by enacting the Education of the Handicapped Act (EHA) in 1975[55] in response to intensive litigation seeking to ensure the rights of children with disabilities. The challenge that drove PL 94–142 was the 1972 lawsuit in *Pennsylvania Association of Retarded Citizens (PARC)*.[56] Although many states provided some special education services, provisions often were minimal, permissive, or nonexistent. Decided for plaintiffs, *PARC* unleashed a series of lawsuits aimed at forcing states to provide special education services to all children. With

---

53 PL 89–910.
54 PL 94–142.
55 PL 94–142.
56 Pennsylvania Association of Retarded Citizens (PARC) v. Pennsylvania, 343 F.Supp. 279 (1972).

congressional passage of the EHA, states failing to provide services were denied federal aid to schools. To help states provide services, Congress appropriated $300 million and authorized itself to provide up to 40% of special education costs. Although federal support has never come close to the 40% goal, federal aid and pressure by courts have discouraged states from refusing to provide services. Special education laws have undergone periodic revision, including reauthorization of the Individuals with Disabilities Act in 2004.[57]

Federal interest in elementary and secondary education has continued to the present day. Recent laws have included the Civil Rights Act of 1991,[58] the 1994 passage of Goals 2000: Educate America Act,[59] the School-to-Work Opportunities Act of 1994,[60] the Safe Schools Act of 1994,[61] and the Improving America's Schools Act,[62] which revised the ESEA. Topping the list of recent laws having significant impact is, of course, the No Child Left Behind Act[63] of 2001, which reauthorized the ESEA and mandated high-stakes testing, accountability, early reading programs, and parental choice programs—requirements later heightened in intensity by the proposed reauthorization in *Building on Results: A Blueprint for Strengthening the No Child Left Behind Act.*[64] These efforts show that while the federal government has no direct duty to education, it has taken great interest and at times has even commandeered a central role. The only reasonable conclusion is that if the K–12 services funded in part by the federal government were left to local or state units of government, the impact would be enormous—an impact equal to $76 billion, 12.7% of school districts' revenues (see Table 2.6).

State Support for Schools

In the absence of a federal duty to education, states have had to create education finance distributional formulas in order to fund the services demanded by citizens or risk telling local communities that they must rely on local taxes to pay for schools. The inequalities of local ability to pay have been so great, however, that virtually all states over the last century have assumed some level of responsibility for funding schools, albeit reluctantly in some cases.

Although public elementary and secondary education is a state responsibility, its funding has been a highly contentious debate over the years that has caused a huge and still unsettled shift in the balance of power between local and state governments. In this

---

57 PL 108–466.
58 PL 102–166.
59 PL 103–227.
60 PL 103–239.
61 PL 103–227.
62 PL 103–382.
63 PL 107–110.
64 U.S. Department of Education, 2007. https://www2.ed.gov/policy/elsec/leg/nclb/buildingon results.pdf.

striking fiscal interplay, states moved, on average, from funding only 16.5% of school costs in 1920 to 43.4% in 2010.

Table 2.6 reflects that three levels of government share schools' costs. As we have seen, the federal role is limited. Because the Constitution grants plenary powers to states, a major portion of school costs has fallen to the states, who in turn have delegated some level of that responsibility to local school districts. Although slow to accept major responsibility, states have, over time, assumed greater proportions of these costs out of necessity and because the courts have found a weighty duty to fund education within the individual states' constitutional provisions. States have accepted their funding role quite unevenly. On average, in 2010, states and local school districts shared funding education equally, each contributing 43.4%. However, across states, the percentage varied greatly, from 28.4% to 81.6%. It is relatively simple to describe how the federal government has aided education—but in contrast there are 50 states, each with its own constitution, and so a nearly equal number of ways to fund schools has emerged.

Nevertheless, each state provides aid for schools. The amount and method depend on several factors. The first factor is usually the wealth of each local school district.[65] Generally speaking, states try to equalize school spending by granting more fiscal aid to poorer school districts; politically, however, this is difficult. A second factor is the amount of federal school aid flowing to a given state. A good example is federal impact aid. In some states, the amount of land exempt from local taxes due to federal installations is high; in such cases, state aid has been important, but the presence of impact aid may have moderated state aid amounts. A third factor is the operation of political philosophies that have driven the design of state education finance distribution formulas. For example, some states have adopted equalization aid formulas that inversely link local wealth and state fiscal aid. Other states have chosen minimum foundation plans to help school districts reach a base expenditure level before leaving the balance of costs to local taxpayers. Only a few states have even proposed full state funding (see Chapter 3 for a full discussion of state aid formulas). A fourth factor of growing importance has been the force of law via education funding lawsuits. The result is that state education finance distribution formulas are a function of political, legal, and economic realities. As noted previously, the level and type of state financial support for education has developed unevenly across states and over time, resulting in widely varied mixes of federal, state, and local revenues we see today.

The fragmentation brought about by state authority over many years, restrained mostly by politics and courts and fitful surges in federal interest, has left a patchwork effect in terms of how each state funds public schools. The result has been that the state education finance distribution formulas for elementary and secondary education mirror

---

65 It is important to note for the student of education finance that the authors use the term "school district" in a generic manner throughout the text. The local educational agency providing public education goes by different statutory names, e.g., school corporations in Indiana, school divisions in Virginia.

the economic and political realities of each state. It is unfortunate in some ways that such variability has been able to develop because—to whatever extent money buys quality—the value of an education may be highly unequal across states since the range of expenditures and programs is great. In some states educational facilities are not a high priority, while other states give it great emphasis. Consequently, beliefs regarding the value of public education have had a powerful impact on the amount of money invested in state education finance distribution plans. Although it can be argued that needs and costs differ among states, as well as the ability of the state to raise revenues, it is difficult to see that wide expenditure differences per pupil are a result of careful analysis of educational needs. Inversely, it is also difficult for school leaders to explain why spending for schools should increase when the public often is convinced that pupil achievement is unsatisfactory. And it is ultimately more difficult to explain these realities when expenditure levels differ greatly not only across states, but also across school districts within single states as well. Regardless of these disparities, however, the record shows an increasing state role in funding elementary and secondary education over time, but it remains to be seen whether or not recent attempts by states to take greater control of education will result in a larger state funding role.

Local Support for Schools

Even though citizens are often aware of state aid, they are convinced that education remains a locally funded enterprise. This conviction arises from the fact that schools are highly visible in every community and have been regarded as locally controlled from the earliest days of the nation. It is difficult to live and work today without being aware of the turmoil surrounding local school boards, the high profile of local school leaders, and the tensions affecting the portion of local property taxes dedicated to schools. As discussed within this chapter, states have assumed a much larger role in educational issues, especially via mandating accountability. This discussion also makes the case that not all states have assumed equal responsibility for school costs so that wide variance in method and amount of fiscal support continues to affect public elementary and secondary education. Thus, the examination of local cost-share issues is necessary in order to gain a complete snapshot of school funding.

According to Table 2.1, decreasing reliance on local funding for public schools evolved over time. Beginning in 1920 with the first reported divisions of costs, 83% of the total $970 million funding fell on local districts. The first big shift came in 1940, as the local share of the $2.26 billion dropped to 68%. By 1970, the local share of the $40.27 billion available to schools had dropped to 52%. By 1990, the local share made up 47% of the $208.5 billion cost for public K–12 schools. By 2011, the local share stood at about 44% of the total amount available for K–12 education.

Although the proportion of local spending fell over the last century, the picture is actually unstable. For example, it is true that local support for schools in the nation's earlier days was high as a percentage of total costs compared to today. But by many accounts, local dollars have not declined, either in total or in aggregate burden. Locally, gross dollars supplied by taxpayers have increased due to inflation and as a result of increased costs tied to other factors, such as expanded programs arising either by local choice or in response to federal and state mandates. Likewise, aggregate tax burden has not declined much overall and actually may have increased, as the additional dollars needed in modern complex school organizations have soared and as other governmental units have increased taxes simultaneously. Although the term *municipal overburden* was coined to depict demand on urban taxpayers from multiple taxing units such as cities, counties, police and fire departments, central water and sewage systems, schools, and other services, tax levels in rural and urban settings alike have led tax critics to charge that there has been very little easing of taxpayer burden.

A second issue of local responsibility lies in recognizing the different realities of elementary and secondary education funding in the 50 states. States have been free to create funding systems to meet the states' constitutional obligation except for the pressure of politics, which can force similarities between states, and the demand by the courts to fund education in compliance with the state constitutional mandate. Thus, reform has occurred over the years. But despite such events, experience in individual states has not led to equal shifts in local school districts' share of costs. Tax burdens are very different among states, and national averages do not capture differences between states.

A third issue of local responsibility rests in the basic nature of how local shares are determined. School districts typically derive revenue from a local *tax base*. Although some states tax more than one type of object to raise school revenue, most states rely on *real property* to define a school district's tax base. This means that real estate is often the main source of tax revenue at the local level. No two school districts contain exactly the same property values, so that highly unequal *tax capacity* may be evident from one school district to the next. A simple illustration makes this clear. Urban properties are often quite valuable, with businesses, homes, and land commanding high prices. Rural land is often less so because it consists predominantly of land used for agriculture. Unless rural land has other attributes such as natural resources to make it more valuable, urban areas will have much higher *property wealth*. That wealth, or *assessed valuation*, is generally the basis for deriving school revenue by assessing taxes against each property. State statutes define assessed valuation methodologies and collections. For example, an acre of urban land might sell for millions of dollars depending on location. In a rural area, a one-acre home site might sell for $3,000—far less if it is remotely located. A *tax rate* of 10 *mills*[66] on the urban acre would yield $10,000 in school tax revenue, while the rural home site would yield only $30—a vast difference, with implications for the ability of a local district to provide adequate funding for schools. See the equation below:

Assessed Valuation × Millage Rate = Yield

---

66 A mill equals 1/1,000 of a dollar. Therefore, 1 mill equals $1 tax revenue per $1,000 assessed value (AV). The formula for tax yield is AV × mills = tax yield. Therefore, $1,000,000 × 0.001 = $1,000. Likewise, $3,000 × 0.001 = $3. This does not consider fractional assessment, a practice in many states that takes only a portion of the market value of a piece of property.

Even the implications are complex. These data might suggest a clear rural disadvantage and unfairly high urban wealth while the opposite may be true. For example, it is certain that one feature of an urban area is population density. Thus, high property wealth spread over a large population may actually yield low *per capita* wealth. The urban condition may bring higher costs associated with economically disadvantaged populations and tax base competition (i.e., municipal overburden). Some urban property owners are absentee individuals or businesses, having no community loyalty and interested only in taking profits without reinvesting. Rural conditions are equally complex. Although property may be less costly, ownership rests in fewer hands, which translates into a heavier tax burden per capita than in more populated areas. Also, the lack of urban problems in rural areas does not necessarily result in lower education costs, as smaller populations result in higher per-pupil costs due to diseconomies of scale. In addition, low income families and children are also found in rural communities; in fact, some rural areas have a higher incidence of poverty than some cities.

A fourth feature of local responsibility is actually a complication of how local school districts determine the cost share and—to some extent—the level of total spending. This phenomenon takes several forms and is made more complex by how school district budgets are determined, the interdependency of tax bases, and intergovernmental competition. The concept of municipal overburden was raised earlier, and the broader concept of *tax overburden* applies in some way to almost all school districts, including rural areas. A by-product of overburden is the hostility encountered by many local school districts when seeking to increase education funding through an increase in the local property tax. In addition, in a number of states, the community must vote to approve school budgets. And even though some states allow for *local option leeway*; that is, giving school boards the option of additional local *tax effort* for schools, local voter approval is required. As state aid plans limiting voter leeway have come into existence and as overall tax burdens have grown, voter approval has become harder to obtain. A further complicating factor in some states is the issue of *fiscal dependence* where local school budgets are submitted to a higher authority in tandem with budgets of other taxing units such as cities and counties. In these circumstances, fiscal dependency creates problems because local school districts may have trouble securing adequate revenue when competition for a finite tax pool includes multiple units of local government.[67] In sum, depending upon state law, local school district budgets can be constrained in a number of ways.

The issues driving local responsibility and ability to pay for schools are so numerous that it is difficult to tell from percentages alone why the local share in a particular state has declined or increased. What is clear is that school districts differ in ability to pay and that experience in the individual states varies widely. It is also clear that if local districts depended entirely on local tax bases, unconscionable disparities would follow.

---

67 See, e.g., Carlee Poston Escue, "Adequate Yearly Progress as a Means of Funding Public Elementary and Secondary Education for Impoverished Students: Florida Funding," *Journal of Education Finance* 37 4 (Spring 2012): 347–373.

TABLE 2.6 Revenues for Public Elementary and Secondary Schools by Source and State: 2009–2010

State	Dollars (in thousands)				Distribution by %		
	Total	Federal	State	Local	Federal	State	Local
United States	597,485,869	75,997,858	259,809,768	261,678,243	12.7	43.5	43.8
Alabama	7,239,691	1,168,016	3,800,153	2,271,522	16.1	52.5	31.4
Alaska	2,338,215	369,729	1,461,906	506,580	15.8	62.5	21.7
Arizona	10,069,959	1,893,298	3,896,117	4,280,545	18.8	38.7	42.5
Arkansas	5,160,401	819,459	2,686,231	1,654,711	15.9	52.1	32.1
California	64,130,242	8,855,246	34,743,249	20,531,747	13.8	54.2	32.0
Colorado	8,852,609	730,363	3,860,026	4,262,220	8.3	43.6	48.1
Connecticut	9,895,487	854,645	3,463,790	5,577,052	8.6	35.0	56.4
Delaware	1,784,101	218,204	1,046,317	519,580	12.2	58.6	29.1
Florida	26,056,857	4,200,101	8,216,579	13,640,177	16.1	31.5	52.3
Georgia	17,835,791	2,645,785	6,764,686	8,425,320	14.8	37.9	47.2
Hawaii	2,564,855	382,399	2,093,299	89,157	14.9	81.6	3.5
Idaho	2,222,539	462,867	1,284,139	475,533	20.8	57.8	21.4
Illinois	28,263,059	3,508,917	8,021,217	16,732,925	12.4	28.4	59.2
Indiana	13,641,695	1,513,137	6,441,408	5,687,150	11.1	47.2	41.7
Iowa	5,541,140	743,561	2,217,893	2,579,686	13.4	40.0	46.6
Kansas	5,487,071	641,619	2,893,517	1,951,936	11.7	52.7	35.6
Kentucky	6,873,286	1,139,931	3,582,406	2,150,950	16.6	52.1	31.3
Louisiana	8,215,973	1,572,272	3,533,026	3,110,675	19.1	43.0	37.9
Maine	2,639,779	315,277	1,079,330	1,245,173	11.9	40.9	47.2
Maryland	13,352,511	1,039,305	5,544,364	6,768,842	7.8	41.5	50.7
Massachusetts	15,570,234	1,175,524	6,476,420	7,918,291	7.5	41.6	50.9
Michigan	19,401,180	2,575,799	10,516,655	6,308,726	13.3	54.2	32.5
Minnesota	10,639,251	1,326,127	6,309,625	3,003,499	12.5	59.3	28.2
Mississippi	4,443,683	945,971	2,109,083	1,388,629	21.3	47.5	31.2
Missouri	10,157,112	1,515,939	2,971,265	5,669,907	14.9	29.3	55.8
Montana	1,616,262	259,304	753,976	602,983	16.0	46.6	37.3
Nebraska	3,693,930	469,503	1,220,466	2,003,961	12.7	33.0	54.3
Nevada	4,310,014	367,140	1,406,630	2,536,244	8.5	32.6	58.8
New Hampshire	2,810,018	351,279	902,020	1,556,719	12.5	32.1	55.4
New Jersey	25,856,286	2,422,449	9,412,795	14,021,042	9.4	36.4	54.2
New Mexico	3,760,801	789,309	2,384,730	586,762	21.0	63.4	15.6
New York	57,146,375	5,122,664	23,438,008	28,585,703	9.0	41.0	50.0
North Carolina	13,056,767	1,991,491	7,602,930	3,462,346	15.3	58.2	26.5

TABLE 2.6 *continued*

State	Dollars (in thousands)				Distribution by %		
	Total	Federal	State	Local	Federal	State	Local
North Dakota	1,256,048	277,989	552,862	425,197	22.1	44.0	33.9
Ohio	22,729,890	2,452,032	10,017,540	10,260,318	10.8	44.1	45.1
Oklahoma	5,699,758	978,847	2,726,116	1,994,795	17.2	47.8	35.0
Oregon	6,211,294	820,955	2,945,986	2,444,352	13.2	47.4	39.4
Pennsylvania	26,408,846	2,887,079	9,456,502	14,065,265	10.9	35.8	53.3
Rhode Island	2,262,193	259,486	790,260	1,212,447	11.5	34.9	53.6
South Carolina	7,837,314	1,092,174	3,431,142	3,313,999	13.9	43.8	42.3
South Dakota	1,300,147	253,761	404,402	641,985	19.5	31.1	49.4
Tennessee	8,528,047	1,158,247	3,842,346	3,527,454	13.6	45.1	41.4
Texas	50,045,607	7,787,692	19,714,162	22,543,753	15.6	39.4	45.0
Utah	4,464,562	560,352	2,283,683	1,620,527	12.6	51.2	36.3
Vermont	1,638,396	174,139	1,337,034	127,223	10.6	81.6	7.8
Virginia	14,692,849	1,527,093	5,485,997	7,679,759	10.4	37.3	52.3
Washington	11,817,488	1,401,295	6,931,627	3,484,566	11.9	58.7	29.5
West Virginia	3,432,220	536,424	1,899,967	995,830	15.6	55.4	29.0
Wisconsin	11,104,749	1,163,103	4,975,033	4,966,614	10.5	44.8	44.7
Wyoming	1,708,365	124,360	880,853	703,152	7.3	51.6	41.2

Source: *Digest of Education Statistics 2010*. Table 203. Washington, DC: NCES, Institute for Education Sciences, U.S. Department of Education, 2012.

And finally, it is clear that the federal, state, and local partnership is both variable and essential: Education has long been a partnership in America—the real issue is refinement of that partnership in ways that enhance fiscal adequacy and equity for every child.

WHAT CONSTITUTES ADEQUATE AND EQUITABLE FUNDING FOR SCHOOLS?

The importance of adequate and equitable funding is heightened by the vast scope and costs of education, changing demographics, and links between education and economic and social progress. Even though current research cannot specify with exactitude the link between student achievement and money, there is a longstanding belief that society must guard against underinvesting in education in order to avoid destructive economic and social consequences. In this uncertain context, policymakers have been challenged to fund education at an appropriate level.

The result has been an unending debate over money and schools. While some views deal with what schools mean to different members of society, perhaps the greatest issue is over how school money is distributed. Part of the struggle arises because there will never be enough funds to address every educational and societal need there, so that distribution becomes even more critical. By all accounts, the differing views have escalated due to greater willingness to pursue confrontational remedies such as legal challenges to state education finance distribution formulas. Some researchers are quick to assert that more money makes better schools, arguing that schools distribute economic and social opportunity and that equal opportunity depends on the quality of schools children attend. They further contend that despite lack of a tight link between money and outcomes, school quality is powerfully affected by purchased resources such as highly qualified teachers and modern facilities. They offer the challenge that people who argue the irrelevance of money still prefer more money be spent on the education of their own children. Under these conditions, litigants have aggressively sought fair and adequate funding, believing that how states fund education has a direct effect on social and economic justice.

Origins of School Funding Challenges

For more than a century, the financing of public elementary and secondary education has been a deep concern for courts and policymakers. Although education finance as a discipline only emerged during the early 20th century, issues of school taxation have been a flashpoint since the early days of the nation. Likewise, schools have long been the object of intense conflict regarding equality of educational opportunity as it relates to discrimination, and it is easy to link discrimination to disparities in funding across and within schools, districts, and states.

The history of education finance litigation has played out in federal and state courts. At the federal level, litigation has focused on the interpretation of the United States Constitution in regard to federal responsibility for education, hoping to read a *guaranteed right* into the Constitution. At the state level, litigation has focused on both the *constitutional* and *statutory* demands of each state. State constitutional interpretations have been swayed by the times and attitudes of courts, particularly when there were wide variances among states in the constitutional and statutory provisions for school funding. In both federal and state cases, litigants have sought rulings regarding the meaning of equal opportunity and sought to test the strength of constitutional and statutory language regarding elementary and secondary education. Traditionally, state constitutional challenges have followed three claims: education as a *fundamental right*, the *equal protection* of laws, and the *education articles* of state constitutions. Each of these can be traced from the federal and state origins into modern school finance litigation strategy.

Federal Origins

Although school finance litigation is largely regarded as state-specific, the federal case actually predates all other strategies. Plaintiffs first sought equality in funding by seeking a favorable United States Supreme Court ruling as the supreme law of the land. The logic was that if a ruling were favorable, states would have to follow federal law.

Bringing a federal lawsuit was an understandable act. Equality had been important since the days when the colonial charters sought freedom from British rule. Equality was a key part of the Bill of Rights, and the Fourteenth Amendment to the Constitution guaranteed equality under federal law. The Fourteenth Amendment was critically important because its provisions applied to the individual states:

> No State shall make or enforce any law which shall abridge the privileges or immunities of citizens of the United States; nor shall any State deprive any person of life, liberty, or property, without due process of law; nor deny to any person within its jurisdiction the equal protection of the laws.[68]

A case for school funding fairness was laid in a series of suits testing the limits of equality under the United States Constitution. Earlier cases had laid a groundwork, including overturning of racial segregation, where the practical implications included the costs and organization of schools. The next step was to ask whether unequal money in schools is a type of impermissible inequality under law.

This strategy was actually an extension of judicial sympathy that already existed for other assured fundamental rights. In addition to named rights in the Constitution, the United States Supreme Court had previously ruled on other rights that it found so basic that they could not be denied except by due process of law. The importance of establishing a fundamental right could not be overstated, in that the equality requirement was so strong that these rights must be protected at all costs—a guarantee could possibly link school funding and equal rights under the Fourteenth Amendment's *equal protection* clause. This line of thinking produced two litigation thrusts. One thrust came from defining unequal treatment of *suspect classes*: school funding litigation might prevail, plaintiffs thought, if they could show that money was tied to a protected social class in schools. The second thrust came from seeking ways in which some other fundamental right might be violated by unequal funding. The strategy was perilous—if neither a fundamental right to education nor a suspect class (e.g., poor people) could be established, lawsuits would have to focus on individual state constitutional clauses.

The Early Federal Case

Although federal racial equality litigation actually spanned many decades, it was in *Brown v. Board of Education* in 1954 that equality of educational opportunity found its footing as the United States Supreme Court overturned "separate but equal" education provisions, which had allowed racially segregated schools.[69] Overturning the

---

68 U.S. Const. Amend. XIV, Sec. 1.
69 *Brown v. Board of Education*, 347 U.S. at 493.

entire social and economic history of the United States, the court held that separate but equal was inherently unequal and that education was vital to the health and well-being of the nation. The court stated that education

> is perhaps the most important function of state and local governments. . . . It is the very foundation of good citizenship. . . . In these days, it is doubtful that any child may reasonably be expected to succeed in life if he is denied the opportunity of an education. Such an opportunity, where the state has undertaken to provide it, is a right that must be made available to all on equal terms.[70]

Emboldened by *Brown*, reformers turned to fiscal inequality, believing that the same analysis could apply to the funding of public elementary and secondary education because it was easily proposed that money and educational opportunity varied greatly based on residence in school districts of unequal wealth. Of great value to this theory was a line of argument that unequal school district wealth made a case for wealth discrimination, so that the happenstance of residence could be interpreted as a wealth-based suspect class. By this logic, wealth-disadvantaged children by virtue of their accident of residence in poor school districts were a perfect case in point.

The first federal suit took shape in Virginia in *Burruss v. Wilkerson* in 1969.[71] Plaintiffs based their claims on the Fourteenth Amendment, arguing that state aid was not given to school districts on the basis of educational needs. The United States District Court, however, held that whereas "deficiencies and differences are forcefully put by plaintiffs' counsel . . . we do not believe they are creatures of discrimination by the State. . . . We can only see to it that the outlays on one group are not invidiously greater or less than that of another." The court added "the courts have neither the knowledge, nor means, nor the power to tailor the public moneys to fit the varying needs of these students throughout the state."[72] The tone of *Burruss* foretold much of the potential failure of a federal case. Over the coming years, plaintiffs experienced the same logic, often as federal courts repeatedly drew on the words of previous court decisions to express their own limitations. The near lone exception came in 1972 in *Van Dusartz v. Hatfield*,[73] as a Minnesota federal court held that wealthy districts not only had greater revenue per child but also paid lower tax rates—conditions tied to the child's residence. *Van Dusartz* was hardly the rule, however, as other federal courts complained that their hands were tied by a lack of judicially manageable standards. Equality in federal court was stated negatively, in that absence of money was not the same as discrimination.

---

70 Ibid.
71 *Burruss v. Wilkerson*, 310 F. Supp. 572 (1969).
72 Ibid. at 574.
73 *Van Dusartz v. Hatfield*, 334 F. Supp. 870 (Minn. 1971).

San Antonio v. Rodriguez

The application of this concept was argued before the United States Supreme Court in 1973. In *San Antonio Independent School District v. Rodriguez* the United States Supreme Court overturned the plaintiffs' claims that the state of Texas must be neutral in aiding schools.[74] Additionally, the Supreme Court overturned the plaintiffs' claim that education was of fundamental interest to the state. *Rodriguez* was on appeal to the United States Supreme Court, where plaintiffs argued that the Texas funding system violated federal equal protections by discriminating against a suspect class of poor and that students making up that class were denied the right to equal education. The United States Supreme Court rejected the suspect class argument, however, as it saw only students living in poor school districts, rather than being poor themselves. The Court noted that individual income did not correlate with school district wealth and that even if the link were strong, the Court's view of wealth suspectness was limited to absolute deprivation. Because no student was absolutely deprived of an education, fiscal inequalities were of only relative difference.

The Court also rejected education as a fundamental right. Plaintiffs had argued that education was so prerequisite to other rights that it created a nexus to other established fundamental rights. The Court disagreed, seeing no link between education and other rights. Although the Court criticized the disparities among Texas school districts, a *rational basis* was required to defend the state education finance distribution formula absent invidious discrimination. A rational basis could be found in the Texas goal of promoting local control of schools, and the Court refused to intervene in such a complex and political arena.

Subsequent Federal Litigation

Although *Rodriguez* had a chilling effect on new federal lawsuits, other cases were brought to keep the question alive, especially in light of the fact that the Supreme Court did not completely close the door on future claims. Three cases illustrate the importance of the federal courts in defining a federal role in educational equality.

Thirteen years after *Rodriguez*, plaintiffs in Mississippi sued in *Papasan v. Allain* for equal protection on revenue disparity based on Section Sixteen lands lost during the Civil War.[75] Although the state provided aid to offset losses in affected school districts, by 1981 state funds were only $0.63 per pupil compared to $75.34 per pupil in districts where land had not been taken. Though the case was dismissed in federal district court, the Fifth Circuit Court held on appeal in *Papasan* that although the Eleventh Amendment to the U.S. Constitution did not bar equal protection claims, *Rodriguez* was the standard regarding fiscal disparity. The United States Supreme Court affirmed, but it also sent the case back for further development. *Papasan* was therefore notable for two reasons. First, the complaint was narrowly taken, never drawing the issue of

---

74 *San Antonio Independent School District v. Rodriguez*, 411 U.S. 1 (1973).
75 *Papasan v. Allain*, 478 U.S. 265 (1986), 756 F.2d 1087 (5th Cir. 1985).

fundamentality into the claims. Second, remanding to the lower court, as the Supreme Court noted that unreasonable government action would attract the court's interest, opened a small window of federal interest in school funding.

A second important case arose in Texas as the United States Supreme Court ruled in *Plyler v. Doe* that refusal by a state to educate illegal aliens could invoke federal equal protections.[76] Although the Court stopped short of declaring education a fundamental right, it did approve a higher level of scrutiny in cases of absolute educational deprivation. The court pointed to its hesitancy to forestall any attempt in the federal courts, as it stated:

> Education provides the basic tools by which individuals might lead economically productive lives to the benefit of us all. In sum, education has a fundamental role in maintaining the fabric of our society. We cannot ignore the significant social costs borne by our Nation when select groups are denied the means to absorb the values and skills on which our social order rests.[77]

The third important federal case came in *Kadrmas v. Dickinson Public Schools*, as plaintiffs in North Dakota alleged that fees for bus service denied equal protection because the plaintiff child could not afford to pay for transportation.[78] The United States Supreme Court held for the state, but its 5–4 vote was a bare majority and indicated the unsettled nature of federal education claims. The court warned that *Rodriguez* was not the last word in that there were nuances that deeply interested the court.[79] The minority opinion expressed this well:

> The Court . . . does not address the question whether a state constitutionally could deny a child access to a minimally adequate education. In prior cases this court explicitly has left open the question whether such a deprivation of access would violate a fundamental constitutional right. That question remains open today.[80]

Although *Rodriguez* has been said to close off hope for a successful federal claim, the record disagrees. Federal courts are sympathetic to judicially unmanageable standards, and they are inclined to defer to legislative prerogative. Likewise, the nation's highest court is reluctant to declare education a fundamental right. But it is also clear that the Supreme Court takes an interest in education, as over time it revisits and refines earlier rulings. More recently, plaintiffs have attempted to overturn state education finance distribution formulas arguing the racial intent and thus discrimination against

---

76 *Plyler v. Doe*, 457 U.S. 202 (1982).
77 457 U.S. 202 at 221.
78 *Kadrmas v. Dickinson Public Schools*, 487 U.S. 450, 108 S.Ct. 2481 (1988).
79 See, R. Craig Wood, "*Kadrmas v. Dickinson Public Schools*: A Further Retreat From Equality of Educational Opportunity," *Journal of Education Finance* 15 3 (Winter 1990): 429–436.
80 108 S.Ct. at 2491.

minority children.[81] Again, these attempts have not met with success for the reasons contained herein. In the end, however, it is clear that the case for school finance reform has had to turn to state courts to experience meaningful and systematic success.

State Origins

Development of the state case for equalizing money in schools parallels the federal path—in particular, there has been significant overlap of both time and nature of claims. In fact, lawsuits were often brought simultaneously in state and federal courts in the early days of litigation. For example, *Burruss* and *Rodriguez* were both filed in federal court in the 1960s, but the California case of *Serrano v. Priest* actually ended at the California Supreme Court level in 1971 before the United States Supreme Court had ruled in *Rodriguez* in 1973. The nature of claims also overlapped, as state cases like *Serrano* made federal and state constitutional claims conjointly. But whereas success on the federal front was unlikely, state litigation occurred far more frequently and with significantly greater success.

Serrano v. Priest

The first state education finance distribution formula constitutional challenge to gain attention was *Serrano*,[82] as the California Supreme Court ruled in what would become a model for state school finance litigation. Plaintiffs sought a ruling on issues of a fundamental right to education, wealth as a suspect class, and federal and state equal protection on these grounds. Plaintiffs charged that the state education finance distribution formula created disparity and that these differences impacted the quality of schools. Plaintiffs also charged that some taxpayers paid higher tax rates and received poorer education. The net sum of such finance schemes, plaintiffs alleged, was to make the quality of education impermissibly dependent on local property wealth.

In a sweeping victory for plaintiffs, the state supreme court overturned the California education funding formula, finding that it violated both the federal Fourteenth Amendment and the state constitution's equal protection clause. This ruling ran counter to every trend. The California Supreme Court was harsh in its view of unequal opportunity:

> We have determined that this funding scheme invidiously discriminates against the poor because it makes the quality of a child's education a function of the wealth of his parents and neighbors. Recognizing, as we must, that the right to an education in our public schools is a fundamental interest that cannot be conditional on wealth, we can discern no compelling state purpose necessitating the present method of financing.[83]

---

81 R. Craig Wood, "A Critique of the Federal Challenge to Financing Public Education Along Racial Lines in *Lynch v. Alabama*: How the Plaintiffs, the Defendants, and the Federal District Court Erred in Examining the Funding of Public Education in Alabama," *Education Law and Policy Review* 1 (Spring 2014): 123–171.

82 *Serrano v. Priest*, 487 P.2d 1241 (1971).

83 Ibid. at 1244.

The fact that the federal claim was later overturned by *Rodriguez* did not deter the impact of *Serrano* at the state level because state courts might not adopt the same posture as federal courts; that is, state law may be stricter than federal law. *Serrano* provided a blueprint for continued litigation by its success on state-level fundamentality and equal protection claims, and it showed that state constitutions might be vulnerable in ways unavailable at the federal level. Many states immediately saw *Serrano* as a harbinger of the future. As a result, an explosion of school finance reform litigation followed in other states, along with many states voluntarily acting ahead of anticipated lawsuits. Since this time, nearly every state has faced legal challenges regarding the education finance distribution formula and whether it meets the state constitutional standard. These challenges to the manner of funding public elementary and secondary education have met with successes and failures at the state level.

Subsequent Failures in State Litigation

The case for state-level litigation challenging education finance distribution formulas did not enjoy sudden and sustained success. Although a full accounting of the history of litigation is beyond the scope of this book, a few early cases illustrate that the state-level record included significant failures.[84]

Shortly after *Serrano*, the Michigan Supreme Court handed down its decision in *Milliken*,[85] a ruling that changed in a relatively short time. The original ruling was for plaintiffs and was modeled after *Serrano*, but the victory was short-lived because the Michigan Supreme Court experienced a change of sitting judges—a change that ended in reversal of the ruling. The new court vacated the prior decision on the basis that the evidence did not prove that equal protection of children in low-wealth districts was violated. Of particular importance to the court was the question of linkage between fiscal inputs and achievement, so that additional money could not be shown to provide greater and more equal outcomes.

After *Rodriguez*, the Arizona Supreme Court held for the defendant state in *Shofstall*.[86] The court had been asked to decide if that state's school funding statute violated the state equal protection clause and its "general and uniform" provision in the state's constitution. The court interpreted *general and uniform* to mean that the state would provide a minimum school year, certify personnel, and set course requirements and standards. Although the court found a fundamental right to education, it saw legislative redress as the solution to political problems; that is, school funding.

The Illinois Supreme Court ruled on behalf of the state in *Blase*.[87] Plaintiffs had based their claims on the state constitution's strong wording, which said, "the State shall

---

84 For an overview of education finance litigation, see, R. Craig Wood, David C. Thompson, John Dayton, and Christine Kiracofe, *Education Finance Law: Constitutional Challenges to State Aid Plans, An Analysis of Strategy*, 4th ed. (Dayton, OH: Education Law Association, 2015).

85 *Milliken v. Green*, vacated, 212 N.W.2d 711 (Mich. 1973), 203 N.W.2d 457 (Mich. 1972).

86 *Shofstall v. Hollins*, 515 P.2d 590 (Ariz. 1973).

87 *Blase v. Illinois*, 55 Ill. 2d 94, 302 N.E.2d 46 (Ill. 1973).

provide for an efficient system of high quality public educational institutions and services [and that] the State has the primary responsibility for financing the system of public education." Plaintiffs wanted the state to provide no less than 50% of costs, along with other strict equality provisions. The Illinois Supreme Court rejected this view, ruling that the language expressed only a goal rather than a specific command.

An early state challenge from Washington illustrates a stunning defeat for the plaintiffs in *Northshore v. Kinnear*,[88] wherein the plaintiffs' case failed despite all elements of victory seemingly in place. Plaintiffs' claims included the charge that the state had disobeyed a provision of the constitution, which read, "it is the paramount duty of the state to make ample provision for the education of all children," and that the state had failed to provide a general and uniform system of public schools. Although Washington was regarded as one of the states having the most forceful constitutional language, the Washington Supreme Court nonetheless denied these claims, noting that even if the state were only one school district, spending per child would still depend on geography, climate, terrain, social and economic conditions, transportation, special services, and local choices in curricula. The strength of language regarding "ample provision" for education was viewed unfavorably, as the court noted, "constitutionally speaking, the duty or function is the same as any other major duty or function of state government."[89]

Despite numerous suits in state courts over many years, it is important to emphasize the still unsettled condition of states' constitutional obligations regarding the financing of public elementary and secondary education. In nearly all states that have experienced education finance litigation, some multiple times, plaintiffs have prevailed at various times while the state defendants have prevailed at others. In sum, although there have been numerous plaintiff victories, a realistic view recognizes that failure is possible when plaintiffs engage in high stakes constitutional litigation.[90]

Subsequent Successes in State Litigation

Although plaintiffs lost many cases at the state level, especially in the early years of education finance litigation, a number of victories have dramatically affected how schools are financed. A few important state cases wherein the plaintiffs prevailed following *Serrano* illustrate the volatile context of school funding litigation.

The blueprint for funding reform was aided by another victory soon after *Serrano*, as the state supreme court in New Jersey ruled in *Robinson v. Cahill*.[91] The state high court reviewed a lower court's holding for plaintiffs wherein it was charged that the education finance distribution formula violated federal and state equal protections

---

88 *Northshore v. Kinnear*, 530 P.2d 178 (Wash. 1974).

89 530 P.2d 178 at 64.

90 See, e.g., R. Craig Wood and William E. Thro, "Originalism and the State Education Clauses: The Louisiana Voucher Case as an Illustration," *Education Law Reporter* 302 (April 2014); Carlee Escue, William Thro, and R. Craig Wood, "Some Perspectives on Recent School Finance Litigation," *Education Law Reporter*, vol. 268, no. 2, August 18, 2011, 601–618.

91 *Robinson v. Cahill*, 287 A.2d 187 (N.J. Super. 1972), aff'd as mod., 303 A.2d 273 (N.J. 1973).

and denied students' fundamental right to education because tax revenue varied with district wealth and was unequalized. The court denied fundamentality and wealth suspect class, stating that such findings would have the unintended consequence of changing our most basic political structures. But the court still overturned the education finance distribution system by turning to the education article of the state constitution, which demanded a "thorough and efficient" system of schools—a requirement unmet due to lack of equalization in revenues and thereby violating the state's equal protection clause.

Other decisions for plaintiffs followed over the next few years. One of the more expansive state supreme court rulings came from Wyoming in *Washakie* as the court found that poor districts showed a pattern of less revenue due to low assessed valuation.[92] The court accepted plaintiff arguments that the quality of education was related to money. The court cut to the core, stating, "until equality of financing is achieved, there is no practicable method of achieving equality of quality."[93] The Wyoming Supreme Court reached its decision based on the fact that certain provisions of the state constitution were more demanding than federal equal protections and because education was of such compelling value in that state that it was among the protected fundamental rights. Unlike most courts, the Wyoming high court embraced wealth as a suspect class, saying, "the state has the burden of demonstrating a compelling interest . . . served by the challenged legislation and which cannot be satisfied by any other convenient legal structure."[94]

The unsettled nature of education finance litigation is illustrated in Texas where a series of cases have been before the state supreme court over the years. Failing in *Rodriguez*, plaintiffs turned to the Texas Supreme Court, which ruled in their favor in *Edgewood* in 1988.[95] The court ordered the legislature to create a satisfactory remedy within a specific time period—a duty that the state legislature had difficulty meeting and consequently forcing the case to return repeatedly for judicial review. The Texas issues of funding public education moved through subsequent decisions,[96] with the courts reviewing the legislature's efforts to improve equity and adequacy of school funding, in part by recapturing local revenues from the state's wealthier school districts for redistribution to poorer schools. Not surprisingly, such solutions were contentious, so that in 2001 high-wealth school districts sued under *West Orange-Cove*, claiming that a state-imposed property tax lid meant to limit funding disparities was unconstitutional.[97] Plaintiff interveners joined hundreds of school districts to the case and reshaped the basic nature of the suit. The trial court in 2004 held the system of property tax methodology did not allow "meaningful discretion" and was thus

---

92 *Washakie County School District v. Herschler*, 606 P.2d 310 (1980).
93 606 P.2d 310 at 53.
94 606 P.2d 310 at 54.
95 *Edgewood v. Kirby*, 761 S.W.2d 859 (Tex. 1988).
96 *Edgewood Indep. Sch. Dist. v. Kirby*, 804 S.W.2d 491 (Tex. 1991), 777 S.W.2d 391(Tex. 1989).
97 *West Orange-Cove Consolidated ISD v. Nelson*, 107 S.W.3d 558 (2001).

unconstitutional. A subsequent state supreme court ruling enjoining state aid distribution is pending legislative action.[98]

Financing public elementary and secondary education has yet to be fully settled in Texas. In October 2011, the Texas Taxpayer and Student Fairness Coalition filed suit against the state regarding the 2006 legislative changes made to comply with the *West Orange-Cove* decision, in addition to recent cuts in state aid. The case was heard in 2013 and reheard in 2014.[99]

Plaintiff victories are illustrated by two other important longstanding cases in Kentucky and New Jersey, both of which provide insight on the nature of funding challenges. One of the key plaintiff wins that led state legislatures to revise both state academic systems as well as state education finance distribution formulas was the Kentucky Supreme Court's ruling in *Rose* in 1989.[100] In a decision that spurred change in many states' education finance distribution formulas with an increased attention to adequacy issues leading to student achievement, the Kentucky court held that the system of common schools was not efficient. Finding a fundamental right to education, the court concluded that this right was denied when the state's schools were underfunded and inadequate in educational programs—observations that caused the court to order a complete overhaul of the educational system with massive new funds. Simultaneously, the New Jersey case of *Abbott v. Burke* in 1990,[101] a multi-decade continuation of the original *Robinson* case from 1973, stirred national interest as that state's education finance distribution formula was again overruled because it did not meet the needs of poor urban districts and because the formula still violated the thorough and efficient clause of the state constitution. The court stated, "[f]rom this record we find that certain poorer urban districts do not provide a thorough and efficient education to their students. . . . We find the constitutional failure clear, severe, and of long duration."[102] Although the court later found the level of fiscal resources to finally meet adequacy standards—a finding only after subsequent cases[103]—New Jersey's experience represents serial litigation that by its very nature continues for many years in various forms. In 2011, plaintiffs again triumphed in *Abbott XXI*,[104] this time forcing the state legislature to restore funding reductions to *Abbott* districts made as a result of a revenue shortfall facing the legislature due to a weak state economy.

Winless in federal court, plaintiffs have won in numerous states for a variety of reasons. Again, the central question is whether the education finance distribution

---

98 *Neeley v. W. Orange-Cove Consol. Indep. Sch. Dist.*, 176 S.W.3d 746 (Tex.2005).

99 Texas: *Texas Taxpayer and Student Fairness Coalition v. Scott*, Cause No. D-1-GN-11–003130, Travis County District Court, 200th Judicial District. (2013).

100 *Rose v. Council for Better Education*, 790 S.W.2d 186 (Ky. 1989).

101 *Abbott v. Burke*, 575 A.2d 359 (N.J. 1990).

102 Ibid. at 359 at 168.

103 *Abbott v. Burke*, 971 A.2d 989, (N.J. 2009), 693 A.2d 417 (N.J. 1997), 575 A.2d 359 (N.J. 1990); *Robinson v. Cahill*, 303 A.2d 273 (N.J. 1973).

104 *Abbott v. Burke* (M-1293–09), May 24, 2011.

formula is in compliance with the state constitutional mandate in providing public elementary and secondary education. It must be understood that the judicial picture will continue to change each year. Whether the state defendants prevail or the plaintiffs prevail, the key to success is having an excellent legal team, a state education finance formula which is fundamentally sound, and education finance researchers who understand education finance formulas and the measurements associated with the discipline.[105]

EQUALITY, PRODUCTIVITY, AND LIBERTY IN PUBLIC EDUCATION

This chapter has discussed the difficult situation that schools face when trying to satisfy all stakeholders. Some parts of society pursue education for economic reasons, while others see schools as a forum for redressing social injustice. Still other groups view schools as a place where the principles of liberty should reign, though there is strong disagreement about whether liberty means freedom to achieve based on ability or whether freedom is only realized once schools have enabled society's less fortunate members. In all instances, a common thread is the demand for educational productivity however it might be defined, a demand that is becoming ever more strident.

Maintaining—or even establishing—adequate and equitable financial support for schools has become exceedingly complex. As costs have risen, taxpayer burdens have grown at the same time that costs of other social services have skyrocketed. Attitudes about adequate funding for schools are a morass of desires, resentments, and mandates.[106] On one hand, the numbers are so vast that it is hard to imagine revenues

---

105 For example, see R. Craig Wood and George Lange, "Selected State Education Finance Constitutional Litigation in the Context of Judicial Review," *Education Law Reporter* 207, no. 1 (May 4, 2006): 1–16; R. Craig Wood and George Lange, "The Justiciability Doctrine and Selected State Education Finance Constitutional Challenges," *Journal of Education Finance* 32, no. 1 (Summer 2006): 1–21; George Lange and R. Craig Wood, "Education Finance Litigation in North Carolina: Distinguishing *Leandro*," *Journal of Education Finance* 32, no. 1 (Summer 2006): 36–70; R. Craig Wood and Alvin Schilling, "An Examination of *Abbeville v. South Carolina*: Constitutional Challenge in Financing Public Elementary and Secondary Education," *Education Law Reporter* 220, no. 2 (August 23, 2007): 453–470; John Dayton and R. Craig Wood, "School Funding Litigation: Scanning the Event Horizon," *Education Law Reporter* 224, no. 1 (November 29, 2007): 1–19; William Thro and R. Craig Wood, "The Constitutional Text Matters: Reflections on Recent School Finance Cases," *Education Law Reporter* 251, no. 2 (February 18, 2010): 510–532; R. Craig Wood, "Justiciability, Adequacy, Advocacy, and the 'American Dream,'" *Kentucky Law Journal* 98, no. 4 (2009–2010): 739–787; Faith E. Crampton and David. C. Thompson, "The Road Ahead for School Finance Reform: Legislative Trends 2011 and Beyond," *Journal of Education Finance* 37, no. 2 (Fall 2011): 185–204; David C. Thompson and Faith E. Crampton, "The Impact of School Finance Litigation: A Long View," *Journal of Education Finance* 27 (Winter 2002): 783–816; R. Craig Wood and David C. Thompson, "Politics of Plaintiffs and Defendants," in *Money, Politics, and Law*, eds. Karen DeMoss and Kenneth K. Wong (Larchmont, NY: Eye On Education, 2004), 37–45.

106 See, R. Craig Wood and R. Anthony Rolle, "Improving 'Adequacy' Concepts in Education Finance: A Heuristic Examination of the Professional Judgment Research Protocol," *Educational Considerations* 35, no. 1 (Fall, 2007): 51–55.

are inadequate and that to ask for more surely stretches the limits of reason, particularly as education is only one of many important government functions. On the other hand, the depth of need reflects increasing demands on schools from all quarters. And at the same time, the success of public education is being questioned relentlessly.

The struggle comes not so much from whether people want the benefits of schooling, but rather from how to distribute education in ways that respect the common good while respecting individual freedom to accept or reject educational benefits or to obtain them from nonpublic sources. Hence the movement toward charter and virtual schools as well as vouchers. It is exactly this tension that is reflected in schools: a tension among economics, equality, productivity, liberty, and democracy. It is in exactly this context that all education finance policy is made.

POINT–COUNTERPOINT

POINT

The protracted struggle regarding school funding in states and courts is divisive and wasteful. Common sense tells us that children have unequal needs, and common sense tells politicians to quit squabbling over school aid plans, because we have the technical knowledge to do what is right. The controversy is only a ruse that distracts from the underlying fundamentals—those with money do not want to share it with those less fortunate, and to fund schools fairly is political suicide for politicians. In sum, it is easier to outmaneuver court orders than to face political constituencies.

COUNTERPOINT

The long history of school finance litigation has produced a dedicated set of reformers, all of whom seem to argue that no amount of funding will eliminate the perceived equality gap. The fundamental issue is that existing resources are poorly managed and any new money will be misused too. Public schools are inefficient governmental units. Plaintiffs in school finance regularly play on race and class and plead their case in the media ahead of entering the courtroom because their mission is to drive new money into schools regardless of demonstrable benefit. If it is conceded that schools are in fact underfunded, the only solution is to combine existing and new funding with structural reforms in a performance-based system benchmarked to student achievement levels.

- Which of these diametrically opposed perspectives on school funding best represents your own view? Explain.
- Do any arguments presented by either side fail to make sense? Why?
- How can states redress the legitimate issues in this discussion while funding all of the other services that states normally provide in a fair and equitable manner?

CASE STUDY

As the new assistant superintendent for finance in your school district, you sense something is afoot at the school board meeting. Several board members seem vitally interested in media reports that the state might take renewed interest in school size and efficiency and that school district consolidation might be a hot topic in the next legislative session. Having seen the same reports, you know that questions are swirling in the state capital about keeping taxes down and avoiding tax increases at all costs, particularly since the next year is an election year. You are savvy enough to realize that some issues take on a life of their own. In fact, you muse silently that there really is no difference between beliefs and reality, as reality simply is whatever people think in large enough numbers to vote in that direction.

At the administrative cabinet meeting the next day, your superintendent mentions the possibility of district consolidation. Having reviewed national trends, he suggests that many states appear to be jumping on the bandwagon. He mentions a number of examples that have appeared in *Education Week*, including Arkansas's attempt at massive consolidation; a proposal in Maine to reduce the number of school districts; a South Carolina effort to abolish the state's school districts and instead form regional councils; and various proposals in other states, generally at legislative behest and often with governors' backing. Consolidation proponents at the meeting cite savings such as reduced staff and fewer infrastructure demands, along with greater state flexibility in resources. Opponents, however, vociferously counter, citing studies detailing hardships for students when schools close, reduced activity participation due to longer bus rides and loss of local school identity, and increased costs due to expansion of administrative units, greater transportation costs, and the need to construct new schools.

Additionally, and yet interwoven within this discussion is the growing charter school movement in your state. It is most likely that the state legislature will increase the number of authorized providers within the near future. Compounding this issue is the potential approval for virtual schools to operate throughout the state independently of any school district. Presently, you know of no pending charter startups in your district. However, you are aware that at least a few parents may be interested in starting their own charter school or availing themselves to educate their children via a virtual school.

Following both these meetings, your superintendent requests time to discuss with you what the district's position should be if consolidation becomes a local topic. Most important is to consider whether consolidation would help or harm your district since its enrollment size falls squarely in the middle of your state's profile. While the superintendent thinks your district is in no danger of being eliminated, real questions emerge about the impact of consolidation as well as the presence of a charter school or individual children attending a virtual school on staffing, facilities, curriculum, treatment by the state aid formula, and so forth. The point of the conversation comes down to one question: what consolidation scenarios can be anticipated, and with what effect?

Not surprisingly, your superintendent asks you to prepare an analysis of likely scenarios. He indicates he would expect a background review of actions in other states and analysis of those situations that seem most comparable to your own state. Your analysis should consider school districts surrounding your own and how those districts might be viewed through legislative eyes. Additionally, your study should consider the impact if your district needs to absorb enrollments from any closed districts. How is it a charter school could impact your district? How is it that a virtual school could impact your district? Your study, you learn, would be used in lobbying your local legislative representatives, the state school board association, and other power brokers in the state capital.

- What concerns do you believe will be immediately voiced by the community once this topic becomes public?
- How does this district's profile compare to your own in terms of these issues?
- What would be the local reaction in your school district if consolidation, charter schools, virtual schools were proposed?

PORTFOLIO EXERCISES

- Research the history of financing education in your state. (Your state department of education is likely to be a good source of information.) Identify important issues such as the history of school district formation and reorganization, major state initiatives related to the financing of schools, and the relative autonomy (degree of centralization or decentralization) of educational decision making permitted by the legislature over time.
- Identify the major organizations in your state that have direct or indirect influence on educational policymaking at state and local levels. State the nature of their influence and reflect on the degree of impact they have on the financing of education.
- Obtain a copy of the organizational chart in your school district and trace the formal authority and power structure.
- If there has been school finance litigation in your state, list and describe the relevant court cases. Using what you have learned in this chapter, analyze whether or not these cases have improved the equity and adequacy of the state school finance system.

WEB RESOURCES

Association of School Business Officials, www.asbointl.org

Bureau of Labor Statistics, www.bls.gov

Center on Budget and Policy Priorities, www.cbpp.org

Council of the Great City Schools, www.cgcs.org

Education Law Center, www.edlawcenter.org

National Association of State Budget Officers, www.nsbo.org

National Center for Education Statistics, U.S. Department of Education, www.nces.ed.gov

National Conference of State Legislatures, www.ncsl.org

National Education Access Network, wwwschoolfunding.info

National Education Association, www.nea.org

National Education Finance Conference, www.nationaledfinance.com

National Governors Association, www.nga.org

The Rural School and Community Trust, www.ruraledu.org

U.S. Department of Education, www.ed.gov

U.S. Department of Labor, Bureau of Labor Statistics,www.bls.gov

EDUCATION FINANCE LITIGATION CASES BY STATE

Alabama: *James v. Alabama*, 836 So.2d 813 (Ala. 2002); *Opinion of the Justices*, 624 So. 2d 107 (Ala. 1993).

Alaska: *Matanuska-Susitna v. State*, 931 P.2d 39 1(Alaska 1997).

Arizona: *Roosevelt v. Bishop*, 877 P.2d 806 (Ariz. 1994); *Shofstall v. Hollins*, 515 P.2d 590 (Ariz. 1973).

Arkansas: *Lake View v. Huckabee*, 91 S.W.3d 472 (Ark. 2002) *Dupree v. Alma Sch. Dist.*, 651 S.W.2d 90 (Ark. 1983).

California: *Serrano v. Priest*, 557 P.2d 929 (Cal. 1976); *Serrano v. Priest*, 96 Cal. Rptr. 601, 487 P.2d 1241 (Cal. 1971).

Colorado: *Labato v. State*, Case No. 2005CV4794 May 29, 2013; *Lobato v. Colorado*, 218 P.3d 358 (Colo. 2009); *Lujan v. Colorado State Bd. of Educ.*, 649 P.2d 1005 (Colo. 1982),

Connecticut: *Connecticut Coalition for Justice in Educ. Funding, Inc. v. Rell*, 990 A.2d 206 (Conn. 2010); *Horton v. Meskill*, 376 A.2d 359 (Conn. 1977).

Florida: *Schroeder v. Palm Beach County Sch. Bd.*, 10 So.3d 1134 (Fla. App. 2009); *Coalition for Adequacy and Fairness in Sch. Funding v. Chiles*, 680 So.2d 400 (Fla. 1996).

Georgia: *McDaniel v. Thomas*, 285 S.E.2d 156 (Ga. 1981).

Idaho: *Idaho Schs. for Equal Educ. Opportunity v. Evans*, 850 P.2d 724 (Idaho 1993); *Thompson v. Engelking*, 537 P.2d 635 (Idaho 1975).

Indiana: *Bonner ex rel. Bonner v. Daniels*, 907 N.E. 2d 516 (Ind. 2009).

Illinois: *Committee v. Edgar*, 672 N.E.2d 1178 (Ill. 1996); *Blase v. Illinois*, 302 N.E.2d 46 (Ill.1973).

Kansas: Ganon v. State, 3rd Dist. Ct, Topeka, Case no 10C1569. Jan. 11, 2013, *Montoy v. Kansas*, 102 P.3d 1160 (Kan.), *supplemented*, 112 P.3d 923 [198 Ed. Law Rep. 703] (Kan.), *republished with concurring opinion*, 120 P.3d 306 (Kan. 2005), *Unified Sch. Dist. v. Kansas*, 885 P.2d 1170 (Kan. 1994).

Kentucky: *Rose v. Council for Better Educ.*, 790 S.W.2d 186 (Ky. 1989).

Louisiana: *Louisiana Ass'n of Educators v. Edwards*, 521 So. 2d 390 (La. 1988).

Maine: *School Administrative Dist. v. Commissioner*, 659 A.2d 854 (Me. 1995).

Maryland: *Hornbeck v. Somerset*, 458 A.2d 758 (Md. 1983).

Massachusetts: *Hancock v. Commissioner of Educ.*, 822 N.E.2d 1134 (Mass. 2005); *McDuffy v. Secretary of the Executive Office of Educ.*, 615 N.E.2d 516 (Mass. 1993).

Michigan: *Milliken v. Green*, 212 N.W.2d 711 (Mich. 1973).

Minnesota: *Skeen v. Minnesota*, 505 N.W.2d 299 (Minn. 1993).

Missouri: *Committee for Educ. Equality v. Missouri*, 294 S.W.3d 477 (Mo. 2009); *Committee for Educ. Quality v. Missouri*, 878 S.W.2d 446 (Mo. 1994).

Montana: *Columbia Falls Elementary Sch. District No. 6 v. Montana*, 109 P.3d 257 (Mont. 2005); *Helena v. Montana*, 769 P.2d 684 (Mont. 1989); *Montana ex rel. Woodahl v. Straub*, 520 P.2d 776 (Mont. 1974).

Nebraska: *Nebraska Coalition for Education Equity and Adequacy v. Heinman*, 731 N.W.2d 164 (Neb. 2007); *Gould v. Orr*, 506 N.W.2d 349 (Neb. 1993).

New Hampshire: *Londonderry Sch. Dist. SAU #12 v. New Hampshire*, 958 A.2d 930 (N.H. 2008); *Claremont Sch. Dist. v. Governor*, 703 A.2d 1353 (N.H. 1993).*Claremont Sch. Dist. v. Governor*, 635 A.2d 1375 (N.H. 1993).

New Jersey: *Abbott v. Burke*, 971 A.2d 989 (N.J. 2009); *Abbott v. Burke*, 693 A.2d 417 (N.J. 1997); *Abbott v. Burke*, 575 A.2d 359 (N.J. 1990); *Robinson v. Cahill*, 303 A.2d 273 (N.J. 1973).

New York: *Campaign for Fiscal Equity v. State*, 769 N.Y.S.2d 106, 801 N.E.2d 326, (N.Y. 2003); *Reform Educ. Financing Inequities Today v. Cuomo*, 606 N.Y.S. 2d 44 (N.Y. App. 1994); *Board of Educ., Levittown v. Nyquist*, 453 N.Y.S.2d 643, 439 N.E.2d 359 (N.Y. 1982).

North Carolina: See, *Hoke County Bd. of Educ v. State*, No. COA11–1545 Wake Co. No. 95 CVS 1158, Aug. 21, 2012, *Hoke County Bd. of Educ. v. North Carolina*, 599 S.E.2d 365 (N.C. 2004); *Leandro v. North Carolina State Bd. of Educ.*, 468 S.E.2d 543 (N.C. App. 1996), *rev'd* 488 S.E.3d 249 (N.C. 1997); *Britt v. North Carolina State Bd. of Educ.*, 357 S.E.2d 432, (N.C. App.) *aff'd mem.*, 361 S.E.2d 71 (N.C. 1987).

North Dakota; *Bismarck Public Sch. Dist. v. North Dakota*, 511 N.W.2d 247 (N.D. 1994).

Ohio: *Ohio ex rel. Ohio v. Lewis*, 789 N.E.2d 195 (Ohio 2003; *DeRolph v. Ohio*, 780 N.E.2d 529 (Ohio 2002); *DeRolph v. Ohio*, 677 N.E.2d 733(Ohio 1997); *Board of Educ. of the City Sch. Dist. of the City of Cincinnati v. Walter*, 390 N.E.2d 813 (Ohio 1979).

Oklahoma: *Oklahoma Education Ass'n v. Oklahoma*, 158 P.3d 1058 (Okla. 2007); *Fair Sch. Fin. Council v. Oklahoma*, 746 P.2d 1135 (Okla. 1987).

Oregon: *Pendleton v. Oregon*, 185 P.3d 471, (2008). *Withers v. Oregon*, 891 P.2d 675 (Or. App. 1995); *Coalition for Equitable Sch. Funding v. Oregon*, 811 P.2d 116 (Or. 1991); *Olsen v. Oregon*, 554 P.2d 139 (Or. 1976).

Pennsylvania: *Marrero v. Pennsylvania*, 739 A.2d 110 (1999); *Danson v. Casey*, 399 A.2d 360 (Pa. 1979).

Rhode Island: *City of Pawtucket v. Sundlun*, 662 A.2d 40 (R.I. 1995).

South Carolina: *Abbeville v. State*, S.C. Supreme Court, Appellate Case No. 2007–065159, June, 2012. *Abbeville County Sch. Dist. v. South Carolina*, 515 S.E.2d 535 (S.C. 1999); *Richland County v. Campbell*, 364 S.E.2d 470 (S.C. 1988).

South Dakota: *Olson v. Guindon*, 771 N.W.2d 318 (S.D. 2009).

Tennessee: *Tennessee Small Sch. Sys. v. McWherter*, 91 S.W.3d 232 (Tenn. 2002); *Tennessee Small Sch. Systems v. McWherter*, 894 S.W.2d 734 (Tenn. 1995); *Tennessee Small Sch. Systems v. McWherter*, 851 S.W. 2d 139 (Tenn. 1993).

Texas: *Texas Taxpayer and Student Fairness Coalition v. Scott*, Cause No. D-1-GN-11–003130, Travis County District Court, 200th Judicial District. (2013); *Neeley v. West Orange-Cove Consolidated Indep. Sch. Dist.*, 176 S.W.3d 746 (Tex. 2005); *Edgewood Indep.Sch. Dist. v. Kirby*, 804 S.W.2d 491 (Tex. 1991); *Edgewood Indep. Sch. Dist. v. Kirby*, 777 S.W.2d 391 (Tex. 1989)

Vermont: *Brigham v. Vermont*, 692 A.2d 384 (Vt. 1997).

Virginia: *Scott v. Virginia*, 443 S.E.2d 138 (Va. 1994).

Washington: *McCleary v. Washington*, No 84362–7 January 2012, *Federal Way School Dist. v. Washington*, 219 P.3d 941 (Wash. 2009); *School District's Alliance for Adequate Funding of Special Educ. v. Washington*, 202 P.3d 990 (Wash. App. 2009); *Seattle Sch. Dist. v. Washington*, 585 P.2d 71 (Wash. 1978); *Northshore Sch. Dist. No. 417 v. Kinnear*, 530 P.2d 178 (Wash. 1974).

West Virginia: *Board of Educ. of the County of Kanawha v. West Virginia Bd. of Educ.*, 639 S.E. 2d 893 (W. Va. 2006); *West Virginia ex rel. Board of Educ. v. Bailey*, 453 S.E.2d 368 (W. Va. 1994); *Pauley v. Kelly*, 255 S.E.2d 859 (W. Va. 1979).

Wisconsin: *Vincent v. Voight*, 614 N.W.2d 388 (Wis. 2000); *Kuker v. Grover*, 436 N.W.2d 568 (Wis. 1989).

Wyoming: *Campbell County v. Wyoming*, 181 P.3d 43 (Wyo. 2008); *Wyoming v. Campbell County Sch. District*, 32 P.3d 325 (Wyo. 2001), *Wyoming v. Campbell County Sch. District*, 19 P.3d 518 (Wyo. 2001) *Campbell County Sch. Dist. v. State*, 907 P.2d 1238 (Wyo. 1995); *Washakie County Sch. Dist. v. Herschler*, 606 P.2d 310 (Wyo. 1980); *Sweetwater County Planning Committee for Organization of Sch. Districts v. Hinkle*, 491 P.2d 1234 (Wyo. 1971).

CHAPTER 3

Basic Funding Structures

THE CHALLENGE

No one funding formula or set of formulas is right for all states, given voter diversity, tradition and interpretations of state constitutions with regard to education.

Crampton and Whitney (1996)[1]

CHAPTER DRIVERS

Please reflect upon the following questions as you read this chapter:

- What is the context of funding schools in America?
- What is the overarching tax system at the federal, state, and local levels?
- What are state aid formulas?
- What is a fair funding formula?
- How do states fund schools?

---

1 Faith E. Crampton and Terry N. Whitney, *Principles of a Sound State School Finance System* (Washington, DC, and Denver, CO: Foundation for State Legislatures, National Conference of State Legislatures, 1996), 1.

THE CONTEXT OF FUNDING SCHOOLS

Our journey thus far has made apparent that the context of funding public schools is highly complex, in large part due to the turbulent political, economic, and social environment in which education operates. Unlike the private sector, the goal of government is to provide for the public good rather than to pursue profit. Simply stated, the goal of a private sector business in a capitalistic system is to offer products or services that consumers are willing to buy at a price that will yield a profit for business owners and shareholders. If the product or service is overpriced, consumer demand is weak, or if a competitor offers a better/cheaper version, the business must adapt or fail. In contrast, public goods like education historically have relied upon tax revenues, albeit from a sometimes resistant citizenry. At the same time, public schools compete with other government-funded services for limited tax revenues. Furthermore, public schools increasingly compete for tax dollars with nonprofit and for-profit entities through the expansion of charter schools managed by education management organizations (EMOs) and vouchers for students to attend private, nonprofit and religious schools. Given the above statements, we come to the crux of this chapter: Public schools are increasingly called upon to embrace competition and to maximize the efficiency with which they deploy tax revenues. Although business stakeholders generally have a straightforward understanding of the products they offer for sale, there is no broad societal consensus on what education's "products" should be. Rather, education outcomes are multi-dimensional and are often subject to intense disagreement as to their relevance, importance, or priority. In addition, education stakeholders, such as parents, communities, and taxpayers, often lack a clear understanding of the mix of local, state, and federal tax revenues that support public education, such that some never get beyond the general feeling that the taxes they pay to fund schools are too high—regardless of the amount.

Although the topic of education's funding sources is complex, we can obtain a working grasp of the issues by examining the sources and types of revenue used to fund schools. Relatedly, we can gain a deeper understanding of school funding context by considering the elements of school funding formula fairness as it has developed over the last century, largely in response to the legislative and litigative pressures. Finally, we consider the current and prospective status of school funding by exploring how states fund schools. In sum, now that we have a initial grasp of the politics of schools, values, and money, it is time to expand our knowledge to include revenue sources and school funding systems.

WHAT IS THE OVERARCHING TAX SYSTEM?

A theme throughout this book is that revenue for schools is a source of conflict in many states and localities. The roots of this struggle fundamentally derive from disputes over what schools should do and the inescapable fact that school revenues are derived predominantly from taxation, some of which involves little or no direct input from taxpayers. Although other revenue sources may exist, it is unrealistic to think that taxes are less than the lion's share or that taxes will be replaced soon by some magic pool of money.

The history of taxation is extensively covered in many locations, including our own books.[2] Taxes are necessary to support the many public services we enjoy as part of a civilized society. As we saw in the last chapter, a strong national defense, interstate highways, stable social benefits, and intergovernmental revenue-sharing are among the services funded by federal taxation. State tax revenues provide many comparable services, albeit for their specific populations, such as state highways and social safety net programs, but also oversight of the state's natural resources, such as parks, lakes, and rivers. City streets, police and fire protection, and local parks are among the local tax benefits enjoyed by citizens. Of especial importance, local taxes provide many highly visible services, including a significant contribution toward meeting school costs. The overarching tax system therefore has three principal players in the form of federal, state, and local units of government.[3] Each plays a different role although overlap is not uncommon; and each level of government has a relationship to schools in some varying proportion.

What Is the Federal Tax System?

The federal tax system that exists today is far removed from the nation's early, awkward attempts to create a federal tax structure. As we saw in Chapter 2, Figure 2.1, federal tax revenues today are used to support a wide range of programs, from national defense to environmental protection. A number of taxes, as seen in Figure 3.1, are used to finance these. Of these, individual income tax revenues comprise almost half, and payroll tax revenues approximately one-third. Corporate income tax revenues are a distant third at 13%.

Ironically, in a nation born of suspicion toward all central government, the federal tax system today is both massive and complex; it also is frequently the object of criticism from across the political spectrum. For example, fiscal conservatives maintain that federal taxes are too high and bemoan the complexity of the tax system. They generally advocate for simplifying the tax code and granting across-the-board tax cuts particularly, but not exclusively, to the private sector in order to stimulate the economy and create jobs. In addition, they are usually critical of the number of social benefit programs, including education, along with the levels of tax revenues dedicated to them, arguing for a more limited role of government. At the other end of the spectrum are those who assert that the federal tax system is regressive and in need of a major overhaul to tax those with the greatest ability to pay, be they individuals or corporations, so that

---

2 For a brief history of taxation for public education illustrating contentiousness, see "Revenue Sources for Education," in *Fiscal Leadership for Schools: Concepts and Practices*, by David C. Thompson, R. Craig Wood, and David Honeyman, 131–172 (New York: Longman, 1994).

3 In addition, many states have what are termed "intermediate" units of government. The types of intermediate units vary greatly across states along with their powers to tax (or lack thereof) and responsibilities. One of the most common intermediate units in the U.S. is the county. For further information, see the National Association of Counties, www.naco.org.

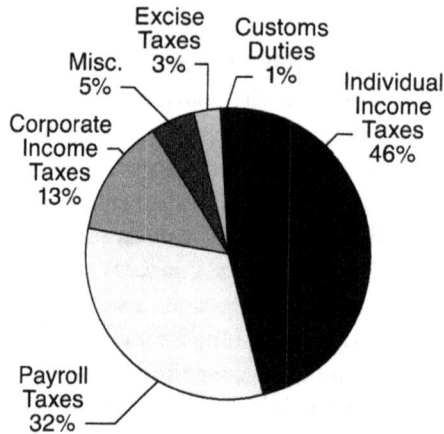

FIGURE 3.1 Federal Tax Revenue by Type of Tax for Fiscal Year 2015 (projected)

Source: National Priorities Project. "Federal Revenue: Where Does the Money Come From?" https://www.national priorities.org/budget-basics/federal-budget-101/revenues.

all pay their fair share. In general, they are more tolerant of a complex tax system, asserting that complexity is an integral part of a progressive tax system. In addition, they advocate for a robust, tax-funded social safety net as a public good that yields both immediate and intergenerational benefits to individuals and the country.

At its most fundamental level, the debate over federal taxation takes root in efforts to limit the role of central government. Historically a nation of tax protesters, Americans fought federal taxation. Numerous attempts at centralized taxation dating from the 1600s were bitterly opposed by the colonists and underlay the Revolutionary War in 1776. Even the war itself was a target of tax protest, marking the first instance of a budget deficit as the new nation struggled with war debt. Early presidents and congressional leaders were themselves mostly anti-tax, leading to a weak federal tax system that depended mostly on tariffs and customs for the first 125 years of nationhood. Repeated efforts to establish a federal income tax failed or were rescinded shortly after passage into law, including a lawsuit in which the U.S. Supreme Court declared invalid an 1894 income tax law on the grounds that the federal constitution did not expressly authorize Congress to collect such a tax.[4]

The needs of a growing nation, however, caused an impoverished Congress to propose the structure that eventually evolved into the tax system that exists today. In 1909, Congress proposed the Sixteenth Amendment to the Constitution, granting Congress the power to "lay and collect taxes on incomes, from whatever source derived, without apportionment among the States, and without regard to any census or enumeration." The amendment was finally ratified in 1913, whereupon Congress enacted a tax of 1% on personal income which subsequently has been expanded and

---

4 Pollock v. Farmers Loan & Trust Co. Supreme Court of the United States, 158 U.S. 601; 15 S.Ct. 912 (1985).

TABLE 3.1 Federal Tax Revenues by Source (in billions of dollars): 1940–2015

Fiscal Year	Individual Income Taxes	Corporate Income Taxes	Social Insurance and Retirement Recipts	Excise Taxes	Other	Total Federal Receipts
1940	892	1,197	1,785	1,977	698	6,548
1950	15,755	10,449	4,338	7,550	1,351	39,443
1960	40,715	21,494	14,683	11,676	3,923	92,492
1970	90,412	32,829	44,362	15,705	9,499	192,807
1980	244,069	64,600	157,803	24,329	26,311	517,112
1990	466,884	93,507	380,047	35,345	56,174	1,031,958
2000	1,004,462	207,289	652,852	68,865	91,723	2,025,191
2010	898,549	191,437	864,814	66,909	140,997	2,162,706
2011	1,091,473	181,085	818,792	72,381	139,735	2,303,466
2012	1,132,206	242,289	845,314	79,061	151,294	2,450,164
2013	1,316,405	273,506	947,820	84,007	153,365	2,775,103
2014	1,386,068	332,740	1,021,109	93,528	168,276	3,001,721
2015	1,533,942	449,020	1,055,744	110,539	188,180	3,337,425

Note: 2014 and 2015 receipts are estimated.

Source: Adapted from "Historical Tables." Table 2.1. U.S. Office of Management and Budget. www.whitehouse.gov/omb/budget/historicals.

modified in numerous ways on many occasions to accomplish a broad range of policy goals. Administration of federal tax laws that emanated from ratification of the amendment has evolved into a large federal agency in the form of the Internal Revenue Service, yielding revenues that most people find incomprehensible. By 2015, federal tax collections are projected to total $3.3 trillion. Of that amount, individual income tax revenues are projected to be $1.5 trillion, corporate income tax $449 billion, social insurance and retirement $1.1 billion, and excise taxes $110.5 billion (see Table 3.1).

Although the federal tax system and its revenues have grown substantially over time, the path has not been smooth. Even at times when Congress has faced voter pressure to reduce taxes, people still expect a strong national defense, a sound retirement system, and safe highways. Education too has been a beneficiary of federal funding, although the federal role has been limited because the Tenth Amendment leaves education to the states. Nonetheless, federal involvement in and funding of education have a long history. Ever since the Northwest Ordinance in 1787 first granted land to states for educational purposes, the federal government has tried to assist states in areas of federal interest. As we saw in the last chapter, the list of federally aided education programs is long and includes programs like special education, school meals,[5] and vocational education, to name just a few. Although the federal role has often been

---

5 Note that the U.S. Department of Agriculture (USDA), rather than the U.S. Department of Education, administers school meal programs.

indirect, the dollars have not been trivial. Federal funds for elementary and secondary education in 2011 through the U.S. Department of Education totaled $79 billion,[6] a sum which excludes other federal agency programs that directly or indirectly benefit schools such as the U.S. Department of Agriculture's child nutrition programs (school breakfast, lunch, and afterschool snacks); Health and Human Services' Head Start program; and the U.S. Department of Labor's youth employment and training programs.

What Is the State Tax System?

An important aspect of taxation in the United States has been the simultaneous development of multiple tax systems. States have played a central role in the nation's history, so much so that even today we hear issues of states' rights debated vigorously in respected forums. People feel strongly about the relationship of government to its constituents, and the authority of states has been jealously guarded.

The extensive tax nature ascribed to the federal government is true of state tax systems too. The dissimilarity, of course, is the number of variations on tax themes, as there are 50 states but only one federal government. As a result, each state's tax system has been affected by unique social, economic, and political factors, and further affected by the relationship of states to the federal government.

As we saw earlier, colonial tax systems predated federal efforts to levy taxes. In fact, the system of elected representation to Congress guaranteed that states would closely guard their autonomy, as the U.S. Constitution granted to the states all powers not reserved to Congress itself. Differences in geography, climate, economy, and preferences further ensured that states would approach taxation differently. Many of the earliest colonial government structures were directly aimed at counteracting a strong federal seat of power, beginning with the Virginia legislature's defiance in 1619 of the Virginia Company's attempts to revoke certain freedoms. By 1700, all colonies had written charters guaranteeing liberties born of conflict between the Crown and independent-minded colonialists.

Not surprisingly, colonial—and later state—systems of taxation were tightly linked to local politics and economies. As the need for revenue expanded with population growth, the New England colonies tended to tax personal property, land, and houses in the belief that every person's taxpaying ability was different and that everyone should pay. Concentrated wealth in the South meant only a few persons would bear the brunt of taxation, so a revenue system based on exports and imports was developed to shift taxes away from the wealthy. Other taxes, such as poll and faculty taxes, were used as early, primitive forms of income tax.[7] The middle colonies picked up this system and

---

6 *Digest of Education Statistics 2013*, "Revenues for Public Elementary and Secondary Schools, by Source of Funds and State or Jurisdiction: 2010–11," Table 235.10, http://nces.ed.gov/programs/digest/d13/tables/dt13_235.10.asp.

7 A poll tax, also referred to as a "head tax," was levied per individual, generally as a matter of convenience in Colonial times when the individual voted. It, however, was later used to discriminate against African-American voters, primarily in the South, although it affected all voters too poor to pay

made refinements to these taxes. Colonies also ran lotteries or invented other special revenue sources.

From the outset, strong state curbs on federal power were deliberate. The U.S. Constitution gave the federal government only limited power to levy taxes for the purpose of paying debts and for the general welfare of the nation. States, however, were granted full powers, including control of local government; chartering of towns; building of roads and bridges; protection of civil liberties; and, of course, care of the federal government via representation in Congress. Such responsibility was not free to states, however. By the end of the Civil War, colonial-style tax systems were no longer adequate given these broad responsibilities and a growing population, and the answer seemed to be state authority to tax all property—both real and personal. However, widespread tax evasion was rampant, in that land, buildings, and livestock were visible while other property, such as bonds, notes, and negotiable instruments, was easily concealed. The unintended effect was shifting of the tax burden to property owners who could not hide their wealth.

Around 1880, study commissions began exploring ways to improve state tax systems, especially administration of the property tax. This resulted in creation of tax equalization boards, efforts to improve property assessments, prosecution of tax evasion, and refinement of tax requirements on various property types. Efforts still met with limited success as equalization proved politically unpopular, and evasion and resistance to taxes were impossible to eliminate. The numerous woes of property tax administration ultimately led to many recommendations that states should abandon the property tax in favor of other tax bases. Faced with such problems, states began to rely less on property, and by 1920 several states had adopted both individual and corporate income tax plans. Although the property tax at the state level has not been completely eliminated, the majority of states now have enacted income taxes, as well as other taxes on commercial transactions such as sales and excise taxes (see Table 3.2).

Over the last century, growth in state taxation has been phenomenal. The earliest records, from 1902, indicate that states were levying only small property taxes and other miscellaneous taxes,while now they assess and collect a much wider range of taxes, as seen in Table 3.2, with substantial revenues from sales, gross receipts, and income taxes. Table 3.3 traces the growth of state tax collections from $156 million in 1902 to an astounding $846 billion a century later in 2013.

State aid to elementary and secondary education today constitutes, on average, about one third of state budgets,[8] in large part because the U.S. Constitution prevents the federal government from assuming a direct educational role. As a result, states provide a significant portion of the cost associated with elementary and secondary education, resulting in the complex state aid formulas to be discussed later in this chapter.

---

the tax. The 24th Amendment ratified in 1964 outlawed its use in federal elections. A faculty tax was an early form of income tax whereby individuals were taxed a flat amount based upon their profession.

8 National Association of State Budget Officers, "State Expenditure Report: Examining Fiscal 2011–2013 State Spending," www.nasbo.org/sites/default/files/State%20Expenditure%20Report%20%28Fiscal%202011–2013%20Data%29.pdf.

TABLE 3.2 State Reliance on Major Tax Sources: 2013

State	General Sales and Gross Receipts	Individual Income	Selective Sales Taxes	Corporation Net Income	Property Taxes	Other Taxes
U.S. Average	30.1%	36.6%	16.3%	5.3%	1.6%	10.1%
Alabama	25.2%	34.6%	25.6%	4.1%	3.5%	7.0%
Alaska	n.a.	n.a.	4.9%	12.3%	1.9%	80.9%
Arizona	48.0%	25.2%	12.9%	4.9%	5.7%	3.3%
Arkansas	33.0%	30.9%	13.8%	4.7%	11.9%	5.7%
California	25.5%	50.2%	10.6%	5.6%	1.5%	6.6%
Colorado	21.5%	49.2%	16.6%	5.8%	n.a.	7.0%
Connecticut	23.9%	48.4%	17.9%	3.5%	n.a.	6.2%
Delaware	n.a.	33.8%	14.6%	9.3%	n.a.	42.4%
Florida	60.1%	n.a.	22.4%	6.0%	0.0%	11.5%
Georgia	29.7%	49.3%	12.0%	4.5%	0.3%	4.2%
Hawaii	48.3%	28.5%	16.2%	2.0%	n.a.	4.9%
Idaho	37.0%	36.1%	12.5%	5.6%	n.a.	8.7%
Illinois	21.1%	42.7%	16.9%	11.5%	0.2%	7.6%
Indiana	40.1%	29.4%	20.7%	4.6%	0.0%	5.1%
Iowa	30.1%	41.0%	13.0%	5.1%	n.a.	10.7%
Kansas	38.0%	38.8%	11.1%	5.0%	1.0%	6.0%
Kentucky	27.9%	34.4%	19.3%	6.0%	5.2%	7.2%
Louisiana	30.6%	29.7%	23.3%	2.7%	0.6%	13.1%
Maine	27.6%	39.4%	18.2%	4.4%	1.0%	9.3%
Maryland	22.7%	42.5%	17.8%	5.3%	4.1%	7.6%
Massachusetts	21.7%	53.9%	9.5%	7.9%	0.0%	7.0%
Michigan	33.6%	32.8%	15.3%	3.6%	7.8%	6.9%
Minnesota	23.8%	42.6%	15.6%	6.5%	3.9%	7.6%
Mississippi	43.1%	23.7%	18.6%	5.6%	0.3%	8.6%
Missouri	28.3%	48.3%	14.7%	3.4%	0.3%	5.0%
Montana	n.a.	39.5%	21.1%	6.5%	9.9%	22.9%
Nebraska	35.4%	44.5%	11.2%	5.8%	0.0%	3.0%
Nevada	51.8%	n.a.	26.1%	n.a.	3.3%	18.8%
New Hampshire	n.a.	4.2%	39.9%	23.3%	16.9%	15.7%
New Jersey	29.1%	41.6%	12.9%	7.8%	0.0%	8.5%
New Mexico	37.8%	23.9%	13.1%	5.1%	1.4%	18.6%
New York	16.4%	54.6%	15.1%	6.7%	n.a.	7.2%
North Carolina	23.5%	46.6%	17.3%	5.4%	n.a.	7.2%
North Dakota	23.9%	12.1%	9.3%	4.3%	0.1%	50.3%
Ohio	31.6%	36.1%	18.3%	1.0%	n.a.	13.0%

TABLE 3.2 *continued*

State	General Sales and Gross Receipts	Individual Income	Selective Sales Taxes	Corporation Net Income	Property Taxes	Other Taxes
Oklahoma	28.3%	32.8%	15.0%	6.6%	n.a.	17.3%
Oregon	n.a.	68.3%	14.9%	5.0%	0.2%	11.5%
Pennsylvania	27.2%	31.7%	23.1%	6.5%	0.2%	11.2%
Rhode Island	30.0%	37.0%	21.6%	4.9%	0.1%	6.4%
South Carolina	36.7%	38.5%	14.6%	4.4%	0.1%	5.6%
South Dakota	55.7%	n.a.	24.4%	2.4%	n.a.	17.5%
Tennessee	53.6%	2.1%	20.2%	10.2%	n.a.	13.9%
Texas	50.5%	n.a.	25.4%	n.a.	n.a.	24.0%
Utah	29.8%	45.1%	13.5%	5.2%	n.a.	6.4%
Vermont	12.1%	23.0%	22.1%	3.7%	33.8%	5.4%
Virginia	19.3%	56.8%	12.9%	4.0%	0.2%	6.7%
Washington	59.6%	n.a.	18.9%	n.a.	10.4%	11.1%
West Virginia	23.3%	33.4%	24.6%	4.5%	0.1%	14.0%
Wisconsin	26.7%	43.7%	16.2%	5.8%	0.9%	6.7%
Wyoming	32.1%	n.a.	5.7%	n.a.	15.2%	47.0%

Note: n.a. = not applicable.

Source: National Conference of State Legislatures. www.ncsl.org/research/fiscal-policy/state-reliance-on-major-taxes-2010.aspx.

TABLE 3.3 State Tax Revenues (in thousands of dollars) for Selected Years: 1902–2013

Year	Total (in thousands of dollars)
1902	156,000
1913	301,000
1922	947,000
1932	1,890,000
1940	3,313,000
1950	7,929,881
1960	18,035,927
1970	47,961,994
1980	137,075,178
1990	300,488,565
2000	539,655,337
2010	705,929,253
2011	761,836,690
2012	797,740,658
2013	846,214,995

Note: Data are in current (unadjusted) dollars.

Source: U.S. Census Bureau. "State Government Tax Collections: Historical Data." www.census.gov/govs/statetax/historical_data.html.

What Is the Local Tax System?

What many people think of as local taxes are, in reality, state taxes; that is, local governments, including school districts, have no taxing authority outside state statutory permission. Hence, the "local" property tax, often a major funding source for school districts, is actually a tax that the state has delegated to local government. In addition to state aid, school districts in most states rely upon local property tax revenues for a significant portion of their funding even though they normally share that tax base with other local government units. A number of states also allow localities to levy a local sales tax. In 2014, local governments in 38 states levied sales taxes, ranging from 0.003% in Mississippi to 4.89% in Louisiana.[9] However, it is unclear as to what portion, if any, of local sales tax revenues directly benefits school districts.

Although federal and state governments have tended to be centrally structured, local government is generally more fragmented, including multiple jurisdictions, such as counties, cities, school districts, villages, and townships, as well as special taxing districts for entities like sanitation systems and public libraries. Because local units of government are created and controlled by state government, they are limited in what they can tax, and the level of that taxation. Yet the amount of tax revenues collected by localities is not insignificant (see Table 3.4). In 2011, they collected over half a billion dollars, of which $429 billion was property tax revenues. The sales tax accounted for $93.1 billion in local revenues, with selective sale tax revenues yielding $27.6 billion. Other noteworthy local taxes include those on individual income ($25.6 billion) and corporate income ($7.1 billion).

TABLE 3.4 Local Sales Taxes and Revenue (in thousands of dollars): 2011

Total	$578,177,391
Property	429,086,267
Sales and gross receipts	93,078,804
General sales	65,430,782
Selective sales	27,648,022
Motor fuel	1,344,338
Alcoholic beverages	511,719
Tobacco products	403,210
Public utilities	14,056,299
Other selective sales	11,332,456
Individual income	25,628,794
Corporate income	7,163,771
Motor vehicle licenses	1,662,382
Other taxes	21,557,373

Source: U.S. Census Bureau. *State and Local Government Finance: 2011*. www.census.gov/govs/local.

---

9 Scott Drenkard. "State and Local Sales Tax Rates in 2014" (Washington, DC: Tax Foundation, March 18, 2014), http://taxfoundation.org/article/state-and-local-sales-tax-rates-2014.

Like other units of local government, schools depend upon a mix of revenue sources, and the particular mix varies from state to state and within states. In general, schools rely equally upon state aid and local property taxes, with federal aid a distant third. This represents an evolution from the beginnings of the common school movement in the 19th century when schools were almost completely dependent on local property tax revenues.

Tax System Summary

It is important to note that school districts draw upon a number of revenue sources—federal, state, and local—each with its own advantages and disadvantages. First, federal aid to education is limited in scope, given federal Constitutional constraints, and often is targeted for specific purposes. Second, over time, state aid has become increasingly important, as states have responded to school finance reform and to litigation testing states' fiscal responsibilities to schools.[10] Third, in many states, school districts still depend upon the local property tax to fund a significant portion of their expenditures, such that in 2011 the average mix of school district revenues was: 44.1% state; 44.1% local; and 12.5% federal (see Table 2.1 in the previous chapter).[11] Fourth, schools usually have been prevented from tapping tax bases other than property, as most states do not allow schools to tax sales, income, or other kinds of wealth. The net sum is that schools are primarily supported by state and local taxes, with limited but meaningful federal assistance.

The overarching tax system in the United States is comprised of federal, state, and local tax structures, with the federal system relying heavily on individual income tax revenues, and providing only a small portion of school district revenues. State tax systems rely primarily on revenues from individual income and general sales taxes, with the magnitude of state aid to school districts dependent on the social, economic, and political environment in a particular state. At the local level, tax systems derive a large percentage of their revenues from real property taxation, and a significant portion is used by school districts—a reality that has caused the property tax to be seen (incorrectly) as the "school tax." Under these conditions, the local relationship to school funding is very strong. From this flows the observation, then, that the revenues available to schools are fundamentally sales and income taxes through state aid and property taxes at the local level. Finally, it is starkly clear that schools compete at all government levels for tax revenues because there are practical limits on the amount of tax dollars that can be generated—and those same dollars must be apportioned among the many worthy programs that serve the public good.

---

10 See, "Origins of School Funding Challenges," in Chapter 2.

11 However, it is important to note that this revenue mix varies greatly state-by-state. For example, local support ranges from 7.6% in Vermont to 57.8% in Illinois in 2011. Conversely, South Dakota has the lowest level of state support (29.1%) while Vermont has the highest (81.7%). With regard to federal support, New Jersey is lowest at 5.3%, while Mississippi receives the highest level at 22.4%. See, *Digest of Education Statistics*, "Revenues for Public Elementary and Secondary Schools, by Source of Funds and State or Jurisdiction: 2010–11."

STATE FUNDING FOR SCHOOLS

With this basic grasp of tax systems, we turn now to an overview of state aid to school districts. This is an issue that goes deeper than overarching tax systems, as it raises questions of distributional fairness and equality of educational opportunity. If we believe, as stated in the first chapter, that the amount of money available is important to the success or failure of schools, then it follows that how money flows from the state to local school districts is a critical question of fundamental sufficiency and fairness; that is, adequacy and equity.

In this last part of this chapter, we turn to exactly those issues. Our first priority is to gain an understanding of how states distribute aid to schools. From there, it becomes important to understand the principles of fair formulas and other aid mechanisms for distributing money to individual districts. We tackle these issues now because all the subsequent topics in this book will have no real world consequence if revenues for schools are inadequate and inequitable. In sum, sound tax systems should provide adequate revenue from multiple sources distributed to school districts using equitable aid formulas—only then can school leaders successfully undertake the budgeting behaviors that comprise the remaining chapters of this book.

THE DEVELOPMENT OF STATE AID FORMULAS

The previous section makes clear that money for public schools comes primarily from tax revenues. In most states, the real property tax is a major source of local revenue for schools. At the same time, virtually no school district in the United States is completely at the mercy of its local tax base for funding education. Variations in the size of the local tax base across any given state, often expressed as the measure of school district wealth, are so extreme that even the most fiscally conservative state lawmaker recognizes a role for state aid. Indeed, most states have tried to develop state school aid schemes that speak to some basic elements of adequacy and equity. School aid formulas thus attract a great deal of attention at federal, state, and local levels, although states have been the primary player in designing and implementing aid formulas both by choice and by force of litigation.

Under these conditions, state aid formulas are legislative and are policy tools used to address disparities in educational opportunity that would be present if schools were entirely dependent on their respective local tax base. It is not hard to imagine the size of such disparity absent intervention, as most states have wide extremes of local wealth, i.e., tax capacity. A fairly common case, for example, is a public utility power plant in a low enrollment school district that creates vast wealth per pupil in the form of taxable property. In contrast, another district in the same state of similar enrollment size may have only marginal agricultural property as its tax base. Disparities in wealth per pupil in such cases can easily be 100:1 or greater, meaning that the property-wealthy district can raise $100 for every $1 raised in the property-poor district—using the same tax rate! The example in Figure 3.2 is quite common, with the wealthiest district able

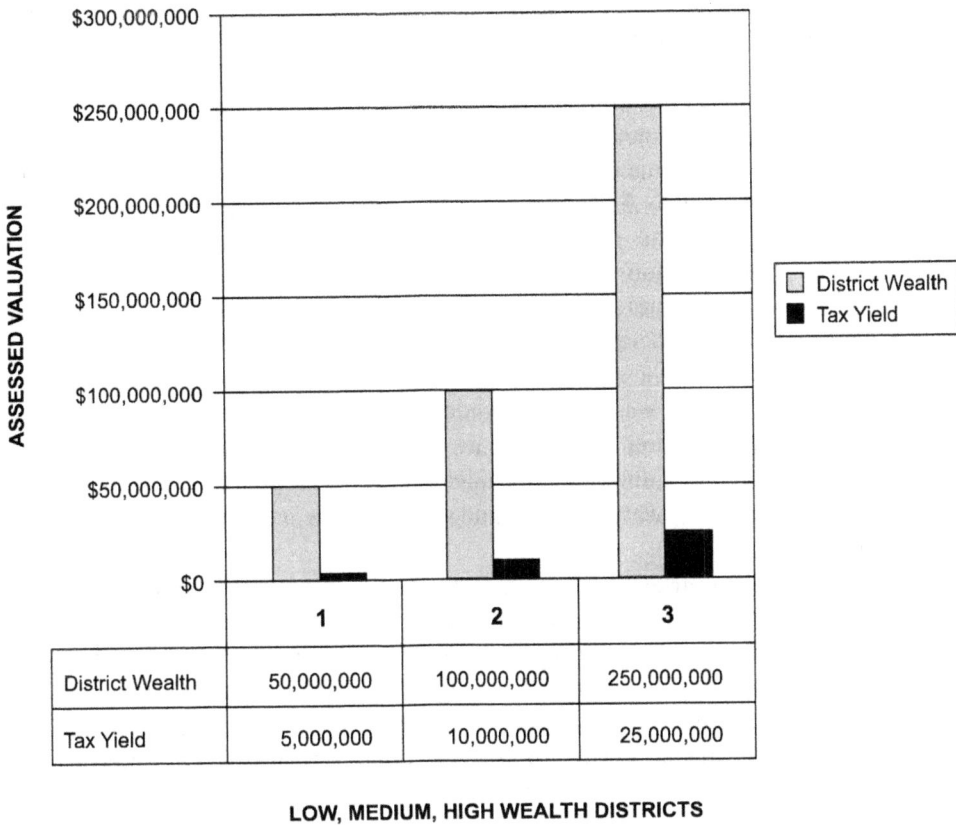

	1	2	3
District Wealth	50,000,000	100,000,000	250,000,000
Tax Yield	5,000,000	10,000,000	25,000,000

LOW, MEDIUM, HIGH WEALTH DISTRICTS

FIGURE 3.2 Tax Capacity at 100 Mills Uniform Effort

to raise $25 million locally, five times more than the poorest district—all at a uniform tax rate of 100 mills (or $100 per $1,000 of assessed property valuation)—ignoring the fact that a property-poor district almost never can tax itself at such a high rate. The effect is vastly different tax rates to produce the same amount of revenue per pupil, or vastly different expenditure levels per pupil. Any number of variations on this example can be created to fit any state's circumstance. For example, urban school districts often have less per-pupil property wealth than their surrounding, more affluent suburbs due to their higher student enrollments and lower tax bases. In sum, a state school aid formula seeks to reduce or eliminate tax base differences by offsetting the effects of wealth disparity on educational opportunity.

Americans have not been enthusiastic about paying taxes at any time in the nation's history. A big part of the reluctance to pay taxes has been cultural, but real problems have existed in tax administration, aggravating an already sensitive situation. As discussed earlier, tax evasion has plagued all levels of government, both because people sometimes have refused to pay taxes and—in the more modern case—because they have found ways to avoid taxes, legally and illegally. The many tax problems faced by government led to the study of tax fairness and administration, so that knowledge about good tax systems, with implications for schools, grew rapidly during the first half of the last century.

Growth of schools in the nation, accompanied by growth in state responsibility for education, also led to state interest in providing at least some fiscal aid to local schools. Although we are skipping much historical development here, it is the case that by 1890 states were providing nearly $34 million in aid to schools, or approximately 24% of revenues. A goodly portion of such aid was stimulated by the fledgling concept of educational program equity that followed on the heels of the first studies within states revealing vast disparities arising from exclusively local tax base reliance. Although state aid predates the work of Elwood P. Cubberley, he is credited with initiating the dramatic rise in interest in state aid in his 1906 monograph that set the tone for the future.[12] Cubberley's point was simple by today's standard, but profound for his time: He argued that all the children of the state are equal and entitled to equal advantages. In studying several states, Cubberley concluded that few, if any, shared this philosophy because educational quality varied greatly and generally rose or fell in tandem with local property wealth.

Cubberley's work sparked an entire growth industry, as other scholars undertook similar studies. Harlan Updegraff's work in 1922 extended his line of thinking another step.[13] Studying rural schools in the state of New York, he argued that state aid should vary by local wealth and in relationship to local tax effort. Where Cubberley had validated the need for aid and created the concept of equality, Updegraff introduced the ideas of equalization and reward for tax effort; that is, districts could receive more state aid by taxing themselves at higher rates. The next major advance came in 1923 with the work of George Strayer and Robert Haig.[14] Accepting all that had already been done, Strayer and Haig took another giant step forward by advocating that concepts of equality and equalization should also result in a degree of minimum educational opportunity. Their view bound the state to go beyond just providing money to include some measure of program equality. Additionally, they argued that such a program should be available under uniform tax effort. The result was a foundation program, whereby the state would guarantee a fiscal foundation on which local districts could then build.

Yet another significant step was taken by Paul Mort in 1924.[15] Mort extended the minimum program concept by defining the weighted pupil, arguing that educational programs will have different costs in order to be equal. For example, small enrollment schools cost more due to diseconomies of scale. His contribution was to critically press

---

12 Elwood P. Cubberley, *School Funds and Their Apportionment* (New York: Columbia Teachers College, 1906).

13 Harlan Updegraff, *Rural School Survey of New York State: Financial Support* (Ithaca, NY: Author, 1992).

14 George D. Strayer and Robert M. Haig, *The Financing of Education in the State of New York,* Vol. 1 (New York: Macmillan, 1923).

15 Paul Mort, *The Measurement of Educational Need* (New York: Columbia Teachers College, 1924).

how states determine aid to districts, arguing that aid should vary along multiple criteria based on trying to estimate true educational costs rather than just distributing aid in a blindly neutral fashion.

The ideas of these early researchers were widely utilized as states struggled to conceptualize how they should aid schools. One last major breakthrough was less enthusiastically received, however. Henry Morrison, writing in 1930, was so disturbed by the extremes in quality of educational programs that he argued strongly for abolition of all school districts, while favoring a complete state takeover.[16] This was not at all radical in his view because he believed that since states had the ultimate duty to control education, fiscal inequality would never be resolved until tax base and educational program control were entirely statewide affairs. Obviously, such thinking ran counter to local control and was not warmly embraced—a sentiment that endures today despite the obvious minimization of variability that comes with a uniform statewide funding system.

Development of state aid plans clearly had basic fairness in mind, at least in terms of what these theorists intended, by suggesting ways to make educational opportunities more equal through the use of money. A state aid formula should fit the unique needs and features of school districts within each state, and the plan should apply universally within the state's borders. States worked at developing aid plans using these criteria, with each plan further reflecting certain educational, fiscal, and political philosophies and realities. For example, states taking an aggressive view of state responsibility for education developed school aid plans that made the state a fuller funding partner. Conversely, states favoring local control tended to devise aid plans that left considerable local freedom to exceed a set of educational minimums. These facts were the basis for the development of state aid plans that fall into several general types, based on what states conceptualized as fair. Over the years, grant-in-aid plans have become known as flat grants, equalization grants, multitier grants, and full state funding grants.

Flat Grants

The earliest form of state aid, a flat grant, is a flat sum of money per unit, such as student or teacher, paid to districts without concern for a local share or local ability to pay. This plan was justified by its advocates as distributionally neutral. Critics, however, argued that wealth disparity remained unchanged and that aid amounts were often too low to make a real difference. Flat grants proved popular, however—at the beginning of the 20th century, 38 states were using them to aid public schools. Popularity fell only as school finance litigation escalated in the 1970s. As Table 3.5 shows,[17] no state now relies solely on flat grants as the principal finance scheme although they are still used for other purposes or in multitier combinations.

---

16 Henry C. Morrison, *School Revenue* (Chicago: University of Chicago Press, 1930).

17 Although it is impossible to publish up to the minute, 50-state funding information due to the constantly changing political arena, Table 3.5 represents the most current, authoritative compilation of state school aid features.

TABLE 3.5 Major Features of State Aid to Education Plans by State

State	Formula Type (2009)	Expenditure per Pupil (2011)	State Aid Percent (2011)	Lottery Earmark (2013)	Tax and Expenditure Limits (2010)	Categorical Aid or Weighting Factor (2011)		
						Special Education	Poverty/ Compensatory	ELL
U.S. Average		10,658	44.1	–	–	–	–	–
Alabama	Foundation	8,726	51.8	n.a.	No	Yes	Yes	Yes
Alaska	Foundation	16,663	61.7	n.a.	Yes	Yes	Yes	Yes
Arizona	Foundation	7,782	40.2	No	Yes	Yes	No	Yes
Arkansas	Foundation	9,496	51.3	Yes	No	Yes	No	Yes
California	Foundation	9,146	56.6	Yes	Yes	Yes	Yes	Yes
Colorado	Foundation	8,786	40.1	No	Yes	Yes	Yes	No
Connecticut	Foundation	16,224	34.3	No	Yes	Yes	Yes	Yes
Delaware	Flat Grant+Equalization	12,467	58.6	No	Yes	Yes	Yes	No
Florida	Foundation	9,030	34.4	Yes	Yes	Yes	No	Yes
Georgia	Foundation/Guaranteed Yield	9,259	41.7	Yes	No	Yes	Yes	Yes
Hawaii	Full State Funding	11,924	83.4	n.a.	Yes	Yes	Yes	Yes
Idaho	Foundation	6,821	63.3	No	Yes	Yes	No	Yes
Illinois	Foundation/Flat Grant	11,742	32.2	No	No	Yes	Yes	Yes
Indiana	Foundation	9,251	55.6	No	Yes	Yes	Yes	Yes
Iowa	Foundation	9,795	43.2	No	Yes	Yes	Yes	Yes
Kansas	Flat Grant+Equalization	9,802	52.5	No	No	Yes	Yes	Yes
Kentucky	Foundation/Guaranteed Tax Base	9,228	51.8	Yes	No	Yes	Yes	Yes
Louisiana	Foundation	10,799	42.2	No	Yes	Yes	Yes	Yes
Maine	Foundation	12,576	40.5	No	Yes	Yes	Yes	Yes
Maryland	Foundation/Guaranteed Tax Base	14,123	41.0	No	No	Yes	Yes	Yes
Massachusetts	Foundation	14,285	37.8	No	Yes	Yes	Yes	Yes
Michigan	Foundation	10,577	55.1	Yes	Yes	Yes	Yes	Yes
Minnesota	Foundation	10,674	58.5	No	No	Yes	Yes	Yes
Mississippi	Foundation	7,926	46.2	n.a.	Yes	Yes	Yes	No
Missouri	Foundation	9,461	29.6	Yes	Yes	Yes	Yes	Yes

TABLE 3.5 *continued*

	Type	Expenditure	Percent					
Montana	Foundation/Guaranteed Tax Base	10,719	43.7	No	Yes	Yes	No	No
Nebraska	Foundation	11,540	30.3	No	No	Yes	Yes	Yes
Nevada	Foundation	8,411	33.0	n.a.	Yes	Yes	No	No
New Hampshire	Foundation	13,548	36.6	Yes	No	Yes	Yes	Yes
New Jersey	Foundation	16,855	37.3	No	Yes	Yes	Yes	Yes
New Mexico	Foundation	9,250	64.7	Yes	No	Yes	No	Yes
New York	Foundation	18,834	40.1	Yes	No	Yes	Yes	Yes
North Carolina	Flat Grant+Equalization	8,267	58.1	Yes	Yes	Yes	Yes	Yes
North Dakota	Foundation	10,898	50.0	No	No	Yes	No	Yes
Ohio	Foundation	11,395	43.2	Yes	Yes	Yes	Yes	Yes
Oklahoma	Foundation	7,631	46.9	Yes	Yes	Yes	Yes	Yes
Oregon	Foundation	9,516	45.6	No	Yes	Yes	Yes	Yes
Pennsylvania	Foundation	13,096	34.5	No	No	Yes	Yes	No
Rhode Island	General Aid	14,948	36.4	No	Yes	No	No	Yes
South Carolina	Foundation	8,903	43.4	Yes	Yes	Yes	Yes	No
South Dakota	Foundation	8,931	29.1	No	No	Yes	No	No
Tennessee	Foundation	8,484	44.8	Yes	Yes	Yes	Yes	Yes
Texas	Foundation/Guaranteed Yield	8,685	40.2	Yes	Yes	Yes	Yes	Yes
Utah	Foundation	6,326	50.9	n.a.	Yes	Yes	No	Yes
Vermont	Full State Funding	14,707	81.7	Yes	No	Yes	Yes	Yes
Virginia	Foundation	10,363	37.0	Yes	No	Yes	Yes	Yes
Washington	Foundation	9,619	57.3	No	Yes	Yes	Yes	Yes
West Virginia	Foundation	11,978	55.8	No	No	Yes	No	Yes
Wisconsin	Guaranteed Tax Base	11,946	45.9	No	Yes	Yes	Yes	Yes
Wyoming	Foundation	15,815	53.3	No	No	Yes	No	Yes

Sources: Compiled from multiple sources. U.S. Department of Education, *Digest of Education Statistics*, "Total and Current Expenditures per Pupil in Fall Enrollment in Public Elementary and Secondary Education, by Function and State or Jurisdiction: 2010–11," Table 236.75, http://nces.ed.gov/programs/digest/d13/tables/dt13_236.75.asp. U.S. Department of Education, *Digest of Education Statistics*, "Revenues for Public Elementary and Secondary Schools, by Source of Funds and State or Jurisdiction: 2010–11," Table 235.10, http://nces.ed.gov/programs/digest/d13/tables/dt13_235.20.asp. Deborah A. Verstegen, "A Quick Glance at School Finance: A 50-State Survey of School Finance Policies (2011)," http://schoolfinancesdav.wordpress.com. Bert Waisanan, "State Tax and Expenditure Limits—2010," National Conference of State Legislatures www.ncsl.org/research/fiscal-policy/state-tax-and-expenditure-limits-2010.aspx. Elle Hull and Jennifer Burnett, "State Lotteries," Council of State Governments, June 17, 2013, http://knowledgecenter.csg.org/kc/content/state-lotteries.Vermont Department of Education, "Vermont's Education Funding System," June 2011, http://education.vermont.gov/documents/EDU-Finance_Education_Funding_System_2011.pdf. Independent research by the authors.

The operation and effect of a flat grant is illustrated in Figure 3.3. The figure shows that while a $1,000 flat grant per pupil surely would be welcomed in low, medium, and high wealth districts alike, its impact is completely unrelated to local ability to pay for schools. It is likely most desperately needed in the low-wealth district, and it certainly represents a larger proportion of total expenditure per pupil.

However, a flat grant has absolutely no impact on equalization; that is, wealth-based inequalities are untouched while expenditures in all districts simply go up by exactly $1,000; or, alternatively, the district might choose to reduce local tax effort by an equivalent amount so that students are no better off dollar-wise. The net sum for poor districts is no change in equalization, while the net sum for wealthy districts is enrichment unrelated to educational need or tax relief. Although flat grants represented a step forward in terms of states participating in education's costs, they did not reduce property tax base inequalities.

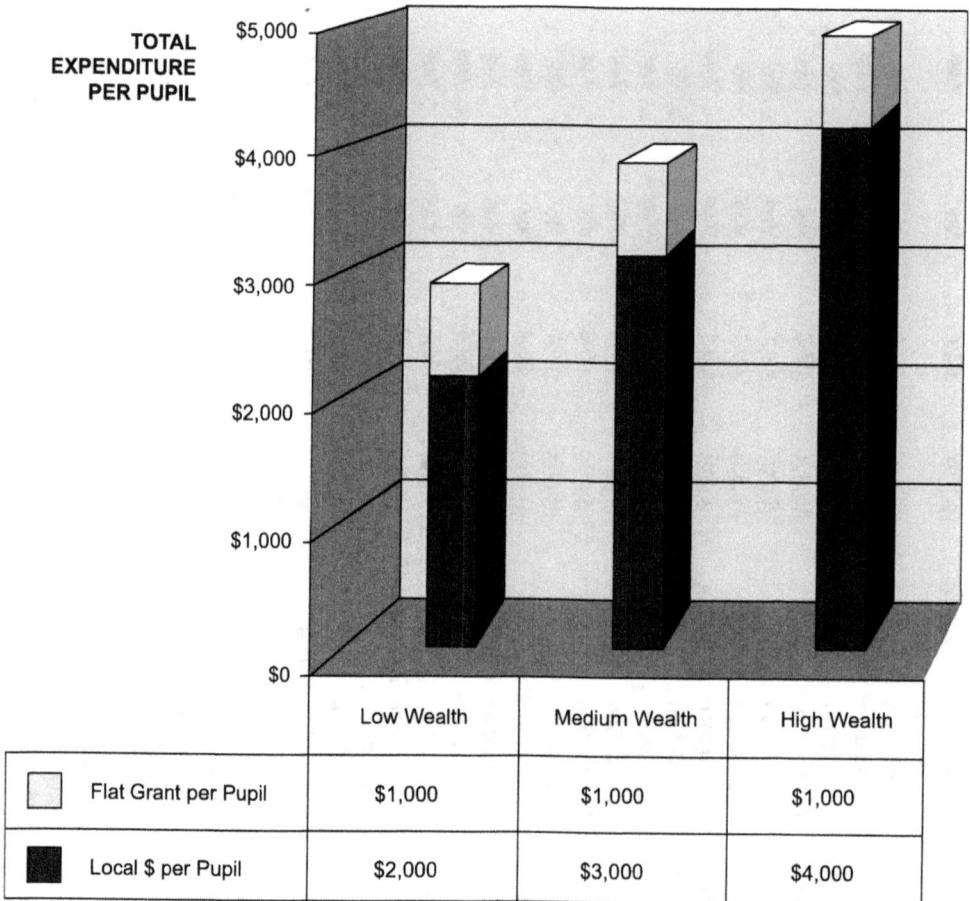

TOTAL EXPENDITURE PER PUPIL	Low Wealth	Medium Wealth	High Wealth
☐ Flat Grant per Pupil	$1,000	$1,000	$1,000
■ Local $ per Pupil	$2,000	$3,000	$4,000

FIGURE 3.3 Effect of a $1,000 Per-Pupil Flat Grant

Equalization Grants

Equalization plans include a wide variety of state aid formulas seeking to grant aid inversely to local ability to pay for schools. Largely in response to the nonequalizing effect of earlier aid plans, equalization grants were designed to bring expenditure levels in rich and poor districts closer together, or at least to better equalize poorer districts' opportunity to spend at the same level as wealthier districts. Although many kinds of equalization grants exist, all such plans are based on the idea of increasing state aid to local districts with the least fiscal capacity. Differing political philosophies have driven formula designs in individual states, primarily by virtue of two decisions that must be made: first whether the state should set expenditure levels and tax rates, and, second, whether the state should let districts set their own tax-and-spend limits.[18] Major equalization plans flowing from these decisions became known as foundation plans and resource accessibility plans.

Foundation plans were originally based on a minimum concept. This meant several things. First, a foundation plan is politically and factually effective in that equality is achieved by requiring a uniform minimum expenditure level and a uniform minimum tax rate in each school district throughout the state. Second, the state requires districts to provide a minimum standard educational program. Third, a foundation plan allows higher local spending by permitting additional local tax effort. Fourth, the minimum costs are equalized because the amount of state aid is inversely related to local ability to pay for schools. However, to be effective, the minimum required expenditure levels must be meaningful, and the state cost-share must be high enough to encourage local effort above the minimum. Foundation plans are the most popular form of equalization aid today, with more than 40 states using them as their primary means to distribute state aid. Several states use a foundation in combination with other aid programs.

Resource accessibility plans seek to equalize school revenues by taking a different approach. While a foundation plan has historically focused on statewide minimum standards in tax rate and expenditure levels, resource equalization plans try to empower districts to make their own fiscal and program decisions unhindered by local wealth limitations. This means that variability in programs and expenditures is acceptable as long as availability of revenue is not the reason for such variability, so while foundation plans have sought minimum equality, resource accessibility plans attempt to balance wealth, or ability to pay, in each district through formulas that adjust for tax base differences. The result has been various percentage equalizing plans, and these plans

---

18 Note that Table 3.5 has a column indicating which states have tax and expenditure limits (TELs). The structure of TELs varies greatly across states. Some have a direct effect on a school district's ability to increase expenditures or property tax revenues (even both, in some cases). Other TELs place limits on a state's ability to increase existing taxes or expenditures. In either case, i.e., local or state limits, less revenue is available to school districts. For further information, see Bert Waisanan, "State Tax and Expenditure Limits—2010," National Conference of State Legislatures, www.ncsl.org/research/fiscal-policy/state-tax-and-expenditure-limits-2010.aspx.

have been further refined to include variations such as guaranteed tax base (GTB), guaranteed tax yield (GTY), and district power equalization (DPE). Each of these plans approaches the problem of unequal resources differently. Percentage equalizing plans guarantee a constant percentage of budget from the state based on local ability to pay, with the local district setting costs and programs. GTB and GTY equalize revenues by assuring districts the same tax capacity as every other district. DPE carries the resource accessibility concept to its ultimate potential of recapture of excess revenue capacity by requiring that districts with wealth greater than the state's per-pupil guarantee remit excess revenue to the state for redistribution to poorer districts. Compared to the popularity of foundation plans, far fewer states have adopted resource accessibility formulas, and most states adopting some version of the latter plans have modified the most politically unpopular features or combined them with a foundation plan in a two-tiered funding system. Only six states use GTB or GTY, of which five pair it with a foundation plan. Wisconsin is the only state to use a resource accessibility plan (GTY) as its sole form of basic or general aid. No state uses DPE (see Table 3.5). Equalization plans have served a useful purpose, in that school finance reform in the 1970s gave impetus to self-scrutiny by states, with resultant improvement of equalization.

The operation and effect of a foundation plan is illustrated in Figure 3.4. The figure illustrates a uniform tax rate and a $5,000 per-pupil expenditure target or "foundation level." The low-wealth district can raise only 20% of the target from local tax effort, and so the state provides 80%. Conversely, the wealthiest district raises 100% of the target at the uniform minimum tax rate. Countless variations on this scheme are possible. Some states provide local option leeway above the minimum expenditure, and the leeway may or may not qualify for state aid depending on the structure of the state aid plan. Recapture can be built in by setting the statewide tax rate high enough to produce more revenue than wealthy districts can legally spend per pupil. The possible variations are too numerous to illustrate here, but the effect of aid inversely related to local ability to pay is clearly the aim of any equalization formula. Equalization plans can be costly to states, both in terms of actual dollars when setting adequate resource levels and in political terms because concepts like low aid, zero aid, or recapture can prove politically unpalatable to property-wealthy communities.

Multitier Grants

To make state aid plans acceptable to many constituencies, policymakers have sometimes created formulas that combine parts of two or more plans. For example, a state might enact a foundation program combined with a percentage equalizing formula (DPE, GTB, or GYF) that provides greater local leeway in spending to appeal to a broader range of school districts, similar to the two-tiered plan mentioned in the previous section. Variations might include capping the matching feature of the percentage equalizing grant; equalizing it at the same aid ratio as the foundation amount; or equalizing the percentage equalizing grant up to a certain point. Other types of aid, such as a flat grant, could also be attached to the basic formula structure. Only one state, Illinois, takes this approach.

**FOUNDATION PLAN UNDER UNIFORM TAX RATE WITH
A STATE COST-SHARE RATIO 0–80%**

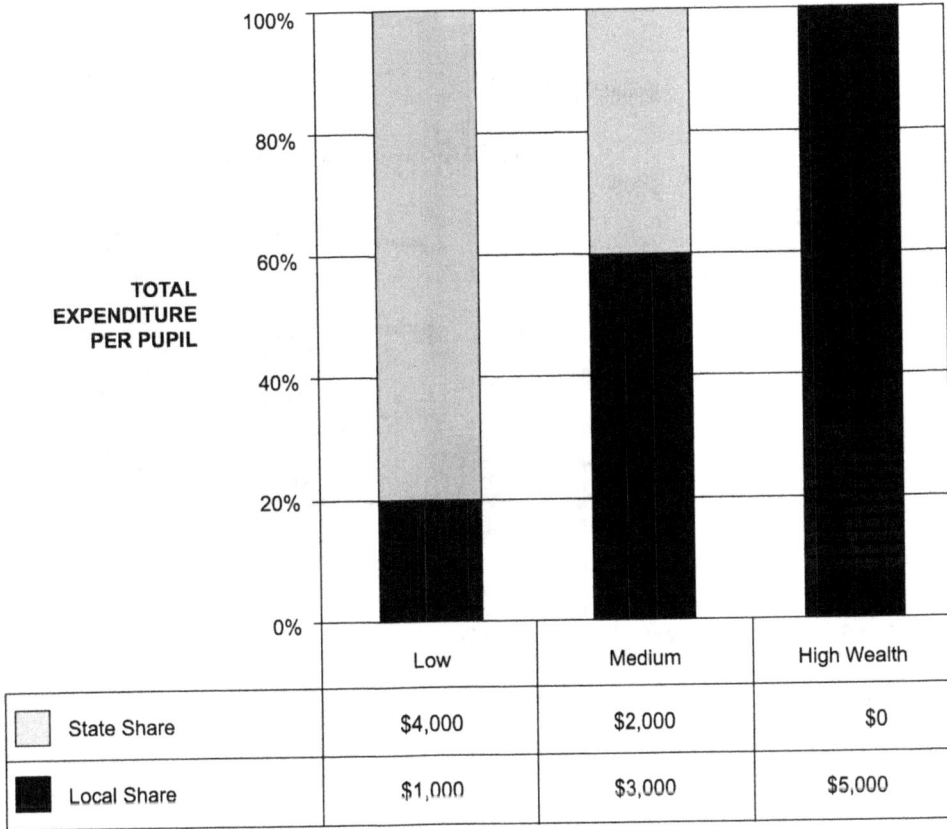

	Low	Medium	High Wealth
State Share	$4,000	$2,000	$0
Local Share	$1,000	$3,000	$5,000

FIGURE 3.4 Effect of a Foundation Grant

Figure 3.5 illustrates a aid formula that combines a foundation of $5,000 per pupil, coupled with a 25% local option leeway aided at the same aid ratio as the foundation amount. In this example, districts can choose to spend up to $6,250 per pupil, but they must tax themselves voluntarily for the portion identified as the local share of the local leeway option. The state's aid ratio, however, is guaranteed up to the maximum per-pupil expenditure level, so choosing to increase local tax effort means more state aid. Of course, districts can choose not to make the extra tax effort and forego additional state aid. Politically motivated strategies can be embedded in these designs. For example, the local leeway option may represent a concession to high-wealth districts because without it, this group of districts would receive no state aid. Such strategies are sometimes used as compromise measures by state lawmakers to gain buy-in from a majority of the state's school districts in order to enact reforms in the state funding system.

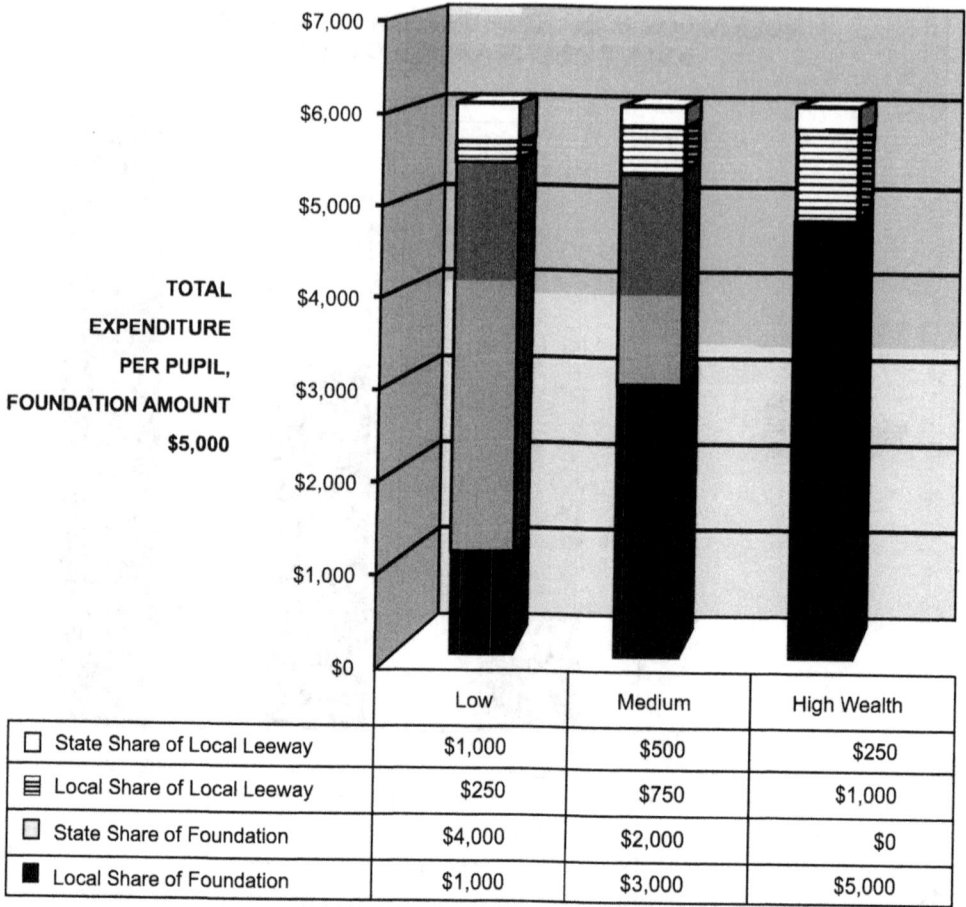

	Low	Medium	High Wealth
☐ State Share of Local Leeway	$1,000	$500	$250
☰ Local Share of Local Leeway	$250	$750	$1,000
☐ State Share of Foundation	$4,000	$2,000	$0
■ Local Share of Foundation	$1,000	$3,000	$5,000

FIGURE 3.5 Effect of a Foundation Grant with Equalized Local 25 Percent Option Leeway

Full State Funding Grants

Regarded as a potential threat to local control, full state funding is rare. The rationale for full state funding is a state's acceptance of responsibility with regard to education as plenary. Operationally, full state funding is simple. It places all the resources of a state within reach of every child through changing that portion of the local property tax dedicated to school support to a state tax so that it can be pooled at the state level and redistributed as aid to schools without regard to local property wealth. As a result, individual school districts no longer have local discretion to spend more or less than other districts. In addition, recapture, widely held as politically unpalatable, is inherently included in full state funding because a uniform statewide property tax rate will yield differing amounts from communities based upon their property wealth, with some communities generating revenue above state mandated education expenditure levels.

As such, full state funding differs radically from the other state aid plans previously described.

With these stipulations, only two states have adopted full state funding. Hawaii's single school district structure represents a type of de facto full state funding. Vermont is the second state, with 81.7% of school district expenditures provided by state aid. Overall, the U.S. average for state aid was 44.1% in 2011, although it is important to note that some states like Illinois, Missouri, Nebraska, Nevada, and South Dakota provide less than one-third.

Figure 3.6 depicts a full state funding plan, albeit an oversimplified one because it lacks vertical equity adjustments or additions (to be discussed in the next section). Each district spends $5,000 per pupil, with the local share financed by a uniform tax effort of 20 mills. The low property-wealth district can raise only $40 per pupil in local revenue, while the higher property-wealth district's tax yield per pupil exceeds the required uniform expenditure per pupil. The result is that the state provides sufficient aid to less wealthy districts so that they are able to spend $5,000 per pupil when combined with their local tax effort. At the same time, the state finances this plan, in part, with funds recaptured from the wealthiest districts.

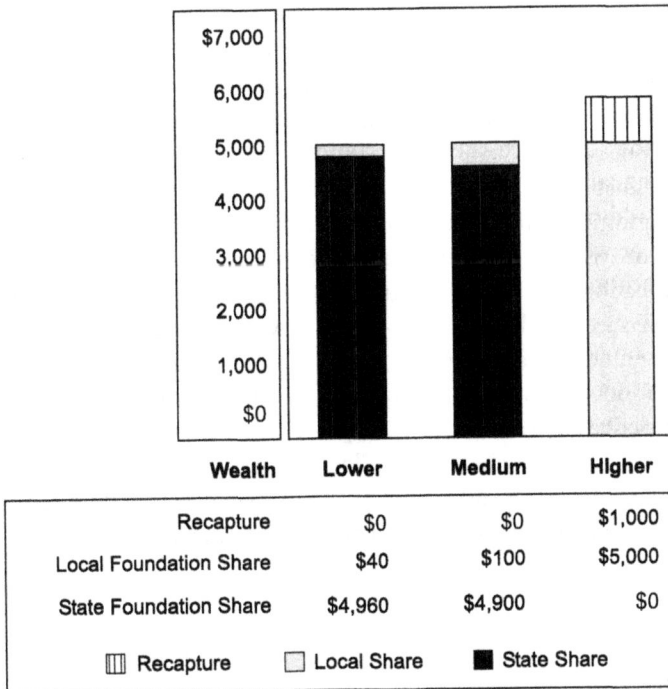

Wealth	Lower	Medium	Higher
Recapture	$0	$0	$1,000
Local Foundation Share	$40	$100	$5,000
State Foundation Share	$4,960	$4,900	$0

▥ Recapture   ☐ Local Share   ◼ State Share

FIGURE 3.6 Full State Funding Per-Pupil Grant under 20 Mills Local Tax Effort with Recapture Provision

ADJUSTMENTS AND ADDITIONS TO BASIC AID FORMULAS

Our discussion to this point has considered general or basic state aid, with no consideration for vertical equity adjustments to school aid formulas based on student differences. Although horizontal equity, defined as "the equal treatment of equals,"[19] requires all students to be funded as equals, all students are not the same in that some may require additional resources to be academically successful. Hence, state school funding systems also need to incorporate funding mechanisms for vertical equity, or "the appropriately unequal treatment of unequals."[20] Generally speaking, these adjustments or additions fall into categories of need equalization and cost equalization.

Need Equalization

Under state and federal law, every child is entitled to an education appropriate to his or her needs. The concept of need speaks directly to vertical equity, i.e., differences among children relating to those who are considered educationally disadvantaged by virtue of conditions outside their control. Although there is not universal agreement on the definition of "educationally disadvantaged," education research often refers to these students as "at-risk" [of academic failure] and has identified them as children from low income families; those with disabilities; racial/ethnic minority students; English language learners; children in urban schools; and students from families with low parental education attainment.[21] Need equalization therefore is a critical component of state school funding systems. A range of aid programs has sprung up around the concept of need equalization, of which the most common are special education, compensatory education, bilingual education,[22] and early childhood education. Today most states provide some additional financial support to these students, usually in the form of categorical aid or weighting of per-pupil basic aid.

Special education has been the most visible need equalization program for many years. Although special education programs have existed for many decades, special education took on new meaning in the 1970s with enactment of federal legislation and aggressive litigation surrounding the rights of children with disabilities to be educated in the least restrictive environment. Although other need equalization adjustments may receive only modest, or even no, attention in some states, addressing the needs of special education students has been the center of intense advocacy, with every indication of continuing far into the future as a powerful political and legal force.

---

19 Robert Berne and Leanna Stiefel, *The Measurement of Equity in School Finance* (Baltimore, MD: Johns Hopkins University Press, 1984), 406.

20 Ibid.

21 See, e.g., Randall S. Vesely, Faith E. Crampton, Festus E. Obiakor, and Marty Sapp, "The Role of States in Funding Education to Achieve Social Justice," *Journal of Education Finance* 34 (Summer 2008): 56–74.

22 Bilingual education is also referred to as education for limited English proficient (LEP) students and English Language Learners (ELL).

States generally fund special education in much the same way as other need equalization programs, but the mandated nature of special education has resulted in close governmental monitoring, particularly because special education funding involves a mix of federal, state, and local moneys. States typically fund special education by pupil weighting, categorical aid, cost reimbursement, or census.[23] States that use a weighting factor often weight pupils by type or severity of disability. In reality, states often pay only a portion of school districts' actual costs, leaving school districts to fund the remainder after taking into consideration federal funding. Forty-nine states provide special education aid, with Rhode Island the only exception.

The purpose of compensatory aid is to redress social and economic inequality by targeting additional funding to low income students. The federal government has long had an interest in compensatory education aid through a range of programs, e.g., Title I funding, free and reduced-price school meals and afterschool snacks, and Head Start. Thirty-seven states provide some level of aid for compensatory education.

With growth in immigration, aid to bilingual education has become increasingly important to states and local school districts. Various court rulings have spurred the need for bilingual programs, in that civil rights legislation has been held to encompass language barriers. Court rulings and other federal legislation have caused states to provide bilingual programs or risk lawsuits or loss of federal funding. The response has been varied, with 43 states providing some level of aid for bilingual education.

A number of studies indicate that there is a significant return on investment on preschool programs, particularly for low income and special needs children, that accrue to both schools and society.[24] Because federal Head Start funding allows only a small percentage of these children access to quality early childhood education, more states have become involved in either supplementing Head Start funding or providing funding to school districts for pre-K programs. Forty states provide some types of early childhood education services, but only a handful of states provide such programs to a majority of eligible children (see Figure 3.7). Newer research indicates that all children derive some benefit from early childhood education, which has renewed interest on the part of the federal government in increasing access to high quality early education programs.[25] However, as Figure 3.8 indicates, no state yet offers universal access.

---

23 Census-based funding in special education is based upon a fixed percentage of total school district enrollment set by the state, not the actual number of students identified as having special needs in a particular district. See, William T. Hartman, "The Impact of Census-Based Special Education in Pennsylvania," *Journal of Special Education Leadership* 14, no. 1 (2001): 4–12. www.csef-air.org/publications/related/jsel/hartman.html.

24 See, e.g., Clive Belfield, "Does It Pay to Invest in Preschool for All? Analyzing Return-on-Investment in Three States?" NIER Working Paper (New Brunswick, NJ: Rutgers University Press, 2006), http://nieer.org/resources/research/DoesitPay.pdf.

25 U.S. Department of Education, "Early Learning: America's Middle Class Promise Begins Early," www.ed.gov/early-learning.

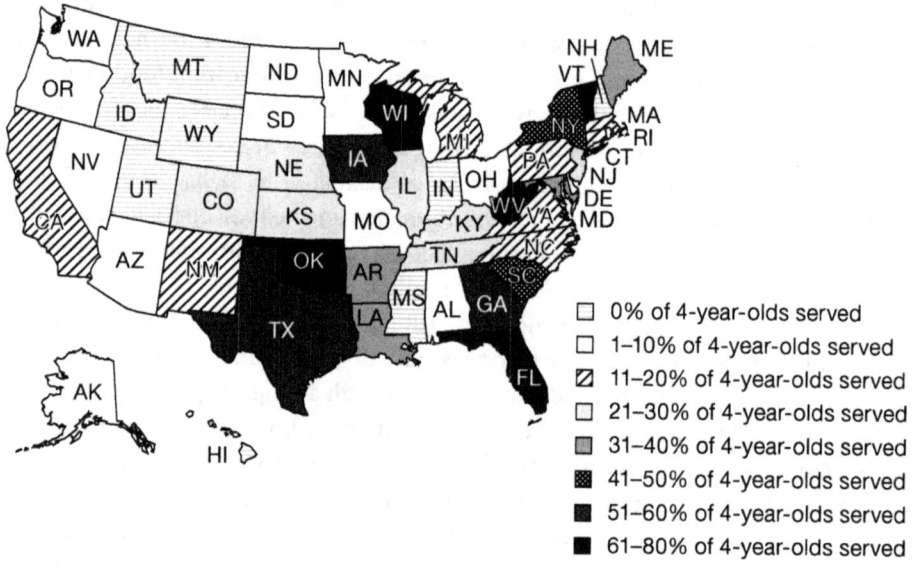

FIGURE 3.7 Percent of Four-Year-Olds Served in State Pre-Kindergarten Programs

Source: National Institute for Early Education Research. *The State of Preschool 2013*. http://nieer.org/publications/state-preschool-2013.

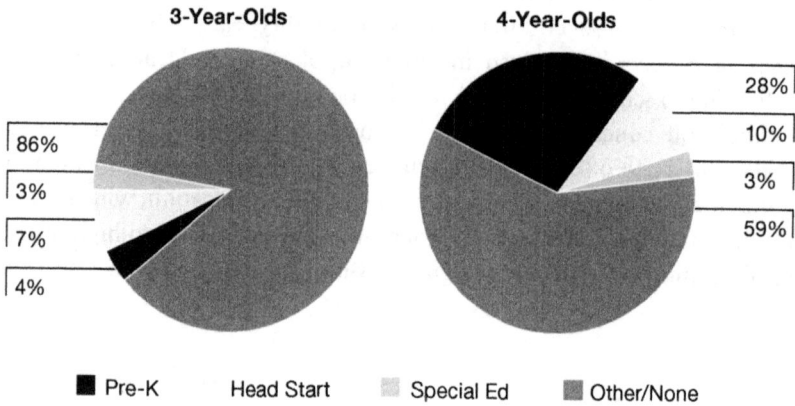

FIGURE 3.8 State Pre-K and Head Start Enrollment as Percentage of Total Enrollment

Source: National Institute for Early Education Research. *The State of Preschool 2013*. http://nieer.org/publications/state-preschool-2013.

Cost Equalization

The differing economic, demographic, and geographic characteristics of states have resulted in cost equalization adjustments or additions to state school funding systems. Cost equalization in state aid usually takes two forms. One form recognizes that different costs may arise due to diseconomies of scale, while the second attempts to compensate districts for market-based cost differentials. For example, higher costs may stem from the price of urban life. Conversely, rural districts may face higher costs when trying to attract and retain personnel. Similarly, rural school districts may face higher costs related to transportation over sparsely populated but geographically large school districts (in terms of square miles).

States choosing to engage in cost equalization may do so based more on political pressure than research evidence. Cost equalization is addressed most often through categorical aid or pupil weightings attached to basic or general aid, e.g., adding factors such as enrollment density or sparsity and declining or increasing enrollment. A few states have tried to create education cost indices based on market-based cost differences within the state, but the lack of detailed data, coupled with the complexity of constructing a valid index and political sensitivities, has generally served as a deterrent.

WRAP-UP

Our discussion throughout this chapter has illustrated that states have many goals when designing school aid formulas.[26] At the most basic level, aid formulas are an attempt to redress local tax base inequalities, i.e., high vs. low property wealth. Such inequality, if not abated, would result in unacceptable disparities in number, type, and quality of educational programs and, hence, equality of educational opportunity. The first goal of general or basic aid formulas, then, is to make adequate funding available to all districts using state resources. Other goals are equally important. Among them are the need to address special human conditions, to reflect the unique problems of individual states, and to convince taxpayers that their voices are heard and that their resources are not wasted. At the same time, state aid formulas must satisfy legal mandates found in state constitutions and statutes as well as in the U.S. Constitution. In addition, state policymakers must be attuned to political philosophies as they try to create aid plans that neither infringe on local control nor are too weak to be effective.

---

26 See also, Faith E. Crampton and Terry N. Whitney, *Principles of a Sound State School Finance System* (Denver, CO, and Washington, DC: Foundation for State Legislatures, 1996), where the authors enumerate five major policy goals that state policymakers should strive to incorporate in their education funding plans—equity, adequacy, efficiency, accountability, and stability.

POINT–COUNTERPOINT

POINT

States face many funding obligations of which public schools are only one. Of all the many obligations faced by states, public schools should be the first priority—even at the expense of other social programs—given how inadequate funding of education eventually translates into higher social service costs.

COUNTERPOINT

When states experience revenue shortfalls, all state spending—including spending for public schools—must be reduced because states generally cannot engage in deficit spending. In terms of state support, education is no more important than any other program or service the state funds. It is only fair that schools take their fair share of cuts in state aid to help balance the state's budget.

- In your opinion, which state services are most important to fully fund in a budget shortfall? Why?
- How do states come to experience budget shortfalls, and what should they do to address and prevent such situations?

CASE STUDY

As one of the more established superintendents in your state, you have been asked to testify next month before a legislative interim committee studying school finance. You are no stranger to state politics, and it has long been your belief that your state's school funding formula is outdated and deficient in some important ways. More specifically, you have spoken out in the past in favor of increasing state aid in the belief that it is insufficient if school districts are to meet new, more rigorous state standards. You have further lobbied for increased recognition of adjustments to the state funding system that would increase funding to students who might have difficulty reaching those standards without additional resources, like tutoring. As you have considered the invitation to testify, it has occurred to you that you will be questioned closely because some members of the interim committee likely will represent school districts that would not benefit from your views.

As you begin to prepare for your testimony, you run through all the possible viewpoints you might face. Certainly, your own school board will want you to advocate positions favorable to your district—i.e., a fairly well-to-do community whose children perform well on state assessments. Your district has one of the highest graduate rates in the state, and the vast majority of your high school graduates pursue postsecondary education. Relatedly, your state allows school districts to raise additional property tax revenues for program enhancements without getting local voter approval, and your district currently levies at the maximum allowed in order to fund exemplary curricular and cocurricular programs that might have to be cut if the state changed or eliminated this option. At the same time, other types of school districts will advocate for their needs. For example, many of the small, rural school districts face stagnant or declining enrollments, and are experiencing challenges in offering just the state's basic mandated curriculum under the current funding system. They want an across-the-board increase in per-pupil state aid, although they would also welcome more state aid for transportation, particularly because of rising fuel costs. The state's urban school districts, on the other hand, face crowded classrooms and crumbling infrastructure. At the very least, they would like to see a state aid for class size reduction added to the current school finance system. Second on their list is the state funding for school construction and modernization. They have buildings more than a century old that are unsafe, expensive to heat, and ill-equipped for technology. Of course, there are the many districts resembling yours, i.e., doing well and mostly wishing for new money to do more good things for children, but generally not wanting to rock the boat in the state capital.

The agenda for next month's legislative meeting devotes an hour to your testimony. You know the committee has already heard from experts on the elements of good school aid formulas. Your testimony will conclude the information gathering phase, after which public comments will be taken. The committee's goal is to recommend changes to the state funding system in the next legislative session.

Below is a set of questions. As you respond, consider your learning throughout this chapter and apply your knowledge and views to the situation:

- What will be the major talking points in your upcoming legislative testimony?
- How will you go about satisfying the expectations of your school district while taking into consideration the needs of other school districts in the state?
- Using your own state's school aid formula as a basis, what would you recommend to the legislative committee? What counterarguments could you expect from legislators, other school districts, and general critics of education spending; and how would you respond?

PORTFOLIO EXERCISES

- Obtain documents explaining the state aid formula(s) in your state. (These are often available through your state department of education and online.) Identify the type of general or basic aid formula used in your state. Identify state revenue sources used to fund education (e.g., income taxes, sales taxes, lottery profits, etc.). Identify from these documents, if possible, your state's policy goals and priorities with regard to aid to local school districts.

- Identify how your state aid formula addresses student and taxpayer equity as well as adequacy. Consider how horizontal equity is addressed, and identify any adjustments or additions to basic aid to address vertical equity. Identify the amounts of money allocated to general aid, categorical aid, pupil weighting, and need or cost adjustments. Determine whether there has been any recent research on the equity or adequacy or your state's funding system and, if available, examine the results.

- Interview leaders of educational organizations (e.g., school board, parent–teacher associations, teachers' unions, administrators, state agencies, professional associations) to learn what they perceive as the strengths and weaknesses of your state's school funding system. Ask them what needs to be done to improve any weaknesses they perceive.

- Watch for meetings addressing school funding you can attend. These might include legislative committee meetings, legislative issues town meetings, teacher association meetings, local school board meetings. Take notes on the issues and attitudes expressed, and try to identify the most influential players. Take note of any changes proposed to financing schools.

- Compare how your state funds education to other states in your region. Consider the numbers of students to be educated, dollars legislatively appropriated, choice of state aid formula design, and revenue (tax) sources for education. Assess which states provide the greatest degree of equity and adequacy in their funding systems.

WEB RESOURCES

Council of State Governments, www.csg.org

National Association of State Budget Officers, www.nasbo.org

National Conference of State Legislatures, www.ncsl.org

National Institute for Early Childhood Education. "The State of Preschool 2013: State Profiles." http://nieer.org/publications/state-preschool-2013-state-profiles

Tax Foundation, www.taxfoundation.org

U.S. Census Bureau, www.census.gov

U.S. Department of Education, Early Learning: America's Middle Class Promise Begins Early, http://www.ed.gov/early-learning

U.S. Department of Education, National Center for Education Statistics, http://nces.ed.gov

U.S. Office of Management and Budget, www.whitehouse.gov/omb/budget

RECOMMENDED READING

Barnett, W. Steven, Megan E. Carolan, James H. Squires, and Kristy Clarke Brown. *The State of Preschool 2013*. New Brunswick, NJ: National Institute for Early Education Research, 2013. http://nieer.org/publications/state-preschool-2013.

Belfield, Clive. "Does It Pay to Invest in Preschool for All? Analyzing Return-on-Investment in Three States." NIER Working Paper. New Brunswick, NJ: Rutgers University, 2006. http://nieer.org/resources/research/DoesitPay.pdf.

Crampton, Faith E., and Terry N. Whitney. *Principles of a Sound State School Finance System*. A monograph of the Education Partners Project. Denver, CO, and Washington, DC: Foundation for State Legislatures, 1996.

Hartman, William T. "The Impact of Census-Based Special Education in Pennsylvania." *Journal of Special Education Leadership* 14, no. 1 (2001): 4–12. www.csef-air.org/publications/related/jsel/hartman.html.

National Association of State Budget Officers. "State Expenditure Report: Examining Fiscal 2011–2013 State Spending." Washington, DC: 2013. www.nasbo.org/sites/default/files/State%20Expenditure%20Report%20%28Fiscal%202011–2013%20Data%29.pdf.

Thompson, David C., R. Craig Wood, and David S. Honeyman. *Fiscal Leadership for Schools: Concepts and Practices*. New York: Longman, 1994.

PART

II

Operationalizing School Money

School Funds: Accountability and Professionalism

THE CHALLENGE

To assess accountability, citizens as well as legislative and oversight bodies want to ensure that resources are used in accordance with appropriations. Overspending may indicate poor financial management, weak budgetary practices, or uncontrollable and unforeseen circumstances. Underspending may indicate effective financial management that provides the necessary quality and quantity of services within the available appropriations or a decision by management to accumulate a surplus of resources for future use. A comprehensive education information system gives a broad view of budgetary concerns, ratherthan simply a bottom line.

Financial Accounting for Local and State School Systems (2009)[1]

CHAPTER DRIVERS

Please reflect upon the following questions as you read this chapter:

- What is fiscal accountability?
- What are the fiduciary responsibilities of school districts and administrators?
- How does the accounting process help establish accountability?
- What are the purposes of accounting?
- How are educational budgets allocated?
- How are school moneys tracked?
- How do revenue and expenditure structures assist in tracking money?
- How do audits improve school districts' abilities to track money?
- What ethical standards should guide school leaders' professionalism in handling school money?

---

1 Gregory S. Allison, Steven D. Honegger, and Frank Johnson, *Financial Accounting for Local and State School Systems: 2009 Edition* (Washington, DC: U.S. Department of Education, Institute of Education Sciences, National Center for Education Statistics, June 2009).

SCHOOL FUNDS ACCOUNTABILITY

Citizens, with a wide range of views on the value of education, are increasingly involved in schools. At the same time, the issues faced by federal, state, and local governments are extraordinarily complex as every governmental agency attempts to satisfy the demands of all constituencies. Elementary and secondary schools are part of the fabric of the larger society, and citizens have the power to cause lasting change, either by forcing change or resisting it. Many school leaders have learned the hard way that the public is becoming bolder regarding voicing disagreement with what administrators have long regarded as routine policy in budgeting, curriculum, and even the day-to-day operations of schools. This chapter is an introductory discussion of fiscal accountability and fiduciary trust because the best-laid educational plans mean nothing without a sound financial plan—a plan based on the highest ethical and professional accounting standards.

This chapter turns to the specific elements of implementing school budgets—the operational aspects of putting money to work in schools. Money is an issue of accountability and trust because only a few people in a school district really understand the complex expectations to which administrators and others are held when handling public funds. Consequently, new and experienced school leaders alike must be thoroughly versed in the concepts of *fiscal accountability* and the *fiduciary trust*. Simultaneously, this chapter examines the *receipt of revenues* and the *restrictions on expenditures* and also provides a panoramic view of *how money flows* through a school district from beginning to end. Finally, this chapter describes the *code of ethical standards* for handling public moneys. Many school leaders have difficulties in this arena—most frequently due to ignorance of good practice and a lack of sufficient training. In sum, the complexity of appropriate stewardship of school money is still less complex than facing the consequences of mishandling public funds.

For many individuals, the concept of accountability for school funds is intimidating, well deserving the fear and respect it invites. There is no defense for people who do not take time to fully grasp the weight of accountability for public money, because all aspects of education suffer irreparable damage when proper accountability measures are not followed; that is, failure to establish good fiscal accountability results in pervasive distrust of everyone involved. As a consequence, this chapter examines the concept of accountability itself, followed by a deeper discussion of how money flows through schools.

FISCAL ACCOUNTABILITY

Accountability is a term greatly overused in education. This does not mean that too much accountability exists, but rather that the word is applied too casually to a wide scope of activities ranging from curriculum and student achievement to mapping bus routes and winning ball games. As a result, accountability is not always well defined, and its meaning is made more elusive by a lack of precise tools to measure what people hope to achieve when they think about accountability. In the discipline of education finance, accountability has a clear meaning. Fundamentally, accountability in fiscal terms means that those responsible for an activity involving money must provide evidence of appropriate care as conservators, which includes the *wise use* of all resources. Importantly, the scope of accountability continues to expand so that wise use is being redefined constantly.

Accountability can be conceptualized on numerous levels. At its root, it describes the practice of sound business principles when handling money regardless of whether the source of money is public or private. This definition can be traced back centuries. Growth in schools in the United States forced formal recognition of the importance of good business practice in education, with the first known business manager's position created in 1841 when the schools in Cleveland, Ohio, hired a manager to care for the accounting functions of the school district. The ever-increasing complexity of managing millions of dollars that characterizes virtually every modern school district has added greatly to needs for accountability awareness because the rising price of education increases the need for confidence that good business procedures are in place.

More broadly, accountability also has come to mean wise use of all resources in the care of the school district. This includes not only the accounting function, of course, but also the decision-making process by which funds are spent and the outcomes linked to such expenditures. Most individuals would agree that spending resources on things that hold little chance of helping students is not a wise business practice, yet the issues as discussed within this text suggest that wise resource utilization does not come easily. In other words, an increasingly distrustful public is no longer satisfied with evidence of good accounting procedures. In addition, many citizens ask pointed questions about whether increasing teachers' pay or creating new programs is wise from the perspective of both educational and fiscal accountability. Struggles over which programs obtain funding or are eliminated stand as proof of emerging applications of accountability, as do legislative and local debates on the relationship between funding and student achievement. This latter issue reached historic proportions with the passage of the No Child Left Behind Act of 2001,[2] which mandated states to require schools to increase academic performance standards, commonly referred to as "adequate yearly progress," or face increasingly harsh sanctions for both the state and underperforming schools and school districts. Therefore, the topics of resource decision making and fiscal accountability are concepts which are discussed frequently in this book, particularly in later chapters that address budgeting for educational programs.

Fiduciary Responsibilities

Central to the concepts of professionalism and accountability is the role of the school leader as a *fiduciary*. The origin of the word, *fiducia*, is Latin for "trust." As a noun, a fiduciary is a *trustee*. Trusteeship is itself an intriguing term, having heavy weight attached by virtue of *trust* as its root. More specifically, fiduciary responsibility carries

---

2 PL 107–110.

many pointed elements, inclusive of "the power and obligation to act for another [often called the beneficiary] under circumstances which require total trust, good faith and honesty."[3] The fiduciary is required to place the beneficiary's interests above his or her own. The seriousness needs no development except to underscore the weighty language. For purposes of this text, a person with fiduciary responsibility is someone placed in charge of any kind of property and in whom others—the public, in the case of public schools—have placed trust, so much so that one's personal reputation and professional livelihood are dependent on public confidence and support in wise use and conservatorship. Under these conditions, the level of trust is enormous—indeed, it is hard to conceive a more serious charge than that of a fiduciary, and the responsibility for millions of dollars entrusted to schools and their leaders is staggering.

As accountability has risen to a new level of public scrutiny, so have the duties and responsibilities of persons with fiduciary obligations. The duties of a fiduciary from the particular perspective of a school business manager have been identified for many years. The fiduciary role also touches school boards, administrators, teachers, staff, policymakers, and laypersons to varying degrees; that is, anyone who comes in contact with school resources in some manner. The duties have been identified as the following:

- *Planning:* the process of looking to the future, identifying resources and needs, and creating a master plan to follow
- *Decision making:* the process of choosing among options, knowing that setting a course of action is not easy to reverse and that making choices precludes other options
- *Organizing:* the process of preparing a plan for identifying needed human and fiscal resources and a sequence of events to reach a set of stated goals
- *Directing:* the process of accepting responsibility to see that plans are implemented and carried out
- *Controlling:* the process of monitoring progress against the original goals so that errors can be corrected during the implementation phase
- *Evaluating:* the ultimate responsibility for determining if goals were met and whether resources were wisely used[4]

These responsibilities have direct application to the financing of schools. For example, school administrators, teachers, and other staff have a shared responsibility for making schools successful so that only the level of direct involvement differs. As a rule, instructional staff conduct these duties in ways related to teaching and learning, although school site councils, decentralized budgeting, salary negotiations, and other aspects of participatory management have expanded formerly centralized fiduciary roles. Building principals, school superintendents, and chief finance officers as well as local

---

3 Legal Dictionary, http://dictionary.law.com/Default.aspx?selected=744.

4 R. Craig Wood, David C. Thompson, Lawrence O. Picus, and Don I. Tharpe, *Principles of School Business Management*, 2nd ed. (Reston, VA: Association of School Business Officials, 1995).

boards of education have more direct hands-on control of financial resources, although limited significantly by laws governing resource utilization and shared decision making. At the same time, state and local policymakers are involved in setting financial guidelines and controls, in many instances providing primary leadership for increased accountability. Laypeople are increasingly involved, particularly in approving or rejecting budgets, serving on site councils, and either directly or tacitly controlling all planning activities through the democratic process. Indeed planning, organizing, directing, controlling, and evaluating are no longer discrete functions as these critical duties increasingly involve interactions among multiple interest groups.

Although roles drive an individual or group's level of direct involvement in budget matters, interest in the fiduciary trust relating to schools and money always comes to the same end. Ultimately, the fiduciary interest relates to fulfilling the primary mission of schools—an accountability question; that is, are schools doing what is expected of them? The fiduciary path to answering this question also answers a second query: What are the essential fiduciary duties associated with schools? The bulleted list, as follows, indicates that meeting schools' primary mission is a multifaceted task:

- General management
- Office management
- Personnel management
- Staff development
- Collective negotiations
- Legal control
- Financial planning and budgeting
- Fiscal accounting and financial reporting
- Cash management
- Fiscal audits and reports
- Payroll management
- School activity and student body funds
- Purchasing and inventory
- School insurance and risk management
- Plant security and property protection
- School property management
- School plant maintenance
- School plant operations
- Educational facility planning
- School construction management
- Debt service and capital-fund management
- Information management and technology
- School transportation services
- School food services
- Grants and contracts
- School–community relations

The Purposes of Accounting

Though not widely understood, the accounting process is *the* vehicle by which a substantial portion of accountability is carried out. Although not sufficient alone to reach issues of school effectiveness under the meaning of broader accountability, the accounting process serves a critical function by managing the single resource (money) that controls the purchase of all other human and material resources used to carry out the educational mission. Importantly, emerging developments suggest that linkages will be increasingly established between the financial data examined in accounting and other forms of public calls for accountability.[5] In other words, tying school money to student outcomes will continue to grow in importance.

Broadly speaking, most people view accounting as a tool used in business to report profits and losses and to detect financial wrongdoing. That perception is accurate, although incomplete, because it does not capture the full range of benefits to be gained from the accounting cycle, nor does it acknowledge that financial accounting equally applies to nonprofit and governmental entities. In addition, in the case of elementary and secondary education, accountability and funding and student learning come together in a school district through the budget. We have held for many years that a budget is the *fiscal expression of the educational philosophy* of a school district and its schools; that is, a budget is the implementation of the district's *educational plan*. By creating a budget, school districts identify how money will be spent to achieve the stated educational goals. Only by accounting for how the budget is spent can it be known whether—in fiscal terms—the school district is satisfying its educational expectations. These realities establish five key purposes of the accounting function, all of which are meant to keep the organization focused on its educational mission.

The first purpose of accounting is to establish a procedure, by which all fiscal activities in a school district can be accumulated, categorized, reported, and controlled. Each of these terms has specific meaning and value. Accumulating transactions sets up a method of data collection in one location (a set of "books")[6] that allows people to view the school district's fiscal transactions. Categorizing transactions separates the various fiscal activities according to similarities; it implies that grouping those transactions will provide useful analysis about where money is going. Reporting transactions makes the results of all activities known. Controlling transactions is essential because resources are finite, while needs are infinite.

The second purpose of accounting is to provide a means to judge progress toward goals. This is a cornerstone of the accountability issue, as schools increasingly must show wise use of resources beyond traditional methods that have relied on standardized testing or locally constructed achievement measures. The accounting function can provide a tool for assessing progress in several ways, and new directions are being sought

---

5 See, for example, the extensive and important revisions to fiscal reporting contained in the U.S. Department of Education's most recent accounting handbook, *Financial Accounting for Local and State School Systems: 2009 Edition*, by Gregory S. Allison, Steven D. Honegger, and Frank Johnson (Washington, DC: National Center for Education Statistics, June 2009).

6 Today, financial data are not recorded in physical "books" or "journals," but rather recorded using accounting software and electronic spreadsheets.

constantly, particularly given public debate on school funding policy. One way in which the accounting function is able to assess goal attainment is by tracking the financial condition of a school district. For example, the accounting function monitors changes in balances of all funds and accounts held. To illustrate, if only 10% of instructional supply money remains by the end of the first month of the school year, the accounting function should flag a serious problem unless there has been a conscious decision to spend this amount to capture some other benefit such as bulk purchasing. Performance budgeting is discussed at a later point—an activity aided by the accounting function that assists in evaluating progress concerning academic goals by tying fiscal information to student achievement data. The accounting function therefore helps assess whether expenditures and educational programs are in proper alignment.

The third purpose of accounting is complementary by providing hard evidence to the state that schools are meeting required educational responsibilities that are laid down in statutes, as well as promulgated rules and regulations. Accounting helps the state as well as its agencies, i.e., the state education agency, evaluate whether school districts, as legal arms of the state, are fulfilling the state's constitutional duty to educate children. Every state has an inescapable duty to educate children, and accountability data—including financial data—are indicators by which states may be judged. In addition, states' interests have increased as state financial aid to schools has grown, with many states now demanding extensive reporting of school revenues and expenditures, on which policy decisions may ultimately be based. These realities have led to more states requiring school districts to use uniform accounting codes and standardized reporting formats to ensure consistent and comparable data collection across school districts throughout the state. States face accountability in the form of federal reporting to qualify for federal grants and aid as well as to demonstrate compliance with federal laws relating to educational equity.

The fourth purpose of accounting is to aid in budget preparation. The task of building a budget at district and school levels requires historical data for baseline purposes. Indeed, budgeting is the act of placing money on line items in the total budget for the sole purpose of carrying out the school district's educational plan. The process is bidirectional: the accounting function is satisfied in part by budgeting, and budget preparation requires accounting data. More specifically, accounting establishes both initial and end products by creating the funds and line items to which budget allocations are made, while the process of executing a budget creates data needed to carry out the accounting cycle *and* to establish a baseline for the next budget cycle.

The fifth purpose of accounting is to ensure proper handling of money and to guard against misuse of the fiduciary trust. Given the public's growing mistrust of government, this aspect of the accounting function is crucial to many issues discussed in earlier chapters of this text. One direct outcome of this mistrust is suspicion aimed at public officials, including school administrators, making it critical for schools to observe the highest standards of transparency and integrity. Nearly everyone can relate to instances of real or perceived abuse of public trust, and media reports speculating about misuse of public moneys have become commonplace. A critical aspect of the accounting function is to provide *proof* that public confidence is well placed. Accounting is thus a powerful tool for carrying out educational planning, control, and stewardship through budget structures and organization, while the budget itself is the accompanying vehicle on which accountability rests. Accounting therefore provides a major accountability feature when it does the following:

- *Creates a complete record* of all financial transactions at district and school levels
- *Summarizes financial activities* of the schools in reports required for proper, effective, and efficient administration
- *Provides information* used in budget preparation, adoption, and execution
- *Provides safeguards* on use of money and property, including protection against waste, inefficiency, fraud, and carelessness
- *Creates a longitudinal record* to aid administrators, teachers, boards, and laypersons in program decision processes

ALLOCATION OF EDUCATION BUDGETS

The previous section introduced reasons for and benefits of an accountability structure for tracking money, but it did not discuss or examine what happens when money comes into a school district. The question of how educational budgets are allocated actually has several embedded questions that are discussed in greater detail in later chapters. For example, related questions arise regarding how to determine amounts of money to be assigned to budget lines during the budget-building process. These issues are highly interwoven within the accounting and budgeting functions. The first issue for examination is the overall revenue structures for a typical school district.

Fund Structure

School districts receive money from multiple sources, primarily federal, state, and local governments. Regardless of how revenue sources are arranged in a given state, certain accounting principles apply that make it possible to permanently record revenues and—eventually—expenditures. For accounting and accountability purposes, we refer to the overarching record system as a *fund structure*.[7] Within the fund structure are the broad categories of *governmental* funds, *proprietary* funds, and *fiduciary* funds. Each of these must be clearly defined if one is to grasp how revenues are allocated at any level.

As a preface to examining each operational fund's purpose, it must be understood that the fundamental point is that schools operate under a system of fund accounting. *Fund accounting* is a term describing how the types of revenue and expenditure are organized and reported for (in this case) an educational organization. Fund accounting's primary value is based in the requirement that each fund may be used only for specific

---

7 From this point forward, a *fund* is an accounting entity for segregating types of money for receipt and expenditure purposes, and no longer refers to money itself. Careful examination from this point forward will reveal that use of the word *fund* adhered to the definition in this note.

purposes and that the various separate funds in the fund accounting system must not be commingled. By way of specific example, school districts must credit state transportation aid only to the transportation fund for exclusive use in transportation-related expenditures as defined by the state accounting code. Analogously, special education money may only be credited to the special education revenue and expenditure categories. Thus the purpose of fund accounting is to recognize distinct or "segregated" fiscal operations, to track revenues and expenditures by function and to provide accountability for these functions according to intended use.

Governmental Funds

The broad fund structure is actually comprised of individual funds. Governmental funds make up most of the various fund types in school districts, receiving most of the actual money receipted and spent by schools. Generally, school districts operate four types of governmental funds. While eventual fund structure is broken down further than these four funds suggest, the broad fund structure comprises the following:

- *General fund.* All money not reserved to other funds is placed in the general fund—hence its name, implying a general use fund. The general fund is the largest of all funds in a school district because most current annual instructional expenditures are paid from it, including teacher and administrator salaries, teaching supplies, insurance, and utilities.
- *Special revenue fund.* Money restricted to specific purposes, such as for compensatory education or special education programs, is placed in various special revenue funds. The purpose is to earmark moneys to ensure they are spent only for specified purposes.
- *Capital projects fund.* A capital projects fund allows deposit and expenditure of money from a variety of sources (usually bond revenues) used to finance long-lived assets such as buildings, durable equipment, and land. A capital projects fund is distinct from other operating funds such as capital outlay and debt service funds, which might also be used to buy some long-lived assets.
- *Debt service fund.* A debt service fund allows receiving and expending money used to amortize long-term debt, including bond issues for school infrastructure, or major equipment purchases. Bond issues usually require establishment of debt service funds, with a separate fund established for each bond issue.

Proprietary Funds

Not all money received by school districts is governmental, requiring a separate accounting for such money. The convention for receiving and expending the most common types of nongovernmental moneys is creation of separate *proprietary* funds. Proprietary funds often involve fees for services and may be used to create a method of internal billing; as implied by the name, these are moneys generated and "owned" differently than governmental money, which is the property of the state or other taxing unit. In contrast, proprietary funds are created to fit local needs and ways of doing business. They are further identified as either *enterprise* or *internal service* funds, a distinction made clear as follows:

- *Enterprise funds.* These funds handle money from "local" activities such as athletics, school newspapers, and student bookstore operations. The idea is that these activities are like private enterprises, with services provided in exchange for fee, and may be self-supporting. As a result, enterprise revenues and expenditures are maintained separately.
- *Internal service funds.* Large school districts often produce goods or services within the organization that are purchased and consumed by other parts of the same organization. Examples include central printing or maintenance services. Such large districts may have an internal charge-back system, which also assists in tracking the cost and profitability of these various services.

Fiduciary Funds

Not all revenues fall neatly into either governmental or proprietary funds. One type of revenue of growing importance to school districts is money received from external nongovernmental organizations such as business partnerships, major gifts, endowments, donations, and other benevolent trusts. Although the vast majority of school districts do not have extensive fiduciary funds, a structure is available in case the opportunity arises. Such funds are known as *fiduciary* funds.

A district managing fiduciary funds is actually only a trustee, as the name implies. Appropriate revenue is deposited to a fiduciary fund, and expenditures are controlled by an agreement detailing the purpose of the fund, how the fund is to be managed, and the disposition of the proceeds if the agreement is ever dissolved. In general, fiduciary funds include two basic types:

- *Trust funds.* These may be of several different types. In all cases, however, the school district has trusteeship and acts as the fund's manager. A pension trust fund is a common type and may exist when the district offers local pension benefits in addition to, or in lieu of, a state retirement system. Pension funds as described herein are highly state-specific as state statutes govern the creation and administration of such funds. An investment trust fund is another type and is used to account for the external portion (the part that does not belong to the school district) of investment pools operated by the district. Again, investment funds are generally highly regulated by state statute and vary among the states. Private-purpose trust funds are the final type: these may include nonexpendable trusts where the principal amount must remain intact, with the interest available for school district benefit. Similarly, an expendable trust fund may be set up, wherein both the principal and earned interest are available for school district use. Again, it is stressed these types of funds vary from state to state and are highly regulated by state statutes.
- *Agency funds.* Agency funds are moneys held in trusteeship by a school district for individuals, private organizations, or other governments. Examples include accounting for student activities or taxes collected for another unit of government. A historically common use of agency funds has included setting up a central payroll fund to reduce the number of accounts needed for payroll transactions to

the various entities in a school district—for example, teachers, administrators, support staff, and food service workers. Under one central fund, all data on wages, fringe benefits, tax withholding, and workers' compensation may be more efficiently monitored.

An Intermediate Overview

It is critical to grasp that there is a *structure* for school money that allows it to be *receipted, expended,* and *tracked* by its intended purpose. The picture is clearer if the total accounting system is viewed as a pyramid. From the broadest view, one can see that the total *accounting system* is first made up of various *funds.* Districts in all states operate *governmental* funds made of up a *general* fund and *special revenue* funds, and most school districts also have *capital project* and *debt service* funds. Similarly, all school districts use *proprietary* funds to some extent, particularly for common operations such as *enterprise* funds, and many school districts also have *internal service* funds. Far fewer school districts will have extensive *fiduciary* funds. Ultimately, pursuant to state statutes, the board of education is the final *custodian* of all funds, and building administrators are often charged with administering *activity* funds. Boards of education delegate and charge the superintendent of schools with his or her staff to manage such funds. Policymakers and higher units of government rely on fund accounting to direct the flow of school money, including state aid, and to judge the impact of educational and tax policy decisions. And community members depend on fund accounting to ensure educational experiences for students and to protect the fiduciary trust. In sum, accounting through the fund structure is a critical component of education accountability.

TRACKING SCHOOL MONEY

To fully understand fiscal accountability, we turn now to the examination of how money is handled within the fund structure once it is received. The twin concepts of *revenue* and *expenditure* are examined as well. Second, the *accounting cycle* is examined. These conceptual underpinnings are foundational to the actual budget process discussed in later chapters; that is, how resources are assigned in the budget.

Revenue Structure

For accounting purposes, a district's financial affairs are presented on a two-dimensional plane—*revenue* and *expenditure*—even though we moved beyond this earlier when we stated that the budget expressed the school district's educational plan. Hence, the budget is actually three-dimensional—a budget triangle—where accountability for program planning is linked to revenue and expenditure. But for present purposes, the first picture is simply revenue as money going *into* schools, as contrasted to expenditure, which is that same money going back *out* in support of teaching and learning.

Revenue to education generally involves a three-tiered classification. The first tier is the *fund*, which was discussed earlier in this chapter. The second tier is the *source* of revenue. The third tier is the *type* of revenue. These concepts are interrelated.

The earlier discussion regarding *fund* structure re-enters the picture in that revenue received must be recorded in one of the funds operated by the school district. For example, revenue earmarked for transportation must be earmarked to the transportation fund, and revenue for any other restricted or categorical purpose must be recorded in its appropriate special fund. Revenue not reserved to special funds is usually placed in the general fund.

When the actual budgeting behaviors are presented in later chapters, it will be evident that the revenue side of a budget requires placing each revenue receipt on a line noting its source. While each state department of education has its own unique budget forms, the practice is universal: placing money on a source line in the revenue side of the budget is required because it allows the school district to report fiscal data to the appropriate state agency and to establish lobbying positions during legislative sessions; that is, fund accounting is required by law, and accounting data reveal a great deal of information. Three revenue sources apply to school budgeting and accounting:

- *Local and intermediate sources*: Local sources include money raised by the school district, usually from local property taxes. Intermediate sources include money from governmental units that exist in many states that stand between the local school district and the state, such as cities and counties.
- *State sources* include money raised within the state in which the district is located: generally state aid, but excluding funds passed through the state from the federal government.
- *Federal sources* include direct federal aid or state flow-through money, usually categorical aid.[8]

Type of revenue refers to both source and use. Local revenues often include property tax, tuition, student transportation fees, investment earnings, student organization fees, and revenue from textbook rentals. Intermediate and state revenues may include unrestricted grants-in-aid and revenue in lieu of taxes under tax exemptions or tax abatements granted by other taxing units. Types of revenue from federal sources include unrestricted grants-in-aid received either directly from the federal government or as restricted grants-in-aid from the federal level distributed through the state. Figure 4.1 illustrates how fund, source, and type of revenue come together in the revenue side of a school district's budget. In Figure 4.1, the *fund* is the general fund. *Sources* include local, intermediate (county in this illustration), state, federal, and other. *Types* include, for example, ad valorem property taxes levied and a personal property

---

8 Gregory S. Allison, Steven D. Honegger, and Frank Johnson, *Financial Accounting for Local and State School Systems: 2009 Edition* (Washington, DC: U.S. Department of Education, National Center for Education Statistics, June 2009).

tax on recreational vehicles.[9] Source codes are part of the system for reporting to the federal government.[10] Importantly, budget documents in the various states may look different from Figure 4.1 because of differences in the underlying tax scheme, but the essential elements of fund accounting apply universally.

The system of revenue structure is important because it is used to allocate money to the different funds constituting a school district's total budget. Revenues are thus first classified by fund and source, and then broken into governmental, proprietary, and fiduciary groups for further distinction by fund, source, and type. Not all of these distinctions are apparent in Figure 4.1, which only shows governmental general fund revenue, but the figure clearly illustrates that the very first step to creating an educational plan is receiving and depositing revenue so that an expenditure plan can be built—a plan in the case of Figure 4.1 that takes into consideration the school district's historical revenue trends when setting a new year's budget.

Expenditure Structure

Expenditure structure is significantly more complex than revenue. Revenue sources typically fit into only three categories, while expenditures are broken into many different classifications. This means that school districts have only a few sources of revenue while they have many expenditure categories in order to understand the actual expenses.

Budget documents in every state classify educational expenditures in a program budgeting format. Expenditures are classified by *fund*, *function*, and *object*, and may be further broken down by *project*, *instructional level*, *operational unit*, *subject matter*, and *job classification*. States and local school districts vary greatly in the amount of such detail they provide, although states generally specify a minimum amount of coding districts must provide. Such a classification scheme permits accumulation of data that may be used for a wide variety of purposes, the first of which is tracking expenditures for program accountability. Each level in the expenditure classification scheme has discrete codes hierarchically arranged to track expenditures from broad to narrow. For example, although the general fund is very broad, object codes break functions into various subcodes for more detailed reporting and analysis.

Extensive detail of how detailed expenditures can be broken down is again beyond the scope of this discussion. For general purposes of understanding expenditure structure, however, the following statements describe how coding moves from the broad to the specific:

---

9 Describing each state's taxable property scheme is beyond the scope of this text. In Figure 4.1, for school purposes *real* property (real estate) is subject to taxation, as are the improvements on that land (*ad valorum*, or added value tax). The sample state in Table 4.1 also taxes *personal* property in the form of motor homes and other recreational vehicles, but exempts automobiles as a direct source of school tax revenue. The nuances among states are significant: for example, in Table 4.1, automobiles are not taxable locally but the state itself collects a motor vehicle tax, some of which finds its way into the state school aid distribution formula as state general fund revenues.

10 Allison et al., *Financial Accounting for Local and State School Systems.*

01 GENERAL	12 months 2013–2014 Actual	12 months 2014–2015 Actual	12 months 2015–2016 Budget
Unencumbered cash balance July 1			
Unencumbered cash balance from transportation, bilingual education, and vocational education funds			
Revenue:			
1000 Local sources			
1110 Ad valorem tax levied			
2010 $			
2011 $			
2012 $			
2013 $			
1140 Delinquent tax			
1300 Tuition			
1312 Individuals (out-district)			
1320 Other school district in-state			
1330 Other school district out-state			
1410 Transportation fees			
1700 Student activities (reimbursement)			
1900 Other revenue from local source			
1910 User charges			
1980 Reimbursements			
1985 State aid reimbursement			
2000 County sources			
2450 Recreational vehicle tax			
2800 In lieu of taxes IRBs			
3000 State sources			
3110 General state aid			
3130 Mineral production tax			
3205 Special education aid			
4000 Federal sources			
4590 Other reserve grants-in-aid			
4591 Title I (formerly Chapter I)			
4592 Title (math/science)			
4599 Other			
4820 PL 382 (Exclude Extra Aid for Children on Indian Land and Low Rent Housing) (formerly PL 874)			
5000 Other			
5208 Transfer from supplemental general			
Resources Available			
Total expenditures and transfers			
Excess revenue to state (recapture)			
Unencumbered cash balance June 30			

FIGURE 4.1 Sample Revenue Side of a Budget

- *Fund.* Expenditures are first classified as an expenditure from a governmental fund, proprietary fund, or fiduciary fund. The purpose of starting with the fund is clear: since revenue is first assigned to a fund on the basis of use in support of some educational activity, expenditures consequently must be assigned to the corresponding fund—for example, Code 01 to designate general fund.
- *Function.* Expenditures can be classified by function, which refers to the general activity for which a purchased good or service is acquired. Function describes the areas of instruction, support services, operation of noninstructional services, facilities acquisition and construction, and debt service. These codes track expenditures more closely by identifying functions carried out—for example, Code 2300 to designate an expenditure for general administration support services within the general fund.
- *Object.* Finally, expenditures are classified by object, or the item or service acquired. This includes nine major object categories (numbered 100–999), which can be further subdivided. The major categories include areas such as salaries, employee benefits, purchased professional and technical services, purchased property services, and supplies. For example, Code 310 might designate a board-level salary expense within the general fund.

Figure 4.2 illustrates this complex structure. Figure 4.2 is the expenditure side of a school district's general fund budget document. Assume the school district has received and deposited revenue into each of its operating funds. Assume also that the budget process is complete and that a budget has been legally adopted—a procedure explored further in later chapters. Now the school district has authority to spend money. More importantly, several other things are in place. Figure 4.2 reflects expenditure classification as follows: The *fund* is the general fund. *Functions* in the general fund include instruction (Code 1000), support services (Code 2000), school administration (Code 2400), operations and maintenance (Code 2600), and so on up to architectural and engineering services (Code 4300). These expenditure codes are broken down further by *object*, for example, teacher salaries (Code 1000–110), teacher benefits (Code 1000–200) and general administration salaries (Code 2300–100). The benefits are multiple. First, federal and state data tracking are satisfied by uniform reporting methods. Second, the school district may choose to analyze the minimum required data further by expanding it to include codes that report at progressively more detailed levels, wherein the purchase of teaching materials could be tracked to each school and even each classroom. In other words, accounting is not just an assurance against ineptitude, carelessness, or fraud; rather, it is the other dimension of accountability in that costs of programs can be calculated, and those costs can be linked to student outcome data if the system is properly structured. For example, if low performance and underfunding simultaneously appear at an identifiable grade level, appropriate interventions can be made: Perhaps new instructional materials must be bought; teachers may need targeted professional development; or teacher aides or a reduction in class size might be needed because of large class sizes that result in inadequate individualized attention—a host of options can be explored using data available through accounting in combination with education information.

01 GENERAL EXPENDITURES	12 months 2013–2014 Actual	12 months 2014–2015 Actual	12 months 2015–2016 Budget
1000 Instruction			
100 Salaries			
110 Certified			
120 Noncertified			
200 Employee benefits			
210 Insurance (employee)			
220 Social Security			
290 Other			
300 Purchased professional and technical services			
500 Other purchased services			
560 Tuition			
561 Tuition/other state LEAs			
562 Tuition/other LEAs outside the state			
563 Tuition/private sources			
590 Other			
600 Supplies			
610 General supplemental (teaching)			
644 Textbooks			
680 Miscellaneous supplies			
700 Property (equipment and furnishings)			
800 Other			
2000 Support services			
2100 Student support services			
100 Salaries			
110 Certified			
120 Noncertified			
200 Employee benefits			
210 Insurance (employee)			
220 Social Security			
290 Other			
300 Purchased professional and technical services			
500 Other purchased services			
600 Supplies			
700 Property (equipment and furnishings)			
800 Other			
2200 Instructional support staff			
100 Salaries			
110 Certified			
120 Noncertified			
200 Employee benefits			
210 Insurance (employee)			

FIGURE 4.2 Sample Expenditure Side of a Budget

01 GENERAL EXPENDITURES	12 months 2013–2014 Actual	12 months 2014–2015 Actual	12 months 2015–2016 Budget
220 Social Security			
290 Other			
300 Purchased professional and technical services			
500 Other purchased services			
600 Supplies			
640 Books (not textbooks) and periodicals			
650 Audiovisual and instructional software			
680 Miscellaneous supplies			
700 Property (equipment and furnishings)			
800 Other			
2300 General administration			
100 Salaries			
110 Certified			
120 Noncertified			
200 Employee benefits			
210 Insurance (employee)			
220 Social Security			
290 Other			
300 Purchased professional and technical services			
400 Purchased property services			
500 Other purchased services			
520 Insurance			
530 Communications (telephone, postage, etc.)			
590 Other			
600 Supplies			
700 Property (equipment & furnishings)			
800 Other			
2400 School administration			
100 Salaries			
110 Certified			
120 Noncertified			
200 Employee benefits			
210 Insurance (employee)			
220 Social Security			
290 Other			
300 Purchased professional and technical services			
400 Purchased property services			
500 Other purchased services			
530 Communications (telephone, postage, etc.)			
590 Other			
600 Supplies			

FIGURE 4.2 *continued*

01 GENERAL EXPENDITURES	12 months 2013–2014 Actual	12 months 2014–2015 Actual	12 months 2015–2016 Budget
700 Property (equipment and furnishings)			
800 Other			
2500 Operations and maintenance			
100 Salaries			
120 Noncertified			
200 Employee benefits			
210 Insurance (employee)			
220 Social Security			
290 Other			
300 Purchased professional and technical services			
400 Purchased property services			
411 Water/sewer			
420 Cleaning			
430 Repairs and maintenance			
440 Rentals			
460 Repair of buildings			
490 Other			
500 Other purchased services			
520 Insurance			
590 Other			
600 Supplies			
610 General supplies			
620 Energy			
621 Heating			
622 Electricity			
626 Motor fuel (not school bus)			
629 Other			
680 Miscellaneous supplies			
700 Property (equipment and furnishings)			
800 Other			
2600 Operations and maintenance (transportation)			
100 Salaries			
120 Noncertified			
200 Employee benefits			
210 Insurance (employee)			
220 Social Security			
290 Other			
300 Purchased and professional technical services			
400 Purchased property services			
500 Other purchased services			
600 Supplies			

FIGURE 4.2 *continued*

01 GENERAL EXPENDITURES	12 months 2013–2014 Actual	12 months 2014–2015 Actual	12 months 2015–2016 Budget
610 General supplies			
620 Energy			
621 Heating			
622 Electricity			
626 Motor fuel (not school bus)			
629 Other			
680 Miscellaneous supplies			
700 Property (equipment and furnishings)			
800 Other			
2700 Student transportation services			
2710 Supervision			
100 Salaries			
120 Noncertified			
200 Employee benefits			
210 Insurance			
220 Social Security			
290 Other			
600 Supplies			
730 Equipment			
800 Other			
2720 Vehicle operating services			
100 Salaries			
120 Noncertified			
200 Employee benefits			
210 Insurance			
220 Social Security			
290 Other			
442 Rent of vehicles (lease)			
500 Other purchased services			
513 Contracting of bus services			
519 Mileage in lieu of transportation			
520 Insurance			
626 Motor fuel			
730 Equipment (including buses)			
800 Other			
2740 Vehicle services and maintenance services			
100 Salaries			
120 Noncertified			
200 Employee benefits			
210 Insurance			
220 Social Security			

FIGURE 4.2 *continued*

01 GENERAL EXPENDITURES	12 months 2013–2014 Actual	12 months 2014–2015 Actual	12 months 2015–2016 Budget
700 Property (equipment and furnishings)			
800 Other			
2500 Operations and maintenance			
100 Salaries			
120 Noncertified			
200 Employee benefits			
210 Insurance (employee)			
220 Social Security			
290 Other			
300 Purchased professional and technical services			
400 Purchased property services			
411 Water/sewer			
420 Cleaning			
430 Repairs and maintenance			
440 Rentals			
460 Repair of buildings			
490 Other			
500 Other purchased services			
520 Insurance			
590 Other			
600 Supplies			
610 General supplies			
620 Energy			
621 Heating			
622 Electricity			
626 Motor fuel (not school bus)			
629 Other			
680 Miscellaneous supplies			
700 Property (equipment and furnishings)			
800 Other			
2600 Operations and maintenance (transportation)			
100 Salaries			
120 Noncertified			
200 Employee benefits			
210 Insurance (employee)			
220 Social Security			
290 Other			
300 Purchased and professional technical services			
400 Purchased property services			
500 Other purchased services			
600 Supplies			

FIGURE 4.2 *continued*

01 GENERAL EXPENDITURES	12 months 2013–2014 Actual	12 months 2014–2015 Actual	12 months 2015–2016 Budget
940 Driver training			
943 Extraordinary school programs			
944 Food service			
946 Professional development			
948 Parent education program			
949 Summer school			
950 Special education			
951 Technology education			
952 Transportation			
954 Vocational education			
955 Area vocational school			
963 Special liability expense fund			
972 Contingency reserve**			
974 Textbook and student materials revolving fund			
TOTAL EXPENDITURES AND TRANSFERS			

FIGURE 4.2 *continued*

The Accounting Transaction

A brief description of the accounting transaction is needed in order to have a complete overview of how money is tracked in public schools. Administrators and school board members need such understanding because they are ultimately the responsible agents. Teachers rarely study accounting, although they are negatively affected if someone engages in poor financial management.

Earlier discussion in this chapter demonstrated how the various funds provide a structure for grouping the financial activities of a school district by revenue and expenditure dimensions. This is an important first step in the accounting process because it segregates money according to its use. The next step is to establish individual *accounts* within each fund wherein the actual money transactions occur. These accounts make up the record of assets, liabilities, revenues, and expenditures that occur in the broader fund context.

Generally, five classifications of accounts are established within any given fund, such as the general fund. The five accounts are *expense, income, asset, liability*, and *net worth* or *fund balance* accounts. The purpose of each is singular: all transactions involving revenue or expenditure or increases or decreases in the value of assets are entered (posted) to these accounts. Schools use the *double entry* method of posting transactions to the various accounts in a fund. Double entry involves entering both a *debit* (an entry on the left-hand side of the account ledger) to one account and a *credit* (an entry on the right-hand side) to another account for each transaction. Asset and expenditure accounts (left-hand side accounts) are increased by debiting and decreased by crediting. Conversely, an income account (a right-hand side account) is decreased by a debit and increased by a credit.

The double entry posting of a transaction can be illustrated using a school district that has just received a general fund tax distribution of $1,000,000. Using a double entry system, this payment involves two general fund account groups: the income account and the asset account (the cash account). The income account increases as the transaction is entered as a credit. The cash account also increases as the transaction is entered as a debit to its side of the ledger. If the district then hires a new teacher at a salary of $35,000, a new transaction in the general fund occurs. Categories affected are the cash account and the appropriate expenditure account containing teacher salaries. As a result, cash balance in the asset account is credited (decreased), and the expenditure account for salaries is debited (increased). The purpose of this complex process is important: double entry is a tool that creates *a self-balancing set of books*, so that the assets of the district are not inflated. If this were not done, assets and liabilities would not balance, falsifying the actual cash position of the fund because appropriate additions and subtractions would not cross-balance revenue and expenditure activity—an error in financial position that would worsen if subsequent decisions were made on the basis of bad information.

The individual accounts in each fund are listed in the *general ledger*, a set of "books" that keeps all records in a single location. Each transaction is recorded in the general ledger by a complicated process. Before being entered in the general ledger, revenue and expenditure transactions are first recorded in a *general journal,* which is a chronological listing of transactions as they were initiated. Transactions are transferred from the general journal and posted to the appropriate accounts on the general ledger, again using double entry. This process brings together (summarizes) all similar accounts. Figure 4.3 is a sample journal entry for a given day showing the unpaid bills and charges to the appropriate expense and asset accounts. Figure 4.3 also shows how double entry creates a self-balancing set of books; that is, expenses are debited in the amount of $3,238.84, thus increasing the expense account, while assets are credited $3,238.84, thereby decreasing the district's assets. From this transaction, the district knows exactly how much it owes compared to its assets—a reflection of true cash position.

This process is repeated for each fund and transaction during the accounting cycle. Each accounting transaction is one of ten steps:

1. Journalizing transactions
2. Posting transactions
3. Preparing a trial balance
4. Preparing a work sheet
5. Preparing financial statements
6. Journalizing closing entries
7. Posting closing entries
8. Balancing, ruling, and bringing forward balances of balance sheet accounts
9. Ruling temporary accounts
10. Preparing post-closing trial balance[11]

---

11 Ronald E. Everett, Raymond L. Lows, and Donald R. Johnson, *Financial and Managerial Accounting for School Administrators: Superintendents, School Business Administrators and Principals,* 4th ed. (Lanham, MD: Rowman & Littlefield, 2003).

Expense Accounts			
Debit No.	1	Supplies	$3,175.63
	18	Miscellaneous	63.21
			$3,238.84
Asset Account			
Credit No.	20	Accts. Payable	$3,238.84

FIGURE 4.3 Typical Journal Entry for the Journal Period Ending June 1

The complexity of the accounting cycle underscores the need to account for all fiscal activity in a tax revenue-based organization. To that end, it is important that school districts hire qualified professionals with the expertise to carry out these fiscal tasks, such as a chief financial officer (CFO) or school business administrator along with accountants, fiscal analysts, and accounting clerks, as needed depending upon the size of the school district and its budget. In addition, it is important to remember that these employees need regular professional development just like other school district employees in order to remain current on best practices and changes in state statutes. In small school districts, it may be more cost-effective to secure qualified outside assistance for some of these activities. Importantly, these professionals provide school leaders with financial data that in conjunction with other types of data allows them to make sound educational program decisions.

Auditing

Finally, we turn our attention to auditing to complete the understanding of tracking money in schools. Auditing is absolutely vital to understanding schools and money because accounting and reporting would have no authority without the critical contribution of auditing. Auditing is the independent examination of accounting systems to ensure the accuracy and completeness of the accounting records in a school district.

Auditing is the best protection for anyone in a fiduciary role within a school district as it assures the public, employees, and the board of education that the financial affairs of the school district meet state statutory and accounting guidelines. The purposes of audits are several. First, audits are meant to detect errors in accounting. Given the enormous amount of financial data in a school district, errors can occur easily. Errors can be accidental or intentional. Auditing serves a second purpose of suggesting changes in accounting procedures in order to improve fiscal operations. Finally, auditing demonstrates to the state, the federal government, and local taxpayers that tax revenues are being used appropriately and lawfully. Thus, audits advance the educational mission of the school district, strengthen stakeholder trust, and protect school officials' professional reputations.

There are several types of audit, each serving a different need. Audits fall into two broad categories of *internal* and *external*. Audits are also known as *preaudits*, *post*-audits, or *continuous* audits based on the timing and purpose. Finally, external audits are classified as *general comprehensive* audits, *state* audits, or *special* audits. Each type has a unique purpose based on the data being sought.

Internal Audits

Internal financial auditing within a school organization is meant to provide a system of self-checks. Internal auditing ranges from basic monthly board of education reports to a full system of continuous internal monitoring, generally with accountants employed by the school district to study and improve accounting systems. All school districts, regardless of size, should engage in rigorous internal auditing. Internal auditing is required to produce monthly financial statements because journals and ledgers must be examined to generate income and expense statements. Mandatory state reports require internal auditing to produce and verify the data on which state aid requests are based.

Internal audits are usually either preaudits or continuous audits. A preaudit ensures proper accounting procedures in advance of a transaction. A continuous audit implies constant observation of the accounting system. Continuous auditing occurs through the system of checks and balances in place in most school districts whereby multiple approvals must be secured to spend money. The hierarchy from one actual district, shown in Figure 4.4, shows protections in place to guard against error or wrongdoing. Although internal auditing is never sufficient alone, it is an important tool of good management.

External Audits

External auditing is a formal examination of financial records in a school district by an outside expert to verify accuracy and legal compliance. External audits are always conducted by an independent auditing organization such as a certified public accounting firm or, in some instances, by state auditors checking for compliance with state regulations.

External audits yield an audit report with recommendations on the audit findings. External audits are accompanied by a letter of transmittal stating the purpose of the audit, procedures followed, a statement of findings, and a list of recommendations. In most instances, the audit is conducted at the same time as preparation of the school district's comprehensive annual financial report. As a general rule, most external audits are *general comprehensive audits* occurring at the close of an accounting period, usually an entire fiscal year. The report generally contains summaries of revenues and expenditures and compares cash balances against encumbrances to determine if statutory requirements were met. Governmental funds are examined separately under statements of budgetary accounts, and other funds such as fiduciary expendable trust funds and proprietary funds are also separately examined. If no problems were noted, the report would yield an *unqualified opinion* because its findings were not qualified by any *audit exceptions*. If concerns were present, the report would yield a *qualified opinion*. Audit reports are presented to the board of education, with the board required to show receipt of the audit in its minutes and to show action to correct audit exceptions.

Accounting and auditing affects everyone connected to schools. Trouble-free audits are the ultimate affirmation of trust, in that administrators, school boards, teachers,

Feedback loop may engage at any point if error is detected. The choices are to trace the system backward, or to restart the process from the beginning.

Revenue, received.

Issue receipts for all moneys received.

Prepare daily listing of revenue receipts.

Listing of revenue receipts forwarded to designated administrator.

Check listing of revenue receipts against ledger of deposits bank balance for depository coverage.

Forward to designated secretary approved list of receipts and depository coverage.

Designated secretary forward approved list of receipts and depository coverage.

Clerk review all receipts listings and depository coverage.

Finance secretary make appropriate entries in clerk record books.

Investment patterns reviewed, investments determined.

Investment and deposit slips prepared.

Investments and deposits completed.

Deposit slips forwarded to financial secretary.

Revenue receipt list and deposit slip copies forwarded to treasurer.

Appropriate entries completed in clerks books.

Compare bank receipts to bank deposits and bank statements from Central Office.

Record interest earnings from revenue receipts prepared by Central Office.

Compute interest earnings. Match with interest receipts received from Central Office.

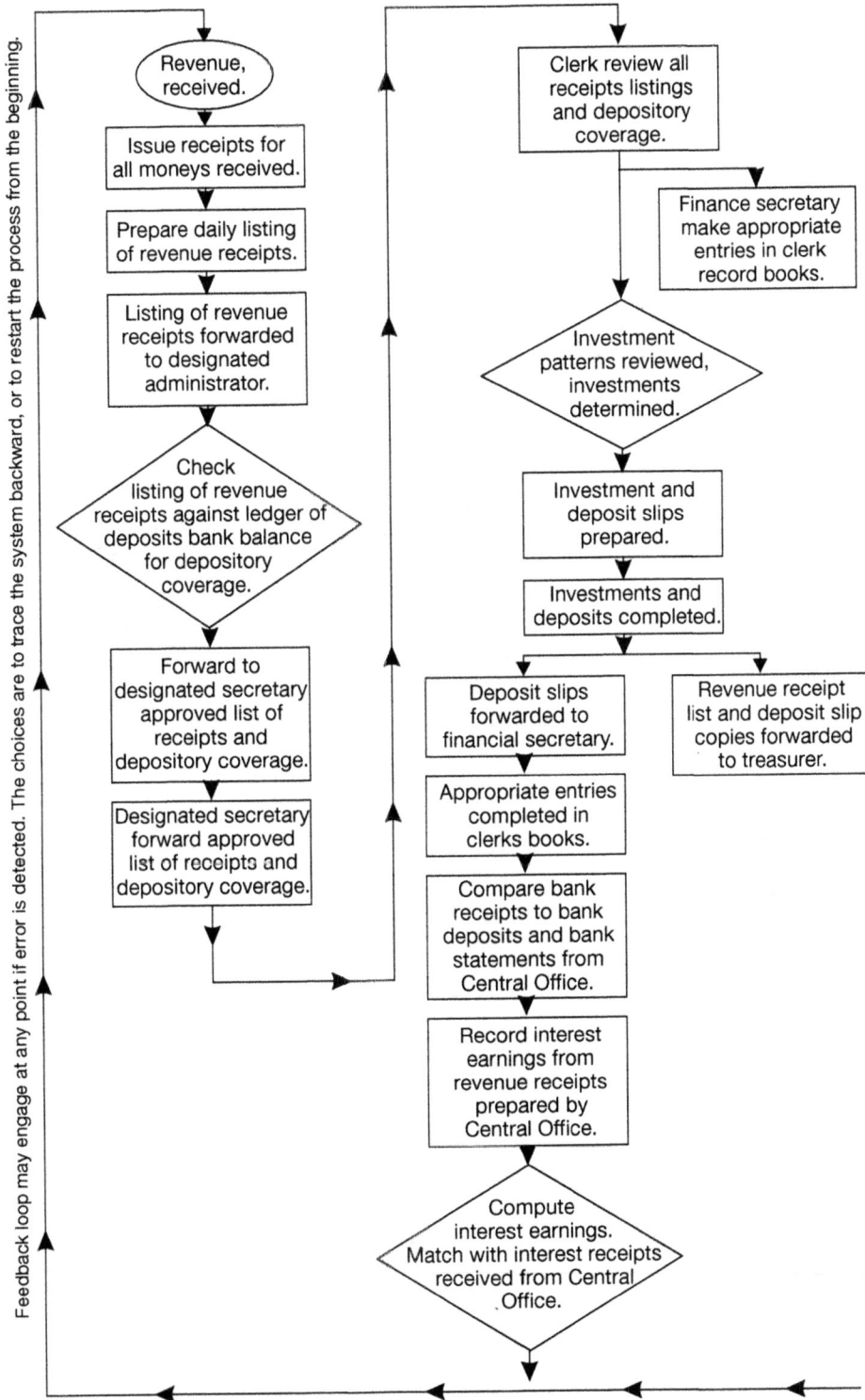

FIGURE 4.4 Accounting Checks and Balances

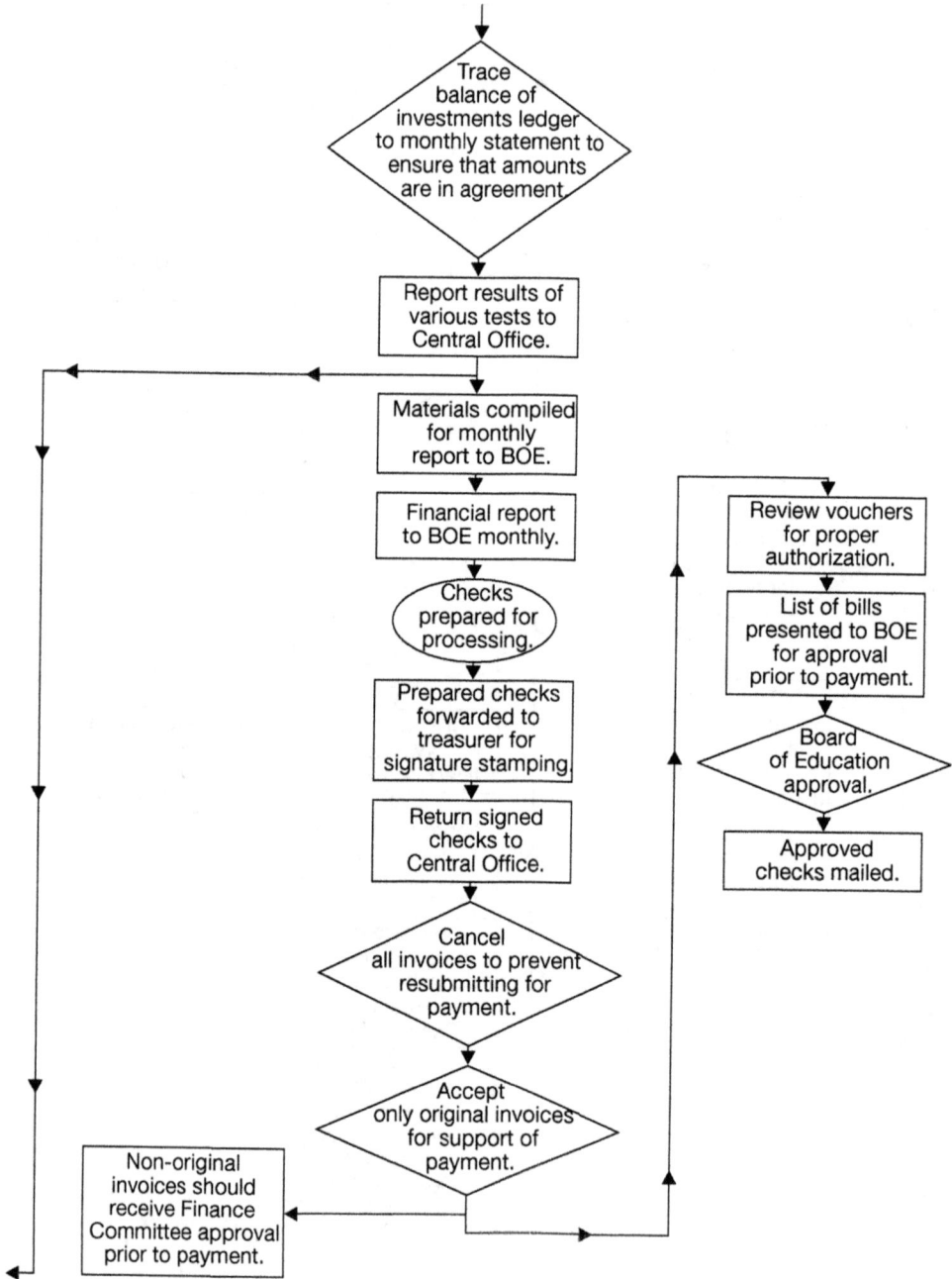

FIGURE 4.4 *continued*

staff, children, and the community are well served by good financial management. On the other hand, everyone suffers if bad fiscal management goes undetected. The price paid for accounting and auditing is money wisely spent, although these tools still do not ensure accountability for wise educational decision making. Nonetheless, accounting and auditing play an important part in overall accountability by assuring the public of conformity with the law.

State Audits

In addition to internal audits and external audits, a variety of *state* audits may occur in school districts. State audits serve a different purpose and are designed to monitor compliance with statutes and regulations involving state or federal money.

The variety of individual state audit requirements makes it difficult to generalize regarding specific details. Many differences rest primarily in how states choose to control elementary and secondary education. In states in which the state emphasizes local control, state audits may serve to meet minimum compliance standards. In states where control has been placed at the state level, state audits may be interested in a more exhaustive review of finances and programs.

All state audits have a common goal of determining whether the state's financial stake in schools is protected. State audits thus focus particularly on those funds to which the state either supplies aid directly or to which the state agencies act as a channel for federal aid to local school districts. In the case of federal funds, state agencies are interested in maintenance of applications, expenditure reports, and transmittal documents. In the case of state funds, state agencies are vitally interested in all documentation relating to state aid claims. For example, transportation claims are often closely examined because many states invest large sums in student transportation services. Likewise, state agencies closely audit school districts to ensure that federal moneys are not commingled or improperly spent. State audits are state-specific, although the goal is always to verify that the state's educational obligations and priorities are met.

Accounting standards for public school districts are determined by the Government Accounting Standards Board (GASB).[12] Generally accepted accounting principles (GAAP)

> require the use of the modified accrual basis of accounting for governmental funds. This means that revenues are recognized when they become both measurable and available to finance expenditures of the fiscal period. Expenditures are generally recognized when the related fund liability is incurred, if measurable.[13]

---

12 The reporting model for school districts is based on GASB Statement 34, Basic Financial Statements—and Management's Discussion and Analysis—for State and Local Governments, and is updated through GASB Statement 63, Financial Reporting of Deferred Outflows of Resources, Deferred Inflows of Resources, and Net Position, and GASB Statement 65, Items Previously Reported as Assets and Liabilities.

13 *Financial and Program Cost Accounting and Reporting for Florida Schools*, Florida Department of Education, Chapter 1, Section 1–3.

Special Audits

Finally, school districts may be subject to *special* audits. Although fairly uncommon, the purpose of a special audit may relate to suspicion of serious error or fraud. One of the logical ways special audits occur is as an offshoot of a normal state audit. For example, a transportation audit might reveal that a school district was claiming more children than were actually being transported. Likewise, internal auditing might cause a school district to voluntarily seek a special audit; for example, inability to reconcile expense claims with receipts could result in a special audit. Other events such as inventory loss might result in a special audit. Unfortunately, these examples are not entirely implausible as it is not possible to completely control individual behavior.

Accounting and accountability are constant companions for school administrators, board members, policymakers, teachers, and the general public. The correct way to engage in financial transactions requires at least the following:

- Strong internal accounting procedures, including segregation of duties based on checks and balances (see Figure 4.4)
- Competent employees with sufficient time to do the work of accounting in order to avoid making errors
- Extensive documentation based on a system that includes the following:

  — Proof of board of education approval of expenditures
  — Statements showing receipts and disbursements
  — Reconciled bank statements, including all canceled checks
  — A system of purchase orders
  — A strict no-cash disbursement policy.

A FINAL WORD CONCERNING PROFESSIONALISM

This chapter has emphasized that the gravity of fiduciary trust cannot be overstated. This is the issue of *professionalism* in handling school money. Although professionalism in the broad context has been addressed, the published ethical standards of the education finance profession should be followed in every school district throughout the nation.

Codes of ethics exist for most professions. Administrators, teachers, and many community members belong to professional or trade organizations that have adopted ethical conduct codes. Standards are essential to the integrity of the entire social order; and people with fiduciary capacity for public moneys have an extraordinary duty to ethical conduct. The Association of School Business Officials, International, has established a code of ethics that is fundamental to fiduciary relationships—a code whose applicability extends beyond those persons whose professions lead them to be ASBO members. The Association of School Business Officials Code of Ethics states:

> The public is giving more attention to the relationship between a school's sound business practices and the quality education of students. Legislative mandates, such

as the "No Child Left Behind Act" in the United States, from all levels of government have drawn more scrutiny to the utilization of resources in schools. School business officials have been recognized as being central to the successful operation of the educational enterprise. School business practices permeate the entire school district. The local education enterprise often maintains the largest budget in the community. Therefore, due to the public's increased demand for accountability, transparency, and independence; the challenge to do more with less; and the needed expertise to manage the financial resources of the school, the school business official must endorse certain [professional] standards in organization and administration, public policy and intergovernmental relations, and the legal framework of our public school districts.[14]

This excerpt below, also from ASBO, captures fully the points of this chapter; that is, increasingly broad definitions of accountability, including accountability for student outcomes, are a defining feature of the future of education:

Ethical Standards

Keeping the well-being of students at the forefront, members and associate members shall fulfill all aspects of their professional responsibilities with honesty and integrity and without intent for personal gain.

Ethical Conduct

To adhere to the ethical standards, members and associate members shall be fair and objective in the interpretation and implementation of policies and practices, supportive of their employer and employees, and accurate and timely when reporting data.

Expectations of Personal and Professional Integrity

In the course of daily business, members and associate members shall be honest; shall avoid conflicts of interest and preferential treatment involving individuals, groups, and themselves; and shall accept leadership responsibilities in support of the profession.[15]

---

14 Association of School Business Officials International, *International School Business Management Professional Standards and Code of Ethics* (Reston, VA: 2006), 4.

15 Association of School Business Officials International, "Professional Standards and Code of Ethics," Executive Summary, asbointl.org.asbo/media/documents/Resources/ASBOExecSummary.pdf.

POINT–COUNTERPOINT

POINT

Educational leaders operate in a highly complex business environment in schools where they must balance the best interest of students with fiscal accountability to local, state, and federal entities. As administrators, they are responsible for the academic and fiscal success of schools, and they should be held strictly accountable for failures in either of these areas.

COUNTERPOINT

Current and future school administrators are educators, not business executives. Their first priority is the education of students. Managing the "business" or finances of schools should be left to the district's school business manager or chief financial officer.

- Which of the two points of view above most closely resemble yours? Explain.
- Are there budget responsibilities in your school district that fall to school-level administrators? If so, how can these school leaders ensure that their school budgeting, accounting, and fiscal management knowledge is adequate to fulfill their responsibilities to students, staff, and the community?
- How can a school leader ensure that those performing the daily work of budgeting and accounting under his or her supervision are carrying out their duties accurately and ethically?

CASE STUDY

As the chief financial officer in your school district, you are surprised to find three school board members waiting outside your office one morning. You quickly learn this is no social call. As the conversation unfolds, you begin to be alarmed by what might well develop into a scandal involving the use of school district credit cards.

Although you are not new to the district, you have been in your position less than six months. You know that district credit cards are in wide use, although you are unaware that anyone might see that practice as a misuse of privilege. But now the board members explain that a school district employee has complained that the superintendent uses his district credit card to make purchases at local restaurants, supply stores, nearby and distant hotels, and shops and casinos. The complaint also alleges that the brightly colored cards bearing your district's mascot have been a topic of conversation in the community, since other district employees have been seen using these cards "often and at strange times."

Given the severity of these claims, your first reaction is to ask the board members if they have talked to the superintendent. They indicate the topic has come up before, but the superintendent dismissed it as "imaginations running wild." You know the superintendent is at a national conference until the end of the week, so you promise the board members you will check into the situation and report back through proper channels.

You schedule a meeting with the superintendent for the next Monday. To prepare for the meeting, you meet with your budget director to learn all about the district's credit card practices. The budget director explains that the district distributes credit cards broadly to employees across the school district's 15 school buildings for airline expenses, hotels, meals, supplies, and gasoline purchases. Central office staff have several cards available too, and the superintendent has a separate set of cards that he carries—in all, more than 50 credit cards are in play every day. The budget director explains that credit cards make it faster to obtain items, that many businesses no longer accept purchase orders, that a credit card is required to make travel arrangements by phone, and that credit cards make bookkeeping easier in many ways. When you quiz her at length about requisitions and approvals and submitting itemized receipts, she reveals that principals do not follow a purchase preapproval process relating to credit cards, that staff are inconsistent about turning in receipts, and that the superintendent approves his own purchases without submitting receipts. Only the monthly credit totals are presented for board payment.

Although you still have much to learn, you know that both new safeguards and strong action are needed. The problem, though, is that you have to deal with this situation in a manner that will garner support, which, given the combination of allegations and suspicions, will be difficult—and now you need a strategy by next Monday morning.

- What are the pitfalls to be avoided as you resolve this situation?
- What are your legal and ethical duties in this situation?
- What are the criteria and procedures that should be established for appropriate use of credit cards in school districts?
- How will you approach this matter with your superintendent?

PORTFOLIO EXERCISES

- Obtain a copy of your school district's budget and identify the fund structure for revenues and expenditures. Identify which funds beyond the general fund your district operates. Identify special revenue funds, capital projects funds, and any debt service funds.

- Closely examine the general fund in your school district. Interview your chief fiscal officer to determine what expenses are paid from the general fund. Discuss cash flow and fiscal resource management to determine how the district optimizes its assets. Ask about any problems the school district encounters in this area.

- Obtain a copy of the monthly revenue and expenditure report for your school or program. Identify account codes and learn how the school district accumulates and reports its revenues and expenditures, including any program planning uses. Interview a school district accounting staff member to trace one or more receipts and disbursements through the entire accounting cycle. Ask how the school district ensures the safe handling of money and disbursements, and compare these to the safeguards mentioned in this chapter.

- Obtain a copy of your school district's annual audit and identify the strengths and weaknesses of your school district's accounting system. Interview the school district's chief accountant to ask what audits are conducted in the school district, how often, and for what purposes. Ask what training activities the school district's business office provides for administrators and staff to ensure that they understand sound fiscal management, and when these are offered.

WEB RESOURCES

American Institute of Certified Public Accountants, www.aicpa.org

Association of School Business Officials International, www.asbointl.org

Financial Accounting Standards Board, www.fasb.org

Government Finance Officers Association, www.gfoa.org

Governmental Accounting Standards Board, www.gasb.org

The Institute of Internal Auditors, www.theiia.org

National Business Officers Association, www.nboa.net

National Center for Education Statistics, www.nces.ed.gov

RECOMMENDED READING

Allison, Gregory S., Steven D. Honegger, and Frank Johnson. *Financial Accounting for Local and State School Systems: 2009 Edition.* Washington, DC: U.S. Department of Education, Institute of Education Sciences, National Center for Education Statistics, June 2009.

Everett, Ronald E., Donald R. Johnson, and Bernard W. Madden. *Financial and Managerial Accounting for School Administrators: Tools for Schools,* 2nd ed. Lanham, MD: Rowman & Littlefield, 2007.

Government Finance Officers Association."Fiscal First Aid." www.gfoa.org/index.php?option=com_content&task=view&id=937&Itemid=416.

Granof, Michael H., and Saleha B.Khumawala. *Government and Not-for-Profit Accounting*, 5th ed. Hoboken, NJ: John Wiley, 2011.

Hartman, William T. *School District Budgeting*, 2nd ed. (Lanham, MD: Rowman and Littlefield, 2003).

Mead, Dean Michael. "Tips for Schools Districts: GASB's New Fund Balance Standards." *School Business Affairs* 76 (November 2010): 8–11.

Okrzesik, Daryl J., and Bert G. Nuehring. "Reduce Fraud Risk in Your District with Stronger Internal Controls." *School Business Affairs* 77 5 (May 2011): 20–22. http://files.eric.ed.gov/fulltext/EJ966676.pdf.

Ratcliffe, Thomas A., and Charles E. Landes. *Understanding Internal Control and Internal Control Services*. New York: American Institute of Certified Public Accountants, Inc., 2009. http://media.journalofaccountancy.com/JOA/Issues/2009/09/Understanding_Internal_Control_Services_2.pdf.

CHAPTER 5

Budget Planning

THE CHALLENGE

The school budget is basically an instrument of educational planning, and, incidentally, an instrument of control.

Ray, Candoli, and Hack (2005)[1]

CHAPTER DRIVERS

Please reflect upon the following questions as you read this chapter:

- What is the primary purpose of a budget?
- What is a budget at its most basic level?
- What is a sound budget philosophy?
- What are common approaches to budgeting?
- What is the general budget process?
- How are budgets constructed?
- How are individual schools funded?
- What are the roles of stakeholders in budgeting?

---

1 John Ray, I. Carl Candoli, and Walter G. Hack, *School Business Administration: A Planning Approach*, 8th ed. (Boston: Allyn & Bacon, 2005), 120.

BUDGETS AND SCHOOLS

Considered in context of how this book has sequentially linked each topic, we turn to the specific elements of building budgets. We now have an understanding of the social context of schools, including recognition of a participatory and sometimes demanding constituent base. Second, we have gained respect for the gravity of handling school money and have an initial grasp of how revenues and expenditures are accounted for via fund structures. Third, we have been introduced to the many decisions underlying the construction and operation of state aid formulas. In all, we have built a framework for understanding money and schools. Consequently, we now start to address and apply the elements of budgeting.

We begin by examining school district budgets from a broad perspective. Later chapters will explore additional aspects of budgeting in greater detail, but this chapter creates a foundation to which we will return often. In this chapter, we gain an overview of how budgets are built, with some attention to how money is directed to individual schools. To achieve these aims, we first define a budget conceptually. We then turn to a discussion of common approaches to budgeting, including appraisal of those approaches in terms of a sound budget framework. The last half of the chapter is devoted to describing the general budget process and the roles of various stakeholders. In this manner, we become familiar with a complicated process while staying true to our goal, i.e., to gain a better understanding of how school and district budgets are operationalized.

BASIC BUDGET CONCEPTS

Earlier chapters revealed that public education is facing a paradigmatic shift in policy; that is, there are increasingly urgent calls for higher student achievement as U.S. student scores continue to trail those in other developed as well as some developing countries. These calls come amidst demands from some of the same voices for a new level of fiscal conservatism, based upon a desire to limit the role of government that borders upon fiscal austerity. At the same time, the nation continues to recover from an economic recession second only to that of the Great Depression of the 1930s, with record levels of student poverty that have spillover effects on schools. In light of the above, public schools face greater state and local scrutiny of their financial operations in the name of efficiency, cost-effectiveness, and accountability. As such, how budgets are envisioned, constructed, and implemented are topics of vital importance to school leaders.

In today's political and fiscal environment outdated assumptions about school budgeting must be set aside. For example, some view education budgeting as a relatively low priority for educators, one that should be the exclusive domain of accountants. Nothing could be further from the truth. Budget planning is inseparable from educational planning. Specifically, the primary purpose of a budget is to translate educational priorities into programmatic and financial terms; as such, the budget is a fiscal expression of the educational philosophy of the school district.

Furthermore, budgets do not just happen. Rather, they require acts of leadership. Leadership is quite broad and includes the community at large; the school board, which is legally charged with approval of the district budget; and school personnel who design and implement educational programs. All of these groups play crucial roles. School and district administrators are hired to build the district's financial plan and to provide philosophical leadership and technical expertise—leadership that should be shared with the instructional staff. Board members bring their educational and political views, which are often influenced by the community. At the same time, it is critical to remember what enables educational programming—it is money, pure and simple—tax dollars taken from a public whose desire to support schools depends in great part on their confidence in school and district leadership.

Budgets are political as well as financial tools in that they reflect the attitudes and values of community-elected school board members. Again, money talks loudly, and the budget process is highly political. Although politics are often viewed negatively by educators, in many instances these realities represent opportunities as well as obstacles. For example, community engagement and advocacy in the budget process has saved important education programs, such as music, art, and student activities, from the chopping block in more than one school district. Failure to engage the public in the budget process is a serious mistake because ownership and enthusiastic support of schools is vital to their success. Conversely, a disengaged community is often apathetic or even hostile.

Rather than seeing budgets as dry documents interesting only to accountants and clerks, school leaders need to understand them as tools that enable schools to function. A budget is a description of a desirable educational program. Second, a budget is an estimate of expenditures needed to carry out the program. Third, a budget is an estimate of revenues available to meet expenses. Our definition is thus three-sided. Although different from an accountant's view that sees only revenue and expenditure, the three-dimensional view best expresses a sound budget philosophy, one that acknowledges that programs should drive both revenues and expenditures. Figure 5.1 illustrates this philosophy, with the educational program serving as the base of the budget triangle. Although fiscal problems may threaten to invert the triangle as programs are constrained by resources, it is important for community members, parents, boards, administrators, teachers, and other stakeholders to not lose sight of the goal that budgets should be built on the basis of program needs. As the budget triangle illustrates, the definition of a budget is first based on quality programs and then supported by revenue and expenditure plans that make envisioned outcomes possible.

ORGANIZING FOR BUDGETING

Our discussion to this point leads to one conclusion: Budgeting is critical to the success of everything that happens in schools. Needless to say, something so important demands a high degree of organization, attention to detail, and accuracy. Historically, school budgets have been an intensely local matter, with minimal state control relating to a few reporting procedures in order to qualify for state aid. With greater calls for fiscal

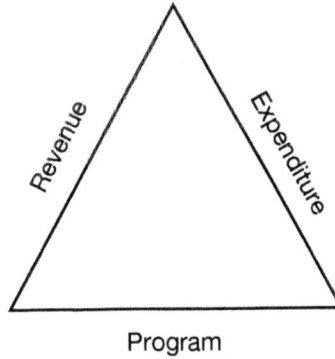

FIGURE 5.1 Ideal Budget Triangle

accountability from seemingly every quarter, the budget process must include the development of a budget framework consistent with the district's vision and operational philosophy. A brief look at common approaches to budgeting is helpful in understanding the various ways in which districts can choose to organize their budgeting activities.

What Are the Common Approaches to Budgeting?

Efforts to improve budget practices have led to common approaches, particularly at the district level. These include incremental budgeting; line-item budgeting; program, planning, budgeting, and evaluation systems (PPBES); zero-based budgeting (ZBB); school site budgeting; and outcome-based budgeting. For the most part, the order of this list relates to their chronological appearance. The main purpose of any approach to budgeting is to detail where resources are targeted in response to students' needs. As we will see in the descriptions that follow, each approach has benefits and drawbacks.

Incremental Budgeting

Incremental budgeting is a simplistic model that uses the prior year's expenditures as a base for creating the next year's budget. It takes its name from the assumption that each budget line should receive the same increment (usually a percent) increase or decrease for the next budget cycle. The process of incremental budgeting can be attractive to school districts as it is easy to understand, even for those unfamiliar with budgeting, and seems, on its face, to be fair in that each major line of the budget receives the same percentage increase or decrease. Incremental budgeting's major flaw, however, is the assumption that next year's combined federal, state, and local allocations will always represent an increase over the prior year's funding.[2] In reality, this has never been the case in public education, but now more than ever, given today's turbulent economic, political, and social environment, districts cannot count upon ever-rising revenues, even in affluent school districts. Importantly, political discourse today is often

---

2 In all fairness to school districts, it should be noted that governors, legislatures, and state education agencies themselves often couch budget discussions in terms of overall percentage changes from year to year.

dominated by the rhetoric of fiscal restraint and accountability, such that many school administrators feel fortunate if next year's budget does not contain reduced revenues and hence necessitate cuts in programs and expenditures.

Incremental budgeting also lacks budget strategies, such as targeting and reallocation of existing funds to maximize educational impact, most likely because it was developed at a time before high stakes testing and value-added evaluations of teachers.[3] Finally, it is obvious that incremental budgeting results in largely unquestioned equal increases to each budget line, potentially causing overfunding or underfunding of individual areas. Overall, this approach fails to consider strategic allocation or returns on investment in educational programs.

Line-Item Budgeting

An improvement over incremental budgeting is line-item budgeting. This tool has been widely used for many years to assign different amounts to each line of the budget. In line-item budgeting, emphasis is placed on the specific objects for which funds are spent. As a result, budgets are planned around each budget line. Typically, line-item budgets have as their base three broad "lines": personnel; maintenance and operations; and supplies and equipment. Personnel costs include salaries, wages, and benefits for all school district employees. Maintenance and operations include day-to-day operational expenses, ranging from utilities to upkeep; and supplies and equipment cover everything from cleaning supplies and textbooks to computers and photocopiers.[4]

Line-item budgeting has several advantages. First, it is simple to understand even for those largely unfamiliar with budgeting who might find a more detailed budget format intimidating. Second, there are those audiences who do not want to peruse a detailed budget and find a line-item budget provides them with concise information. Third, each line item can be expanded to provide more detail if desired. For example, the personnel line can be disaggregated by instructional vs. noninstructional expenditures. Others might want to know what portion of personnel costs are dedicated to benefits, or how much the district is paying for substitute teachers. The other two line items, maintenance and operations, and supplies and equipment, can be disaggregated in a similar manner. Because line-item budgeting has been in place for many years and because it is easily understood, it has survived despite the availability of newer budgeting approaches.

Despite its popularity, line-item budgeting has drawbacks. Although a line-item budget can be used as a building block for a program budget, alone it does not provide program costs. As such, a line-item budget is not an effective tool for educating the public as to expenditures on various programs in the district. Particularly when a district wants to add, cut, or expand programs, it is helpful for both internal and external audiences if administrators are able to clearly present and discuss program costs. In that

---

3 Value-added models evaluate teachers based upon gains in standardized test scores by students in an individual teacher's classroom over the course of an academic year. For a more detailed description and analysis, see Daniel F. McCaffrey, J. R. Lockwood, Daniel M. Koretz, and Laura S. Hamilton, "Evaluating Value-Added Models for Teacher Accountability" (Santa Monica, CA: Rand Corporation, 2003), www.rand.org/content/dam/rand/pubs/monographs/2004/RAND_MG158.pdf.

4 Budgets for capital expenditures are generally developed separately.

sense, a line-item budget is open to criticism for lacking in transparency, which can make it harder for districts to demonstrate to stakeholders that they are willing to be held accountable for the ways in which school moneys are spent.

Planning, Programming, Budgeting, and Evaluation Systems

Planning, Programming, Budgeting, and Evaluation Systems (PPBES) arose from a realization that the budget should be more clearly tied to the educational program. This approach requires each unit in a district or school to establish goals and measurable educational objectives through systematic planning that reviews programs before determining expenditures. The process requires an educational plan where each unit seeks to meet its instructional objectives—a plan for spending, initially justified by needs. Money then follows the plan. The benefits of PPBES are real. This model represents a major conceptual shift from line-item budgeting by deliberately linking programs and expenditures to a presumed cause-and-effect of money. PPBES contributes to accountability, both by its focus on program goals and measurable objectives and by its potential to assess cost-effectiveness.

Like other budgeting approaches, PPBES has drawbacks. School districts must invest significant time and expense upfront in professional development to educate staff on how the PPBES model works and their related responsibilities. Importantly, the district must provide staff with sufficient out-of-classroom time to develop and implement the model. Clearly, PPBES requires a paradigm shift for many schools and districts, making it a challenging approach to budgeting. Yet schools and districts have been forced to consider program budgeting and evaluation of outcomes at increasingly higher levels, as the imposition of more stringent accountability structures has forced this concept on them, ready or not.

Zero-Based Budgeting

The advent of zero-based budgeting (ZBB) in schools coincided with fiscal problems that began to surface during the high inflation years of the 1970s. ZBB was first instituted in the federal government under President Jimmy Carter as an effort to control federal spending by enacting sunset laws to zero-out unproductive government programs. Popular with anti-tax constituencies, ZBB was also implemented by many local governments in response to taxpayer discontent, and it was only a matter of time until schools experimented with the concept. The basic premise of ZBB is that budgets must be justified each year, with the central goal of cutting waste and improving efficiency.

Over the years, many school districts have adopted a modified ZBB model. A typical procedure is to build new budgets based on a percentage reduction from the prior year, with maintenance of prior year funding requiring extensive justification. The rationale is that greater efficiency can be injected into any district, and reductions as a matter of course help achieve that end. Another form of ZBB requires staff to prepare multiple scenarios and to justify each scenario, e.g., decreased, static, and increased expenditure. The first scenario requires extensive description of the educational plan, with the new budget target set at a specified percentage below current funding. The second scenario requires maintenance of both the educational plan and the budget at the same level as the current year. The third scenario allows improvement or expansion of services and expects the budget to increase above the current year. In all instances, each scenario must detail differences between the current year and the next budget cycle, with full expenditure justification.

Benefits of ZBB are many. The product of an era of high inflation and perceived government waste, ZBB represents an opportunity to appease critical taxpayers by taking strong action to reduce waste and increase efficiency. Particularly sound is the idea that budget growth should not occur absent questions about actual contribution to the organization. The idea of multiple spending scenarios is sound, in that planning may improve if expenditures must be fully justified. Finally, districts may be better prepared for reductions if systematic groundwork is laid ahead of actual need to do so. On the other hand, drawbacks are real because the process of zeroing budgets is complex and time-consuming. Some critics hold that ZBB is a cost-reduction tool that can require more resources for effective strategizing than is saved in the end. Also, the potential for internal conflict exists with ZBB, e.g., elective and enrichment courses must make the same justification for existence as core subjects. In extreme cases, animosity among staff can linger long after the budgeting process and even affect morale. In light of these drawbacks, ZBB is generally not used by school districts except in extremely challenging fiscal situations.

School Site Budgeting

School site budgeting is a school-based management tool following closely after the popularity of decentralized administration, with budget decisions pushed downward to the individual school level. It can be said that school site budgeting is a variant of program budgeting applied to each individual school within a district. Under this plan, each site is assigned resources based on a district-level distribution formula that takes into account the number of students at each site in each grade level and program. Typically, the principal and a school site council, comprised of community members, parents, and staff are given responsibility for developing and managing a budget within limits of the total allocation. Depending on state statute or local preference, the council may be authorized to make decisions in such areas as salaries, supplies, and activities— all within the requirement of not violating bargaining agreements, regulations of federally funded programs, and any statutory requirements such as class size limits, or district policies such as school calendar or length of school day.

School site budgeting is appealing because it complements the philosophical underpinnings of site-based management. In concept, site budgeting supports recent advances in learning theory because it values the impact of resources at the point of utilization—i.e., resources are most meaningful at the individual classroom level under the care of the teacher as applied to student needs. Site budgeting is sound in that it involves key stakeholders, especially parents and teachers, in the education of children. The concept is especially attractive as an incentive for greater parental involvement because it asserts the role of the home and community in each student's progress. The special value, then, is in providing a more holistic view of education, making school site budgeting a viable option.

School site budgeting also has some drawbacks. A primary disadvantage is its complexity, wherein school sites are asked to take on new roles related to decision making. Throughout history, schools have been semi-closed social systems, and the addition of community members and parents to budgeting can create new tensions and stresses. Site-based budgeting requires meaningful training for stakeholders, as administrators, teachers, and parents must learn about organizational and technical aspects of funding and must learn to work together cooperatively. And there are real dangers in the concept; that is, unless close attention is paid, equity among schools within a district may be affected through site-based budgeting in that some schools will enjoy greater participation and advocacy. Likewise, there is danger to site decisions in personnel matters, raising legal and ethical questions. However, given current trends, school site budgeting is a likely companion for the foreseeable future—a fact borne out when we return in a later chapter to take a more intensive look at implementing site-based budgeting.

Outcome-Based Budgeting

Outcome-based budgeting is the practice of connecting the aims of the allocation of resources to measurable outcomes, such as test scores. It has grown in popularity in governmental circles in recent years in direct response to interest in accountability. Fiscal austerity, along with competition for finite resources, has only served to increase this approach's attractiveness.

Although this approach to budgeting is still not widely used in school districts, patterns in state aid allocations across the last decade have headed in this direction. Likewise, sanctions in the federal No Child Left Behind Act go directly to increased emphasis on outcome-based budgeting. The advantages are clear: It is intuitive that an organization whose financial support depends on some performance measure will be much more attuned to fully meeting the standard, and it is unarguably legitimate to demand performance in exchange for continued taxpayer support. The disadvantages are equally clear: Organizations facing threats to survival are likely to become victims of damaging stress, and the unintended consequence of slavish devotion to test scores as outcomes ignores the broader aim of educating the whole child. Notwithstanding, outcome-based budgeting combined with a site-level focus is a harbinger of the future.

The choice of a budgeting approach must be carefully considered in order to ensure that districts and schools do not naively seize on a good idea that later proves unworkable. As a consequence, there are several considerations to adopting a budget framework. Hartman proposed issues to be raised when adopting a financial structure at either district or individual school levels.[5] These issues relate to style, preference, and congruency of stakeholders in the budget process. Consideration must be given to the district's history, in that rapid or abrupt changes in budget policies and operations may be met with indifference or resistance. For example, if the district has a history of stakeholder apathy in budget affairs, dramatically increased community involvement is unlikely unless much time is devoted to changing the district's culture. Likewise, budget decisions must be made in light of the historic role of the school board, in that districts

5 William T. Hartman, *School District Budgeting* (Englewood Cliffs, NJ: Prentice Hall, 1988), 28–29.

with a history of strong board control may experience tensions and conflict when trying to move quickly to decentralized models such as site-based budgeting. Likewise, the fiscal condition of the district must be analyzed, as districts in precarious fiscal health may want to stabilize their financial position before introducing a new approach to budgeting.

Constructing Budgets

At the local level, the budget construction usually consists of four sequential, interrelated activities. The first activity is estimating revenue for the new budget year. Envisioning the educational program is usually the second step. The third step is estimating the expenditures required to support the program, while the fourth is a set of decisions designed to balance program needs against revenue and expenditure realities. Ideally, programs should be determined first as seen in the budget triangle, but often revenues drive both expenditures and programs. Although this should be resisted to keep focus on a district's goals, leaders know that the budget process first calls for revenue estimation.

Estimating Revenues

As noted earlier, revenue sources for school districts are federal, state, and local. Federal revenues are established at the national level and usually flow through a state agency with notice of entitlement sent to qualifying districts. State revenues are determined through the legislative process, and districts allocations are calculated through state aid formulas with entitlement notice sent to each district. Each district then calculates its local tax requirement, subject to any existing state limits.[6] For example, states with aid formulas based on a classroom unit may permit total instructional costs of $30,500 per unit, with the state aid formula supplying $20,000 per classroom. If federal aid were equal to $500 per classroom, then $10,000 must be raised locally. A variation achieving the same result might be through a state aid plan that requires a uniform local tax rate of 20 mills, with revenues generated paid to the state, which in turn redistributes it through a statewide staffing formula and salary schedule paying for 55 professional staff positions per 1,000 students. If local option tax leeway is permitted, any additional costs would be funded by local option levy—which might or might not require local voter approval. Likewise, in states funded on a per-pupil basis, the formula might determine the local tax requirement by providing aid in an equalized ratio between 0% and 100% where the unfunded portion must be met by whatever local tax rate is required to raise the necessary funds. Many other highly state-specific configurations exist, in that each state's funding mechanism determines how resources are raised.

---

6 As introduced earlier in Chapter 3, local tax effort is calculated in most states using mill rates. A mill is 1/1000 of a dollar or $1 of tax yield for every $1,000 assessed valuation. A property valued at $100,000 market value and fractionally assessed at 12% for tax purposes and to which a 20 mill tax rate is applied would result in a tax bill of $240 (i.e., $100,000 × 12% = $12,000 × 0.020 = $240). A district's tax rate is found by dividing the local tax requirement by the sum of the district's total assessed valuation (e.g., $5,000,000 local share ÷ $250,000,000 assessed valuation = 0.020 mills).

01 GENERAL	12 months 2012–2013 Actual	12 months 2013–2014 Actual	12 months 2014–2015 Budget
Unencumbered cash balance July 1	683,202	4,657	13,893
Unencumbered cash balance from transportation, bilingual education, and vocational education funds	2,368	12,368	0
Revenue:			
1000 Local sources			
1110 Ad valorem tax levied			
2002 $	407,781		
2013 $	435,968	199,680	
2014 $		414,810	262,990
2015 $			433,712
1140 Delinquent tax	14,897	16,648	6,779
1300 Tuition			
1312 Individuals (out-district)			
1320 Other school district in-state			
1330 Other school district out-state			
1700 Student activities (reimbursement)			
1900 Other revenue from local source			
1910 User charges			
1980 Reimbursements			
1985 State aid reimbursement			
2000 County sources			
2400 Motor vehicle tax	276,484	258,224	252,155
2450 Recreational vehicle tax		6,642	14,166
2800 In lieu of taxes IRBs			
3000 State sources			
3110 General state aid	2,298,537	3,620,788	4,005,159
3130 Mineral production tax			
4000 Federal sources			
4590 Other reserve grants in aid			
4591 Title I (formerly Chapter I)			
4592 Title (math/science)			
4599 Other	14,365	15,864	
4820 PL 382 (Exclude Extra Aid for Children on Indian Land and Low Rent Housing) (formerly PL 874)	39,642	42,888	10,000
5000 Other			
5208 Transfer from local option tax	0	0	0
Resources available	4,173,244	4,592,569	4,998,854
Total expenditures and transfers	4,168,587	4,578,676	4,998,854
Excess revenue to state			0
Unencumbered cash balance June 30	4,657	13,893	

FIGURE 5.2 Sample General Fund Revenue Structure

An example of revenue estimation for a hypothetical school district's general fund is shown in Figure 5.2, where, for the 2014–2015 school year, state aid is estimated at $4,005,159, and local property tax revenues at $433,712. Total general fund revenue is $4,998,854.[7]

In most states, revenues are estimated for each individual fund using state-approved worksheets and information from other agencies. As we saw in Chapter 4, fund accounting sets up multiple separate funds for revenue and expenditure purposes. For example, a state may require that all financial transactions be made from one of the following funds: general; vocational education; special education; capital outlay; bond and interest; food service; transportation; adult education; bilingual education; and in-service/staff development. Fund-based budgets permit analysis of how money is spent and further permit states and the federal government to ensure that funds are spent on their intended purpose. For example, federal special education aid must be segregated in a school district fund dedicated to special education services. At the state level, transportation aid to school districts often comes with the requirement that it too be placed in its own fund account so that it is spent only on transportation. This is especially important, for example, if a state decides to provide additional transportation aid to sparsely populated rural areas with high transportation costs.

In some states, revenue estimation by fund may include the ability (or requirement) to levy different amounts of local tax for each individual fund. For example, a uniform tax rate requirement usually refers only to the general fund from which the bulk of education's costs are paid. Many states do not aid capital outlay or bond indebtedness and therefore permit or require districts to levy a special tax for these funds. As a result, the series of funds operated by school districts can result in multiple revenue estimations and tax levies. However, it must be remembered that other local governmental units levy property taxes for services and operate fund-based budgets that also may require multiple tax levies.

Envisioning Educational Programs

The second activity in the budget process calls for review and establishment of the educational program. This process often seeks to maintain or improve the present situation as well as undertake new initiatives. At times, fiscal issues may force program reductions or elimination, but districts should try to maintain or improve services consistent with their mission statement and educational philosophy.

Envisioning programs takes many forms. One method assumes the present program is adequate and that the budget should be built around the cost of program maintenance. A second method proposes improvements or new initiatives based on consultation with various constituencies. This method has gained popularity with the advent of school

---

7 Note that this school district estimates additional revenues for the general fund budget from the local, state, and federal levels. It estimates $6,779 in tuition. This generally means that a student from another school district is in attendance, and its home district pays the cost of educating him/her. This particular district also estimates a little over $266,000 from county sources related to vehicle taxes. Finally, the district estimates receipt of $10,000 in federal revenues. Note that the district will likely receive more than that amount in federal revenues, but because of the targeted nature of much federal education aid, these revenues will likely be placed in segregated fund accounts.

reform, with many districts having school improvement plans linked to federal and state mandates, e.g., those aimed at increasing student achievement of at-risk students. Such plans may include curriculum committees, task forces, site councils, community–school partnerships, and business and industry partnerships. As a rule, envisioning programs is undertaken to better align curriculum and to specify outcomes in return for resources invested.

Regardless of how schools assess their programs, the underlying point is that programs cost money. The purpose of program description in budgeting is to identify program needs in order to translate them into fiscal terms in the budget document. If program maintenance is the goal, the district can use prior year data as the basis, with allowance for increased costs in the new year, e.g., salaries, supplies, equipment. If improvements are being considered, the district generally turns to its proposed program description, which should include action statements about resources. A budget development calendar may be used to gather input and build the budget. The district's fiscal philosophy, such as site budgeting, will have a powerful impact on educational programs.

Envisioning the educational program is a complex process that requires a commitment of time and resources, but it should be the heart of budgeting because unless it is thoughtfully carried out, nothing more than maintenance of the status quo will occur. In sum, envisioning the program is the critical link between estimating revenues and estimating expenditures.

Estimating Expenditures

Estimation of expenditures needed to support the educational program is the third activity in preparing a budget. Like revenue estimation, expenditure plans must follow state requirements for form and content. The process generally calls for placing revenue on the various proposed expenditure lines of each fund in the budget. Although it is difficult to say that any one step is most important, expenditure estimation is one of the most critical because underestimation of costs is disastrous. For example, failure to accurately calculate the costs of a new teacher salary schedule could result in unmet payroll, suit for breach of employment contract, and force school closures because revenues must equal or exceed all expenditures.

Expenditure estimation identifies the major cost determinants and makes best estimates of all changes for the new budget year. Estimating general fund expenditures generally involves determining employee salaries, wages, and benefits; the number of positions required; movement of each staff member on the applicable salary/wage schedule; maintenance and day-to-day operations costs; quantities and costs of supplies; equipment costs; and costs of services such as professional development, legal fees, auditing, insurance, printing, security, and information technology. The exhaustive nature of these activities is seen in Figure 5.3, which shows the expenditure side of a hypothetical district's general fund budget document. Importantly, these steps are repeated for each separate fund the district operates.

In most districts, every item in the budget is driven by enrollment. Staff, supplies and equipment, as well as the size and number of buildings are a function of the number of students. Estimating enrollment is a critical, but challenging, task because no single

01 GENERAL EXPENDITURES	12 months 2012–2013 Actual	12 months 2013–2014 Actual	12 months 2014–2015 Budget
1000 Instruction			
100 Salaries			
110 Certified	1,688,504	1,799,864	1,872,000
120 Noncertified	25,682	28,243	29,000
200 Employee benefits			
210 Insurance (employee)	28,949	33,640	34,000
220 Social Security	131,083	138,764	140,000
290 Other	3,039	3,642	3,800
300 Purchased professional and technical services			
500 Other purchased services			
560 Tuition			
561 Tuition/other state LEAs			
562 Tuition/other LEAs outside the state			
563 Tuition/private sources			
590 Other	9,241	10,953	9,000
600 Supplies			
610 General supplemental (teaching)	85,984	102,760	104,000
644 Textbooks	52,486	62,384	65,000
680 Miscellaneous supplies	4,685		3,960
700 Property (equipment & furnishings)	51,863	5,543	6,000
800 Other			62,000
2000 Support services			
2100 Student support services			
100 Salaries			
110 Certified	60,504	64,164	65,500
120 Noncertified			
200 Employee benefits			
210 Insurance (employee)	562	699	750
220 Social Security	4,630	4,984	5,200
290 Other	59	100	100
300 Purchased professional and technical services	7,982	9,641	10,000
500 Other purchased services			
600 Supplies			5,000
700 Property (equipment & furnishings)	4,291	5,007	
800 Other			
2200 Instructional support staff			
100 Salaries			
110 Certified	91,860	96,541	98,000
120 Noncertified			
200 Employee benefits			
210 Insurance (employee)	1,072	1,286	1,400

FIGURE 5.3 Sample General Fund Expenditure Structure

01 GENERAL EXPENDITURES	12 months 2012–2013 Actual	12 months 2013–2014 Actual	12 months 2014–2015 Budget
220 Social Security	7,070	7,509	8,500
290 Other	112	148	200
3300 Community services operations	3,064	3,704	4,000
3400 Student activities	28,564	34,296	35,000
4300 Architectural and engineering services			
300 Purchased professional and technical services			
500 Other purchased services			
600 Supplies			
640 Books (not textbooks) and periodicals	14,389	16,841	18,000
650 Audiovisual and instructional software	12,684	15,092	17,000
680 Miscellaneous supplies			
700 Property (equipment and furnishings)	4,066	4,905	5,000
800 Other			
2300 General administration			
100 Salaries			
110 Certified	38,184	40,448	41,500
120 Noncertified	49,860	53,624	54,600
200 Employee benefits			
210 Insurance (employee)	984	1,206	1,300
220 Social Security	7,115	8,492	9,000
290 Other	103	200	200
300 Purchased professional and technical services	17,054	20,384	21,000
400 Purchased property services			
500 Other purchased services			
520 Insurance			
530 Communications (telephone, postage, etc.)	4,643	5,605	5,900
590 Other			
600 Supplies	8,106	9,653	10,000
700 Property (equipment and furnishings)	7,964	9,582	10,000
800 Other	13,165	16,769	16,000
2400 School administration			
100 Salaries			
110 Certified	211,864	220,843	227,000
120 Noncertified	84,286	89,300	91,000
200 Employee benefits			
210 Insurance (employee)	4,995	6,001	6,500
220 Social Security	2,505	26,984	28,000
290 Other	324	411	500
300 Purchased professional and technical services			
400 Purchased property services			
500 Other purchased services			

FIGURE 5.3 *continued*

01 GENERAL EXPENDITURES	12 months 2012–2013 Actual	12 months 2013–2014 Actual	12 months 2014–2015 Budget
530 Communications (telephone, postage, etc.)	1,793	2,174	2,200
590 Other			
600 Supplies			
700 Property (equipment & furnishings)	4,001	4,624	5,000
800 Other			
2600 Operations and maintenance			
100 Salaries			
120 Noncertified	192,386	200,784	205,000
200 Employee benefits			
210 Insurance (employee)	1,995	2,396	2,500
220 Social Security	15,750	16,863	18,000
290 Other	209	255	500
300 Purchased professional and technical services	1,248	1,498	1,500
400 Purchased property services			
411 Water/sewer	8,150	9,750	10,000
420 Cleaning			
430 Repairs and maintenance	161,745	188,640	264,860
440 Rentals		61,980	42,840
460 Repair of buildings	218,714	251,574	388,431
490 Other	37,984	45,472	55,000
500 Other purchased services			
520 Insurance	32,345	36,542	37,000
590 Other		13,052	
600 Supplies			
610 General supplies	42,387	50,845	51,000
620 Energy			
621 Heating	45,190	46,842	48,000
622 Electricity	67,810	69,742	71,000
626 Motor fuel (not school bus)			
629 Other	22,196	32,482	26,000
680 Miscellaneous supplies		12,052	4,000
700 Property (equipment & furnishings)	4,284	8,244	6,000
800 Other	2,361	2,876	3,000
2500, 2800, 2900 Other supplemental services			
100 Salaries			
110 Certified			
120 Noncertified			
200 Employee benefits			
210 Insurance			
220 Social Security			
290 Other			

FIGURE 5.3 *continued*

01 GENERAL EXPENDITURES	12 months 2012–2013 Actual	12 months 2013–2014 Actual	12 months 2014–2015 Budget
300 Purchased professional and technical services			
400 Purchased property services			
500 Other purchased services			
600 Supplies			
700 Property (equipment and furnishings)			
800 Other			
5200 Transfer to:			
932 Adult education			3,000
934 Adult supplemental education			
936 Bilingual education			
938 Capital outlay	75,246	94,400	97,315
940 Driver training	5,000	5,000	5,000
942 Education excellence grant program		10,000	5,000
943 Extraordinary school program			
944 Food service			
946 In-service education	5,136	4,533	11,798
948 Parent education program			
949 Summer school		10,000	10,000
950 Special education	130,000	100,000	125,000
951 Technology education			
952 Transportation	313,080	323,070	360,000
954 Vocational education	6,000	12,864	15,000
955 Area vocational school			
956 Disability income benefits reserve			
958 Health care services reserve			
959 Group life insurance reserve			
960 Risk management reserve			
962 School workers' compensation reserve			
968 Cooperative elementary guidance			
972 Contingency reserve			
Total expenditures and transfers	4,168,587	4,578,766	4,998,854

FIGURE 5.3 *continued*

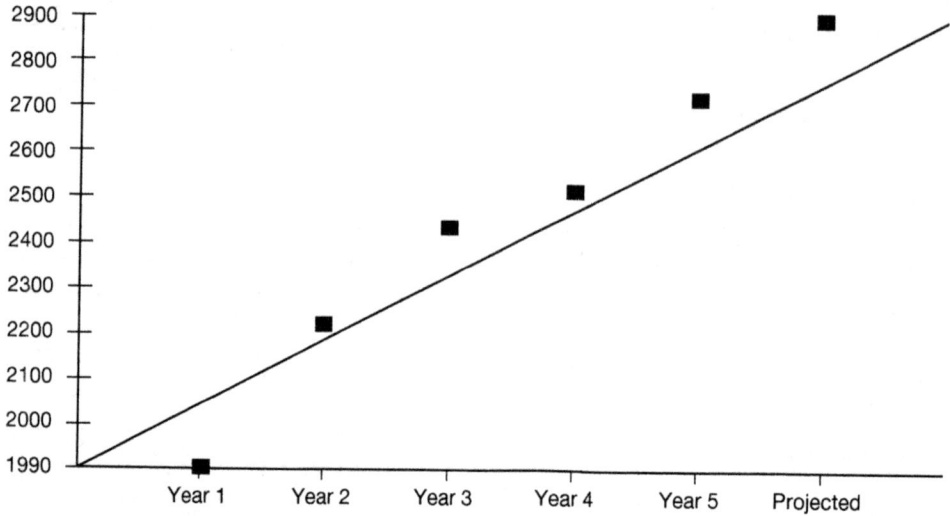

FIGURE 5.4 Trend Line Analysis of Enrollments

method is always completely accurate. Even with powerful population mapping tools, sudden in- and out-migrations due to human variables and economic shifts can affect accuracy. Enrollment projection techniques are remarkably useful, however, because they are all based on two important features. The first feature is an expectation that the conditions characterizing the past will continue. The second feature softens the apparent error of that assumption by requiring constant re-evaluation and updating of the model's underlying assumptions. In essence, tracking shifts in population over time provides a smoothing effect to the data, a technique used in the two most common methods of enrollment estimation: trend analysis and cohort survival.

Trend analysis is the application of regression models to predicting enrollment based on previous years of enrollment data. In its simplest form, trend analysis predicts future enrollments based on the manner in which previous enrollments deviate from a straight line. The formula for the regression line (fitted line) is $Y = Mx + b$ where Y is the future enrollment, M is a coefficient used in the model, x is a future year, and b is a constant showing the relationship between enrollment and year. Using multiyear historic data, a future year is entered, and the result is a predicted enrollment. Figure 5.4 shows a sample trend analysis. The regression formula casts a line of best fit, yielding projected enrollment for next year (Year 6). In the sample district's case, historic data indicate a steadily increasing enrollment trend, with Year 1 enrollment beginning at 1,990 students and increasing to 2,710 by Year 5. Figure 5.4 projects ahead one year, in this case, an enrollment of 2,900 students.

Trend analysis is most appropriate in larger districts because the averages in a regression line do not affect the district to the extent that would be true for a smaller district, where the loss of each student represents a greater proportion of the total budget. As a result, medium and smaller size districts often prefer techniques that are more arithmetically straightforward, more intuitive, and more sensitive to small changes in head count.

Cohort survival is an enrollment projection tool that groups students by grade level at entry to school and tracks them through each year they remain in the school district. In concept, cohort survival looks at entering kindergarten students in Year 1 and calculates how many enter first grade in Year 2, second grade in Year 3 and so on until graduation. Such a system more closely accounts for grade failures, dropouts, and migratory trends impacting student population.

Cohort survival requires enrollment data from previous years as well as the current year for each grade. It calculates the percentage of change and survival as a percentage of the previous year's grade-level enrollment. For example, Part 2 of Figure 5.5 shows that historically enrollments from first to second grade averaged only 94% of the prior year's grade-level population. This means that out-migrations or grade failure resulted in a 6% average loss between first and second grades. This allows entry of the multiyear average into Part 3 of the analysis, where current first grade enrollment can be multiplied by 94% to project 376 students in second grade next year compared to 400 students in first grade in the present year. This process is repeated for each grade for several years into the future, whereupon enrollments are totaled by grade level. Figure 5.6 then graphs the school district's total enrollment trends from 2011 to 2016. One additional point should be made. Kindergarten estimation tends to be unreliable and constitutes a special case in most school districts, requiring use of multiple indicators like birth records, roundups, and local preschool attendance. Except for kindergarten, these numbers are used with relative confidence to assign staff, purchase supplies, plan facility use, and calculate other aspects of revenue and expenditure estimation. Since virtually all budgeting is based on enrollments, cohort survival is a good tool due to its immediate sensitivity to changes in population.

The sheer volume of activities involved in estimating expenditures precludes their explanation in a single textbook chapter. For example, the next major activity after enrollment projection is projecting staffing needs. This involves a complex set of activities involving labor negotiations, salary/wage schedules, and fringe benefits. Student enrollment and staff numbers also drive the purchase of teaching supplies and equipment as well as facilities. We cover these topics in later chapters, e.g., budgeting for personnel in Chapter 6 and budgeting for school infrastructure in Chapter 9.

Balancing the Budget

The fourth step in the budget process aligns estimated costs for each fund with anticipated revenues. This process is straightforward in states that tightly control revenues by mechanisms such as allocating the number of classroom units to each district. For instance, it takes little time to find salary costs if the state allocates 55 professional positions per 1,000 pupils—in such states, school districts will spend the bulk of their time deciding how to meet their instructional needs (given a set staff size) because no options exist for increased staffing except increasing local property taxes. In states with more staffing flexibility, districts may spend more time deciding the allocation of money to various lines in the budget to achieve the best balance for their particular situation. In states where tax rates can vary through local option leeway, districts may also consider raising taxes to pay for additional staff. The process in all states, though, calls for balancing the revenue and expenditure sides of the budget because most states forbid deficit spending by schools.

Part 1: Historic Enrollments							
Grade	2005–06	2006–07	2007–08	2008–09	2009–10	2010-11	Average
Pre-K	500.0	500.0	499.0	502.0	500.0	503.0	500.7
One	490.0	501.0	498.0	499.0	501.0	400.0	481.5
Two	627.0	499.0	478.0	466.0	489.0	410.0	494.8
Three	590.0	611.0	497.0	477.0	477.0	488.0	523.3
Four	491.0	593.0	601.0	488.0	482.0	469.0	520.7
Five	399.0	478.0	578.0	615.0	479.0	489.0	506.3
Six	617.0	389.0	502.0	477.0	610.0	477.0	512.0
Seven	591.0	616.0	399.0	499.0	470.0	600.0	529.2
Eight	499.0	588.0	618.0	381.0	489.0	479.0	509.0
Nine	650.0	482.0	549.0	729.0	377.0	488.0	545.8
Ten	533.0	623.0	492.0	532.0	716.0	369.0	544.2
Eleven	811.0	540.0	622.0	499.0	415.0	616.0	583.8
Twelve	710.0	815.0	539.0	627.0	481.0	421.0	598.8
TOTAL	7508.0	7235.0	6872.0	6791.0	6486.0	6209.0	6850.2

Part 2: Survival Ratio							
Grade	2005–06	2006–07	2007–08	2008–09	2009–10	2010-11	Average
Pre-K		100%	100%	101%	100%	101%	100%
One		100%	100%	100%	100%	80%	96%
Two		102%	95%	94%	98%	82%	94%
Three		97%	100%	100%	102%	100%	100%
Four		101%	98%	98%	101%	98%	99%
Five		97%	97%	102%	98%	101%	99%
Six		97%	105%	83%	99%	100%	97%
Seven		100%	103%	99%	99%	98%	100%
Eight		99%	100%	95%	98%	102%	99%
Nine		97%	93%	118%	99%	100%	101%
Ten		96%	102%	97%	98%	98%	98%
Eleven		101%	100%	101%	78%	86%	93%
Twelve		100%	100%	101%	96%	101%	100%

FIGURE 5.5 Cohort Survival Technique

		Part 3: Enrollment Projections through 2016					
Grade	Multiyear Average	2010–11 (actual)	2011–12	2012–13	2013–14	2014–15	2015–16
Pre-K	100%	503.0	503.6	504.2	504.8	505.8	506.4
One	96%	400.0	482.5	483.1	483.6	484.2	485.2
Two	94%	410.0	376.5	454.2	454.7	455.3	455.8
Three	100%	488.0	409.2	375.8	453.2	453.8	454.3
Four	99%	469.0	484.5	406.3	373.1	450.0	450.6
Five	99%	489.0	466.0	481.4	403.6	370.7	447.1
Six	97%	477.0	473.2	450.9	465.8	390.6	358.7
Seven	100%	600.0	475.8	471.9	449.7	464.6	389.5
Eight	99%	479.0	594.3	471.2	467.4	445.4	460.1
Nine	101%	488.0	485.4	602.2	477.5	473.7	451.3
Ten	98%	369.0	479.1	476.6	591.2	468.8	465.1
Eleven	93%	616.0	344.4	447.1	444.8	551.8	437.5
Twelve	100%	421.0	614.7	343.6	446.2	443.8	550.6
TOTAL		6209.0	6189.0	5968.4	6015.7	5958.4	5912.3

FIGURE 5.5 *continued*

Efforts to balance revenues and expenditures result in cause-and-effect scenarios, with nearly inescapable instructional impacts. For example, revenues may need careful review if program needs significantly exceed available funding. Alternatively, program expenditures may have to be reduced if it is clear that revenues will continue to be inadequate. Although state-specific conditions sometimes limit available options, these activities—called budget adjustments—usually involve one of three common scenarios. The first scenario happens when school districts receive increased revenues through federal, state, or local sources. The second scenario occurs when revenues are static, and the third appears when revenue declines. Each of these situations has been faced at some time by every school district, and the process for dealing with each one can be difficult and complex.

In Chapter 1, we recommended that school districts plan for the various scenarios described above through prioritization of programs and expenditures. We suggested the use of PPBES as one budgeting approach that builds in program priorities as they relate to the district's mission, vision, and educational goals. Here we focus on potential strategies to increase efficiency and hence reduce costs. These are particularly helpful when a district faces static or declining revenues. However, even when a district enjoys increased revenues, implementation of these strategies is helpful because it frees up additional funding for instructional programs.

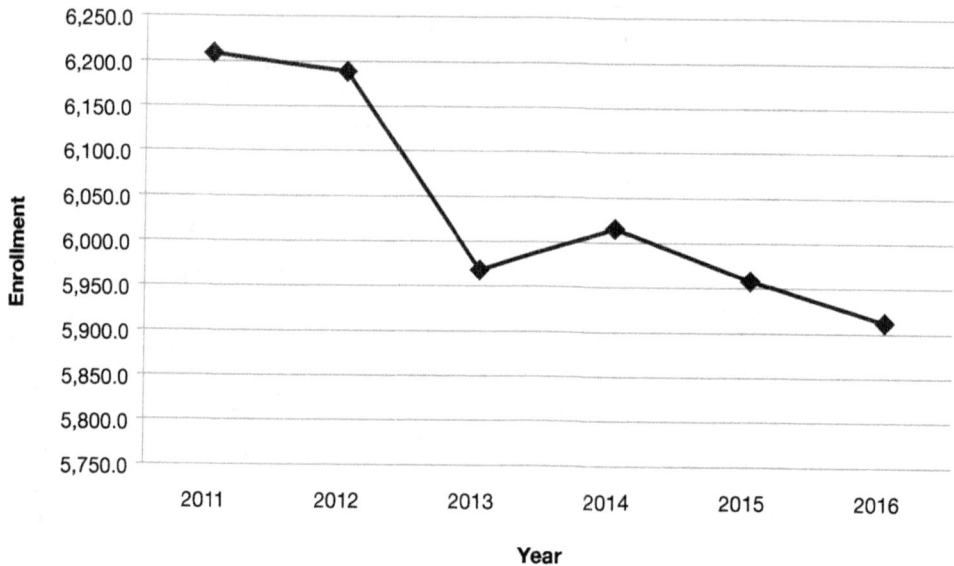

FIGURE 5.6 District Enrollment Trend: 2011–2016

Examples of strategies actually used by districts are as follows:

- Energy efficiency: Chapter 9, on school infrastructure funding, contains a number of short- and long-term strategies for schools to reduce energy consumption. These benefit both the environment and the bottom line. When faced with the need to immediately reduce expenditures, districts typically look for low to no-cost strategies. The U.S. Department of Energy offers a number of cost-reduction techniques through its "EnergySmart Schools" initiative which includes a website and a number of concise publications with easy to implement suggestions, e.g., shutting down boilers during unoccupied times when there is no danger of freezing; lowering the temperature on water heaters; and using daylighting in classrooms.[8]
- More efficient purchasing: In times of limited or reduced budgets, districts must carefully distinguish between "wants" and "needs" with regard to purchasing supplies and equipment. For better or worse, this may require more centralized oversight of purchasing including greater use of written justifications by those making requests. Other approaches to lowering costs include bulk discount buying and "just-in-time" purchasing. Smaller school districts may realize cost savings through cooperative purchasing with neighboring districts or municipalities.
- Deferral of equipment purchases and maintenance: Deferral of purchasing new equipment carries with it potential benefits and costs. For example, delaying bus

---

8 U.S. Department of Energy, *EnergySmart Schools Tips: Retrofitting, Operating, and Maintaining Existing Buildings* (Washington, DC: Office of Energy Efficiency and Renewable Energy, Building Technologies Program), http://apps1.eere.energy.gov/buildings/publications/pdfs/energysmartschools/ess_quick-wins_fs.pdf.

purchases may result in older buses with higher operating and maintenance costs. At some point such buses may become unsafe or simply lack up-to-date safety features, posing a liability risk for the district that is far greater than the price of a new bus. In addition, purchasing a new "green" bus that uses less fuel or less costly fuel may actually reduce transportation costs. Similarly, deferral of facilities maintenance may result in higher costs later. This issue is covered in more detail in Chapter 9.

- Improved cash management: Districts are well-advised to hire a savvy school business manager who understands the importance of investing every dollar of idle funds. Although it may be tempting to turn to "temporary" measures like drawing down reserves, districts would be well advised to consider the wisdom of doing so. Reserves often exist for emergencies like a boiler breaking down in the middle of winter. In such an instance, if reserves are insufficient to replace it immediately, the district may be forced to engage in short term borrowing at noncompetitive interest rates—a situation that embodies the saying "penny wise and pound foolish."

- Improved risk management: Raising insurance deductible amounts, assessing the potential benefits and risks of self-insuring, and competitive bidding of insurance coverage are strategies to reduce risk management costs. However, each of these deserves serious cost–benefit analysis.

- Refinancing long-term debt: Here too savvy business managers more than earn their annual salaries given their expertise in fiscal matters. Refunding bonds to take advantage of lower interest rates can save districts thousands of dollars annually in lower interest costs. However, it is unwise to extend bond payments over a longer period of time. This may reduce the annual payment, but overall it will result in an increase in interest costs.

- Incentives for employee retirement: Providing incentives for eligible employees to retire might be another strategy to consider. Experienced employees are generally more expensive, and so their retirement coupled with replacement by less experienced employees can be a substantial savings to the district. However, we offer several cautions. First, seek legal counsel because there are a number of state and federal laws that may affect the crafting of such incentives, including but not limited to discrimination against older employees. Second, consider the educational cost–benefit of such programs; that is, losing the expertise and leadership of experienced staff can be damaging to educational programs and staff morale. Also to be successful, the incentives must be not only attractive and large enough to result in actual retirement, but at the same time small enough to effect a reduction in expenditures.

- Reduction of employee costs: When all of the above measures prove insufficient, districts may be forced to consider reducing employee costs. A district that has engaged in long-range planning and uses budgeting systems like PPBES is better situated to make informed decisions that minimize potential damage to instructional programs. Temporary measures like increasing class sizes and reducing electives and extracurricular programs are sometimes taken as first steps. Sometimes with retirements and resignations, reduction in force (RIF) is unnecessary. Salary and wage freezes may also be a possibility if labor agreements permit. If not, unions might be asked to make concessions in order to avoid lay-offs. Some districts have used furloughs to make temporary reductions in salary and wage costs. Others have asked employees to shoulder a greater percentage of benefit costs, like insurance and retirement contributions. Outsourcing of some services might be examined as a possibility. However as noted in other chapters, outsourcing requires careful cost–benefit analysis to determine if savings are actually realized as well as consideration of community reaction to the change.

Nonetheless, in some situations, even these measures may not be sufficient to balance a budget. In that case, the one remaining alternative is to cut programs. Care must be exercised, however, not to violate contracts or state laws. For example, in many states length of school day, hours of work, and class schedules are part of negotiated agreements, and many states have mandated preschool and extended day programs. Although cuts are never easy, reductions in staff and programs are the most painful and destructive. As a result, such measures should be used only as a last resort.

Completing the Budget Process

Budget construction is nearly complete when programs are envisioned, revenues and expenditures are estimated, and a balanced budget is achieved. The budget still must be approved, however. Approval steps differ across states, but the end result is always legal adoption of the budget under statutory requirements. For example, in states where school districts are fiscally dependent on some other unit of government, the budget is forwarded to a higher authority, such as a city council or county board, for final approval. In states where districts are fiscally independent, approval is more complex in that several events usually occur sequentially. Although highly state-specific, a general procedure calls for official publication of a budget summary, usually in a newspaper of general local circulation, followed by a waiting period, public hearing, formal adoption of the budget, and certification of the proposed or amended budget to some other governmental unit such as a county taxing authority. Publication is meant to give notice to the public of the budget hearing, with the waiting period to allow citizens a chance to prepare comments and to attend the hearing. State statutes usually call for the school board to vote in open session. The budget, if adopted, must be certified according to state statute. These laws are meant to guard against secrecy and impropriety, and they must be strictly observed.

HOW ARE INDIVIDUAL SCHOOLS FUNDED?

The process discussed to this point details budgeting at the district level, but it says nothing about funding individual schools. This is a challenging topic because states generally have not enacted statewide school-level funding laws, leaving most of the nation's roughly 14,000 districts free to adopt their own school site budget philosophy.

That is exactly the point of our earlier focus on adopting a local budget philosophy, i.e., districts have great freedom to create internal budget structures, and those choices have a tremendous impact on individual schools. As a result, how individual schools are funded is as different as the number of districts that exist. Nonetheless, some common ways that districts fund schools can be reviewed.

Most school districts operate from a budget calendar such as the one in Figure 5.7. Budget calendars range from very simple to highly complex. Figure 5.7 is fairly uncomplicated and is taken from an actual district of about 7,000 students. The calendar identifies all areas of the budget, assigns responsibility to an administrator, and lays out the budget process with deadlines. An important feature is that budgeting is a multi-month process that includes a flow chart of responsibility and (in this case) involves many people, including principals and other staff. The processes of estimating revenues, envisioning school programs, estimating expenditures, and balancing the budget are all evident in the sample budget calendar, as is the overall coordination of the budget process at the district level that brings these separate activities into a completed total budget prior to a new school year.

The budget calendar in Figure 5.7 also notes another aspect of school budgeting in that building principals are assigned a formal role. Although again dependent on local district preference, this budget calendar shows principals involved at almost all stages including the initial planning stage, program planning, preliminary budget review, requisition and purchase order preparation, and the daily administration of school budgets. Figure 5.7 might be used in a relatively centralized district, but it could apply just as easily to a district using site-based budgeting. In the first case, school principals would be asked about program needs, supplies, equipment, and facilities. In the latter case, principals would have significant control over daily resource utilization; the individual school would operate independently with ultimate accountability for productivity. We will explore these ideas later when we look at budgeting for instruction, and again when we look more closely at site-based leadership and the future.

The process of budgeting at this point can be pictured as an inverted pyramid, flowing mostly from state to local. It begins with federal and state policies that make revenue available to school districts. Each district determines its program requirements, matches revenues and needs, and adjusts local revenue and programs to fill the deficit. Districts then allocate revenue to individual schools based on a preferred budget philosophy, using such concepts as fairness; horizontal and vertical equity; and preferences about decentralization and accountability. For example, a district may decide it wishes to assign block grants to each elementary school in exchange for the promise to increase student achievement on test scores by a certain amount next year. Principals and staffs may then consult with site councils and opt, for example, for more teacher aides and slightly larger class sizes instead of hiring a new teacher. Another school, however, might take a different path by hiring a grant writer to seek additional funding and using the enhanced revenue to provide extra supplies, equipment, and instructional staff to meet some other set of learning goals. The range of possibilities depends on state laws and available revenues, in combination with local ingenuity.

Budget Area	Staff Responsible
General Fund	Board/central administration
Administration	Superintendent
School budgets	Principals
Travel: administrator and teacher	Director of Personnel
Special programs	Director of Special Services
Adult education	Coordinator Adult Education
Bilingual programs	ESL Coordinator
Capital outlay	Director of Maintenance
Driver education	Business Manager
Food service	Director of Food Service
Transportation	Transportation Director
Special education	Director of Special Education
Bond & interest budgets	Business Manager
In-service budget	Director of Curriculum
Vocational school budget	Director of Curriculum
Special projects and grants	Business Manager
Other budgets	As assigned

Preparation Calendar

Date	Description	Responsible
January	Distribute planning guide Meet with principals and program directors	Business Manager
March	Requests for new programs and personnel due	Superintendent, Business Manager, and Personnel Director
April	Seek board input on programs and new personnel	Superintendent, Curriculum, and Personnel Director
April	Building, program, and capita repair/improvements due	Directors and Principals
May	Bid capital outlay, instructional items and advise of bids	Principals and Business Manager
June	First draft of total budget	Superintendent and Business Manager
July	Board budget workshop	All administrators
July	Budget publication and hearings	Admin, Board, public
August	Adoption and certification	Business Manager

FIGURE 5.7 Sample Budget Calendar with Staff Responsibilities

WHAT IS THE ROLE OF STAKEHOLDERS?

Every chapter in this book has implied that school money is a legitimate place for multiple stakeholders to make their voices heard. This chapter is no different. We have underscored that there is a place in school budgeting for everyone—administrators, boards, teachers, policymakers, parents, and community members. If the purpose of budgets is to identify the needs of schools, prioritize those needs, match resources with needs, and operationalize educational goals, there is much to be gained by their broad participation.

Although we believe everyone should take initiative and responsibility for school budgeting, we especially believe that educational leaders should deliberately use the budget for specific stakeholder benefits. Leaders should use budgets to structure the educational plan, assess progress toward outcomes, to evaluate accomplishment of the plan, and to make adjustments when needed. Budgeting is not only a central office function; increasingly, principals must account for program decisions, with greater responsibility for money under site-based leadership. Boards are legally charged with the responsibility for expending funds and must take responsibility for prudent fiscal stewardship. The expertise of teachers and other instruction-related professional staff should be fully utilized in the creation of the educational plan expressed by the budget. Policymakers need knowledge about educational programming, and feedback loops help them reach the decisions about funding schools that they are constitutionally required to make. Finally, no audience is more crucial than parents and community members whose taxes pay for schools and whose approval every district must have in order to fulfill its educational aims. The interaction of these constituent roles is made clear in Figure 5.8—it is not by accident that the link between strategic planning and school budget outcomes involves many stakeholders who ultimately decide how schools are funded.

Carrying out the educational plan requires financial resources, professional judgment, and the linking of resources and outcomes in an integrated budget plan. School and district administrators must guard against losing sight of the purpose of budgets and stand as strong leaders. As Ward avowed, education finance is not a "technical and sterile area of study employing complex mathematics, arcane algebraic formulas [nor] a refuge for the methodologically minded to be avoided by those humanists in education who see their emphasis as being on children, instruction, and qualitative aspects of schooling."[9] Instead, a budget is the fiscal expression of the educational philosophy of a school district.

---

9 James G. Ward, "An Inquiry into the Normative Foundations of American Public School Finance," *Journal of Education Finance* 12 (Summer 1987): 463.

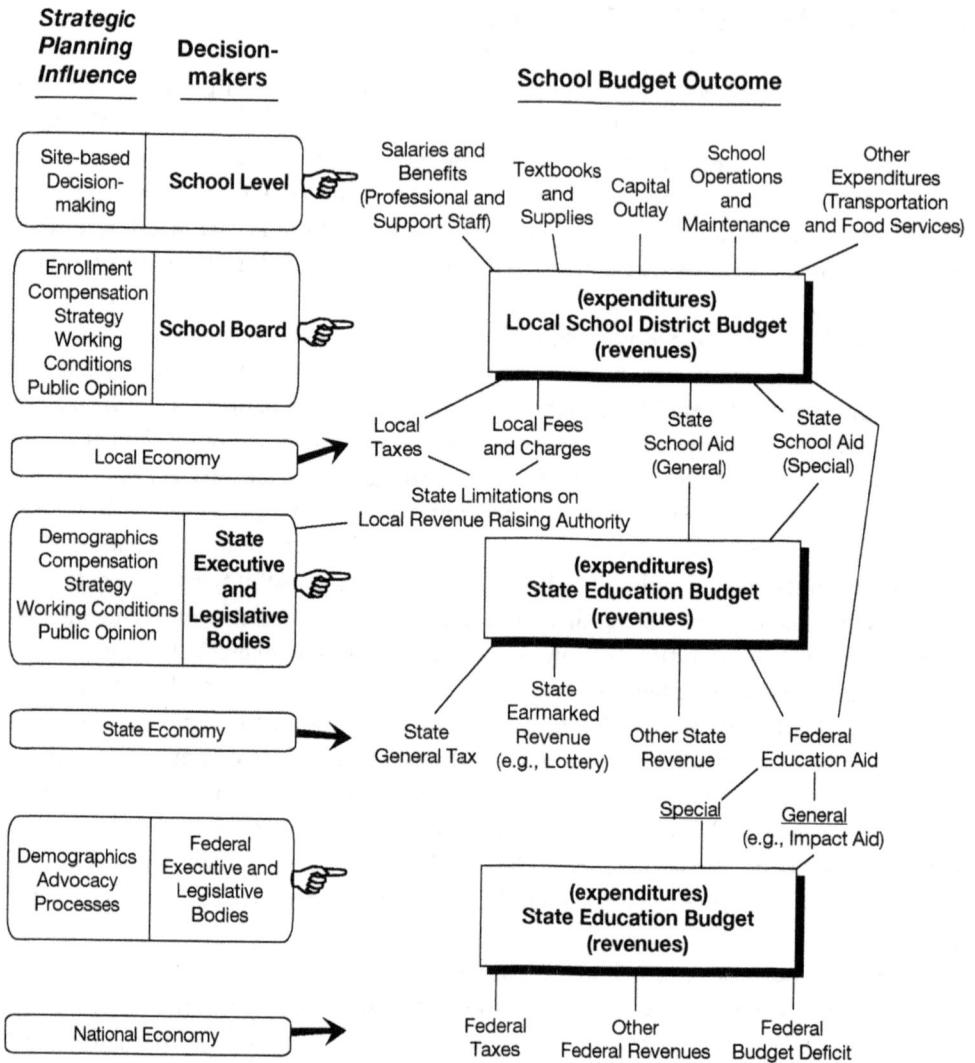

FIGURE 5.8 School Budget Arena

POINT–COUNTERPOINT

POINT

School leaders today, especially principals, are charged with the success of high stakes educational programs and must be given responsibility for designing and executing site-level budgets if they are to meet their increased accountability expectations.

COUNTERPOINT

School leaders today, especially principals, are so engulfed by instructional leadership duties, high stakes accountability, and day-to-day operations that school districts should not require budget involvement by school site administrators—instead, districts should increase central support services to fulfill this "management" responsibility.

- Which view best represents your philosophy of budgeting? Explain why.
- How are principals, central office staff, teachers, and others involved in budget construction and daily budget administration in your own school district?
- If you were an administrator in your school district, how would you wish budgeting to be structured? Explain why.

CASE STUDY

As a long-time principal in your school district, you were surprised at last week's administrative cabinet meeting when the new superintendent announced her desire to redesign the district's budgeting practices. As you listened, you learned she hoped to move many resource decisions to the school site level. As the discussion developed, you became both intrigued and worried when you realized that she was suggesting increased stakeholder participation and increased site level accountability for the outcomes of expenditure decisions.

Inasmuch as all district and site-level administrators were in attendance at the weekly cabinet meeting, a vigorous discussion ensued. Several administrators, notably some of your fellow principals, seemed eager to seize the reins and accept responsibility for how money gets spent at the school site. Others seemed more reluctant, raising questions about how a new system would be structured, including concerns about individual school profiles, determination of each school's programmatic resource needs, and—of course—how evaluation of site-level resource decision making would be carried out. As the conversation progressed, it became clear that while the superintendent's idea was widely recognized as having merit, the district's administrative cabinet needed a blueprint for how such a plan would be constituted before everyone would unreservedly endorse such a dramatic change.

To move to the next level, the superintendent indicated that she would form a study group to consider and propose a redesign. She indicated that a workable proposal was due on her desk by the end of the school year—about eight months from now. As the most experienced principal in the school district, you were asked to co-chair the study group along with the associate superintendent for management services. As the meeting broke up, your co-chair asked you to step into his office, whereupon he requested that you take the lead in organizing the work to be undertaken at the committee's first meeting. Although you privately pondered that his job title might be better suited to the task at hand, you recognized that his motivation included the fact that you would have a better grasp of concerns likely to be held by the district's numerous school site administrators and that your insights might help avoid some pitfalls. In that you hope to move into a central office role shortly, you expressed willingness to accept the task and determined to yourself that you would be both careful and exhaustive in your approach.

Below is a set of questions. As you respond, consider your learning in this chapter and apply your knowledge and emerging beliefs/preferences to the situation:

- Do you believe the process this district is pursuing is wise? Why or why not? What advantages do you see? What problems might follow from this process?
- What steps should you take to begin this planning process? What factors need to be taken into account? What do you believe are the critical elements for such organizational changes to succeed?
- How are your school district's budgeting practices organized? What do you believe would happen if such a proposal were raised in your district? If such a practice is already in place in your district, assess how effective it is.
- If you had been the superintendent in this case study, would you have embarked on this course? If so, explain why. If not, what would you have done differently?

PORTFOLIO EXERCISES

- Interview the appropriate central office leader(s) to discuss the relationship between budgeting and strategic planning in your school district. Explore how the district conceptualizes its budget and the processes by which budgeting occurs. Discuss the overall process of estimating revenues and expenditures, including how the district involves stakeholders in the process. Discuss the act of balancing the budget and the district's efforts to maintain and improve instructional programs.

- Obtain a copy of your district's most recent enrollment projections and interview the author as to how the projections were developed, e.g., methodology and data sources. Discuss the assumptions that were used for the projections. Consider how different assumptions or different methodologies might affect the projections now being used. Explore how the projections affect budget planning in the district.

- Talk to one or more school site administrators in your district to determine how they are involved in the budgeting process. Ask how they involve their staffs and other stakeholders, and how they prioritize requests when expenditures exceed budget allocations. Ask how they would improve the budget planning process.

- If your state, district, or school uses school site councils, find out the extent to which councils are involved in budget planning activities. Review state or school district policy documents and analyze the strengths and weaknesses of the decision-making roles these bodies play.

- Obtain a copy of your school district's budget calendar. Determine how and when your district obtains public input into the budget process at both formative and final stages. Interview your district's business manager or chief financial officer to determine how the district tries to ensure smooth passage of the final budget.

- Obtain a copy of your school and district budgets. Which budgeting approach described in this chapter is used in each? In your estimation, is this the optimal approach for your school or district? Explain your answer.

WEB RESOURCES

American Association of School Administrators, www.aasa.org

American Federation of Teachers, www.aft.org

Association of School Business Officials International, www.asbointl.org

U.S. Department of Energy, www.energy.gov

National Conference of State Legislatures, www.ncsl.org

National Education Association, www.nea.org

National Governors Association, www.nga.org

National School Boards Association, www.nsba.org

RECOMMENDED READING

Crampton, Faith E., and Randall S. Vesely. "Resource Allocation Issues for Educational Leaders." In *Handbook for Excellence in School Leadership*, 4th ed, edited by Stuart C. Smith and Philip K. Piele, 401–427. Thousand Oaks, CA: Corwin, 2006.

Foley, Ellen. "Student-Based Budgeting: The Potential for More Equitable Funding for Schools." Providence, RI: Brown University, Annenberg Institute for Education Reform, February 21,

2011. http://annenberginstitute.org/commentary/2011/02/student-based-budgeting-potential-more-equitable-funding-schools.

Government Finance Officers Association. "Making the Budget Document Easier to Understand." February 2014. www.gfoa.org/making-budget-document-easier-understand.

Kavanagh, Shayne. *Making the Grade: Long-Term Financial Planning for Schools*. Chicago: Government Finance Officers Association, 2007. www.gfoa.org/sites/default/files/GFOA MakingtheGradeLTFPforSchools.pdf.

Hartman, William T. *School District Budgeting*. Englewood Cliffs, NJ: Prentice Hall, 2002.

McCaffrey, Daniel F., J. R. Lockwood, Daniel M. Koretz, and Laura S. Hamilton. "Evaluating Value-Added Models for Teacher Accountability." Santa Monica, CA: Rand Corporation, 2003. www.rand.org/content/dam/rand/pubs/monographs/2004/RAND_MG158.pdf.

Ray, John, I. Carl Candoli, and Walter G. Hack. *School Business Administration: A Planning Approach*, 8th ed. Boston: Allyn & Bacon, 2005.

REL West. "School-Based Budgeting and Management." San Francisco, CA: WestEd, August 2009.

Sorensen, Richard D. and Goldsmith, Lloyd M. *The Principal's Guide to School Budgeting*. Thousand Oaks, CA: Corwin, 2006.

CHAPTER 6

Budgeting for Personnel

THE CHALLENGE

Elementary and secondary education is labor intensive; that is, much of the work educating children and young adults requires direct contact with education employees, be they teachers, professional and support staff, or administrators. School district budgets reflect the labor-intensive nature of pre-kindergarten through 12th grade education. It is not uncommon for 80% of the typical district budget to be personnel costs, which include salaries, wages, and benefits of all district employees.

Crampton and Vesely (2006)[1]

CHAPTER DRIVERS

Please reflect upon the following questions as you read this chapter:

- What is the scope of the personnel function in school districts?
- How are staffing needs determined?
- How do school districts successfully recruit and select staff?
- What other personnel budget issues must school districts consider?
- What are the issues in personnel compensation?
- What role do negotiations play in personnel and budget functions?
- What is current thinking about alternative reward systems?
- What are the fiscal and legal ramifications of RIFs and dismissals?
- Why is due process important in RIFs and dismissals?
- What are the roles of various stakeholders in personnel matters?

---

1 Faith E. Crampton and Randall S. Vesely, "Resource Allocation Issues for Educational Leaders," in *Handbook for Excellence in School Leadership*, 4th ed., edited by Stuart C. Smith and Philip K. Piele (Thousand Oaks, CA: Corwin, 2006), 401–427.

THE GENERAL LANDSCAPE

The opening quotation to this chapter and the combined weight of this text thus far point to a highly complex relationship between the aims of schooling and the adults in schools charged with carrying out the educational mission. The introduction to the budget process in the last chapter noted that the single largest proportion of public elementary and secondary education's costs is the human resource function. Today's school budgets are under significant stress, especially given the considerable costs of education reform. States have increased academic requirements for schools without corresponding increases in funding, and federal education reforms, such as the No Child Left Behind Act, have resulted in new costs for schools. These changes have repercussions throughout the entire school district budget. Personnel costs are the single largest item in public school budgets, a fact underscored in the previous chapter where it was emphasized that after estimating enrollments and envisioning educational programs, determining the total financial costs of salaries, wages, and benefits is the next most important task in balancing revenues and expenditures. As a consequence, this chapter examines the act of budgeting for personnel. It begins by considering the scope of the personnel function, followed by an examination of determining staffing needs for each school throughout a school district. The chapter then examines recruitment and selection along with an analysis of issues affecting compensation structures including those associated with traditional salary schedules and alternative reward systems. Finally, the chapter examines the legal context of budgeting for personnel; that is, the personnel budget cannot be separated from the myriad risks and obligations that have implications for school district resources. In sum, the act of budgeting for personnel consumes a major portion of a school district's finances—an act that in large measure determines the school district's ability to accomplish its educational mission.

THE PERSONNEL FUNCTION

As noted at the outset of this chapter, public elementary and secondary education is a labor-intensive industry. As such, it is often the focus of taxpayer concern when the annual school district budget is presented for public comment, debate, and input. However, it is important to remember that expenditures for salaries, wages, and fringe benefits have a positive impact on the total economy because school personnel are active consumers who spend substantial portions of their salaries in the local economy for necessities like food, housing, and clothing as well as discretionary expenditures such as restaurants and movies. Their consumption actually sustains or increases employment in community businesses. An additional point often missed by public education's critics is that school personnel also pay taxes—property, sales, income—that in turn contribute to the support of public schools as well as a variety of other tax-supported services. As such, the personnel function represents an investment rather than an expenditure over time. As a result, the personnel function is both a human resource and a fiscal resource.

The personnel function takes into account everyone who is employed by a school district. When the general public thinks of school employees, they immediately think of teachers. Although teachers are at the core of what schools do, this view is incomplete because the personnel function embraces both certificated staff (teachers, administrators, and other professionally licensed employees), noncertificated professional staff (accountants, technology and data specialists), and classified staff (secretaries, custodians, bus drivers, teacher aides, and cafeteria workers). All these individuals have indispensable roles in operating a school district. As school districts have become more organizationally complex and inclusive of the many elements that contribute to equal educational opportunity, the number of certificated and noncertificated employees has increased over time.

The size of the personnel function is exceeded only by its importance to successful school district operation. In fact, regardless of how well the fiscal operations of a school district are managed, the true success of a school district ultimately depends on the people who work with students each day. Recruitment, selection, employment, and retention of competent employees are the keys to cost-effective operation of elementary and secondary schools. The critical role of the personnel function has led most school districts to centralize this operation, with one person having line authority over all aspects of this function. Although administrative titles vary with local custom and even by school district size, an assistant superintendent for personnel, a director of human resources, or the superintendent may have direct responsibility for the personnel function. As school districts increase in size, responsibility often is further subdivided.

Regardless of how the personnel function is structured within the school district, good personnel administration requires clear written policies that assist in furthering the work of the school district and that link all operations under one authority. The specific authority and linkages should be specified in the school district policy manual that specifies all aspects of personnel policy. Good policies assure uniform communication and help monitor relationships between the goals of the school district and the expectations of personnel. Policies must be clearly stated in order to avoid confusion for either the employer or employee, promote accurate interpretation and legal evaluation in the event of serious disagreement and be clearly based on applicable state statutes. An added benefit of school district policies is to provide a blueprint for consistent action that will simultaneously enhance employee morale and increase productivity. Because program quality is a direct result of the skill of all staff working in unison, an effective and efficient school district wisely invests time and money in creating and maintaining sound personnel policies and operations.

When the personnel function is correctly assigned to an individual or office, governed by written policies and procedures, and organized efficiently, the benefit is evident in the form of strong leadership and good management. A school district that merely maintains the status quo cannot consistently improve its programs. Alternatively, reliance on charismatic leadership to the neglect of proper management of the personnel function endangers the school district in many ways, including liability for the many problems and conflicts that can arise between and among employees in a labor-intensive organization. The school district's overall goals and objectives cannot be met except by proper management of all instructional and support staffs. Although it is sometimes hard to distinguish between the nuances of leadership versus management, the point is that the organizational and directive functions of personnel must be carefully led and managed if the school district is to function effectively because schools rely on competent personnel to fulfill their goals.

The scope of the personnel function is broad, encompassing six major tasks:

1. Determining staffing needs
2. Recruiting and retaining the most competent staff
3. Assisting in individual development of competencies
4. Ensuring that staff are assigned and used efficiently
5. Increasing and improving staff satisfaction
6. Establishing clear expectations and ensuring competent performance evaluation

The critical nature of these tasks underscores the need for both leadership and management. The personnel function requires good leadership for school improvement, and good management is needed to ensure effective performance assessment. The personnel function thus *assesses staffing needs* and *recruits, selects, inducts, compensates, evaluates,* and *retains* employees. The personnel function also embraces other duties, including *discipline* and *dismissal* of unsatisfactory staff. These tasks are explored more fully here due to their close relationship with the act of creating a good budget.

Determining Staffing Needs

Ability to properly determine staffing needs is a function of organizing and using information concerning the school district and its current and prospective staff. All school districts maintain a database of employee information, if for no other reason than to calculate payroll. A basic database contains information on each employee's salary or wage; fringe benefits and their cost to employer and employee; and record of leave days. Personnel files generally include projected retirement information as well as records of employees' additional coursework, professional development, and training that may qualify them for raises and other types of monetary rewards pursuant to state statutes, collective bargaining agreements, and district policies. All school district employees, including part-time and temporary, should be included in the employee database although they may not have the same level of fringe benefits as permanent, full-time staff.

Information concerning the school district and staffing is interrelated and should be designed to permit electronic linking because, in every instance, the school district's profile drives staffing patterns.[2] The database should contain other information, such

---

2 Much information in personnel files is confidential and protected by federal and state privacy laws. When a school district builds linkages between databases (e.g., personnel and community demographics), it must take care to build in appropriate security measures so only those authorized

as population of the community, population of the schools, percentage of households with school-age children, ages of children in preschool through twelfth grade, in- and out-migration patterns, commercial and industrial characteristics of the district, major sources and types of employment, income and age of residents, and, of course, fiscal data on the school district itself. This information is useful as a general backdrop to a school district's annual enrollment projections. In most states, enrollment is the basis for state fiscal aid to the school district, and the population of a community drives student enrollment. It should not be missed that demographic data can be useful in predicting community attitudes toward schools and budgets.

While many school districts keep much employee information on file, it is often not effectively organized for projecting staffing needs. For example, small school districts may still keep employee information in paper files whereas larger school districts are more likely to use electronic databases. Although there is specialized software for management of human resources, many small school districts may find the cost prohibitive. However, they should not overlook database management software that now comes standard with many desktop computers as a possible resource for organizing personnel information electronically.

As a school district grows in size, the personnel database may contain information on prospective employees and projections of staff attrition by area and level. However, regardless of school district size, the creation of databases with community profiles and employee information is essential because they can be used to project whether staffing needs can be met internally, whether it will be necessary to hire new employees, or whether it will be necessary to reduce staff. Thus, the employee database should be broader than simple retrieval of professional licensure information; it should also permit other projections, such as calculating the cost of existing or proposed early retirement incentives.[3] Such information intersects with the budget function, in that the cost of early retirement plans (compared to other scenarios such as savings accrued through hiring less experienced staff) must be available when making long-term policy and staffing decisions. Likewise, projections indicating a need for new staff also require budget input. The use of extensive databases makes it possible to descriptively assess present reality and to forecast future scenarios—an obviously critical function for the budget side of planning and organization. In most instances, the basic database is built and maintained in the personnel office and electronically linked to the budget office.

Although each school district must develop databases to meet its unique needs, the goal is always the same. The personnel and budget functions in a school district

to view confidential personnel information have access to that data. See, e.g., "Public Sector Employee Privacy," in *Employment Law for Business*, 7th ed., by Dawn D. Bennett-Alexander and Laura P. Hartman (Boston: McGraw-Hill, 2011), 661–671.

3 It has been shown that early retirement plans, dependent upon the specifics, may not save public school districts moneys over lengthy periods of time. See, R. Craig Wood, "The Early Retirement Concept and a Fiscal Assessment Model for Public School Districts," *Journal of Education Finance* 7, no. 3 (1982): 262–276.

must share information, but the most frequent interaction occurs when staffing needs are reviewed. The personnel function annually considers whether the employment of current staff will continue, and those decisions must be coordinated with the budget office, which must find money for projected salaries. Sometimes, of course, the scenario is reversed: if the budget office finds that personnel costs are too high, then the personnel side must find ways to deal with economic reality. Although these functions are interdependent, the realities of the modern comprehensive school district cause the personnel function to most often drive the fiscal side by communicating to the business office staffing projections for the next school year.

Although a comprehensive community and staff database is essential, the technical side of determining staffing needs differs across states and individual districts. For example, some state education finance aid provisions calculate the number of pupils at each grade level and allocate staff positions to districts on a per-classroom basis. In this case, the school district has little meaningful control over the most basic personnel function of determining how many teachers it will hire because it can afford to hire only those teachers reimbursed through the state education finance distribution formula. In other states, local boards of education are free to decide how many staff members to hire by choosing among competing expenditure categories within overall budgetary constraints; for example, a choice to reduce overall class size may be at the expense of expanding extracurricular or academic enrichment programs. An example of a centralized system would be where a state education finance distribution formula converts full-time equivalency (FTE) students into staff units, which are then multiplied by a statewide salary and benefits schedule, with additional allocations for nonpersonnel-related costs. This formula has the practical effect of leveling expenditures (with staffing implications) downward in some school districts in order to bring greater fiscal parity across school districts in the state. At the opposite extreme are states that have tried to reduce class size, where state-initiated reform mandated lower pupil/teacher ratios with the practical effect of driving up staffing requirements for nearly all school districts at significant costs to local taxpayers. A middle-ground example of local decisions driving staffing is found in school districts with board of education policies limiting class size, with resultant staffing increases. A more complicated but common situation occurs when local boards of education have either been required by state law to negotiate class size or have voluntarily negotiated such agreements. In all these examples, it is clear that the personnel and budget functions are tightly linked.

Regardless of local circumstance, once a policy or law governing staffing is set, it is possible to apply the appropriate staffing formula to enrollments. After projecting enrollment, the process calls for applying a staffing formula, usually by dividing the number of students at each grade level by the approved ratio, yielding the required number of staff members. The process is typically carried out at the district level, with input from individual schools. A simple illustration using a single high school would result in the following staffing pattern:

Formula: *Enrollment + Approved Ratio = Staffing Needs**

421 ninth graders + 20:1 ratio = 21 ninth-grade teaching positions

373 tenth graders + 20:1   = 18.6 tenth-grade teaching positions

297 eleventh graders + 20:1   = 14.8 eleventh-grade teaching positions

312 twelfth graders + 20:1   = 15.6 twelfth-grade teaching positions

1,403 pupil FTE   = 70.0 teaching staff FTE

*This example considers only teaching staff—separate discussions about other staffing needs also must be carried out.

Of course, funding these positions is more difficult than simply calculating staffing needs, at times requiring adjustments to the staffing formula if funding is insufficient. This is especially true when enrollment fluctuates across years, across grades, or across school buildings. If the database reveals, for example, that other schools in the district are gaining enrollment and if our sample high school presently has 78 existing faculty (instead of the 70 needed next year), the school district could reassign the eight surplus teachers to other schools if their professional licensure matches vacancies. Obviously, this solution becomes more feasible as school district size increases because small school districts may have only one teacher per grade or only one high school. If reassignment is not feasible, reduction of full-time to part-time positions or layoffs may need to be considered.

Determining staffing is at once simple and complex. It is mathematically easy, but it is complex because such decisions affect real people and because governmental policy may limit the options. Regardless, sound decisions cannot be made without a comprehensive database that takes into account both community and employee profiles. For example, the school district in the scenario just described might be able to lessen the impact of staff reductions if the database holds information on attrition trends, retirements, or early contract buyouts. In a more positive vein, data can be used for targeted information-sharing such as in-house electronic notices to employees when vacancies arise. For many reasons, an orderly plan for determining staffing needs is the next step after projecting enrollment.

Recruitment and Selection

When openings occur, the next major task is recruitment, followed by selection of personnel. Regardless of the type of position, every employee classification needs a formal recruitment plan. The school district needs to make decisions regarding number and type of positions, as well as minimum and preferred qualifications for each employee classification. The budget and personnel functions intersect at this point once again, particularly regarding pay for current staff and whether the school district must hire entry-level or can afford more experienced or educated staff. The goal is to attract and retain the most highly qualified people. This goal may be difficult to achieve because the purpose is often at odds with the competing goal of minimizing taxpayer costs. Although there are no easy solutions, there are procedures available in the recruiting and selection process that soften the harshness of these realities.

At the outset of the recruiting process, the budget and personnel staffs should jointly produce a manual for the school district with a clear description of the hiring process, starting with application procedures and continuing through descriptions of screening committees, interviews, contract offers, and pay periods and amounts. Every current and prospective employee should be informed of training requirements and opportunities, and this information should be consistent within each employee classification. These procedures should be closely tied to position advertising by the school district and standardized with regard to internal and external search procedures consistent with equal opportunity selection of the best candidate for each vacancy. This manual is so important that it should be posted on the school district's web site.

After policies and procedures for recruitment have been set, the school district is ready to recruit. For large school districts, this may mean hiring on the basis of anticipated vacancies. With regard to teacher recruitment and hiring, large school systems often visit teacher recruitment fairs across the nation, hiring candidates for anticipated vacancies. In many instances, these school districts are taking little risk because they know that they will not be able to hire staff for all openings. In smaller school districts, the process is simpler; for example, these districts might advertise via university placement offices and wait for applications to arrive. Even here, however, the personnel and budget functions continue to intersect, as success in recruiting is related to how well the salary schedule is designed and funded. Because most states do not have uniform or statewide teacher salary schedules or, where state salary schedules do exist, local school districts are permitted to exceed the statewide salary schedule, recruitment is the joint responsibility of prudent personnel and budget planning.

When the school district has successfully determined its staffing needs and has recruited as effectively as it can, the selection process begins. Because success in meeting district goals depends on the quality of personnel, selection is a critical responsibility. Even though the depth of the candidate pool and the marketplace affect who is hired, it must be recognized that the school district's first obligation is to select employees on the basis of skills. Skills must be judged on the basis of documented training, relevant experience, and satisfactory performance. Additionally, many positions in a school district require specific licensure from the appropriate state agency. Every position should be filled only after the appropriate person, often the superintendent, has made a final recommendation to the board of education. As will be seen later in the chapter regarding legal liability, a valid employment offer usually cannot be made unless the board of education has approved the offer in a public meeting pursuant to state statute.

The intersecting and conflicting goals of the personnel and budget needs are most apparent at the time of selection. The goal of the personnel need is to select the most qualified person to perform the duties of a specific position. This applies across all position openings, regardless of whether the person is being interviewed for a teaching position or a custodial position. The goal of the budgetary need is to hire that same person within the constraints of a realistic budget. The budgeted amount for a position clearly affects the stated qualifications in the position opening as well as the recruitment plan. Selection thus involves many steps, all aimed at hiring the best candidate within the financial means of the school district. From the beginning of the process to its end, the relationship between the personnel and budget functions is apparent in that whatever job candidate is chosen, that position will have to be funded.

Other Personnel Budget Matters

Although it is beyond the scope of this text to deeply examine the personnel side of school district operations, as entire education personnel courses are necessary to do so, it is important to note that there are other issues of budgeting for personnel that go beyond recruitment and selection. The most obvious issue is compensation policies and procedures, a topic developed in detail in the last half of this chapter. Other personnel tasks, including induction, orientation, assignment, mentoring and ongoing support, evaluation, and staff development, also intersect with the school district budget because these activities require financial support and are costly if poorly done because the result can be suboptimal job performance. These issues are so important that they consume most of the time of the personnel office.

The scope of the personnel function and its relationship to the budget function is thus highly complex. In general, the personnel function can be described as working closely with the budget office to determine staffing needs based on enrollment projections in the context of salaries or wages and operating costs throughout the school district. More specifically, the personnel function in tandem with the budget function is usually responsible for the following:

- Recruitment and selection
  - Describing role expectations for positions
  - Assessing qualifications needed to fit the role
  - Compiling appropriate information on candidates
  - Evaluating candidates on role and personal expectations
  - Rating eligible candidates on the criteria
  - Making the employment decision from among choices

- Compensation policies and procedures
  - Placing the employee in the most appropriate position
  - Determining appropriate pay structures

- Personnel development
  - Inducting new staff into the district
  - Assigning staff to positions based on program needs
  - Orienting staff to the position and role

— Providing mentoring and ongoing support
— Evaluating staff on objective performance criteria
— Developing staff through additional training

PERSONNEL COMPENSATION POLICIES AND PROCEDURES

As emphasized previously, enrollment drives revenue, which in turn drives expenditures. For better or worse, these realities sometimes drive program decisions. As a result, we examine compensation policies and procedures in this section because inability to fund a sound staffing plan invariably impacts the quality and quantity of services available to students.

What Is the Role of Compensation?

The role of employee compensation is clear in the bulleted list in the previous section. Compensation is the reason most people work—it provides their livelihoods, rewards their professional achievements, and allows them to support their families. Compensation forms the basis for purchased services in schools and covers a range of work including administration; instruction and instructional support; transportation; food service; maintenance; and repair. As noted earlier, compensation is composed of not only salaries and wages,[4] but also fringe benefits offered by and paid for (in part or totally) by the district.[5] These usually include health insurance, pension,[6] and paid leave.[7]

---

4 Salaried employees are exempt from overtime pay but may be eligible for supplemental duty pay. Hourly wage employees are eligible for overtime pay. Districts must be careful to observe state and federal laws regarding overtime pay. For federal guidelines, see "Overtime Pay," U.S. Department of Labor, www.dol.gov/dol/topic/wages/overtimepay.htm.

5 Some employee benefits are required under federal law. These include workers' compensation insurance, unemployment insurance, FICA (Federal Insurance Contributions Act), and Medicare Hospital Insurance. Employers pay for the first two in full, while employers and employees both make contributions to FICA (Social Security) and Medicare.

6 Many states offer or require that school district employees participate in state retirement systems instead of or in addition to federal Social Security. Policies vary by state. In some states, employees are responsible for payments into the state retirement system while in others payments are shared between the district and the employee. In still others, the district pays the employee's share via a contractual agreement. In addition, some urban school districts have local retirement plans in addition to or instead of state retirement plans. For an overview of state education retirement plans see, Robert K. Toutkoushian, Justin M. Bathon, and Martha M. McCarthy, "A National Study of the Net Benefits of State Pension Plans for Educators," *Journal of Education Finance* 37, no. 1 (Summer 2011): 24–51.

7 Paid leave can take several forms, such as sick leave, bereavement leave, and personal leave. Districts can also offer unpaid leave. In addition, employees are entitled to unpaid leave under relevant federal and state laws. At the federal level, this includes unpaid leave under the Family and Medical Leave Act of 1993. See "Fact Sheet #28: The Family and Medical Leave Act of 1993," U.S. Department of Labor, www.dol.gov/whd/regs/compliance/whdfs28.htm.

In sum, the strength of the total compensation package can be the basis for employees' willingness to enter an employment contract.[8]

General Issues

When the topic of public school pay is raised, most people think of salaried employees like administrators and teachers. This section is focused on teachers' salaries not only because they represent a significant portion of a school district's personnel expenditures but also because they receive a substantial amount of public scrutiny, by community members, the state, and also by the media. Historically, single-salary schedules for teachers were developed as a means to correct pay inequities that discriminated according to race, gender, and grade-level differences across the nation. Additionally, in many school districts teachers were paid based on political party affiliation or other nonmeritorious bases. Although modern opponents argue that the single-salary schedule discourages individual merit, proponents have long held that it is superior to other choices because it fosters better working relationships, is less expensive to administer, and avoids problems such as favoritism, discrimination, and retaliation.[9] Nor is the concept of a single-salary schedule unique to school districts since a number of local, state, and even federal governmental units use a similar approach.

Administration of all forms of employee compensation begins with determination and formulation of a job description for each position in a school district. Complete, detailed, written descriptions should be developed for every employee classification. If done properly, job descriptions are based on surveys, interviews, and assessments of what every job classification is expected to contribute to organizational goals. Job descriptions should be very clear so that all parties can agree on the nature, duties, and expectations of the position. Each position should have a performance-based job explanation that includes statements about the method and amount of compensation. Evaluation of performance based on goals can then follow; performance should form the basis for an employee's location on the salary schedule. Obviously, descriptions vary by position. For example, the job description of a school principal is different from and far more complex than the job description for a school secretary. Examples of job descriptions for these two positions are shown in Figures 6.1 and 6.2.

Although job descriptions should result in objective salary decisions based on placement of employees according to school district salary schedule policies, the actual salary structure is usually a function of two realities. In some states, collective bargaining applies to both certificated and classified employee groups. In other states, teachers bargain under collective negotiations, while classified employees and administrators are outside the negotiations law. In such instances, nonteaching staff salaries and wages

---

8 It should be noted that our discussion refers to full-time employees. Fringe benefits for part-time employees may differ significantly.

9 It is noted that some economists attempt to classify all single schedule salary plans as inefficient in that certain teachers are perhaps paid more than they are actually worth, while others are paid less than their level of productivity.

are often a function of prevailing rates obtained by informal and formal comparisons with comparable school districts. Once salaries are in place, annual adjustments across employee groups are often a function of similar percentage increases. For example, it is unlikely that administrators will receive a much higher percentage salary increase than teachers simply because of the negative publicity it would attract. In states where nonteaching staff have no legal bargaining status, it is likely that salaries and wages will be decided after collective negotiations with teachers are complete, with percentage increases closely conforming.

Negotiations

The fiscal aspect of collective bargaining can be time-intensive and complex. Because so much is at stake, both financially and in terms of future working relationships, it is important for all parties to develop trust and respect for each side's information and philosophical position. Many school districts hold informal contract discussions during the school year about employment concerns, including compensation. Discussions should always be with appropriate employee association or union leaders in order to avoid committing an unfair labor practice under applicable state statutes. Throughout the school year and in multiyear contracts as well, dialogue with all groups eases the negotiations process by preventing tensions from growing and silently festering.

The negotiation process is unique in each state because of different bargaining laws. The National Labor Relations Act of 1935[10] dictates that for employees of state, county, and municipal governments, including public school districts, collective bargaining rights are governed by state statutes and are not covered by federal law. Thus, collective bargaining rights and subjects are totally controlled by state laws and state courts. In principle, however, the steps are similar depending on the extent to which outside arbitration is required. At whatever time of year salary and contract discussions begin, the budget office is called on by the personnel division to provide salary data for use in making fiscal projections and to provide cost analyses of any salary proposals. The reason is that short- and long-range costs must be known for all salary and contractual proposals before agreement can be reached regarding a new compensation plan. The budget office must consider not only all direct costs of salary and fringe benefits, but also cash flow, cost of employee time, and any other items placed on the negotiations table by either side. Each of these issues must be analyzed for present and future costs and for the long-range impact on school district financial health. The essence of all these activities is to conduct negotiations in good faith and to accurately anticipate all costs of compensation in order to balance revenues and expenditures in the final budget.

---

10 29 U.S.C. §151–169.

Position Title: Elementary School Principal

Basic Function: Administers the school under the supervision of the assistant
superintendent. Provides leadership to faculty and students; manages
and directs all activities.

Performance Responsibilities:
1. Demonstrates leadership through beliefs, skills, and personal characteristics
2. Ensures that teachers plan and provide effective instruction
3. Monitors, assesses, and supervises the approved district curriculum
4. Develops an effective staff development program
5. Promotes a positive school climate by encouraging capabilities of all
individuals
6. Uses a variety of data to improve the school's instructional program
7. Coordinates development of a written statement of the school's beliefs and
goals
8. Determines whether the individual educational needs of pupils are being
met
9. Evaluates the performance of the certified and classified staff members
10. Interprets, implements, and maintains school board policies and state
school laws
11. Develops a program of public relations to further community support
12. Administers the school's budgeted allocations
13. Directs activities involving pupil and parent contacts concerning
registrations, credits and transfers, suspensions, expulsions, pupil
progress, placement, guidance and counseling matters, and other matters
of a personal nature
14. Possesses a thorough understanding of child growth and development
15. Engages in a program of continuing professional development
16. Orients newly assigned staff members and ensures their familiarization with
school policies and procedures, teaching materials, and school facilities
17. Creates a strong sense of togetherness through human relations techniques
18. Possesses skill in conflict resolution, decision making, and consensus
building
19. Performs other related duties as requested

Requirements: Valid certificate and five years of teaching experience.
Salary commensurate with experience.

FIGURE 6.1 Sample Job Description for Elementary School Principal

Source: Adapted from Denver Public Schools, Division of Personnel Services.

Job Title: School Secretary

Qualifications: Under regular supervision, performs routine to moderately complex clerical and/or secretarial work to ensure efficient and effective office operations

Reports To: This person reports directly to the principal.

Supervises: There are no supervisor responsibilities.

Job Goal: To perform a variety of routine clerical/secretarial duties and some specialized duties as assigned by the principal

Performance Responsibilities:
1. Greet all guests entering the office area and communicate with a variety of individuals and groups, including immediate supervisor, coworkers, other school administrators and staff, district administrators and staff, parents and guardians, students, and the general public
2. Refer all guests to appropriate offices or school personnel
3. Answer telephone and receive and deliver messages
4. Assist with student enrollment and withdrawal application process
5. Update and transfer yearly academic permanent records and transcripts of all students
6. Order and maintain inventory of office and teacher supplies
7. Update employee contact information for phone directory and database system
8. Maintain appearance of front office and workroom
9. Respond to inquiries and requests for information and assistance from school and district personnel, students, parents, and the general public; provide copies of printed informational materials as requested
10. Enter and retrieve computer data
11. Input data from discipline referrals
12. Maintain hard copy of discipline records for all students
13. Collect information on students recommended for expulsion
14. Prepare all records and correspondence for parents and district hearing officer for expulsion hearings
15. Perform all bookkeeping duties as required to maintain accurate school accounting procedures
16. Collect, receipt, record, and deposit various school revenues; prepare billing invoices as required; maintain individual accounts as assigned, including pupil activity accounts
17. Prepare purchase orders and process invoices for payment
18. Prepare records for internal and external audits

Physical Requirements: Requires sedentary work that involves walking, bending, or standing some of the time and involves exerting up to 10 pounds of force on a recurring basis and routine keyboard operations.

Evaluation: Performance of this job will be evaluated in accordance with board policy.

FIGURE 6.2 Sample Job Description for School Secretary

Source: Adapted from Lexington School District 4 Human Resources, www.lex4.k12.sc.us/index.php?option=com_content&view=article&id=246:school-secretary&catid=51:classified-job-descriptions&Itemid=98.

Basic Components of Collective Negotiations

Collective negotiations are governed by state statute. State statutes as well as administrative rules and regulations vary from state to state from those with highly favorable employee relations to a total inability of employees to negotiate in any manner. Thus, this section is an overview that must be applied within pertinent statutes, administrative rules, and regulations. After the relevant salary and contract data are collected and verified by both sides, the negotiations process is ready to begin. Agreement on the facts makes bargaining easier because the school district's position at the table, the potential for favorable review at impasse or arbitration, and the union's receptiveness are all enhanced. Items on which initial agreement should be sought include cash projections, the impact of these data on the school district, historical data related to the issues, and data showing how the school district compares to other school districts of similar profile in the region and state. Careful preparation and presentation always increases the potential for success at the bargaining table, as well as aiding favorable treatment if fact-finding and arbitration should eventually be required.

The principal goal of both sides in contract negotiations should be to have a reasonable discussion regarding the facts in order to agree on a fair salary and benefits package. When agreement is struck, any changes are applied to the appropriate salary and benefit schedules. For example, for certificated teaching staff the first and most direct impact is often adjustment to the salary schedule, both in terms of dollars and any changes to the structure of the schedule itself. For noncertificated staff, the impact occurs either in similar application to the relevant salary or wage schedule or by adjustment to each individual's contracted salary or wage. The goal of fairness must be extended to the fringe benefit package as well. Thus, data reflecting the need to attract and retain high quality staff, as well as to promote employee development, must be balanced with the ability of the school district to fund contractual obligations.

During the negotiations process, both management and labor come to the bargaining table with items they expressly want to negotiate. Preparation on the part of the school district focuses on collecting and examining financial data and any other current concerns of the school district. The employee organization has interest in these same items, although for mostly different reasons. Items brought to the table by both sides are fairly common and include the following:

- *Strengths and weaknesses* of the entire contract
- *Salary schedule*, including number and costs of each cell of the salary matrix over the life of the contract and a projection into the near future
- *Basic data* on minimum, maximum, and average cost per employee over the life of the contract
- *Comparative salaries* in competing school districts and industries
- *Living standards* of the local community
- *Personnel turnover*, including pending retirements
- *Movement on the salary schedule* due to advanced education/training, experience, and other criteria

- *New program needs and curtailments*
- *Future revenues and expenditures*, including tax levies and state aid projections

In addition, the school district and employee groups will need to gather and bring other nonfinancial data to the table. Generally this consists of such issues as the following:

- Are there parts of the contract that have not worked well?
- Is there a pattern of grievances over parts of the contract?
- Should parts of the contract be modified or dropped?
- What new issues may prove problematic?

These data are critical to the negotiations process and to compensation policies because without good data costs cannot be projected and the ability to fund a future contract is unknown. Indeed, the school district's fiscal integrity is at the mercy of accurate data.

Costing-Out Salary Proposals

Although terms and conditions of employment make up a large part of the total negotiations process, the most elemental aspect comes when salary is discussed. It is at salary time when the personnel and budget functions are most closely related because, if contract agreement is not reached, the district is likely to suffer low staff morale.

For certificated staff, discussion of salary is likely to center on improving the basic structure of the salary schedule and on increasing the dollar amount of the base salary while taking into consideration any increase in the cost of fringe benefits. Table 6.1 contains several tables related to a single-salary schedule for a sample school district, and provides an illustration of how contract negotiations occur. The first table shows the index (or percent of base, where base equals $25,000) that computes the dollars for each position. The second table then translates those percentages of the base into salary amounts. The third table applies these salares plus benefits to individual teaching staff for this school year and the next, indicating the additional cost for next year would be $3,000. The fourth table proposes a new base of 26,000. Using the same percentages as the first table, the fifth table presents the new salary amounts. The sixth and final table applies these new salary amounts to teaching staff and adds $300 in fringe benefits to come up with a $13,940 increase over the previous year. Hence, these tables provide concrete information to negotiators as to the impact of a $1,000 increase to the base salary and a 10% increase in the cost of fringe benefits.

In addition to an increase in base salary which we saw in Table 6.1, other enhancements to the salary schedule might be proposed in negotiations. Second, for those districts that do not recognize advanced education and degrees beyond the B.A., adding "columns" to reward these, as done in Table 6.1, may be proposed. A third proposal might be to add steps at the bottom of some or all columns as a reward for years of teaching experience in the school district. Naturally, all of these proposals will increase the district's personnel costs. On the other hand, in order to reduce personnel costs, the district's negotiating team might seek more restrictive language on nonsalary items, such as limiting or refining discretionary leaves. Realistically, negotiating a salary decrease is highly unlikely except under conditions of severe fiscal exigency. Then, at best, the school district might obtain agreement on a salary freeze.

All changes to salary schedules must be considered carefully. The effect of increasing the base 4% or $1,000 is seen in Table 6.1. Importantly, increasing the base by even a modest amount affects the entire schedule because each step is indexed to the base. In addition, current teachers will receive a step increase in the next school year. Also, given the relative maturity of many teaching staffs throughout the United States, care must be taken in salary negotiations because, as salary schedules load on experience, personnel cost rise, although at least in the short run, the higher cost of experienced staff may be offset due to turnover.[11] Hence, a modest $1,000 base increase raises personnel costs by $13,940 as shown in Table 6.1 (Note that $300 was added to fringe benefits to reflect an increase in health insurance costs). The cost of increasing the number of columns cannot be ascertained from data in Table 6.1 although the general impact can be seen. Needless to say, salaries for teachers with advanced degrees are more expensive, so that in spite of the benefits of well-qualified staff, the district must be cognizant of the increased personnel costs involved.

The third proposal, to add steps to existing columns, is also costly. The purpose, of course, is to recognize, reward, and retain experienced teachers. Adding steps, for example, beyond the 18 years of experience in Table 6.1, may be much higher than it first appears. Before a school district enters into such an agreement, it should determine how many teachers would qualify for vertical movement. Additionally, the school district should try to determine how many of those individuals might qualify to move horizontally due to additional coursework or attainment of an advanced degree. In other words, both horizontal and vertical movement on the salary schedule add to the total cost of adding steps.

Data in this brief illustration have many applications. One of the most important benefits is the ability to automate the salary schedule for instant "what-if" scenarios. Salary schedules, such as the illustrated, Table 6.1, can be placed in a spreadsheet, so that as the base changes, all other cells are updated. Also, both sides can immediately see the effect. Both sides also profit from the entire negotiations process in that, although the board of education will have to increase salaries next year at the budget's expense, it does so willingly in exchange for the least dollar amount possible at which it can hire and retain highly qualified employees. It is important for board members, administrators, teachers, and the public as a whole to understand that collective bargaining is a series of compromises and that one side rarely has complete success.

---

11 Edwyna Synar and Jeffrey Maiden, "A Comprehensive Model for Estimating the Financial Impact of Teacher Turnover," *Journal of Education Finance* 38, no. 2 (Fall, 2012): 130–144; Abigail J. Levy, Lois Joy, Pamela Ellis Erica Jablonski, and Tzur M. Karelitz, "Estimating Teacher Turnover Costs: A Case Study," *Journal of Education Finance* 38, no. 2 (Fall, 2012): 102–129.

TABLE 6.1 Sample Salary Schedule

BASE = $25,000

YEAR	BA + 0	BA + 15	BA + 30	Masters	MS + 15	MS + 30	Doctorate
1	100%	102%	104%	106%	108%	110%	112%
2	102%	104%	106%	108%	110%	112%	114%
3	104%	106%	108%	110%	112%	114%	116%
4	106%	108%	110%	112%	114%	116%	118%
5	108%	108%	112%	114%	116%	118%	120%
6	110%	112%	114%	116%	118%	120%	122%
7	112%	114%	116%	118%	120%	122%	124%
8	114%	116%	118%	120%	122%	124%	126%
9		118%	120%	122%	124%	126%	128%
10		120%	122%	124%	126%	128%	130%
11			124%	126%	128%	130%	132%
12			126%	128%	130%	132%	134%
13				130%	132%	134%	136%
14				132%	134%	136%	138%
15					136%	138%	140%
16					138%	140%	142%
17						142%	144%
18							146%

YEAR	BA + 0	BA + 15	BA + 30	Masters	MS + 15	MS + 30	Doctorate
1	$ 25,000	$ 25,500	$ 26,000	$ 26,500	$ 27,000	$ 27,500	$ 28,000
2	$ 25,500	$ 26,000	$ 26,500	$ 27,000	$ 27,500	$ 28,000	$ 28,500
3	$ 26,000	$ 26,500	$ 27,000	$ 27,500	$ 28,000	$ 28,500	$ 29,000
4	$ 26,500	$ 27,000	$ 27,500	$ 28,000	$ 28,500	$ 29,000	$ 29,500
5	$ 27,000	$ 27,000	$ 28,000	$ 28,500	$ 29,000	$ 29,500	$ 30,000
6	$ 27,500	$ 28,000	$ 28,500	$ 29,000	$ 29,500	$ 30,000	$ 30,500
7	$ 28,000	$ 28,500	$ 29,000	$ 29,500	$ 30,000	$ 30,500	$ 31,000
8		$ 29,000	$ 29,500	$ 30,000	$ 30,500	$ 31,000	$ 31,500
9		$ 29,500	$ 30,000	$ 30,500	$ 31,000	$ 31,500	$ 32,000
10		$ 30,000	$ 30,500	$ 31,000	$ 31,500	$ 32,000	$ 32,500
11			$ 31,000	$ 31,500	$ 32,000	$ 32,500	$ 33,000
12			$ 31,500	$ 32,000	$ 32,500	$ 33,000	$ 33,500
13				$ 32,500	$ 33,000	$ 33,500	$ 34,000
14				$ 33,000	$ 33,500	$ 34,000	$ 34,500
15					$ 34,000	$ 34,500	$ 35,000
16					$ 34,500	$ 35,000	$ 35,500
17						$ 35,500	$ 36,000
18							$ 36,500

Projections based on zero dollar increase on base (see asterisk note below).

Name	Current salary	Current benefits	Current pkg.	New salary	New benefits	Proposed pkg.	% increase
Mary A.	$ 25,000	$ 3,000	$ 28,000	$ 25,500	$ 3,000	$ 28,500	1.8%
Bob B.	$ 29,500	$ 3,000	$ 32,500	$ 30,000	$ 3,000	$ 33,000	1.5%
Julie C. (frozen)	$ 31,500	$ 3,000	$ 34,500	$ 31,500	$ 3,000	$ 34,500	0.0%
James D.	$ 26,500	$ 3,000	$ 29,500	$ 27,000	$ 3,000	$ 30,000	1.7%
Janet E.	$ 33,500	$ 3,000	$ 36,500	$ 34,000	$ 3,000	$ 37,000	1.4%
Bill F. (frozen)	$ 36,500	$ 3,000	$ 39,500	$ 36,500	$ 3,000	$ 39,500	0.0%
Paula G.***	$ 35,500	$ 3,000	$ 38,500	$ 36,500	$ 3,000	$ 39,500	2.6%
and so on ...							
TOTALS	$ 218,000	$ 21,000	$239,000	$ 221,000	$ 21,000	$ 242,000	1.28%

COST TO FUND
$ 3,000

***will obtain doctorate by end of current school year.

TABLE 6.1 *continued*

BASE = $26,000

YEAR	BA + 0	BA + 15	BA + 30	Masters	MS + 15	MS + 30	Doctorate
1	100%	102%	104%	106%	108%	110%	112%
2	102%	104%	106%	108%	110%	112%	114%
3	104%	106%	108%	110%	112%	114%	116%
4	106%	108%	110%	112%	114%	116%	118%
5	108%	108%	112%	114%	116%	118%	120%
6	110%	112%	114%	116%	118%	120%	122%
7	112%	114%	116%	118%	120%	122%	124%
8	114%	116%	118%	120%	122%	124%	126%
9		118%	120%	122%	124%	126%	128%
10		120%	122%	124%	126%	128%	130%
11			124%	126%	128%	130%	132%
12			126%	128%	130%	132%	134%
13				130%	132%	134%	136%
14				132%	134%	136%	138%
15					136%	138%	140%
16					138%	140%	142%
17						142%	144%
18							146%

YEAR	BA + 0	BA + 15	BA + 30	Masters	MS + 15	MS + 30	Doctorate
1	$ 26,000	$ 26,520	$ 27,040	$ 27,560	$ 28,080	$ 28,600	$ 29,120
2	$ 26,520	$ 27,040	$ 27,560	$ 28,080	$ 28,600	$ 29,120	$ 29,640
3	$ 27,040	$ 27,560	$ 28,080	$ 28,600	$ 29,120	$ 29,640	$ 30,160
4	$ 27,560	$ 28,080	$ 28,600	$ 29,120	$ 29,640	$ 30,160	$ 30,680
5	$ 28,080	$ 28,080	$ 29,120	$ 29,640	$ 30,160	$ 30,680	$ 31,200
6	$ 28,600	$ 29,120	$ 29,640	$ 30,160	$ 30,680	$ 31,200	$ 31,720
7	$ 29,120	$ 29,640	$ 30,160	$ 30,680	$ 31,200	$ 31,720	$ 32,240
8	$ 29,640	$ 30,160	$ 30,680	$ 31,200	$ 31,720	$ 32,240	$ 32,760
9		$ 30,680	$ 31,200	$ 31,720	$ 32,240	$ 32,760	$ 33,280
10		$ 31,200	$ 31,720	$ 32,240	$ 32,760	$ 33,280	$ 33,800
11			$ 32,240	$ 32,760	$ 33,280	$ 33,800	$ 34,320
12			$ 32,760	$ 33,280	$ 33,800	$ 34,320	$ 34,840
13				$ 33,800	$ 34,320	$ 34,840	$ 35,360
14				$ 34,320	$ 34,840	$ 35,360	$ 35,880
15					$ 35,360	$ 35,880	$ 36,400
16					$ 35,880	$ 36,400	$ 36,920
17						$ 36,920	$ 37,440
18							$ 37,960

Projections based on $1,000 increase on base plus $300 fringe.

Name	Current salary	Current benefits	Current pkg.	New salary	New benefits	Proposed pkg.	% increase
Mary A.	$ 25,000	$ 3,000	$ 28,000	$ 26,520	$ 3,300	$ 29,820	6%
Bob B.	$ 29,500	$ 3,000	$ 32,500	$ 31,200	$ 3,300	$ 34,500	6%
Julie C.	$ 31,500	$ 3,000	$ 34,500	$ 32,760	$ 3,300	$ 36,060	5%
James D.	$ 26,500	$ 3,000	$ 29,500	$ 28,080	$ 3,300	$ 31,380	6%
Janet E.	$ 33,500	$ 3,000	$ 36,500	$ 35,360	$ 3,300	$ 38,660	6%
Bill F.	$ 36,500	$ 3,000	$ 39,500	$ 37,960	$ 3,300	$ 41,260	4%
Paula G.***	$ 35,500	$ 3,000	$ 38,500	$ 37,960	$ 3,300	$ 41,260	7%
and so on ...							
TOTALS	$ 218,000	$ 21,000	$ 239,000	$ 229,840	$ 23,100	$ 252,940	5.87%

COST TO FUND
$ 13,940

***will obtain doctorate by end of current school year.

If the district anticipates staffing needs, recruits and selects highly qualified staff, and prepares and uses budget data for sound personnel compensation policies, both sides have a better chance of reaching an acceptable compromise.

Whatever proposals come to the table, several features must be understood and accepted. Negotiations can be confrontational, but the risk of bad relationships can be minimized through transparency and trust. Second, a decision to meaningfully improve the salary schedule may come at a cost to other operations. However, failing to provide competitive salaries and benefits is destructive to long-term school district health at many levels. Third, it is important to understand that an average 3% increase in teacher salaries, for example, will likely result in a 3% increase for all nonteaching staff, including administrators. In sum, a single decision to increase teacher salaries can have broad implications for all personnel costs across the district. Furthermore, annual state aid increases may not be sufficient to cover all new costs, making it necessary to either raise taxes, where statutorily permissible, or reduce other operating expenditures.

The personnel and budget functions work directly with both sides in the negotiations process through the production of data and determination of the costs of proposals. In many instances, the board of education's chief negotiator may be an administrator such as the superintendent or an assistant superintendent for personnel and/or finance; or the chief negotiator may be an attorney, selected for his or her experience of negotiated collective bargaining agreements in the public sector of a given state. Regardless of who serves as the board of education's spokesperson, the personnel and finance functions should be aware of the progress of negotiations and should be continuously consulted to determine the viability of any proposed actions.

Whoever serves in the lead role must exhibit certain skills and knowledge if the outcome is to be successful. The chief negotiator must be familiar with the state's collective bargaining statutes and knowledgeable about state unfair labor practice rulings, as well as having experience and prior success in such matters. Additionally, the negotiator should be emotionally mature, articulate, flexible, and able to reject ideas without alienating the other side.

In addition to the spokesperson, the board of education's team often consists of the chief fiscal officer for the school district, a recorder, a board subcommittee, and others as appropriate. Team composition varies by local custom. Teachers are often represented by an attorney, a professional association or union official, or a suitable local faculty member; that is, each school district differs in the culture of negotiations. Most negotiating sessions follow certain customs—for example, only spokespersons may speak, written initial nonexpandable proposals must be exchanged in advance, and each team keeps its own set of notes. Generally, caucuses are unlimited unless agreed otherwise. Again, it must be stressed that each state varies in statutory guidelines and local custom; for example, in some states bargaining sessions may be closed to the public. The scope of a sample state negotiations law is provided in Figure 6.3.

Mandatorily Negotiable

1. Salary	14. Jury duty
2. Wages	15. Grievance procedure
3. Pay under supplemental contracts	16. Binding arbitration
4. Hours of work	17. Discipline procedure
5. Amounts of work	18. Resignations
6. Vacation allowance	19. Contract termination
7. Holiday leave	20. Contract nonrenewal
8. Sick leave	21. Reemployment
9. Extended leave	22. Contract terms
10. Sabbatical leaves	23. Contract form
11. "Other" leaves	24. Probationary period
12. Number of holidays	25. Evaluation
13. Retirement	26. Insurance benefits
	27. Overtime pay

Permissibly Negotiable

1. Academic and personal freedom (except constitutional)	7. Teacher copyrights
2. Assignment and transfer of personnel	8. Facilities, equipment, materials, supplies
3. Association rights	9. Grading frequency
4. Class size	10. Security
5. Classroom management	11. Substitutes
6. School library hours	12. Teacher aides

Nonnegotiable

1. Number of days or total hours of school	5. First Amendment issues
2. Nondiscrimination	6. Affirmative action
3. Special education placement procedures	7. Student discipline if constitutional issue
4. Teacher discipline if constitutional issue	8. Federal programs

FIGURE 6.3 Sample Negotiations Law

Impasse Resolution

Despite best efforts, negotiations may fail and move to impasse. Under most states' statutes, school districts are required to recognize impasse and to engage in fact-finding, followed either by binding arbitration or by unilateral board of education contracts. Generally, impasse and fact-finding occur when the parties cannot reach agreement on terms and conditions of a new employment contract by some date specified in state statute. For both the personnel and budget functions, failure to successfully negotiate a new contract introduces uncertainty and tension into employer–employee relations— stress that is difficult to heal.

When negotiations reach impasse, most states statutes invoke a timeline calling for a third party to examine the last best offers from both sides, review the facts, and issue a report. Depending on state statute, this person may be a representative of the state's employment relations board or a person approved by some other state agency. Fact-finding in many states is not binding, but it is persuasive to the parties. In contrast, however, some states require mediation and/or binding arbitration if fact-finding does not produce a settlement. Mediation usually precedes arbitration, although in practice each state's statutes are unique. In several states, binding arbitration is immediately invoked: an impartial panel issues a report and both sides must accept the decision. Such a ruling cannot be challenged unless it can be successfully argued that the arbitrator exceeded legal authority. In other states, the process only calls for impasse, fact-finding, mediation, and issuance of unilateral contracts if agreement has still not been reached. In all instances, a statutory timeline like the one in Table 6.2 must be followed.

TABLE 6.2 Sample Negotiations Timeline

February 1	Exchange of notices and proposals. A petition to the state to declare impasse may be filed.
June 1	Notice of impasse must be filed if applicable.
June 5	Five days set aside for consultation with state on impasse.
June 15	State issues findings. Arbitration process begun if needed.
June 20	Fact-finding board appointed with 5 days.
July 10	Fact-finding report issued within 20 days.
Immediate	Parties must meet to discuss fact-finding results.
July 20	Report made public after 10 days.
July 30	Board may issue unilateral contracts if no agreement has been reached.

In certain states where binding arbitration exists, the budget and personnel functions are unable to issue contracts, set budgets, or engage in most employment contract activities until negotiations are settled. This can be uncomfortable for both sides since they often must continue to work together, especially in states where public employee strikes are prohibited. Even more complex, as a public policy as dictated by the state legislature, however, is the total subjugation of the school district to the will of an outside arbitrator who may make a decision that is financially difficult to fulfill. In states without binding arbitration, issues are tense too, but the budget and personnel functions can resume operation earlier. At the opposite end of the spectrum, the issue of salary costs in unilateral contract states is obviously under far greater control.

Pursuant to applicable state statute, negotiations are repeated with each employee group. When contracts are finally settled, a major task of the budget and personnel functions is complete and these divisions can resume employer–employee relationships in which the new contract is administered on a daily basis.

OTHER ISSUES OF PERSONNEL BUDGETING

Although labor contract negotiations are the most critical element of school district budgets once projecting enrollment and estimating staff needs are complete, there are other important issues in budgeting for personnel. For legislators, school boards, administrators, staffs, and communities, three particular areas are important because they impact compensation structures and financial liability. These areas are proposals for *alternative reward systems, reductions-in-force and other dismissals,* and *due process* concerns.

Alternative Reward Systems

A recurring theme related to compensation in public schools is the concept of alternative reward systems for teachers. Most common and longstanding among these systems is the concept of merit pay. More recently, individuals calling for total redesign of compensation systems have offered up a variety of plans, including salary incentives for knowledge- and skills-based performance; differentiated duty pay; differentiated staffing; extra pay for national board certification; and cash incentives such as signing bonuses and supplemental pay to attract classroom teachers to fields where teacher supply is low or to attract high-performing teachers to low-achieving schools. In all cases, the purpose is evident—to aggressively attract the most competent classroom teachers to the field and to reward them along some discriminating performance dimension. In fact, there is relatively little difference between the aims of traditional merit pay and the aims of these other alternative reward systems; both aim not merely to provide additional compensation for additional duties, but to reward superior performance on school or district goals by identifying performance differences between people with similar jobs.

Although any differential reward system for teacher pay has long been subjected to strenuous criticism, there is evidence that school budgets increasingly will be expected to financially support some type of merit pay plan. Despite opponents' claims that merit systems are often based on unproven evaluation methods, induce discord on goals, and generally fail to accurately measure performance over time in any consistent fashion, merit systems continue to make inroads. Recent examples are found in a number of states where the concept of merit pay by value added measures or otherwise linking student achievement with individual classroom teacher performance awards is being actively explored.[12] Broadly, these performance plans include differentiated pay plans that reward additional responsibilities and offer titles and duties involving mentoring, peer coaching, and serving as lead teachers; differentiated staffing plans recognizing advanced achievement and offering additional responsibilities and longer contract years along with titles such as career teacher or master teacher; knowledge- and skill-based pay aimed at rewarding those persons who demonstrate named competencies at apprentice and mastery levels; and other state and local school-based performance award plans tied to achieving established performance goals.[13] Whether merit pay strictly defined or whether some other performance-based plan is imminent seems not to be the major question; that is, school districts will continue to budget for single-salary schedules, but the public policy of alternative reward systems will increasingly join the compensation picture in a meaningful fashion.

As school districts build budgets, two key concerns regarding alternative pay systems should predominate. First, for the school or district level administrator there is a concern for how redesigned compensation systems will affect the school district's internal working relationships. The vast majority of those advocating such merit pay plans are those outside the public education system.

Second, district administrators should be concerned regarding how alternative pay systems will augment or supplant traditional pay structures and the resultant fiscal impact on the school district. While single-salary schedules are costly affairs, with only modest changes rippling nearly exponentially throughout the entire schedule, it is nearly inviolate that alternative compensation plans cost more, either by supplementing existing salary schedules or by substantially supplanting them. In either case, the costs will be at least additive, and it is rare when political entities driving such reforms also fully fund those same reforms. In sum, school districts have reason to celebrate when compensation systems offer increased rewards, but the consequence and total cost of those systems need to be uppermost—at the legislative lobbying level, at contract negotiation time, and at budget management time.

RIF and Other Dismissals

A second area of concern for the budget process involves reduction-in-force (RIF) and other dismissals. RIFs occur when school districts have more staff than they need, and other dismissals occur for reasons such as unsatisfactory performance. Although dismissals are carried out through the personnel function, the budget is impacted because

12 Stuart S. Yeh, "The Reliability, Impact, and Cost-Effectiveness of Value Added Teacher Assessment Methods," *Journal of Education Finance* 37, no. 4 (Spring, 2012): 374–399.

13 Katharine O. Strunk and Dara Zeehandelaar, "Differentiated Compensation: How California School Districts Use Economic Incentives to Target Teachers," *Journal of Education Finance* 36, no. 3 (Winter, 2011): 268–293.

salary and benefits will be terminated, a new hire may be contemplated, and any dismissal always involves risk related to wrongful acts on the part of the school district. In sum, the budget and personnel functions must minimize the damage and estimate the impact of these actions.[14]

In contrast to merit pay, which offers more money for desired behaviors, RIF reduces expenditure from a school district's budget. In some instances, merit pay and RIF might be joined purposely, but the primary concept behind RIF is to reduce the budget, often in response to enrollment decline or fiscal distress. RIF dismisses tenured or untenured staff for reasons unrelated to performance. Conversely, though, if an employee's performance should lead to enrollment decline, dismissal or nonrenewal may still be treated as RIF. The usual reason for RIF, however, is fiscal insolvency. It must be understood that when fiscal insolvency is claimed by a board of education, counterclaims by the teachers' association will center on validity of the board of education's data. Consequently, the school district must be able to substantiate its actions based on evidence. In this arena, the need for clear and precise data is paramount. When data are clear, dismissals will be supported by the courts.

When RIF is invoked, a series of important and complicated events is put in motion. Generally state law is highly detailed regarding this discussion, although federal employment law is important as well. For example, care must be taken to observe any federal protections, such as free speech; to follow all state statutes and local negotiated contract provisions, such as employee rights to seniority (e.g., "bumping"); and to make certain that no allegations of preferential treatment can be made during the dismissal process. Extreme care must be taken to avoid liability because some courts have liberally granted rights to both tenured and untenured staff. Other courts, however, have ruled that as long as constitutionally protected rights are respected, untenured teachers have no expectation of continued employment and possess none of the rights accorded to tenured employees. The concept of bumping is common in such situations, placing an extra burden on school districts to make certain that both laws and negotiated agreements affected by bumping are correctly followed; that is, in such situations teachers may bump other teachers with less seniority as long as other requirements, such as professional licensure in teaching fields, are met. Public school administrators must be aware that when legally challenged under state law and applicable collective bargaining agreements, courts may watch to make certain that RIF is not a ruse for voluntary budget reduction or a diversionary scheme to avoid a difficult dismissal fight. As a consequence, school leaders must be familiar with every aspect of statutory requirements and local employment contract law.

In addition to RIF, other dismissals sometimes occur. Although it is often believed that a teaching job is a life appointment, the reality is that tenured and untenured staff may be dismissed. There should be no underestimation of the local board of education's

---

14 See, R. C. Wood, "Reduction In Force," in *Principles of School Business Management*, edited by R. C. Wood (Reston, VA: Association of School Business Officials, 1987), 537–557.

power in personnel matters. Boards of education and supervisors have authority to evaluate and dismiss, powers that come by virtue of states granting both implied and delegated authority to operate the public schools.

Even though boards of education can dismiss staff, termination by RIF, or for any other reason, must not be undertaken lightly. This is true because in the vast majority of states significant differences exist between dismissal procedures for untenured versus tenured staff. Tenure grants expectation for a continuing contract and entitles the staff member to due process of law. In contrast, untenured teachers may expect only a term contract under whatever employment and dismissal rights are granted by constitutional and federal or state employment law. This does not mean untenured staff have no protection, because no one can be denied constitutional rights; untenured staff may demand full due process if alleging that fundamental rights such as freedom of speech have been violated. In addition, state statutes govern other rights of untenured staff, making it mandatory to understand state statutes, the termination process, and the terms of the employment contract.

Tenured classroom teachers may be dismissed, but the task may be difficult because state statutes provide specific reasons for termination of tenured employees, and by logic no dismissal can occur in tenured cases except for cause. Under state statutes, cause generally includes such issues as incompetence, immorality, insubordination, felony conviction, unprofessional conduct, incapacity, and neglect of duty. Within limits of seniority and bumping, fiscal exigency also is a defensible cause for tenured dismissal. When any of these reasons is invoked, however, the right of termination falls to employers only if the claims can be substantiated. If challenged, failure to substantiate will likely result in a lawsuit along with liability for various types of restitution and compensation. As a result, great care should be taken when contemplating the dismissal of any employee.

The most challenging dismissal cases typically involve tenured staff. Courts have allowed a broad definition in matters of incompetence, requiring only reasonable evidence relating to lack of ability, lack of legal qualification, or failure to discharge required duties. Proof of incompetence is measured against others having similar duties. Incompetence may be shown by any one of the following criteria or some combination thereof:

- Lack of a proper teaching certificate
- Lack of knowledge of subject matter
- Lack of ability to establish reasonable discipline in class
- Deficiency in teaching methods
- Emotional instability demonstrating inability to teach effectively

Both untenured and tenured staff may be dismissed for these reasons. In dismissing tenured staff, however, great care must be taken to document the charges in case litigation ensues. Additionally, in some states there is a duty to remediate before moving to dismissal. Remediation must also be documented and should include a variety of activities designed to bring the employee up to at least an adequate level of performance. Remediation should help employees to be successful in the specific job, should define activities and duties of all parties, and should demonstrate good faith by the school district to salvage the contractual interest of the employee. Documentation of failure by the employee to respond to remediation must be thorough because the first defense will be to say that the employee is not the worst case in the school district and that the district did not perform in good faith. Serious liability, including award of substantial monetary damages, can accompany improper dismissals, along with reinstatement of the staff member to his or her original position.

As noted, staff may be dismissed for immorality. In the modern context, immorality is not confined to sexual misconduct. In a court, immorality is often based on prevailing community standards, in which the test is whether the act is detrimental to public welfare. Actions such as corruption or indecency constitute immorality, in that the standard may be defined as conduct that offends the morals of a community and sets a bad example for the youth whose ideals a teacher is supposed to foster. Although immorality is broadly defined, care must be taken not to expose the school district to liability for misapplication of the standard. For example, in a conservative community, a sensitive area might be an unwed pregnant teacher. However, courts generally have not supported claims of immorality in such cases due to a lack of proof of immorality. This simply means that it is difficult to prove in the majority of communities that pregnancy results in harm to students in the learning process, or that the teacher's respect in the community has been affected. And, to complicate matters, even though the teacher's pregnancy may offend the moral sensibilities of some in the community, in 1978 Congress passed the Pregnancy Discrimination Act, amending Title VII to include pregnancy under equal benefits coverage.[15]

Dismissal surrounding the issues of insubordination are guided by state statutes and controlling case law. Willful disregard or repeated refusal to obey reasonable and normal professional directives related to the safety, health, and welfare, as well as the educational functions of the school, nearly always constitutes insubordination. Courts place the burden of proof on the school district, however, particularly with tenured staff, given the property rights inherent to a continued employment expectation. The following represent guidelines regarding charges of insubordination in which the school district will generally prevail:

- The employee should be given clear directives and, if at all possible, these directives should be in writing with a written acknowledgement by the employee with copies to the appropriate files.
- There is evidence that the employee understood the directive by signature or other acknowledgement.
- The directive was reasonable and directly work-related to the safety, health, and welfare of students as well as the educational mission of the school.
- The directive did not place the employee in danger of his or her safety or health or was not beyond the scope of their knowledge or expertise.
- The order did not violate public policy in that it would violate the rights of students, fellow employees, or the purpose of schools.

---

15 See, 29 C.F.R. §1604.10.

- The employee was informed of the consequences of not obeying the directive and the employee acknowledged the resultant consequences of their actions including possible termination.

Insubordination and willful neglect must be proved and not merely assumed.

Finally, employees may be discharged without liability for neglect of duty. In practice, neglect of duty may be part of a claim of incompetence. For example, neglect of duty might include failure to follow curriculum standards, failure to maintain discipline, failure to follow teaching lessons, and other similar actions or inactions. Neglect is distinct from insubordination, wherein an employee blatantly disregards directives. To withstand judicial challenge, charges of neglect of duty or insubordination must reflect prior notice and evidence of established policy or directives. Finally, other dismissals for acts such as felony conviction likely will be upheld because such offenses may have an impact on the performance and standing of the employee in the community. In many states, statutes declare that felony conviction is automatic evidence of unfitness. But as always, carelessness in substantiating dismissals for due process purposes may result in great harm to the school district.

Due Process

The seriousness of budgeting for personnel-related issues is clear when it is emphasized that school districts are financially liable for any wrongful acts. Liability is broad and includes risk for improper dismissal, given the near-certainty of forthcoming claims for reinstatement, back pay, and actual and punitive damages for violating the rights and reputation of the accused. These modern realities place a grave duty on school districts to discharge the legal and professional obligations properly and to follow both procedural and substantive due process. Procedural due process ensures that parties are entitled to notice and hearing. Substantive due process is a constitutional guarantee that no one may be wrongfully deprived of rights and must be protected from unreasonable action.

Although the personnel division of the school district has primary responsibility for developing due process guidelines conforming to the requirements of law, the financial implications of liability mean that the budget office is greatly affected and should be involved in development of such policies. A set of policies should be developed, approved by the board of education, and made known to staff. Assuming a tenured employee does not commit an act that is defined by state statute warranting immediate termination, the process of hearings and appeals is normally found within controlling state statutes. Generally, due process as defined by state statutes consists of four elements that also apply to dismissal and should be considered any time there is reason to anticipate that a financial obligation might arise. In the case of contract termination the tenured employee first must receive written notice giving specific reason(s) for nonrenewal—notification must conform to state statutes on timing and method of delivery. Second, an impartial hearing is required so that the employee can hear, examine, and refute any evidence. Third, the employee must be given opportunity to challenge these statements and to call witnesses. Fourth, hearings must occur at several levels in the school district so as to demonstrate that all administrative procedures and remedies were afforded. The process begins with the immediate supervisor and administratively ends with the board of education. This ensures that the employee will have opportunity to be heard and to challenge actions at each level. Failure to provide these proceedings will almost certainly result in severe consequences.

Determining whether due process has been accorded is a function of the external mechanics of proceedings and closer scrutiny of the total process. The administration and the board of education must be careful to deal objectively with the facts and to procedurally follow each due process step. This is especially critical for tenured employees because they may have property rights to continued employment, and procedural and substantive due process must be accorded in that property rights may not be removed arbitrarily. The duty of the school district is grave, as the U.S. Supreme Court has ruled that such interests of employees are "broad and majestic."[16] At the same time, appropriate dismissals should not be avoided because—notwithstanding the seriousness of violating rights and due process—failure to reverse poor employment decisions causes significant harm over time. As noted in this section, the dismissal must be reasonable, reasons for dismissal must not be arbitrary or capricious, defensible documentation must exist, and due process must be properly observed throughout the process.

WHAT IS THE ROLE OF STAKEHOLDERS?

As discussed earlier, personnel costs, on average, drive over 80% of school district expenditures. Public education is a labor-intensive industry. As such, human capital—purchased human resources—is the single largest investment a school district makes. In sum, a school district's ability to reach its educational goals depends heavily on a highly competent staff.

When viewed as a total process, the topics presented in this chapter (projecting enrollments, determining staffing needs, recruiting, selecting, compensating, and retaining highly qualified personnel) constitute critical elements of budgeting. When these elements are properly addressed, the probability of success in providing a sound education for all children is greatly enhanced. If done poorly, the outcome is unsatisfactory. For boards of education, a state constitutional duty to appropriately deliver education rests in large part on the relationship between the budget and staffing. For school administrators, the success of creating and balancing a sound budget is at stake. For classroom teachers, professional success, employment stability, and personal happiness are at stake in the act of budgeting for personnel. And for the general public, the climate of the community and the economic and personal well-being of everyone, including children, is dependent upon offering the next generation a quality education in order to better the specific community and society as a whole. In essence, budgeting for personnel drives revenue, expenditures, and programs at the most fundamental level.

---

16 *Board of Regents v. Roth*, 408 U.S. 564 (1972).

POINT–COUNTERPOINT

POINT

Traditional single-salary schedules based on education and experience do great harm to individual teachers' initiative by eliminating the opportunity to be rewarded for improvements in teacher quality and student performance. Pay-for-performance plans that are independent of years of experience and link pay directly to student achievement offer the best opportunity for schools to recruit and retain top talent and to address staff shortages. Public schools should embrace these plans because traditional single-salary schedules are inefficient.

COUNTERPOINT

Traditional single-salary schedules were developed in response to the failure of merit pay. The history of discriminatory salary practices in public education was overcome only through emergence of the single-salary schedule. It is ironic to suggest that advanced educational levels are an invalid basis for additional pay in schools, and it is nonsensical to argue that skills do not increase with experience. If merit pay systems are reintroduced in schools under the guise of new names like "pay for performance" or "value-added," the culture and productivity of education will change—pitting teacher against teacher and school against school for limited (or nonexistent) financial rewards. Students and learning will suffer.

- Which of these starkly opposite views best represents your beliefs and experience? Explain.
- Would you be willing to accept new employment in a school district that had adopted an alternative compensation system like pay for performance? Why or why not?
- If your current school district announced it was considering a move to a new pay plan designed to improve student achievement, would you be willing to participate in its development? Why or why not?

CASE STUDY

As an experienced, successful principal, you have recently completed your doctoral degree with an emphasis in human resource administration. In fact, your dissertation was a comparative policy and financial analysis of collective bargaining laws in the 50 states. You have accepted a position as personnel director for a school district in another state.

During your first week on the job, you learn several disturbing facts. You are greatly surprised to discover that the teaching staff has been working under an expired contract for the past two years following bitter, protracted negotiations that had ended in a standoff. Your concern escalates when you learn that the school board president served as the board's lead negotiator and that recently he was quoted in the local press as saying, "It was high time teachers in this district got with the program and got paid for results instead of just showing up." You also discover that the president of the local teachers' union fired back in the press, saying that the school board president "apparently planned to continue applying his finely honed skills from the meatpacking industry to the negotiations process where two years ago he dealt a death blow to any hope for a good working relationship with teachers." And to make matters worse, your secretary informs you that the district's building principals have requested a meeting with you to discuss the union members' refusal to perform any unpaid duties (i.e., work-to-rule) until a new master contract has been negotiated. Although you barely have time to realize that none of these issues was made known to you during your hiring interview, it is clear that you have to respond quickly and effectively.

- Identify and describe the major problems confronting you in this situation.
- As you contemplate the need for action, where should you begin? What needs to be done? Who should be involved? What can you do right away that will be positively perceived? What pitfalls should you anticipate? Develop an action plan to address these questions.
- Could this situation occur in your own school district? Have there been instances in which similar tense moments have occurred? If so, what were the circumstances, and how were the problems resolved?

PORTFOLIO EXERCISES

- Talk to your school district's personnel director and outline the functions of the office. Make a list of duties, prioritized from highest to lowest, including estimates of time spent on each of these functions. Explore the coordination between the personnel and budget offices.

- Obtain a copy of your school district's salary schedule(s) for employee groups and analyze the structure of each. Experiment with changes to the salary schedule structure, noting the impact of changes that would be popular in your district—for example, you might analyze changes proposed during recent negotiations.

- Talk to your local teachers' union representative and a school district official to obtain a balanced view of personnel-related budget issues.

- Obtain a copy of your school district's personnel policy manual. Discuss its contents with a range of employees in your school district, such as the personnel director, a site-level administrator, a teacher, a noncertificated staff member, and a union representative. Ask them to assess whether the manual is clear and comprehensive. Ask for their suggestions for its improvement. Summarize these and discuss whether you agree or disagree and explain why.

WEB RESOURCES

American Association of School Administrators, www.aasa.org

American Association of School Personnel Administrators, www.aaspa.org

American Federation of Teachers, www.aft.org

Association of School Business Officials International, asbointl.org

National Center on Performance Incentives, www.performanceincentives.org

National Education Association, www.nea.org

National School Boards Association, www.nsba.org

National School Public Relations Association, www.nspra.org

North American Association of Educational Negotiators, www.naen.org

U.S. Department of Labor, www.dol.gov

RECOMMENDED READING

Azordegan, Jennifer, Patrick Byrnett, Kelsey Campbell, Josh Greenman, and Tricia Coulter. "Diversifying Teacher Compensation." Issue Paper. Denver, CO: Education Commission of the States, December 2005.

Baker, Eva L., Paul E. Barton, Linda Darling-Hammond, Edward Haertel, Helen F. Ladd, Robert L. Linn, Diane Ravitch, Richard Rothstein, Richard J. Shavelson, and Lorrie A. Shepard. "Problems with the Use of Student Test Scores to Evaluate Teachers." EPI Policy Briefing Paper, no. 278. Washington, DC: Economic Policy Institute, August 2010.

Bennett-Alexander, Dawn D., and Laura P. Hartman. "Public Sector Employee Privacy." In *Employment Law for Business*, 7th ed., 661–671. Boston: McGraw-Hill, 2011.

Christie, Kathy, and Jennifer Dounay Zinth. "Teacher Tenure or Continuing Contract Law." *ECS: Teaching Quality*. Denver, CO: Education Commission of the States, August 2011.

Coggshall, Jane G., and Amber Ott, with Molly Lasagna. *Retaining Teacher Talent: Convergence and Contradictions in Teachers' Perceptions of Policy Reform Ideas*. Naperville, IL, and New York: Learning Point Associates and Public Agenda, 2010.

DeMitchell, Todd A. *Labor Relations in Education: Policies, Politics, and Practices*. Lanham, MD: Rowman & Littlefield, 2009.

Dixon, Asenth. *Focus on Teacher Reform Legislation in SREB States: Evaluation Policies.* Atlanta, GA: Southern Regional Education Board, June 2011.

Education Commission of the States. "Teacher Merit Pay: What Do We Know?" *The Progress of Education Reform* 1, no. 3. Denver, CO: ECS, June 2010.

Goodman, Serena, and Lesley Turner. "Teacher Incentive Pay and Educational Outcomes: Evidence from the NYC Bonus Program." Paper presented at the Program on Education Policy and Governance Conference on Merit Pay: Will It Work? Is It Politically Viable? Cambridge, MA: Harvard Kennedy School, June 2010. www.hks.harvard.edu/pepg/MeritPayPapers/goodman_turner_10–07.pdf.

Ravitch, Diane. *The Death and Life of the Great American School System: How Testing and Choice Are Undermining Education.* New York: Basic Books, 2010.

Rice, Jennifer King. "The Impact of Teacher Experience: Examining the Evidence and Policy Implications." Brief no. 11. Washington, DC: Urban Institute, August 2010.

Springer, Matthew G., Dale Ballou, Laura Hamilton, Vi-Nhuan Le, J. R. Lockwood, Daniel F. McCaffrey, Matthew Pepper, and Brian M. Stecher. *Teacher Pay for Performance: Experimental Evidence from the Project on Incentives in Teaching.* Nashville, TN: National Center on Performance Incentives, September 2010.

Toutkoushian, Robert K., Justin M. Bathon, and Martha M. McCarthy. "A National Study of the Net Benefits of State Pension Plans for Educators." *Journal of Education Finance* 37, no.1 (2011): 24–51.

CHAPTER 7

Budgeting for Instruction

THE CHALLENGE

The principal and teacher leaders within each school must engage the faculty and develop a vision of what the school must do if it is to graduate more students who are prepared for life and work in the 21st Century. If state and district leaders have done their jobs, if the vision and desired outcomes are clear and the necessary supports are in place, then the principal and teachers can begin to design and implement solutions tailored to the unique needs of their own students and communities.

Bottoms and Schmidt-Davis (2010)[1]

CHAPTER DRIVERS

Please reflect upon the following questions as you read this chapter:

- What is instructional planning?
- What is the role of districts and schools in instructional planning?
- How do schools organize for instructional budgeting?
- What is the role and size of instructional budgets?
- What are the sources of revenue for instructional budgets?
- What are the elements of budgeting for instruction?
- What are the sources of instructional revenues?
- What does an instructional budget look like?

---

1 Gene Bottom and Jon Schmidt-Davis, *The Three Essentials: Improving Schools Requires District Vision, District and State Support, and Principal Leadership* (Atlanta, GA: Southern Regional Education Board, August 2010).

THE OVERALL PICTURE

This text has provided an introductory discussion of the broad school funding concepts, with the ultimate goal of more closely examining the individual tasks of budgeting. The text has discussed the modern context of schools, the complex social milieu in which school funding policy is made, the sources of school funding, the seriousness of handling school money, the general process of budgeting, and the costs associated with personnel. This overview has been steadily narrowed as the text examined each specific element of budgeting. Thus, *budgeting for instruction* is now examined because it is sensible to study the application and operationalization of money in the classroom—a topic of intense interest to education's many stakeholders.

This chapter, like those previous, begins by moving from a general framework to increasingly specific elements. If school budgets and instruction are to be linked, the starting place is to define instructional planning and the role of districts and individual schools in that process. Underlying these are issues of organizational structure: that is, how schools in a particular school district are organized drives many other structures, including roles and responsibilities in budget decision making. Once these options are developed, instructional budgets are created and implemented, including the sources of instructional revenues and the specific elements of instructional budgeting. As a consequence, this chapter moves us still deeper into the world of school money.

THE PLANNING FUNCTION

While the full range of instructional planning is not the focus of this text, the emphasis on strategizing for effective learning organizations makes it absolutely clear that building a budget based on the instructional goals of a school district is critical. In fact, the whole purpose of budgeting is to build a revenue and expenditure plan to carry out the school district's instructional mission.

What Is Instructional Planning?

Educational research and practice hold many lessons concerning the organizing and operating of schools, with three overriding realities. The first is that successful instructional planning requires the use of experts who envision and direct the teaching and learning process. The second reality is that a sound instructional plan requires the support of a strong financial plan. The third is that effective instruction requires something inseparable from the first two realities; that is, a deliberate plan based on a formal mission and a set of measurable goal statements. In sum, while the budget is the fiscal expression of the educational philosophy of a school district, the instructional plan brings together revenue sources in support of expenditures in order to effectuate the school district's mission and goals.

District Mission and Goals

Mission and goal statements are the cornerstones of education. Much positive benefit has come from consciously focusing on mission and goals. The primary value has been that once such statements are made public, accountability for performance increases noticeably. Although some individuals may question the wide sweep of mission and goal statements, there is an increased duty to the school district when it professes mission statements such as "all children can learn to high standards." Although such beliefs should be unquestioned, history reveals that schools and society have not always believed that all children can learn, and the proof lies in the heated debates concerning the value of special education and compensatory programs. Those debates are beyond the scope of this text, but it is sufficient to say that a mission statement serves to define and drive the organizational culture of the school district such that it has the effect of focusing attitudes and performance on a promise made publicly.

The same is true of goal statements. In contrast to a mission statement, which is meant to be broadly exhortative, goal statements are specific and may be performance-based. For example, school districts may adopt goal statements such as "All children will reach at least the 60th percentile on grade-level standardized tests before passing to the next grade," or "All high school seniors will pass a criterion-referenced test with a state-approved minimum score permitting entry into the state's higher education system without remediation." The range of possibilities for goal statements is endless and ever-increasing, as demonstrated by the challenging standards embedded within the No Child Left Behind Act and Race to the Top program, but the purpose is simple—to focus the school district on outcomes in the larger context of the stated mission and to operationalize the mission in objective, measurable terms. Both mission and goal statements have strong budget implications, so much so that budgeting for instruction is central to all planning aimed at carrying out the mission and actionable, measurable goal statements.

School Mission and Goals

The mission and goal statements also apply to individual schools within a school district. Although it may seem redundant for individual schools to restate school district goals, it is symbolic for schools to spend time and energy building commitment to the larger organization's aims. A simultaneous requirement, however, is that each school will create its own mission and goals specific to its unique culture, needs, and student demographics. Although school mission and goal statements should complement those of the school district, a school's mission and goal statements will also reflect its programs' strengths and target the particular needs of its student population.

If it is financially meaningful for a school district to link mission and goals to the budget, there are equally significant budget implications for school mission and goal statements. As discussed later, school districts often provide some degree of latitude for individual schools to pursue specific goals, and it is unquestioned that needs vary from school to school. Consequently, budget philosophy and fiscal operations at the school site level may differ based on needs and preferences. In other words, mission and goals are not only district-level activities—they are essential budget-building blocks that focus each school's planning on learning outcomes, which in turn should drive instructional spending.

For budgetary purposes, the planning function is the act of determining district and school mission and goals, coupled with an actionable expenditure plan to achieve those outcomes. As discussed in Chapter 6, personnel are a major cost, but there remains a significant portion of every school district's budget that goes to nonsalary instructional expenses. Hence, this is the focus of this chapter, together with how instructional budget decisions are made—decisions affected in significant part by how school systems are organized.

ORGANIZATIONAL OPTIONS

Instructional planning raises the issue of how schools are structured. Chapter 6 introduced organizational options and budgeting strategies. It is clear, for example, that budgeting for schools involved in site-based leadership will be structured differently from schools that operate under a centralized hierarchy. Because instructional decisions are strongly influenced by organizational design, it is important to examine some options before considering how instructional budgeting might occur.

How Are School Districts Organized?

Instructional budgeting is highly dependent on school district organizational design. Although there are many variations, school districts are first driven by central administration's leadership style. As a result, the most common organizational designs include varying degrees of centralization, management teams, and site-based leadership. These designs drive most planning and decision-making processes.

Centralized Structure

Not surprisingly, most decisions in highly centralized school districts are made in a tightly controlled central office environment, with budgets closely held at that same level. As a general rule, highly centralized organizations are committed to line-item or program budgeting, and there is usually an attempt to make uniform allocations to schools as an expression of evenhandedness. Centralization usually is not absolute, however, in that it is often characterized by degrees of delegated responsibility. Ultimately, however, delegation of decision making in such school districts is accompanied by strict central reporting and accountability.

Centralized control has noteworthy benefits and drawbacks. Among the benefits is the concept that the central office is ultimately responsible for everything that happens in the school district and that top leaders are expected to have the necessary expertise to make every important decision. An additional benefit is organizational efficiency, as there is no room for indecisiveness or disagreement if leaders are strong individuals. On the negative side is the obvious fact that decision making and ownership are tightly held, so that unquestioning endorsement of mission and goals and actions by subordinates is mandated. In such organizations, there is typically little staff involvement at any level in budgeting and only marginal involvement in instructional planning.

Management Teams

While highly centralized school districts still exist, use of management teams has grown rapidly. Management teams represent a middle ground between complete centralization and its opposite—decentralization. The management team concept argues that more heads are better than one, although many hallmarks of centralization remain. The basic structure finds most major decisions made by central office staff who advise the superintendent from within a closely held cabinet. Central office staff, however, may offer such advice after having listened to various groups within the district and community.

Management teams also offer benefits and drawbacks. A clear benefit comes from advice more broadly gathered, often by floating trial balloons among senior officials before controversial decisions are made public. Benefits also include the checks and balances of constituent input, and much efficiency inherent to central decision making is preserved. On the downside, individuals or groups may complain that their input is not taken seriously or that input is structured to elicit preferred answers. In such organizations, centralization is still evident, but budgets and instructional decisions are likely to be delegated, albeit to varying degrees.

Site-Based Management

Although no data exist with regard to how many of the nation's roughly 14,000 school districts are still highly centralized, many school districts have stepped away from that particular image. Indeed, it is difficult to imagine that such a design could continue to exist today given demands by employees and community members to have a voice in organizational decision making. Participatory expectations have given rise to site-based management (SBM) on a wide scale, including numerous instances where SBM has been written into statutory guidelines.

The modern impetus for SBM in schools largely began with the sweeping education reform enacted in 1990 in Kentucky, as it responded to a state supreme court order to fix a constitutionally flawed education system. In responding to the court, the state ordered a total restructuring of public elementary and secondary education. The Kentucky Education Reform Act of 1990 was a monumental piece of legislation that required local school boards to implement school-based decision making vested in site councils composed of parents, teachers, and principals. They were given substantial responsibility, including management of schools on a daily basis. For example, the Kentucky law charged site councils with the following:

- Setting school policy to provide an environment to enhance student achievement
- Dividing the staff into committees by areas of interest for the purpose of making recommendations to the council
- Determining the number of persons employed in each job and making personnel decisions on vacancies

- Determining instructional materials and support services
- Determining curriculum, including needs assessment, curriculum development, alignment with state standards, technology utilization, and program appraisal
- Assigning use of staff time
- Assigning students to classes and programs
- Determining the schedule of the school day and week
- Determining use of school space during the day
- Planning and resolving issues of instructional practice
- Implementing discipline and classroom management
- Selecting extracurricular programs and determining policies relating to participation
- Administering the school budget, including discretionary funds, activity funds and other school funds, as well as maintenance, supplies, and equipment funds
- Assessing student progress, including testing and reporting to parents, students, the board, the community, and the state
- Creating school improvement and professional development plans
- Coordinating parent, citizen, and community participation[2]

The demands of the Kentucky law left no question about its intent. The rules had changed, and the purpose of putting stakeholders in charge of a decentralized system was clear. Similar laws have been enacted by many states as numerous others imitated the basic design in subsequent years so that today SBM is pervasive in form and—in many cases—in genuine impact. The underlying rationale is always the same: Stakeholders want a strong voice in schools; expertise exists among educators and non-educators alike; and many decisions are believed to be best made at the school site.[3]

Predictably, site-based leadership designs have benefits and drawbacks. A clear benefit is that SBM stands as the epitome of the concept of shared decision making in which all stakeholders are involved. As such, parents and communities have little ground to stand on if they complain that schools are unresponsive. On the downside, efficiency of professional decision making may decrease when laypeople become closely involved in complex decisions. Additionally, the many sensitive areas in SBM, such as personnel

---

2 The Kentucky legislature approved House Bill 940 on April 11, 1990. It was signed into law as the Kentucky Education Reform Act (KERA) by Governor Wallace Wilkinson (Chapter 476 of the Kentucky Acts of 1990).

3 In 2005, 34 states had relevant statutes on record. Among these were 17 states that had mandated SBM statewide in one form or another (Alabama, Arizona, Colorado, Florida, Georgia, Hawaii, Kansas, Kentucky, Massachusetts, Michigan, New Mexico, New York, North Carolina, South Carolina, Texas, Utah, West Virginia). Two states (Illinois and Ohio) had mandated SBM for specified districts—Illinois required SBM in all Chicago schools, and Ohio mandated that a site council be established in at least one building in districts with more than 5,000 students that had not been identified as "effective" or "excellent" through the state accountability system. A third state, New York, both mandated SBM statewide and also placed additional SBM requirements on the New York City District. See, Jennifer Dounay, "Site-Based Decisionmaking: State-level Policies," *ECS State Notes* (Denver, CO: Education Commission of the States, 2005). An update in mid-2011 found 63 SBM-related bills passed in state legislatures between 2000 and 2011.

decisions made by site councils, can be a source of legal and ethical concern. Further, the potential for inequality may increase as some schools inevitably perform better and more effectively strategize financial and parental support structures.

Budget implications of SBM are self-evident. Although the implementation of the SBM model varies according to local preference or state statutes, schools that engage in SBM are required to accept far more responsibility for budget decisions—tasks formerly reserved to the school district central office. For example, individual schools may have to choose between buying supplies and hiring more personnel, or between maintaining facilities and funding student activities. As a consequence, latitude in decision making is gained, but difficult decisions must by made by individual schools as well as a wide array of stakeholders (boards, central office administrators, principals, staff, parents, and other school site council members) to agree regarding mission and goals, to gather and distribute available resources, and to produce measurable outcomes. The shift is fundamental at all levels; that is, under SBM the school district central office takes on a role of broad oversight, while the individual school becomes the nucleus of authority, power, and direction.

In sum, many individual schools are taking on new powers, even under more centralized organizational designs, because statutes and the general public are seeking more control of public education's goals and outcomes. Accordingly it behooves all leaders to understand issues of organizational design in order to identify the parameters of appropriate and effective leadership, including answers to the following questions:

- Who has primary responsibility for establishing the overall level of expenditure in a district and school?
- Who has primary responsibility for establishing expenditures for each major program or organizational unit?
- Who has primary responsibility for selecting specific resources within the allotted dollar amounts for each program?
- Who has primary responsibility for curriculum selection?
- Who has primary responsibility for new programs or for eliminating or reducing the scope of current programs?
- Who has primary responsibility for establishing salaries and benefits?
- Who has primary responsibility for hiring personnel?
- Who has primary responsibility for establishing capital budgets and deciding how facilities and equipment are purchased and allocated?

INSTRUCTIONAL BUDGET CONCEPTS

As noted previously, all parts of a budget are sequentially linked so that the number of students drives revenues, which in turn drives staffing, thereby driving a huge proportion of total expenditures. But the instructional picture is not yet complete. The next step is to consider the nonsalary portion of instructional costs.

Instructional Budgets

The instructional budget is that portion of a budget remaining after excluding all non-instructional costs. Thus, the costs of food service, capital outlay, transportation, debt service, and most other separate funds are excluded. Under these limitations, the definition of an instructional budget defaults to the *entire* general fund as the best description of instructional expense. Although not entirely accurate, it is useful to picture instructional costs in this manner because direct instructional expense is what most individuals really mean in this instance. Using that logic, it is accurate to think of the general fund in this manner because the general fund truly does pay for the vast majority of certificated and classified staff salaries, instructional supplies, and all other annual operating expenses associated with school buildings and instructional programs. By this definition, 85% to 87% of a typical school district's general fund budget is allocated to instruction (excluding business operations and maintenance—see Figure 7.1). Since everyone working in a school facility or in the central office either has a direct instructional role or an instructional support role, nearly all current expenditures can be viewed as instructional dollars.

The instructional budget can also be interpreted as that portion of a total budget after subtracting all salary and nonteaching supply costs. By this definition, instructional budgets are not as large, but it underscores the reality that the vast majority of education's costs lie in personnel and further illustrates that all other operations are funded by very low percentages of the budget.

Third, the instructional budget also may be defined as all costs attributed directly to students. This would include teachers, supplies, equipment, special education services, and other support services such as librarians, counselors, and nurses, as well as transportation—all of which make up about 76% of the budget (see Figure 7.2). Including the professional and physical environment changes the mix has merit (see Figure 7.3), in that students in fact receive benefits greater than just direct instruction; the cost of education is far more complex than teacher salaries. In fact, the strongest

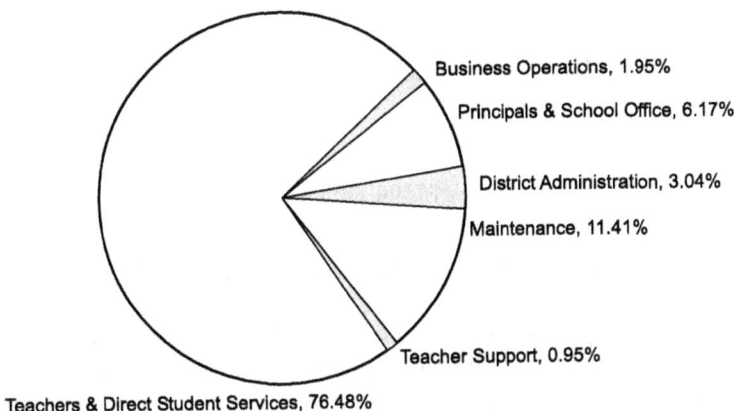

Business Operations, 1.95%

Principals & School Office, 6.17%

District Administration, 3.04%

Maintenance, 11.41%

Teacher Support, 0.95%

Teachers & Direct Student Services, 76.48%

FIGURE 7.1 How Does a District Spend Its Money? Sample School District

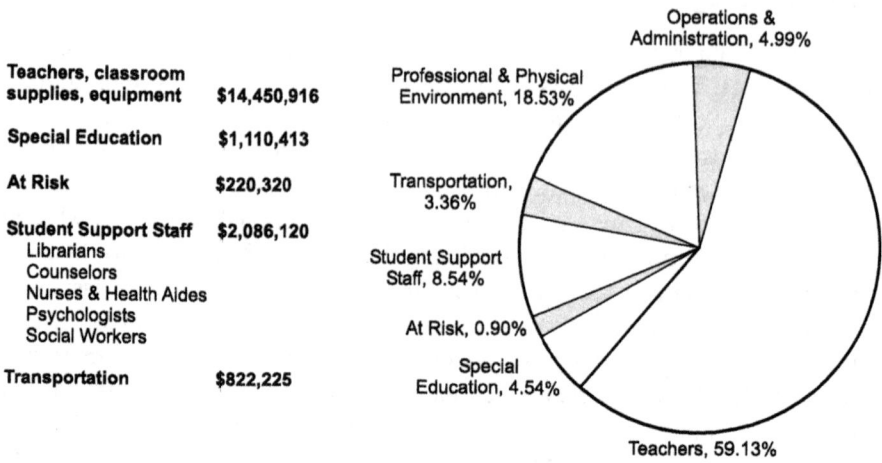

Teachers, classroom supplies, equipment	$14,450,916
Special Education	$1,110,413
At Risk	$220,320
Student Support Staff Librarians Counselors Nurses & Health Aides Psychologists Social Workers	$2,086,120
Transportation	$822,225

FIGURE 7.2 Direct Student Costs: Sample School District

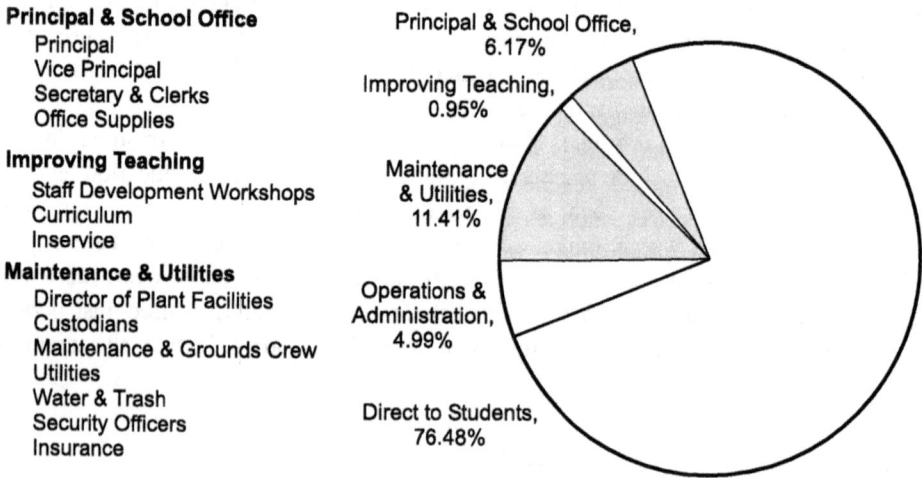

Principal & School Office
Principal
Vice Principal
Secretary & Clerks
Office Supplies

Improving Teaching
Staff Development Workshops
Curriculum
Inservice

Maintenance & Utilities
Director of Plant Facilities
Custodians
Maintenance & Grounds Crew
Utilities
Water & Trash
Security Officers
Insurance

FIGURE 7.3 Professional and Physical Environment: Sample School District

argument for including all such costs is that all parts of the budget go together to create an educational plan; that is, instruction would be far less effective if it were not for the contributions of climate-controlled classrooms, safe and clean buildings and grounds, nutrition and health services, and other system costs (see Figure 7.4).

Although there are additional ways to examine instructional budgets, the most important features have been identified. Probably the most productive way to think of instructional budgets is to use the 80% personnel costs method, remembering that all remaining general fund money must cover all other general fund costs. This view is

District Administration
Board of Education
Superintendent's Office
Assoc. Supt., Site Support
Assoc Supt., Central Support
Research & Evaluation
Election Expense
Legal & Audit Services
Special Education Director
Transportation Director
Human Resources
Information Services

Business Operations
Director of Accounting
Director of Business Services
Payroll
Accounts Payable
Data Processing
Warehousing
Purchasing

Business Operations, 1.95%
District Administration, 3.04%
Maintenance & Utilities, 18.53%
Direct to Students, 76.48%

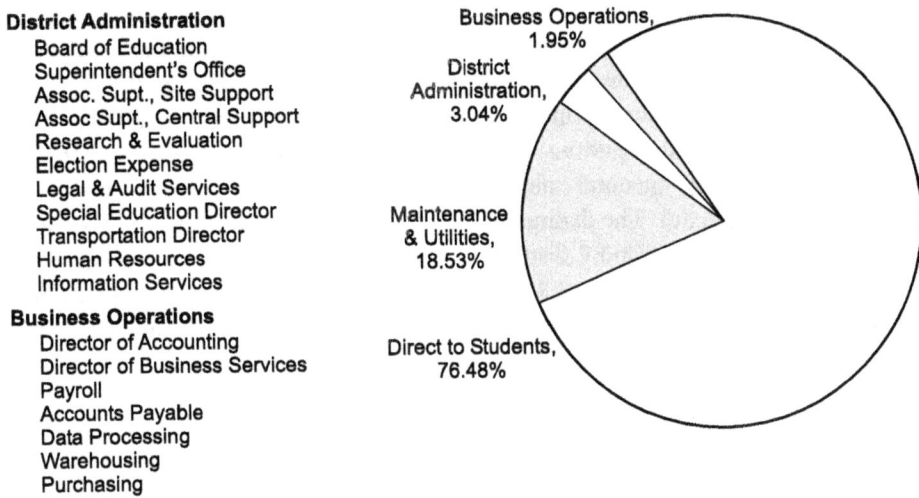

FIGURE 7.4 Running the System: Sample School District

also helpful because it shows the role and size of instructional budgets in relationship to the current operating budget which also contains segregated funds that carry out the other business of schools. The view in this chapter is narrower because the central concern is with that portion after personnel costs and some other general fund operating costs are known.

Sources of Revenue

The discussion in earlier chapters regarding revenue sources for public education deserves expansion. The discussion to this point has laid out a revenue scheme made up of federal, state, and local moneys. However, these sources only represent funds coming into a school district from external sources in the macro view, and the impact of such moneys on individual schools has not been developed. These and other sources actually make up a range of revenues that school districts receive and allocate using one of the budgeting philosophies discussed earlier.

External Sources

Most external revenue comes from three sources. Federal aid to education is mostly targeted at federal priorities such as compensatory and special education. Almost all federal money is flow-through funding, meaning that state agencies are intermediary recipients and are required to pass revenue on to school districts under applicable federal regulations. Additionally, school districts must be able to show that the funds reached individual schools and students and were not commingled with money from other sources. The most distinguishing feature of federal aid, however, is its relatively minor status in the total revenue scheme, approximately 12%.

State revenue is distributed to qualifying school districts through state education finance distribution formulas. Chapter 3 explained that state education finance distribution formulas generally are designed to grant aid inversely to the local ability to pay; that is, poor school districts should receive greater state aid than wealthier school districts. It also described variations on state aid formulas, noting that most states rely predominantly on sales (general sales and gross receipts) and personal income tax revenues to fund state aid. The distinguishing feature of state aid is that it plays nearly as large a role in funding school districts as local revenues do, each at around 44%. This was not always so. As Table 2.1 showed, up until 1980, the percentage was much lower. Even today, state aid varies considerably across states, ranging from 28% to 82% of school districts' operating budgets with an average of 48.5% across all states (See Table 2.6).

Local revenue comes to school districts primarily through property taxes.[4] As seen earlier, local revenue is frequently contentious because citizens may regard local taxes as a direct opportunity to protest the cost of government. Increases in tax levies have become increasingly difficult to pass in the last few decades, with little sign of weakening voter resistance. In a few states, school districts have the authority to levy income, sales, or sumptuary taxes without voter approval—such authority, however, is rare and only modestly productive due to statutory tax limitations and tax base overload. Obviously, the distinguishing feature of local revenue is its visibility to local voters. Nationally, about 44% of school district revenue is raised locally, although the percentage varies widely within and across states.

District Revenue Structures

In a centralized school district, revenues from all sources are gathered in the central office and distributed using a budgetary procedure such as line-item or program budgeting systems as described in Chapter 5. In less centralized school districts, site-based budgeting may be used. But in all instances, care must be taken to provide an overarching budget structure to guard against inequitable distribution, to ensure that all programs are adequately funded, and to guarantee that all children's needs are served.

To meet this goal, school districts exercise the available options. Highly centralized budgeting makes sense initially, as this structure allows the school district to efficiently meet its obligations for neutrality and control. Under this plan, principals gather input from staff and forward purchase requests or work orders to the central office, where senior administrators prioritize requests, making sure that each school receives approximately the same overall budget treatment. This process then continues to spend down available money according to the prioritized master list. The benefits are clear: control is present; efficiency is maximized; staff are not burdened by noninstructional

---

4 It is important to note that while many people associate local property taxes with schools and this perception is often reinforced by local media, the local property tax generally finances a wide range of local services, such as fire, police, and sanitation, and it is frequently an important source of revenue for local municipalities and counties.

financial duties; and all schools are treated equally. The drawbacks are equally clear: control at individual sites is absent; decisions are made far from the point of need; neutrality may not be equitable; and staff are completely uninvolved.

Another option is for central administration to establish allocations to individual schools for selected purposes, while continuing to keep some items centrally funded. This scenario seeks middle ground between centralization and site-based budgeting by arguing that some tasks are best handled at the school level, while other costs are of no interest to individual schools; for example, maintenance of buildings and grounds, utility costs, transportation, insurance, and personnel compensation are typical candidates for centralization in this scenario. Under this plan, individual school allocations tend to be solely for instructional budget purposes, as is also true of any other discretionary money sent to individual schools. The benefits are clear: individual schools are not saddled with tasks that can be handled more efficiently at the school district level; a degree of uniformity across the school district is promoted; and individual schools have latitude within the allocation to fund school site priorities. The one drawback is significant: Because compensation consumes most of a school district's budget, instructional allocations may entail relatively small amounts of money, and schools still must queue up for capital projects and other large purchases such as textbooks and major equipment.

The third option, of course, is site-based budgeting. In its purest form, the school district mostly acts as a funnel, channeling available dollars to individual schools. Under this plan, the board of education gives a formal charge to each school based on the school district's mission and goals, and each school creates its own financial plan to achieve both school district and school objectives. The benefit is clear: Moving money and freedom to the school site confers power on the people who have first hand knowledge of needs and who have the skills to address local problems. The drawbacks are clear as well: Staff may rebel against noninstructional duties; some poor decision-making is inevitable; and there is real danger that unequal resources and unequal outcomes will follow.

Regardless of which instructional budgeting option school districts choose, the flow of money is transparent. Federal and state moneys flow to local school districts through distribution formulas, whereupon (within the limits of federal and state laws and regulations) each school district decides whether to centralize or decentralize fiscal decision making. Resources at the school district level are basically limited to tax dollars, although school districts may benefit from private gifts, grants, foundations, business partnerships, and fund-raising efforts. On the whole, however, these sources contribute a very small percentage of school district revenues.

School Revenue Structures

The great majority of school revenue comes from the district level. Other revenue, however, may be available at the school site. As a result, school revenues derive from two sources: the school district and the individual school site.

School district revenues have been addressed within this chapter. The issue is how much revenue is allocated by the school district to individual schools and how that revenue can be used. As discussed earlier, this revenue often takes the form of a uniform amount (e.g., a per-pupil dollar amount) upon which some school district-controlled restrictions are placed. Figure 7.6 at the end of this chapter develops this idea more fully.

School site revenue refers to money generated at the individual school level beyond what is normally distributed by the school district. Most schools generate some site-level revenue, but must adhere to school board policy regarding revenue generation—and in some cases, must seek board of education permission. For example, individual schools may be able to apply for relatively small grants from the state's department of education, and state agencies often participate in federal grant programs that may result in school site awards. School districts receiving large grants might hold subgrant competitions within the school district, with individual schools competing for funding. Depending upon board of education policy, individual schools might also apply directly to corporations, many of which have a record of funding innovative school projects. Numerous other grants, such as those advertised in the *Federal Register*, are available to either school districts or school sites. In addition, private and charitable foundations are a potential source of school site revenue. Site revenue can also come from local businesses that agree to set up partnerships with individual schools, donating money, time, or materials. Schools sometimes raise money through booster clubs and parent organizations although as we saw in Chapter 8 such groups may be independent of the school. However, although school site revenue can be a benefit by enhancing available revenue for individual schools, it can become a significant concern at the school district and community levels if it results in unequal resources among schools in a district. School-generated revenues, while important, generally represent a very small percentage of total revenues.[5]

THE ELEMENTS OF BUDGETING FOR INSTRUCTION

Regardless of whether a school district chooses to centralize or decentralize instructional budgeting, certain elements are common regarding the budget process. In fact, these elements are repeated to some extent at all levels in a school district—as discussed later in this chapter when the instructional budget for a hypothetical school district is considered. To illustrate this concept, we assume that the hypothetical school district has chosen to engage in some decentralization and simultaneously to retain several activities at the central office level. Thus, a fourfold interest is presented. First, a needs assessment is required to create the educational plan for both the school district and each school. Second, the district must determine its total revenues and make decisions

---

5 See, for example, Faith E. Crampton and Paul Bauman, "A New Challenge to Fiscal Equity: Educational Entrepreneurship and Its Implications for Schools, Districts, and States," *Educational Considerations* 28 (Fall, 2000): 53–61; R. Craig Wood, "New Revenues for Financing Education at the Local Level," in *The Impacts of Litigation and Legislation on Public School Finance*, 59–75. Edited by Julie Underwood and Deborah A. Verstegen (New York: Harper & Row, 1989).

concerning allocations to each school based on the needs assessment. Third, individual schools must use the needs assessment and school-level allocations to establish educational and expenditure plans. And fourth, the school district must provide overall coordination of these activities.

Needs Assessment

Figure 7.5 identifies many of the important data elements required to build an instructional budget. It depicts the environmental scan that should be prepared for both the school district and each individual school. The scan provides data targeting many of the conditions discussed in Chapter 1 so that available resources can be prioritized based on the scan's results. The scan paints a distinct portrait of the community, the school district, and each school so that those in leadership positions can see and understand the unique and shared needs of students. Assuming that the sample school district has set a goal of raising student performance on standardized tests and increasing entry rates into postsecondary education, the environmental scan helps identify weaknesses that should become prime targets for increased spending. The political viability of the educational plan also can be tested through the demographic data in the scan. Results of all these activities will be used by the hypothetical school district at the central office level to establish the district's overall financial support for programs and by the individual schools in deciding how to spend site-level instructional moneys to meet these goals.

Determining Revenues and Educational Plans

As noted earlier, revenues flow from federal, state, district, and school site sources. Chapter 5 identified the steps in creating school district budgets, and the present chapter points out additional revenue sources for individual school sites. In the hypothetical school district, it is assumed that the school district has set uniform per-pupil allocations and that individual school sites have taken the initiative to secure some external funding for program enhancement purposes. At this point, the educational plan can be built and should address the priorities of the district and each school site, as well as any concerns identified by the environmental scan. In effect, the process calls for setting short-term, intermediate, and long-range priorities for the district, each school and grade level, programs, departments, and classrooms in such a way that resources are matched to students' needs by creating program-based budgets.

District Coordination

Regardless of the degree of budget decentralization, all school districts must accept responsibility for overall coordination of every aspect of the budget. Statutorily, only boards of education may spend money, and the statutes assign responsibility for all educational programs to the board of education. Additionally, efficiencies are gained by central coordination and management, and budgets are ultimately the district's

Indirect Influences on Student Performance	Student Descriptors	Student Cognitive Performance	Student Behavioral Performance	Direct Influences on Student Performance
Community Demographics	Gender	Criterion-Referenced Tests	Graduation/Promotion Rates	Instructional Delivery Systems
Number and Types of Community Agencies	Student Perceptions of School	Norm-Referenced Tests	Discipline Referrals	Student Scheduling Patterns
Family Characteristics	Ethnicity	Grades	Attendance/Absentee Rates	Intervention Strategies
Community Crime Rate	Grade Level Enrollment	Student Portfolios	Pregnancies	Use of Technology
Youth-Oriented Community Programs	Staff Perceptions of School	Teacher Anecdotal Records	Extra-Curricular Participation	General Purpose Classrooms
Community Employment Profile	Community Perceptions of School	Teacher-Developed Tests	Student Suspensions	Specialized Learning Labs
	Course Enrollment Patterns/Trends	District-Wide Content Area Tests	Dropout Rate	School Organizational Patterns
	Limited English Speaking Students			Mandated Programs

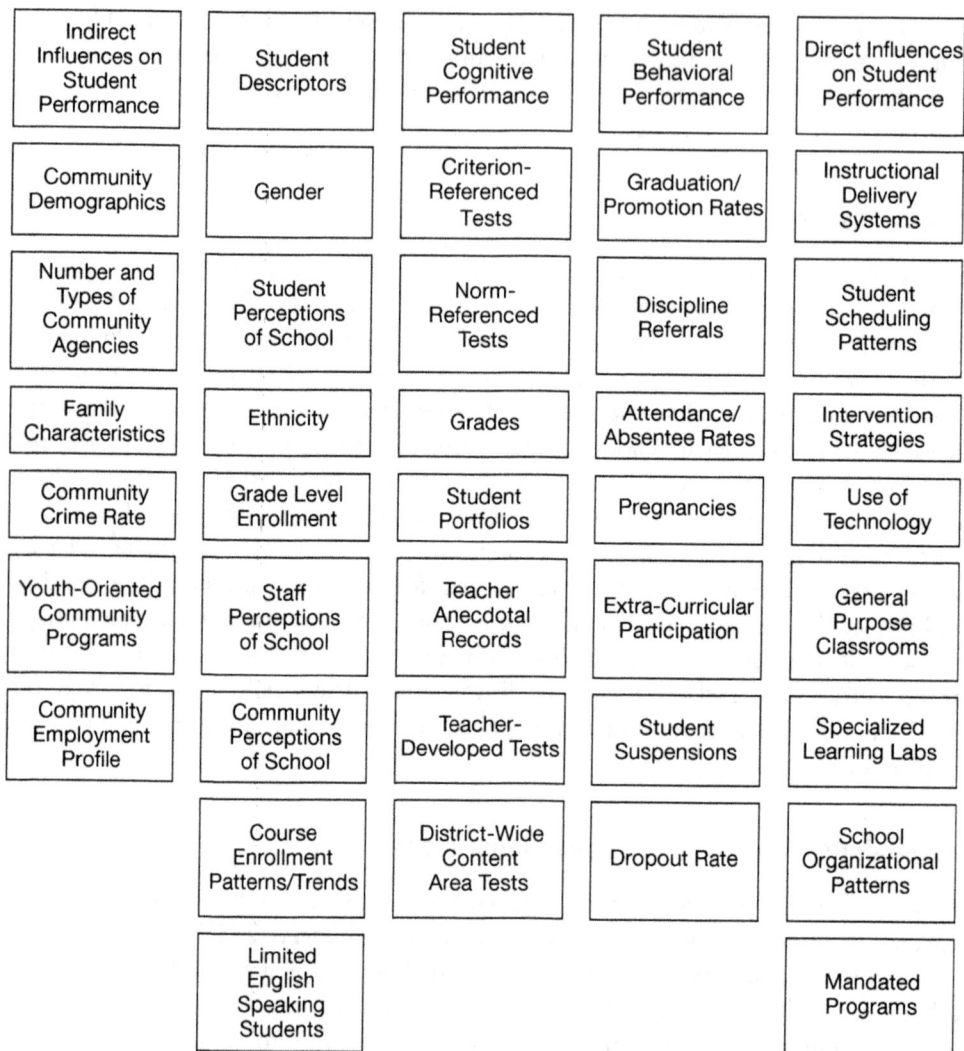

FIGURE 7.5 Environmental Scan

inescapable responsibility. The budget calendar as previously shown in Chapter 5 provided a clear understanding of the school district's role in coordination. In this chapter's hypothetical school district, the board of education has centralized some district-wide activities but has chosen to grant substantial sums of instructional money to individual school sites (See Figure 7.6).

The Instructional Budget

As indicated at the outset of this chapter, the elements of instructional budgeting cannot be carried out in discrete fashion. When conceptualized correctly, the individual elements of instructional budgeting are highly interdependent—demographics and student needs are revealed through scanning environments and other data collection mechanisms; fund accounting tracks and reveals how money is budgeted and spent; state education finance distribution formulas cause educational programs to flourish or starve; liability reduces discretionary spending; personnel costs and enrollments drive available resources; and school district budgeting philosophies determine how much money is available, how it is spent, and who makes spending (and consequently program) decisions. As noted, every aspect of the entire budget of a school district can be viewed as *the* instructional budget, although fund accounting conventions do not see the program side of budgets.

Figure 7.6 presents data for the hypothetical school district and joins concepts from our earlier study of accounting with the concept of instructional budgeting. In fact, Figure 7.6 is comprehensive, covering all issues in all chapters thus far—it also anticipates future chapters by introducing capital outlay and transportation. Figure 7.6 focuses attention on the budgeting implications of the chosen organizational structure in the hypothetical school district, in that the school district has decided to do the following:

- *Track* instructional budgets by accounting codes to permit accumulation of data by individual program
- *Decentralize* many budget aspects while retaining central office oversight through the board of education and central office directorships
- *Allocate* uniform amounts per pupil for instructional program purposes
- *Retain* overall transportation services at the central office level, while also allocating discretionary transportation budgets to schools
- *Decentralize* some aspects of capital outlay and equipment purchases
- *Link* expenditures to expected outcomes in a program budgeting model

The result of this hypothetical school district's budgeting philosophy is illustrated in Figure 7.6, where it is clear that the school district has acted to locate considerable budget and program authority at the individual school site. Great efficiency is gained by school district oversight of functions such as maintenance, repair, and construction of buildings while leaving school sites free to determine how programs are executed. The design results in individual schools accepting responsibility for large sums of money, along with the accompanying expectation for program accountability. In the hypothetical district of about 7,700 pupils, total money assigned to all sites is $892,278 —a sum to be spent on strategically targeted school needs. The fund accounting structure permits program and expenditure analysis, and proposed expenditures are justified by specifying expected outcomes. School staffs, administrators, and site councils have genuine authority to move money among funds.

Figure 7.6 is complex in that it carries out the central task of creating the educational plan for the school district and multiple school sites. The plan must be viewed first in terms of the overarching school district plan and then in terms of what it means to each individual school site. A school principal receiving this document should understand it as a comprehensive planning tool to direct the educational process for the entire school district and each individual school. On the assumption that principals will work closely with their staffs and site councils to create thoughtful instructional budgets for their schools, the following series of questions makes a complex task and a lengthy planning document both purposeful and manageable:

- *General Background Questions*

    — What is the school district's overall mission?
    — What are the school district's goal statements?
    — What is my school's overall mission?
    — What are my school's goal statements?
    — What were the results of the school district's environmental scan?
    — What were the results of my school's environmental scan?
    — Does my school's educational plan address these needs?
    — How can I spend my school's budget to meet these needs?

- *General Budget Questions (and Answers)*

    — Where are the account codes I need to make purchases? (*see the beginning of Figure 7.6*)
    — Can I accumulate program costs? (*use the account codes*)
    — What does my budget have to cover? (*see instructions in Figure 7.6*)
    — How much money do I have for instructional programs? (*see remaining portions of Figure 7.6*)
    — What if I need more money? (*generate site revenue or seek more district funds*)
    — How will I be accountable for outcomes? (*provide program outcomes for each purchase. Account codes will accumulate costs over time. The district will help determine if outcomes are being met.*)
    — What do I do when I have a question? (*contact the central office*)

The budget structure in Figure 7.6 is general in scope, but it clearly illustrates the underlying budgeting philosophy and operational elements that drive this hypothetical school district. From Figure 7.6, the principal, staff, and school site council know to turn to the central office to learn about the school district's mission and goals. They also know they must be intimately familiar with the school's environmental scan, and they know to link the scan to student needs and to use these elements to construct the school's educational plan. They also know that many resource needs, such as textbook adoptions, will be handled by the school district and that each school site has been allotted money on a per-pupil basis—in fact, principals will find their schools listed; see the exact amount of available funds for instructional programs, transportation, and capital outlay; and understand that uniform per-pupil allocation is the basis for all funding in the district. Principals also know that program budgeting is fundamentally in their hands and that performance accountability—tied to mission, goals, and school profile—will follow for resource decisions made at the school site level.

General Fund: School Program Codes

Line-items can be refined or expanded in monitoring activities in your school or program
Contact the Director of Business for information.

ELEMENTARY	Year	Fund	Function	Object	Building	Program
Kindergarten	1	–00	–1000	–610	–xx	–01
Reading						–02
Math						–03
Language Arts						–04
Social Studies						–05
Science						–06
Textbooks						–07
Teaching supplies						–08
School office						–09
Postage						–10
Site council						–11
Grants (list)						–31

MIDDLE SCHOOL						
Physical Education	1	00	1000	610	xx	–01
Vocational Arts						–02
Home Economics						–03
Art						–04
Science						–05
Band						–06
Vocal music						–07
Languages						–08
Math						–09
Social Studies						–10
Publications						–11
Teaching supplies						–12
School office						–13
Postage						–14
Site council						–15
Grants (list)						–31

HIGH SCHOOL						
Physical Education	1	00	1000	610	xx	–01
Vocational Arts						–02
Home Economics						–03
Art						–04
Science						–05
Band						–06
Vocal music						–07
Languages						–08
Math						–09
Social Studies						–10
Publications						–11
Teaching supplies						–12
School office						–13
Postage						–14
Site council						–15
Grants (list)						–31

FIGURE 7.6 Hypothetical Instructional Budget

INSTRUCTIONS TO PRINCIPALS

You are responsible for all instructional money assigned to your school as outlined in this document. You should gather input from staff members and your site council All budget requests and expenditures should be tied to the site plan for your school. These instructions provide: (a) account codes used by central office to track cost of programs in schools—any purchase request needs to show the right codes; (b) general notes to guide you on how the district expects you to code your purchases; (c) a list of instructional programs that have separate budgets; (d) a listing of all general fund budget allocations—it is here that you know how much you have for your school for all accounts; and (e) sample budget request forms.

GENERAL NOTES

1. Teaching supplies includes general supplies, paper, folders, printer cartridges, etc.
2. School office includes general office expenditures, professional materials, printing, student assemblies, and reserve funds.
3. Materials should be purchased from program budgets: Examples include magazine subscriptions, and other direct program expenses. Do not include textbook or equipment purchases here.
4. Remember to include shipping and handling when preparing purchase orders.
5. Transportation costs for program use will be charged to your school. This does not include transportation on regular routes before/after school.
6. Advance payment purchases are not allowed. Staff may not be reimbursed for out-of-pocket purchases.
7. No purchase will be approved without a purchase order in advance.
8. Repair of district-owned equipment will not be charged to schools. Routine expenses like reeds, pads, printer cartridges, etc. will be charged to programs.
9. Major purchases such as textbooks, curriculum adoptions, achievement tests and so forth are budgeted separately—see OTHER PROGRAMS below.

OTHER INSTRUCTIONAL PROGRAMS

CURRICULUM AND INSTRUCTION

Major purchases district-wide are budgeted separately, rather than charged to school budgets. The following categories are developed and administered by the Director of Curriculum and the Directors of Elementary and Secondary Education:

TEXTBOOKS	STAFF DEVELOPMENT	SPECIAL EDUCATION
CURRICULUM	GUIDANCE	TESTING

INSTRUCTIONAL MEDIA

The Director of Media Services coordinates all media services through school principal and librarians.

STUDENT ACTIVITIES

Athletics, debate, forensics, music contests, dramatics, and related equipment purchases will be subsidized by the district. Separate line items will be set up for each activity. Submit all purchase requests according to the budget calendar.

FIGURE 7.6 *continued*

GENERAL FUND INSTRUCTIONAL BUDGETS BY SCHOOL

The board of education annually sets the per-pupil allocation based on revenue availability and the recommendations of principals, staff, and site councils. It must be understood that the board pays many other expenses centrally—amounts shown here should be considered discretionary in terms of how schools expend.

ELEMENTARY INSTRUCTIONAL PROGRAMS ($27.50 per pupil)

Washington School	(230 pupils)	$6,325
Adams School	(326 pupils)	$8,965
Jefferson School	(270 pupils)	$7,425
Madison School	(189 pupils)	$5,198
Monroe School	(276 pupils)	$7,590
J. Q. Adams School	(250 pupils)	$6,875
Jackson School	(479 pupils)	$13,172
Van Buren School	(159 pupils)	$4,372
Harrison School	(233 pupils)	$6,408
Tyler School	(362 pupils)	$9,955
Polk School	(198 pupils)	$5,445
Taylor School	(289 pupils)	$7,948
Fillmore School	(432 pupils)	$11,880
Pierce School	(459 pupils)	$12,622
Buchanan School	(316 pupils)	$8,690
	Instruction-Elementary Totals:	$122,870

MIDDLE SCHOOL INSTRUCTIONAL PROGRAMS ($58 per pupil)

Lincoln School	(601 pupils)	$34,858
Johnson School	(598 pupils)	$34,684
	Instruction-Middle School Totals:	$69,542

HIGH SCHOOL INSTRUCTIONAL PROGRAMS ($75.18 per pupil)

Hayes High	(1076 pupils)	$80,894
Garfield High	(986 pupils)	$74,127
	Instruction-High School Totals:	$155,021
INSTRUCTION TOTAL	7,729 pupils	$347,433

INSTRUCTIONAL MEDIA ($19.25 per pupil)

Books, periodicals, AV supplies, teacher center, staff	$148,783

HIGH SCHOOL ACTIVITY PROGRAMS (each school)

Debate and forensics		$10,500
Dramatics		$1,000
Music contests		$3,250
Band uniform rotation (carries over budget years)		$5,000
ACTIVITY TOTAL 2 HIGH SCHOOLS	(×2) =	$39,500

TECHNOLOGY REQUESTS

Instructional technology and computer services will be coordinated through the Instructional Media Center coordinator, in cooperation with the District Technology Committee.

FURNITURE AND OTHER EQUIPMENT

Direct all requests to central office for district-wide purchasing.

FIGURE 7.6 *continued*

TRANSPORTATION BUDGETS BY SCHOOL

EDUCATIONAL FIELD TRIPS ($3.20 per pupil)

Washington School	(230 pupils)	$736
Adams School	(326 pupils)	$1,043
Jefferson School	(270 pupils)	$864
Madison School	(189 pupils)	$605
Monroe School	(276 pupils)	$883
J. Q. Adams School	(250 pupils)	$800
Jackson School	(479 pupils)	$1,533
Van Buren School	(159 pupils)	$509
Harrison School	(233 pupils)	$746
Tyler School	(362 pupils)	$1,158
Polk School	(198 pupils)	$634
Taylor School	(289 pupils)	$925
Fillmore School	(432 pupils)	$1,382
Pierce School	(459 pupils)	$1,469
Buchanan School	(316 pupils)	$1,011
	Field Trips-Elementary Total:	$14,298

MIDDLE SCHOOL FIELD TRIPS ($3.85 per pupil)

Lincoln School	(601 pupils)	$2,314
Johnson School	(598 pupils)	$2,302
	Field Trips-Middle School Total:	$4,616

HIGH SCHOOL FIELD TRIPS ($3.85 per pupil)

Hayes High	(1076 pupils)	$4,143
Garfield High	(986 pupils)	$3,796
	Field Trips-High School Total:	$7,939
FIELD TRIP TOTALS		$26,852

ATHLETICS

Lincoln School	$9,000
Johnson School	$9,000
Hayes High	$27,500
Garfield High	$27,500
ATHLETIC TOTALS	$73,000

ACTIVITIES ($1.90 mid-high, $5.65 sr. high)

Lincoln School	$1,142
Johnson School	$1,136
Hayes High	$6,079
Garfield High	$5,571
ACTIVITY TOTALS	$13,928

DEBATE and FORENSICS

Hayes High	$7,000
Garfield High	$7,000
DEBATE/FORENSIC TOTALS	$14,000

FIGURE 7.6 *continued*

CAPITAL OUTLAY BUDGETS BY SCHOOL

Major capital projects are the district's responsibility. Schools have a small amount available for minor equipment needs. Money for copiers is available as shown here. Direct all items to central office that are not covered below.

MINOR EQUIPMENT ($4.50 per pupil)

Washington School	(230 pupils)	$1,035
Adams School	(326 pupils)	$1,467
Jefferson School	(270 pupils)	$1,215
Madison School	(189 pupils)	$850
Monroe School	(276 pupils)	$1,242
J. Q. Adams School	(250 pupils)	$1,125
Jackson School	(479 pupils)	$2,156
Van Buren School	(159 pupils)	$716
Harrison School	(233 pupils)	$1,048
Tyler School	(362 pupils)	$1,629
Polk School	(198 pupils)	$891
Taylor School	(289 pupils)	$1,301
Fillmore School	(432 pupils)	$1,944
Pierce School	(459 pupils)	$2,066
Buchanan School	(316 pupils)	$1,422
Lincoln School	(601 pupils)	$2,704
Johnson School	(598 pupils)	$2,691
Hayes High	(1076 pupils)	$4,842
Garfield High	(986 pupils)	$4,437
	MINOR EQUIPMENT TOTALS	$34,780

SCHOOL EQUIPMENT BUDGETS

Elementary total	$10,000
Lincoln Mid-High	$13,000
Johnson Mid-High	$13,000
Hayes High	$25,000
Garfield High	$25,000
Instructional Media Center	$16,000
SCHOOL EQUIPMENT TOTALS	$102,000

COPIER BUDGETS

Elementary total	$16,000
Lincoln Mid-High	$15,000
Johnson Mid-High	$15,000
Hayes High	$15,000
Garfield High	$15,000
Central office	$16,000
COPIER TOTALS	$92,000

GRAND TOTALS

Total Instructional Budgets	$535,716
Total Transportation Budgets	$26,852
Total Athletics, Activities, and Debate	$100,928
Total Capital Outlay Budgets	$228,780
TOTAL SCHOOL BUDGETS	**$892,278**

FIGURE 7.6 *continued*

WASHINGTON ELEMENTARY
2008–09 Budget Year

Program Area: Reading
Code: 4-00-1000-610-80-01
Outcomes: Replaces 2010 copyright collection of storybooks. Children will increase reading time by 20 minutes per pupil.
Supplier: ABC Publishers, Inc.
12345 State Street
Uptown, NY 00000-0000

(See requisition for titles, grade levels, and numbers of books per grade.)

Cost per book:	$9.65
Quantity:	230
Freight:	$267.00
TOTAL:	$2,486.50

FIGURE 7.6 *continued*

WRAP-UP

Not all school districts follow the site-based organizational design set out in Figure 7.6. School district structure drives all resource decisions, and available revenue impacts all decisions. Note that the instructional budgeting consumes most available resources, leaving only the details of how to divide the pieces; that is, school district choices concerning local preference in resource allocation patterns.

Regardless of whether school districts choose to become more performance-accountable or whether a school district is forced to do so by state-mandated constituent involvement in site councils or other similar structures, school and district budgets will continue to be the focus of increased interest and accountability. In the case of budgeting for instruction, it should not be otherwise—*money pays for schools, and schools provide opportunities for children.* In sum, instructional budgeting is the heart of education.

POINT–COUNTERPOINT

POINT

State-mandated site-based management plans, while well-intentioned, have had the practical effect of requiring uninformed and sometimes uninterested people to make decisions concerning school operations. While some genuine level of community involvement is important and even indispensable, this fundamentally political movement has gone too far and has resulted in meddling that—under certain circumstances—can be highly inappropriate.

COUNTERPOINT

For far too long, school boards and district administrators have operated closed educational systems that effectively made a monopoly of society's most important tax-funded enterprise. Site-based management models should serve as a welcome wake-up call to educators, but in true bureaucratic fashion, implementation has managed to trivialize citizen participation by assigning site councils unimportant business while school districts claim legal proscription against citizen involvement in the truly important operations of schools—namely, hiring, evaluating, and firing teachers and administrators. In sum, site-based systems are a significant first step toward school reform, but more is needed to truly accomplish the initial purpose.

- How are principals, central office staff, teachers, and others involved in budget construction and daily budget administration in your school and district?
- What limits, if any, are imposed on site councils in your school district?
- Based upon your readings so far, what do you consider the strengths and weaknesses of your school's and district's instructional budgeting practices? What recommendations would you make for improvements, if needed, and why?

CASE STUDY

You are seeking a position as curriculum director in a public school district. During a lengthy job interview, the superintendent spends considerable time laying out his desire to engage individual school sites more actively in the budget process and particularly to hold school principals and staffs accountable for the use of decentralized moneys through aggressive academic performance targets. As the interview evolves, you learn that the state has recently placed two of the school district's 12 elementary schools, one middle school, and one high school on academic probation for failure to meet state assessment standards and that several other schools in the district might be verging on a similar fate. The superintendent seems convinced that a turnaround could be achieved if principals and staffs were given both the charge to increase performance and the promise of sufficient resources to meet standards. The superintendent makes it clear that he expects the new curriculum director to spearhead this initiative and to put a well-founded action plan into place within a year's time. Upon conclusion of the interview, he notes that he would expect the new director to forward a proposed calendar of events within a matter of weeks.

A week later you receive the job offer from this school district. You gladly accept the offer, knowing that you face a tough challenge. Shortly after accepting your new position, you attend a national conference on raising student performance levels. The many excellent sessions you attend convince you that your new school district indeed can achieve a turnaround by setting high goals, analyzing student data, investing in staff training for school improvement, reducing class sizes, increasing instructional time, implementing best-practice models in teaching and learning, providing extra help for struggling students, engaging parents in students' progress, and creating a community of shared leadership. The problem, you muse, is the typical one school leaders always face—where to begin, how to get others involved, how to build support, what tasks to engage and in what order, and—of course—how to manage high stakes with too little time.

- Is your new school district headed in the right direction? Why or why not?
- Who should be involved in the initial planning stages of this transformation? Who are the most critical players? How will you garner their support? What barriers do you anticipate?
- What are the most pressing priorities in beginning this planning process? What do you believe are the critical elements for change of this magnitude to succeed?
- Do you think your new school district's principals will greet this concept with enthusiasm or reservation? Why? What do you expect will be their most urgent questions?
- What will your proposed plan of action contain; that is, what calendar of events will you propose? In what areas do you anticipate the need for greater resources?

PORTFOLIO EXERCISES

- Make an appointment with your school district's curriculum director to discuss instructional budgeting in your school district. Prior to your meeting, request a copy of the school district's instructional budget. Discuss the curriculum director's perceptions as to how this budget interfaces with the school district's mission and goal statements. Ask if or how the school district goes about development of curriculum-based, instructional budgeting.

- In your interview with the curriculum director, use the series of planning questions appearing in this chapter as a discussion guide. For example, ask questions about who has responsibility for establishing the overall level of instructional spending, who sets budgets for each major program or school, who selects the curriculum, and who has responsibility for new programs or for eliminating current programs.

- If your school district uses site-based budgeting, obtain a copy of your school's budget (for an example, see Figure 7.6, which is a sample school-level instructional budget). Interview your school principal to determine how resource decisions are made at your school site. If your school district does not use site-based budgeting, determine the level of funding available to each school site and discuss the decision-making process with your principal and the school district's chief financial officer. Be sure to include discussion of resource and program accountability.

WEB RESOURCES

American Association of School Administrators, www.aasa.org

American Federation of Teachers, www.aft.org

Association for Supervision and Curriculum Development, www.ascd.org

Association of School Business Officials International, asbointl.org

Education Commission of the States, www.ecs.org

National Conference of State Legislatures, www.ncsl.org

National Education Association, www.nea.org

National Governors Association, www.nga.org

National School Boards Association, www.nsba.org

U.S. Department of Education, www.ed.gov

RECOMMENDED READING

Bird, James J., Chuang Wang, and Louise M. Murray. "Building Budgets and Trust through Superintendent Leadership." *Journal of Education Finance* 35 2 (Fall 2009): 140–156.

Dounay, Jennifer. "Site-Based Decisionmaking: State-Level Policies." *ECS State Notes*. Denver, CO: Education Commission of the States, 2005. www.ecs.org/clearinghouse/61/13/6113.htm.

Eckert, Jonathan, Ed. *Local Labor Management Relationships as a Vehicle to Advance Reform: Findings from the U.S. Department of Education's Labor Management Conference.* Washington, DC: US Department of Education, 2011.

Education Commission of the States. "Recent State Policies/Activities: Governance—Site-Based Management." www.ecs.org/ecs/ecscat.nsf/WebTopicView?OpenView&count=-1&Restrict ToCategory=Governance—Site-Based+Management.

Hadderman, Margaret. "School-Based Budgeting." *ERIC Digest* 131. Eugene, OR: ERIC Clearinghouse on Educational Management, 1999.

Hartman, William T., and William L. Boyd. *Resource Allocation and Productivity in Education: Theory and Practice.* Westport, CT: Greenwood Press, 1998.

Leithwood, Kenneth, Karen Seashore Louis, Stephen Anderson, and Kyla Wahlstrom. *Review of Research: How Leadership Influences Student Learning.* Minneapolis, MN: Center for Applied Research and Educational Improvement, University of Minnesota, 2004.

Ouchi, William G. "Power to the Principals: Decentralization in Three Large School Districts." *Organization Science* 17 (March/April 2006): 298–307.

REL West. *School-Based Budgeting and Management.* San Francisco: WestEd, August 2009.

Trussel, John M., and Patricia A. Patrick. "Predicting Significant Reductions in Instructional Expenditures by School Districts." *Journal of Education Finance* 37 3 (Winter, 2012): 205–233.

World Bank. *What Do We Know About School-Based Management?* Washington, DC: World Bank Education and Human Development Network, November 2007. http://siteresources. worldbank.org/education/Resources/278200–1099079877269/547664–1099079934475/54 7667–1145313948551/what_do_we_know_SBM.pdf.

World Bank. *What Is School-Based Management?* Washington, DC: World Bank Education and Human Development Network, November 2007. http://siteresources.worldbank.org/ Education/Resources/278200–1099079877269/547664–1099079934475/547667–1145313 948551/what_is_SBM.pdf.

CHAPTER 8

Budgeting for Student Activities

THE CHALLENGE

Historically, little attention has been given to accounting for activity funds in school districts. The nature of activity funds, however, makes them especially vulnerable to error, misuse, and fraud. In addition, activity funds often total to large sums of money, especially when capturing the amounts that flow through an educational organization in the form of school board funds, student-generated funds, receipts and disbursements related to athletics, and the myriad cocurricular and extracurricular events sponsored by school districts today.

Financial Accounting for Local and State School Systems (2009)[1]

CHAPTER DRIVERS

Please reflect upon the following questions as you read this chapter:

- What is the role of student activities in schools?
- What are student and district activity funds?
- What are the controls and lines of authority on activity funds?
- What policies are needed regarding segregation of duties, internal controls on handling cash, and disbursement procedures?
- What policies are needed for nonactivity funds such as fee receipts, sales tax, and petty cash?
- What cautions apply to the whole process of budgeting for student activities?

---

1 Gregory S. Allison, Steven D. Honegger, and Frank Johnson, *Financial Accounting for Local and State School Systems: 2009 Edition* (Washington, DC: U.S. Department of Education, Institute of Education Sciences, National Center for Education Statistics, June 2009), 149, http://nces.ed.gov/pubsearch/pubsinfo.asp?pubid=2009325.

ACTIVITIES AND SCHOOLS

The opening quotation suggests yet another critical aspect to funding equal educational opportunity in that educating the whole child includes providing learning experiences for students outside the formal classroom setting. A major aspect of the act of budgeting for schools thus involves providing a sound financial base for the many student activities supported by school districts today.

There is no question that student activities entail significant amounts of time and money. In fact, activities are so central to the life of schools that many public attitudes about education are based almost entirely on the countless activities found in today's schools and districts. Although it is unusual for books about school funding to contain much discussion of activity programs, the topic is so important to a comprehensive view of school money and site-based leadership that we have devoted a chapter to ensuring that student activities are regarded as an essential component of equal educational opportunity.

As with previous chapters, we begin with general concepts and then move to the more specific elements of budgeting—in this case, budgeting for student activities. We first establish the role of activities in schools and then engage a deeper examination of the operational aspects of activity funding. More specifically, we define activity funds and carefully distinguish between student activity funds and district activity funds, followed by an examination of controls on activity funds and relevant lines of authority for receiving and expending those same moneys. We also examine best practices relating to segregation of duties, internal controls on handling cash, and disbursement procedures, as well as present best practices related to treatment of nonactivity funds like fee receipts, sales tax, and petty cash. The chapter ends with a strong caution because, as the opening quote states, lax oversight of activity funds can have serious consequences for those tasked with their oversight.

What Is the Role of Student Activities?

The importance of student activities in the life of schools cannot be overemphasized. An immediate sense of the importance of student activities is captured by simply glancing at the long list of activity programs supported by nearly every school district today. For example, a typical high school may support art clubs, chess clubs, journalism clubs, foreign language clubs, pep clubs, photography clubs, science clubs, chorus, marching band, orchestra, drama, debate teams, drill teams, math teams, and student government. In addition are organized intramural and competitive sports like baseball, basketball, cross-country, football, golf, hockey, soccer, swimming, tennis, track, volleyball, and wrestling. The above activities require one or more resources, like stipends for faculty sponsors, coaching salaries, transportation, equipment, and facilities, some of which can be costly. For example, resurfacing a track can cost in excess of $200,000, in addition to maintenance costs, and it must be recognized that track is a sport that usually generates little in the way of offsetting revenues.[2] The point here is simply that student

---

2 This is offered only as an example. It is not meant to imply that student activities should be self-supporting.

activities represent significant direct and indirect costs for schools and districts. As a result, investment of time and money, as well as issues like liability, establish activities as a major school funding concern.

There is an additional reason why the role played by student activities cannot be overemphasized: their importance in the lives of children and young people. Starting in the early elementary grades, children enthusiastically present vocal and instrumental concerts as well as dramatic performances for proud family and appreciative community audiences. Progressing into the high school years, young people form character, develop self-discipline, and persevere in school as a result of athletic and other student activity programs. In a number of cases, these activities encompass programs related to academics, so, in essence, they represent an extension of the school day. Whether or not school leaders actually enjoy attending every student activity, they generally learn to strongly support them because they rightly come to understand that activities are not extracurricular—rather, they accurately view activities as part of the cocurriculum and, hence, deserving of support.

Finally, beyond the noble reasons for supporting student activity programs is a practical justification: the valuable role they play with regard to public perception and public relations. School leaders sometimes joke that the quality of academic programs is judged by the shine on the floor of the school and the success of student athletic competitions. Savvy school leaders, however, quickly grasp that success in activities and shiny floors boost local pride in all school programs by broadcasting school achievements to the community in highly visible ways. Because a large percentage of people in a typical district do not have school-aged children, it follows that a number of taxpayers and voters see schools only from a spectator's view, e.g., sports fans and consumers of local media. A school district's roster of student activity programs, then, can play a critical role in generating community support, fiscal and otherwise, for local schools.

BUDGETING FOR ACTIVITIES

The sheer scope of cocurricular and extracurricular programs today underscores the fact that a significant amount of money is allocated to and generated by student activities. As we will see, budgeting for activities is at once similar and dissimilar to other budget issues explored in this text. Similarities arise from the fact that many of the accounting principles discussed earlier also apply to activity funds; as such, revenue and expenditure dimensions and various account structures are already familiar. However, differences arise, because, unlike other funds, activity funds typically are more loosely structured in the sense that fewer controls may exist, and revenue and expenditure operations frequently are housed in multiple locations. Similarly, statutes controlling activity funds may be less stringent in some states than others, so some aspects of activity fund accounting might not be strictly prescribed. In sum, the potential for error and fraud is highest in activity funding, making it essential to establish local student activity funding structures that not only support the contribution of activities to school learning, but also defend against error, mismanagement, and abuse.

What Are Activity Funds?

Activity funds are legal entities created by state statute for the purpose of segregating money in support of student activities. The unique nature of activity funds is evident in that statutes often define activities as cocurricular events, which may be further defined as student activities outside the classroom that complement the formal curriculum. Making such distinction has two key advantages. First, it creates the basis for expending district funds in support of activities by linking nonclassroom learning with the academic curriculum. Second, it sets up the mechanism for districts to separately support student activities and to account for money spent on activities. The first distinction is especially important because it is reasonable to believe that districts are not authorized to spend resources on programs unrelated to some curriculum goal. The second distinction is less profound, but it does set up useful controls and permits the existence of student-owned organizations, as will be seen later.

Activity funds are therefore accounting entities analogous to the general and special revenue funds and account structures seen in a school district's regular budget. Each activity fund is an independent accounting entity created to segregate its financial activities from that of all other funds, usually due to special restrictions on how money can be spent. Activity funds may only be spent for statutorily approved purposes, which are usually quite broad and limited only by the intent to spend activity funds for such purposes as athletics, music, and special projects—i.e., activity funds may not be appropriated for any other use. Operation of activity funds, however, is very different from the district's regular budget. As we will see later, the collection, disbursement, and accounting for activity fund moneys usually is housed at the school site level, with building principals designated as the activity fund supervisor. Further, activity funds are distinguished by ownership; that is, whether the funds are owned by the district or by student organizations. In addition, the activity fund supervisor typically is responsible for accounting for all nonactivity fund moneys, including student fee collections, sales tax, and petty cash accounts. To make matters more complex, the ownership distinction creates special collection and disbursement issues. Complicating the mix is a vague (and potentially incorrect) perception among school organization sponsors and students regarding allowable uses of activity funds. Thus, the school principal faces multiple challenges by virtue of being responsible for funds belonging to students, funds belonging to the district, administration of nonactivity funds belonging to the district, collecting and disbursing funds from a school base, and transferring certain funds to the district for disbursement. The potential for error, misunderstanding, and even deliberate wrongdoing is self-evident.

Student Activity Funds

One of the unique features of activity funds is the distinction of ownership. There is no analogous question of who owns the district's regular budget because the school board has complete legal authority and control subject only to applicable statutes. In sharp contrast, activity funds are of two types. Student activity funds are owned by students, i.e., students are the legal owners of certain activity funds and have the right to control how the money is spent, pursuant only to statutes, accounting guidelines, and board policy.

Student activity funds consist of those student moneys that involve a student-owned organization. Operationally, students in such organizations not only take part in the organization's activities but also are involved in the management of the organization. Examples include many of the clubs listed earlier. The definition is important for several reasons. Most obvious is that no one in the school district, other than students, can legally expend money from a student-owned activity fund account. In other words, money on deposit in a district-maintained activity fund is not always owned by the district. The other critical reason is subtler, in that districts must be very careful in subsidizing activities because district money could come under student control if not carefully directed.

District Activity Funds

In contrast, district activity funds belong to the school district. District activity funds support cocurricular activities in which students participate but which are administered by the school district. Examples of district activities include district-sponsored organizations such as choir, band, orchestra, debate teams, and sports. The definition is again important in that the distinguishing feature is that ownership and approval to expend these moneys belongs to the school board, rather than students. The accounting process is different too in that district activity funds are centralized in the district's accounting books, rather than in individual schools (as is the case with student activity funds). District activity fund structures avoid the potential problems cited earlier, in that activities supported by the school district are accounted for at the district level, and all money is deposited through the district treasurer to the district's bank account.

The distinction of district ownership is not trivial. School boards are responsible for maintaining control of district resources used to support student activities, and control would be lost by moving district funds into school-level student activity fund accounts.[3] Although parallel activity fund structures may seem redundant, ownership determines who controls how money is spent.

In addition, distinction of ownership of activity funds may have legal ramifications. For example, school districts have experienced legal problems trying to control organizations like booster clubs and religious groups that may organize around school-based activities, often with a request to be included in the district's chart of activity fund accounts. Because issues of ownership and apparent sponsorship may arise, it is best to require groups not directly sponsored by the district to maintain separate bank accounts.

---

3 The importance of ownership is apparent in the consequences of inattention. If, for example, a school board wished to subsidize a single student event, it should do so by direct expenditure from its own funds. In contrast, if the board were to transfer district moneys directly into a student-owned activity fund account (e.g., senior class), the transferred moneys would immediately become the property of the senior class and the board could no longer require that the money be used for the targeted event.

What Are the Controls on Activity Funds?

The issues raised here suggest that significant amounts of money are involved in student activity budgeting and that a complicated process governs what happens at both the district and individual school levels. This raises questions of controls on activity funds, which logically lead to further examination of issues such as lines of authority and prudent policy development designed to make budgeting and administration transparent. Almost nowhere in school budgeting is the word "control" more welcome than in activity funding, i.e., controls are for the wellbeing of everyone involved. Our many years of experience tell us that more administrators are dismissed for mismanagement of activity funds than for any other reason.

Lines of Authority

The need for clear lines of authority in handling activity budgets is underscored by our discussion up to this point. Segregating activity funds from all other funds in the school district and the complications brought about by numerous school sites handling activity fund moneys indicate a real need to maintain strict control, e.g., gate receipts at an athletic event on a given night may easily exceed $10,000, assuring that activity budgeting and accounting is no small matter. In fact, it is not unusual for the activity fund chart of accounts at a typical high school to have a fund balance well in excess of $100,000. As we have emphasized before, there is almost no stain on a professional reputation as damaging as violating a fiduciary trust, and mismanagement of even a small dollar amount of funds in an activity account has the real potential to place the administrator in question under a cloud of suspicion.

The general guideline for lines of authority for activity funds calls for the district's board of education to adopt clear policies governing establishment and operation of all activity funds. The board treasurer, as the district's fiscal officer, is generally appointed to implement and enforce a system of internal control procedures. These individuals have first-line responsibility for all activity funds in the school district because both district and student activity funds are held on deposit by the district and must be reported in the district's financial statements. In sum, student-owned funds are agency (fiduciary) funds wherein the district acts as agent for these funds, while district-owned funds are classified as special revenue funds intended for support of student activities.

At the school level, the principal is generally designated as the activity fund supervisor. Supervisory designation means the principal is responsible for overall operation of activity funds housed in that school, including collection and deposit of activity fund moneys, approval of disbursements from the activity fund, and all bookkeeping responsibilities. The burden is a weighty one because, although custodial duties in fact may be delegated, final responsibility may not. It is precisely this point that gives rise to many of the policies we will note shortly regarding handling of money and multiple safeguards against misuse, embezzlement, and fraud. In other words, a principal may delegate duties, but responsibility may never be delegated away.

Multiple levels of activity fund ownership, responsibility, and sponsorship give rise to yet one more set of players in the line of authority. Organizational sponsors, often teachers or coaches with little or no financial background, usually initiate an activity fund transaction. Without proper training it is unlikely that they will fully understand either the process or reasons for controls on activity funds. Here, the principal can serve an important role in ensuring compliance with district policies and procedures for safe handling of activity funds by arranging orientation and training for sponsors of school-level student activities at the beginning of each school year so that they understand the process of approved purchases, purchase orders, handling of cash, and issuance of receipts. Generally, someone from the district's business and finance office is more than happy to provide this training. In sum, sponsors serve as a critical first line in ensuring that funds are used appropriately for the particular student activity they oversee.

Recommended Activity Fund Policies

Budgeting for activities is straightforward and prescriptive. The scope and size of activity fund budgets require application of the same professional accounting and auditing standards that apply to all other school moneys. Further, in order to gain control over an arena that sees multiple individuals at multiple sites handling moneys, a set of clear policies and procedures must be established and obeyed by everyone who deals with student activities and, consequently, school money. Although it is not feasible in a text of this nature to go into great detail, we do provide best practices related to management of activity funds, specifically general policies on activity fund operation, segregation of duties, internal controls on handling cash, and disbursement of money, because these are central.

General Policies

Establishment and operation of activity funds requires clear controls to ensure safe and effective management of district and student moneys. Several of the following bulleted items have already been discussed, while others are added here to call attention to additional potential problems:

- Use the services of a professional accountant to set up the activity fund accounting system for the entire school district.
- Provide all staff and organization sponsors with training on activity fund management on an annual basis.
- Task the district treasurer with establishment of standardized forms and procedures. Because the district accumulates and reports all student and district activity fund transactions, the district is responsible for ensuring that standardized controls are in place.
- All activity funds must be approved by the board. Requests to create a student organization include a statement of purpose and potential fundraising activity. To avoid confusion and to aid organizational goals, the name of the organization is descriptive of its purpose.
- Organizations not directly sponsored by the district should be excluded from its financial activities.
- The board formally designates activity fund supervisors. Usually only one supervisor per school or attendance center is appointed.

- All fundraising is approved in advance by the district. All groups included in the district's activity fund chart of accounts receive district approval for their activities, including fundraising. Unauthorized fundraising can create significant community relations problems.
- Activity funds are spent only on students. Although this seems obvious, problems frequently arise when organizations expire with unspent moneys on deposit (e.g., senior class). Insofar as possible, money should be spent on those students who raised it.
- Cash basis strictly applies to student activity funds. Cash basis requires that no money be spent or encumbered unless an equal or greater amount is already on deposit. Strict adherence to advance purchase orders resolves this problem.
- All activity funds are regularly audited along with other funds in the district. Full audits should be done annually.
- Activity funds should never be used for any purpose that results in a benefit, loan, or credit to anyone.

Segregation of Duties

The importance of clear policies on handling activity funds is underscored by sound business practices relating to segregation of financial duties. Bookkeeping errors can occur inadvertently, and the potential for intentional mishandling is always in the realm of possibilities. Risk of error, theft, and fraud can be minimized by segregation of duties meant to reinforce general policies, tighten cash controls, and regulate all receipt and disbursement procedures.

Segregation of duties speaks to both intentional and unintentional error through the principle that no one person should be solely responsible for handling money. Daily instances of cash handling occur in all schools, and segregation of duties helps reduce many attendant problems. At the school level, the activity fund bookkeeper, appointed by the principal, should take the lead on most operations, including collecting activity fund money, preparing deposit slips, making deposits, preparing the fund accounting records, and preparing checks written on the activity fund account. These activities will be examined later during an audit and should be periodically reviewed internally as well. In addition, four particular duties need close attention:

- Although a bookkeeper should prepare checks, a separate signatory should be required.
- The principal as activity fund supervisor should be the primary signatory on checks—in some states, it is required by law that the principal sign all checks.
- All checks should bear two signatures.
- Bank statements must be reconciled regularly with the fund accounting records, and someone other than the bookkeeper should prepare this reconciliation.

These procedures, among others, protect against error and deliberate wrongdoing on the accounting side and serve to back up other internal controls on cash.

Internal Controls on Cash

The number and scope of student activities in schools today guarantees frequent handling of large cash amounts. Yearbook sales, event receipts, fundraisers, student photos, and student class projects such as vocational arts result in many thousands of dollars in cash transactions at the school site. Cash represents the greatest risk of loss, requiring additional internal controls.

The most important aspects of internal cash controls are well-trained employees and careful establishment of an audit trail to provide physical evidence for each step in cash transactions. In fact, the audit trail gives more insight to what might be missing rather than showing something was incorrectly done. Although professional accounting advice is required to properly handle cash, at least the following cash controls must be in place:

- All fund supervisors and sponsors must be trained and provided with written guidelines on handling cash.
- All forms, receipts, and tickets should be prenumbered.
- Prenumbered items should be safeguarded.
- Prenumbered items should not be printed in-house.
- Persons collecting cash should be rotated regularly.
- More than one person should be present when cash is collected.
- No cash collections should be given to another person without a receipt.
- The bookkeeper must use prenumbered, bound receipts for all currency and checks received.
- Cash receipts should be kept intact and may not be used to make change or to make any kind of disbursement.
- The bookkeeper should make daily deposits. Any undeposited cash should be kept locked safely away.
- Everyone handling cash should be bonded.

It may come as a surprise to some readers to learn how often these procedures fail to be followed even though the consequences for not doing so can be devastating. For example: A harried principal or club sponsor sticks school cash into their wallets, purses, or even an unlocked desk drawer for later deposit; volunteer ticket-takers at school events naively tear off extra tickets to make the cash and tickets balance; blank prenumbered cash receipts lie in plain view on a busy secretary's desk; an office clerk leaves cash unattended, even if for only a short time. Especially appalling is the fairly common practice of tossing a bank bag stuffed with athletic gate receipts into a car trunk to be delivered to the school office the following Monday morning. Any one of these examples represents a tragedy-in-waiting not only for the school employee involved, but also for the students who were to benefit from the cocurricular activity that the lost moneys were to support.

Disbursement Procedures

The final activity fund area we should consider is disbursement procedures. Disbursement refers to any financial transaction in which money leaves an account. This discussion can be short, because some of our other discussion involved disbursement as part of the total process. As a result, a bulleted list of guidelines makes these points quickly.

As we noted earlier, activity funds are either district-owned or student-owned. We also noted that student funds typically are handled at the school level, meaning most activity on these accounts occurs at various school sites. District funds are considerably more complicated in that there can be an extra transaction involved because district funds are accounted for at the district level but may have flowed through a school first. An example makes this clearer. Assume the board has agreed to partially subsidize students' woodworking projects.[4] Materials are ordered, and the bill arrives. The district pays the entire bill and calculates how much each student owes. Students then make payment to the school office, which in turn makes a deposit to the revolving woodworking account within the activity fund. The school site activity fund must then transfer these "district-owned" amounts to the district treasurer for deposit back to the district. It is not as difficult as it seems, but this relatively simple example underscores the meticulous nature of activity fund budgeting and accounting.

A more typical daily activity fund transaction involves a student club purchase. In that case, advance approval is obtained, a purchase order is written, goods are received, and the bookkeeper makes payment. Accordingly, disbursement procedures for student activity funds are:

- Disbursement requires approval of the student group's sponsor and the activity fund supervisor (usually the school principal).
- Disbursements should be backed up by a voucher signed by the sponsor and principal.
- Disbursements should be made by prenumbered check with multiple signatures.
- Documentation must show who requested the purchase, what was purchased, which activity fund account should be charged, the amount, and the check number.

In sum, there are three overarching rules with regard to activity funds:

- Be very careful when handling money.
- Spend money only for what it is intended.
- Use fund accounting (the tool for segregating money) so that the first two rules can be efficiently met.

It is prudent to remember that activity funds have the potential to be a major source of financial problems for school leaders if the practices outlined here are not assiduously followed.

---

4 Discussion in the next section will reveal that this transaction actually involves a nonactivity fund account, although it is carried in the activity fund chart of accounts at the school site level. The activity described here is a student fee type transaction. However, it is a common transaction easily recognized by the reader and serves the purpose of demonstrating a disbursement activity.

What about Nonactivity Funds?

In addition to activity funds, school districts and individual school sites collect other kinds of money that must be handled just as securely. This task falls to the same people who are in charge of activity funds although, in a strict sense, we are now talking about nonactivity fund moneys. The money in question here often relates to curricular programs and does not definitionally belong in the activity fund structure. Examples of this type of money include fees related to various programs such as class materials, laboratories, and physical education. Still other kinds of nonactivity fund moneys are handled at district and school levels, such as sales tax and petty cash. Our interest here has less to do with the intricacies of these moneys and more to do with making sure that school leaders know that these moneys exist and must be handled carefully because—once again—this is an area fraught with pitfalls.

The following descriptions are meant to introduce different kinds of nonactivity fund moneys that are typically received by schools. For our purpose, the most important thing to focus on is that these are generally moneys that will be transferred to the district because they are almost always district-owned or received on a fiduciary basis. A more detailed examination is not appropriate for this text because these moneys are merely tools to satisfy certain accounting principles and do not represent educational planning devices—although they do represent opportunities for mishandling.

Fee Funds

As noted earlier, schools usually have several fee fund accounts. For example, schools collect fees for specialized instructional supplies and materials, such as those associated with art classes; advanced placement courses; food service; laboratory usage associated with science classes; and musical instrument rental. These fees represent user charges and are owned by the district, which will, in turn, replenish the appropriate district fund when the school site activity fund bookkeeper remits collections to the district treasurer. The district then uses fee receipts to continue providing services. Fee funds do not represent usable revenue at the school level. Rather, they are "receipt-only" funds, and no disbursements can be made from fee funds. The school merely acts to collect fees on behalf of the district.

Sales Tax

Another type of nonactivity fund money often collected at the school level is sales tax. The concept itself requires little explanation although at times it can be confusing as to when schools need to charge sales tax. The universal rule is that when schools do collect sales tax, the school is merely the collection point and acts as the remitter to another level. School districts usually have the freedom to choose whether to let individual school sites directly remit sales tax collections or whether to centralize tax collection for a single remittance to the state or locality. The confusing aspect is usually related to individual states' laws because it is not always clear whether sales tax should be charged. That issue is answerable only in the context of each state, with the general guiding principle that items for resale are usually subject to sales tax collection in most states.

Petty Cash

The last area of nonactivity funds common to individual school sites is petty cash. Every school in the U.S. likely has a petty cash account, although its appropriate use and accounting requirements are often less well understood. Petty cash is a source of cash used for making small disbursements without writing checks or, alternatively, making payment more quickly than could be done by going through the district's normal bill-paying channels. Petty cash accounts do not involve much money as a general rule, although—as we have repeatedly said—even the smallest sum of money must be handled properly. Examples of uses for petty cash might include paying game referees with a check drawn on the petty cash fund on game night, buying postage stamps, and other small cash purchases.

Because petty cash accounts represent more opportunity for trouble than may be the case for other kinds of school money, petty cash is often statutorily limited in amount. In addition, districts need to establish clear policies on uses of petty cash due to the ease with which these accounts can be defrauded because it is possible, unlike other district funds, to make actual cash payments from petty cash. Board policy should include at least the following:

- The board should set a maximum amount for petty cash accounts and clearly state the intended uses. A maximum disbursement amount should be set, above which board approval is required.
- The activity fund bookkeeper should act as the petty cash custodian. Access to petty cash should be strictly regulated.
- The petty cash custodian should require signed receipts from all persons receiving cash to create an audit trail. Receipts should document the purpose of the disbursement and which fund should be charged when petty cash is replenished at month's end.

What Does an Activity Fund Report Look Like?

Although the different requirements of state laws and wide range of student groups recognized by school districts prevent a universal format for activity fund reporting, the complex picture and set of responsibilities involved in activity funding is best conceptualized visually. Figure 8.1 presents a month-end activity fund balance report for a hypothetical high school in a district of about 7,000 students. Numbers often tell great stories, and Figure 8.1 speaks in telling fashion. First, it can be easily seen that this high school has a wide range of student activities—almost every conceivable organization has a place in this school's programs. Second, it can be seen that some accounts are district-owned, e.g., athletics, while others are student-owned, e.g., choir fundraising. Third, it can be seen that fee funds are reported in the school's activity fund, e.g., parking permits, although the revenue will be transferred to the district at a later time. And fourth, our point about handling significant sums of money is highlighted here, as this single high school in a medium-size district has a month-end cash balance of $69,442.08—not an insignificant amount of money for which the school's leader must take responsibility.

ACCOUNT NUMBER/TITLE		BEGINNING CASH BALANCE	CURRENT MONTH TRANSACTIONS	ENDING CASH BALANCE
109 .XXXXX.XXX.XX.XXX.X	SEASON TICKETS	$ 1,362.03	$ –	$ 1,362.03
110 .XXXXX.XXX.XX.XXX.X	ACTIVITY TICKETS	$ 11,235.09	$ –	$ 11,235.09
111 .XXXXX.XXX.XX.XXX.X	CONCESSIONS	$ –	$ –	$ –
112 .XXXXX.XXX.XX.XXX.X	PARKING PERMITS	$ 8,739.84	$ 565.00	$ 9,304.84
114 .XXXXX.XXX.XX.XXX.X	FOOTBALL	$ 4,114.05	$ 1,871.20 –	$ 2,242.85
116 .XXXXX.XXX.XX.XXX.X	BOYS BASKETBALL	$ 10,131.35	$ 3,182.17 –	$ 6,949.18
117 .XXXXX.XXX.XX.XXX.X	BASEBALL	$ 161.84	$ 187.10	$ 348.94
118 .XXXXX.XXX.XX.XXX.X	BOYS TRACK	$ 140.00	$ 490.00	$ 630.00
119 .XXXXX.XXX.XX.XXX.X	SOCCER	$ –	$ –	$ –
120 .XXXXX.XXX.XX.XXX.X	WRESTLING	$ 8.42	$ –	$ 8.42
122 .XXXXX.XXX.XX.XXX.X	CROSS COUNTRY	$ –	$ –	$ –
124 .XXXXX.XXX.XX.XXX.X	BOYS TENNIS	$ 308.86	$ 120.00	$ 428.86
126 .XXXXX.XXX.XX.XXX.X	GOLF	$ 17.50	$ –	$ 17.50
128 .XXXXX.XXX.XX.XXX.X	BOYS SWIMMING	$ 2,788.38	$ 109.03	$ 2,897.41
130 .XXXXX.XXX.XX.XXX.X	GIRLS TENNIS	$ 469.02	$ –	$ 469.02
131 .XXXXX.XXX.XX.XXX.X	GIRLS SOCCER	$ 33.68	$ 426.10	$ 459.78
132 .XXXXX.XXX.XX.XXX.X	GIRLS VOLLEYBALL	$ –	$ –	$ –
134 .XXXXX.XXX.XX.XXX.X	GIRLS BASKETBALL	$ 6,745.51	$ 1,282.03 –	$ 5,463.48
135 .XXXXX.XXX.XX.XXX.X	SOFTBALL	$ 32.97	$ 111.32	$ 144.29
136 .XXXXX.XXX.XX.XXX.X	GIRLS SWIMMING	$ 1,603.06	$ 129.45	$ 1,732.51
138 .XXXXX.XXX.XX.XXX.X	GIRLS GYMNASTICS	$ –	$ –	$ –
140 .XXXXX.XXX.XX.XXX.X	GIRLS GOLF	$ –	$ –	$ –
141 .XXXXX.XXX.XX.XXX.X	WEIGHT TRAINING	$ 7,035.23	$ 4,076.40 –	$ 2,958.83
142 .XXXXX.XXX.XX.XXX.X	TOURNAMENT ACCOUNT	$ 925.26	$ 1,008.58	$ 1,933.84
143 .XXXXX.XXX.XX.XXX.X	WRITERS CLUB	$ 1.64	$ –	$ 1.64
144 .XXXXX.XXX.XX.XXX.X	STUDENT SUPPORT GROUP	$ 16,602.31	$ 11,040.44 –	$ 5,561.87
145 .XXXXX.XXX.XX.XXX.X	CITY BASKETBALL	$ 3,551.84	$ 110.00 –	$ 3,441.84
146 .XXXXX.XXX.XX.XXX.X	DRAMATICS	$ 1,834.92	$ 41.00	$ 1,875.92
147 .XXXXX.XXX.XX.XXX.X	DRAMA TRIP	$ 19,998.54	$ 14,780.01 –	$ 5,218.53
148 .XXXXX.XXX.XX.XXX.X	THESPIANS	$ 656.88	$ 16,008.06 –	$ (15,351.18)
150 .XXXXX.XXX.XX.XXX.X	DEBATE	$ 920.35	$ –	$ 920.35
151 .XXXXX.XXX.XX.XXX.X	SCHOLARSHIP BOWL	$ 825.00	$ –	$ 825.00
152 .XXXXX.XXX.XX.XXX.X	CAP AND GOWN	$ –	$ –	$ –
154 .XXXXX.XXX.XX.XXX.X	NEEDY STUDENT	$ 355.42	$ 5.00	$ 360.42
156 .XXXXX.XXX.XX.XXX.X	NEWSPAPER	$ 1,400.00	$ 848.00 –	$ 552.00
158 .XXXXX.XXX.XX.XXX.X	MUSIC CONTEST ACCOUNT	$ 216.12	$ 195.19 –	$ 20.93
160 .XXXXX.XXX.XX.XXX.X	MUSIC SUPPORT GROUP	$ 1,517.89	$ –	$ 1,517.89
161 .XXXXX.XXX.XX.XXX.X	VARIETY SHOWS	$ –	$ 1,347.05	$ 1,347.05
162 .XXXXX.XXX.XX.XXX.X	SPECIAL MUSIC	$ 1,916.19	$ 100.00	$ 2,016.19
164 .XXXXX.XXX.XX.XXX.X	CHORALE	$ 4,817.36	$ 4,817.36 –	$ –
166 .XXXXX.XXX.XX.XXX.X	SCHOOLWIDE TALENT	$ 134.92	$ –	$ 134.92
168 .XXXXX.XXX.XX.XXX.X	JAZZ GROUP	$ –	$ –	$ –
170 .XXXXX.XXX.XX.XXX.X	ORCHESTRA	$ 263.00	$ 50.00	$ 313.00
172 .XXXXX.XXX.XX.XXX.X	CHOIR FUNDRAISING	$ 9,679.28	$ 10,530.00 –	$ (850.72)
173 .XXXXX.XXX.XX.XXX.X	PEP CLUB	$ 1,924.66	$ 192.24	$ 2,116.90
174 .XXXXX.XXX.XX.XXX.X	CHEERLEADERS	$ 598.73	$ –	$ 598.73
178 .XXXXX.XXX.XX.XXX.X	STUDENT COUNCIL	$ 12,338.69	$ 2,104.76 –	$ 10,233.93
			FUND BALANCE =	$ 69,442.08

FIGURE 8.1 Sample Cash Balance Report for Activity Fund Accounts

A FINAL WORD OF CAUTION

School activity programs have long been accepted as making a critical contribution to the provision of educational opportunity. Fiscal outlays for support of student activities are much larger than people often realize in that district cash subsidies, student-owned deposits, and the value of facilities and personnel required to carry out a successful activity program are significant, but as we argued at the outset of this chapter, there is a high payoff for everyone involved.

The high profile of student activity programs raises the stakes of budgeting in many ways, and, if such moneys are mishandled, memories can be unpleasant. Two such cases illustrate this point. The first case involved a respected school principal who lost his job and his professional licensure as a result of cash receipts that were stolen from his unlocked car. The second case underscores the latent power that can be aroused when activity programs are threatened. In that case, a district facing a five million dollar shortfall because of state aid reductions decided to cut several athletic programs—a decision that cost several school board members their elected positions and administrators their professional employment. Nearly everyone has heard similar stories, but the central point is that the prominence of student activity programs makes them a dangerous place to engage in lax fiscal practices or short-sighted decision making. The critical feature always ties back to wise leadership in the context of fiduciary trust. Finally, and importantly, in the case of activity funds, it is often school-level leaders who find themselves on the firing line.

POINT–COUNTERPOINT

POINT

School leaders today, hard-pressed to find funding for both academic and cocurricular programs, have been dealt a blow through recent federal and state moves to ban or severely restrict vending machine sales of candy, soda, and chips in schools. These vending contracts, some of which can generate tens of thousands of dollars per year in revenue to individual schools, are critically important because those funds are typically used to support a wide range of student activities.

COUNTERPOINT

Given the growing concern about child and adolescent nutrition in this country, school leaders' first responsibility is to ensure that the school environment is one where healthy eating choices are reinforced. School leaders should welcome federal and state initiatives that discourage if not bar the sale of "junk food" in schools. Furthermore, funding student programs and activities with such money is unethical, analogous to using taxes on tobacco sales to fund smoking cessation programs.

- Which of these views best represents your beliefs and experiences? Explain.
- How are student activities funded in your school and district?
- In your estimation, would your school or district offer more extracurricular or cocurricular activities if there were more funding available? If yes, what types of activities do you think are most needed and why?

CASE STUDY

Upon assuming your new position as principal of a large high school, you undertook a review of your building's activity fund operations with your business clerk.

As you educated yourself about local activity fund practices, you became concerned about lax financial procedures. Among your growing list of anxieties was the fact that last year's comprehensive audit had noted problems in activity fund cash receipts and disbursements. For example, auditors had noted 42 instances of cash entries to the student yearbook account for which no prenumbered receipts were found. Nearly $90,000 in athletic equipment purchases were made for which corresponding requisitions/purchase orders were signed and dated after the vendor's invoice had already been paid. Several activity fund accounts showed negative balances. Moneys received were not always deposited in a timely fashion because on multiple occasions cash deposits were not made for several days after receipt. Your clerk was apologetic but indicated that the district had reduced office staff to such an extent that student office aides were used to carry out tasks such as selling yearbooks. The clerk also indicated that it had been the prior principal's longstanding practice to allow the athletic director to order equipment on the spot from sales calls and to complete the purchasing paperwork later.

As you worked late into the evening, you made even more disturbing discoveries. You knew from your own observations over the last several days that office staff kept the petty cash box in an unlocked desk drawer, and you had personally seen an office worker make a quick run to the supply closet at the back of the office complex while leaving uncounted cash lying on top of a desk. Recently, you also saw cash register drawers at athletic concessions stands left open momentarily while the attendant was distracted by serving multiple customers. So far there had been no reports of missing cash, but on the other hand you had only been on the job for a few short weeks. With nearly half a million dollars total activity fund budget in your care, you knew something had to change—very quickly.

Below is a set of questions. As you respond, consider what you have learned in this chapter and apply your knowledge and experience to the situation.

- What elements of this case study most concern you? Why? What steps should you as principal take immediately to address the most pressing concerns?
- Since these issues seem to have developed over time, what barriers do you anticipate in correcting the situation? How will you go about overcoming these?

- What can and should a school leader do to protect against lax activity fund practices?
- Using your experience as an educator, have you encountered any examples of lax activity fund management accounting? If so, how could these have been avoided?

PORTFOLIO EXERCISES

- Obtain a list of student activities in your district from your district/central office, and determine how each is funded. Distinguish which activities are student-funded and which are district-owned.

- Make an appointment with your district's chief financial officer (CFO) or representative to discuss handling of student activity funding. Obtain a copy of school board policies and guidelines on activity funding. Determine the district's procedures for receipting and disbursing activity fund moneys.

- Obtain a copy of an activity fund report from your school. Determine total revenues and expenditures for activities associated with the school; the number of student groups; and revenues and expenditures by group. Talk to the principal about how the activity fund is supervised and the lines of authority and control that are in place. Identify strengths and weaknesses in the system, and develop recommendations as to how the weaknesses might be remedied.

WEB RESOURCES

American Association of School Administrators, www.aasa.org

Association of Certified Fraud Examiners, www.acfe.com

Association of School Business Officials International, www.asbointl.org

Institute of Internal Auditors, www.theiia.org

National Association for Elementary School Principals, www.naesp.org

National Association for Secondary School Principals, www.nassp.org

National Business Officers Association, www.nboa.net

RECOMMENDED READING

Allison, Gregory S., Steven D. Honegger, and Frank Johnson. *Financial Accounting for Local and State School Systems: 2009 Edition.* Washington, DC: U.S. Department of Education, Institute of Education Sciences, National Center for Education Statistics, June 2009. http://nces.ed.gov/pubsearch/pubsinfo.asp?pubid=2009325.

Cuzzetto, Charles E. "Student Activity Funds: Procedures and Controls." *School Business Affairs* 66 (November 2000): 22–25.

Dessoff, Alan. "Fighting Fraud in Schools." *District Administration*, August 2009. www.districtadministration.com/viewarticle.aspx?articleid=2088.

Everett, Ronald E., Donald R. Johnson, and Bernard W. Madden. *Financial and Managerial Accounting for School Administrators: Tools for Schools*, 2nd ed. Lanham, MD: Rowman & Littlefield, 2007.

Granof, Michael H., and Saleha B. Khumawala. *Government and Not-for-Profit Accounting*, 5th ed. Hoboken, NJ: John Wiley & Sons, 2011.

Hassenpflug, Ann. "Missing Funds." *Journal of Cases in Educational Leadership* 15 2 (2012): 3–9.

Ray, John R., Walter G. Hack, and Carl I. Candoli. *School Business Administration: A Planning Approach*, 8th ed. Boston: Allyn & Bacon, 2005.

CHAPTER 9

Budgeting for School Infrastructure

THE CHALLENGE

In a country where public education is meant to serve as the "great equalizer" for all of its children, we are still struggling to provide equal opportunity when it comes to the upkeep, maintenance and modernization of our schools and classrooms.

President Bill Clinton (2013)[1]

CHAPTER DRIVERS

Please reflect upon the following questions as you read this chapter:

- What is the role of infrastructure in public schools?
- How is school infrastructure defined?
- What is the current condition of school infrastructure?
- What is included in a comprehensive definition of school infrastructure?
- How much money do schools need for infrastructure?
- How is school infrastructure currently funded at state and local levels?
- What are the goals of and activities involved in infrastructure planning?
- What is the role and nature of maintenance and operations?
- How do schools organize for maintenance and operations?
- What is the role of the school site leader in maintenance and operations?

---

1 The Center for Green Schools, "2013 State of Our Schools Report" (Washington, DC: U.S. Green Building Council, 2013), 3, http://centerforgreenschools.org/Libraries/State_of_our_Schools/2013_State_of_Our_Schools_Report_FINAL.sflb.ashx.

SCHOOL INFRASTRUCTURE NEEDS IN PERSPECTIVE

As indicated in the opening quotation to this chapter, no study of school funding is complete without an examination of the role of the physical environment of schools. The staggering cost of school construction, modernization, debt service, maintenance and operations, and associated capital outlays such as those for technology infrastructure has subtly but relentlessly lurked behind the scenes as we have worked our way through the maze of school funding topics. In the case of school infrastructure, some costs may go unnoticed in the rush to adequately fund instruction, but these less visible costs can be as important as the more obvious ones. In other words, while the role of funding school facilities is critically important, other costs consume the vast majority of education's resources. As a consequence, in this chapter we articulate school infrastructure needs and consider how the budgeting process addresses this aspect of equal opportunity.

We begin by exploring the role of school infrastructure, focusing our discussion on its nature and size. We then turn attention to the condition of school facilities in the United States and offer estimates of costs to redress deficiencies. We follow with an extended discussion of how schools' infrastructure needs are funded, with the observation that infrastructure funding lags far behind progress that has been made in funding other areas of school and district needs. With that general framework in place, we are ready to consider a different, but related set of issues: How are school infrastructure planning and maintenance and operations carried out? More specifically, we turn attention to how infrastructure planning occurs; the effect of demographics and education programs on school facility planning; the role of maintenance and operations; and how schools organize their maintenance activities. In sum, although school infrastructure has never enjoyed the high profile of topics like school reform, budgeting for the physical environment of schools plays a crucial role in funding education given the substantial cost of facilities and the relationship between infrastructure quality and student success.

NATURE AND SIZE OF SCHOOL INFRASTRUCTURE

Stated bluntly, public education's infrastructure needs in the United States are shocking and pose a serious—even dire—problem far into the foreseeable future. This assessment derives from the many stressors on school budgets described previously in this textbook, combined with the fact that while much concerted effort has been exerted in recent years to reform schools, far less attention has been given to the need for physical learning environments conducive to teaching and learning. Unfortunately, this is not a new problem. Twenty-five years ago, the American Association of School Administrators (AASA) noted,

> [F]rom every corner have come reports, articles, speeches and goal statements about student achievement, unmet needs and education reform ... but all these

pronouncements have been strangely silent about one essential ingredient . . . that affects every child's health, safety and ability to learn: *the classroom.* [emphasis in original][2]

Pronouncements of this nature are not insignificant in a time when reform of "failing" schools has captured local and national headlines. The source of alarm rests in evidence that education's physical infrastructure is also failing in ways that surely impede education reform. Numerous reports have warned about the condition of school facilities,[3] and school leaders and policymakers have been told of the cost for repair and replacement.[4] Estimates run into hundreds of billions of dollars, mostly because school districts have funded other current needs by delaying maintenance, repair, and modernization of facilities. Often, districts have had to choose between spending for instruction and spending for facilities in which to house those programs. In sum, it is an ever-spiraling crisis that underscores the critical role of planning and budgeting for capital needs, particularly since infrastructure is the single largest investment a school district makes at any one time.

What Is the Role of Infrastructure in Public Schools?

Different language has been used over the years to describe the physical environment of education. "School plant" and "facilities" have historically been used to describe school buildings while "capital outlay" usually has referred to all aspects of paying for the permanent facility and major equipment needs of schools. In a broader and more recent context, the term "infrastructure" has gained acceptance because it captures the full range of capital needs in a single word. All these terms have been useful in describing the role of the physical environment of schools and the critical role it plays in the education of children. The role of infrastructure is captured in the following statement by the AASA:

The most exciting curriculum innovations in the world have trouble succeeding in cold, dank, deteriorating classrooms. If the work environment is unattractive, uncomfortable, or unsafe, school districts have difficulty competing with other sectors of the economy to woo talented teachers . . . Students know the difference too![5]

---

2 American Association of School Administrators (AASA), *Schoolhouse in the Red. A National Study of School Facilities and Energy Use* (Arlington, VA: AASA, 1991), 1.

3 See, for example, Faith E. Crampton and David C. Thompson, "The Condition of America's Schools: A National Disgrace," *School Business Affairs* 68 (December 2002): 15–19.

4 See, Faith E. Crampton, David C. Thompson, and Janis M. Hagey, "Creating and Sustaining School Capacity in the Twenty-First Century: Funding a Physical Environment Conducive to Student Learning," *Journal of Education Finance* 27 (Fall 2001): 633–652; Faith E. Crampton and David C. Thompson, *School Infrastructure Funding Need: A State-by-State Assessment and an Analysis of Recent Court Cases* (Washington, DC: American Federation of Teachers, 2008); and U.S. Government Accountability Office, *School Facilities: Condition of America's Schools* (Washington, DC, 1995).

5 AASA, *Schoolhouse in the Red*, 11.

Obviously, all schools in the United States are not in poor condition. Rather, needs far outstrip resources, and the data point to ever-mounting school infrastructure needs in many states. Over time, the fiscal crisis has broadened from deferred maintenance issues as pressure has been placed on school facilities through the expanding scope of education mandates and reforms, and has been exacerbated by the complex and sometimes arcane ways in which schools are financed and maintained. The role of infrastructure is to support instructional programs by providing a safe, modern, appropriate, and inviting physical environment for learning—a role that often has taken a back seat to expenditures associated with curriculum reform, competitive compensation, and educational mandates. Yet it is clear that the best reforms will fail if the physical environment fails to support or, even worse, impedes learning. In sum, deferring maintenance, construction, and modernization may represent a short-term solution to tight school district budgets, but such decisions ultimately represent a false economy.

The Condition of Schools

Recent headlines heralding school infrastructure decay make it easy to believe that the poor condition of schools in the nation is a newly discovered reality. In fact, problems of school facilities and capital needs have long been noted. In 1831, William A. Alcott graphically described the problems of school facilities, stating:

> Few, indeed, of the numerous schoolhouses in this country are well lighted. Fewer still are painted, even on the outside. Playgrounds for the common schools are scarcely known. There is much suffering from the alternation of heat and cold and from smoke. The feet of children have even sometimes been frozen. Too many pupils are confined to a single desk or bench where they jostle or otherwise disturb each other . . . Hundreds of rooms are so small that the pupils have not on average more than five or six square feet each; here they are obliged to sit, breathing impure air, on benches often not more than six or eight inches wide, and without backs.[6]

Fortunately, no schools today suffer such extreme conditions. Students no longer sit on benches; federal, state, and local health standards have been enacted; and most schools provide more tolerable light and thermal environments than was the case in Alcott's day. Standards for new construction and retrofitting of buildings, including schools, have been articulated by a wide range of U.S. construction-related professional associations, although most of these are voluntary.[7] Today, school facilities, new and old, are subject to their respective local and state building and safety codes, but it

---

6 William A. Alcott, "Essay on the Construction of School-Houses," August 1831, cited in David C. Thompson, *Educational Facility Equity and Adequacy: A Report on Behalf of the Plaintiffs in Roosevelt v. Bishop* (Manhattan, KS: Wood, Thompson & Associates, 1991), 1.

7 A partial listing of such organizations that publish standards includes the American Concrete Institute (ACI), American Institute of Architects (AIA), American Institute of Steel Construction (AISC), Architectural Woodwork Industry (AWI), American Welding Society Code (AWSC), National Building Code (NBC), National Electric Code (NEC), National Fire Protection Association (NFPA), National Illuminating Engineering Society (NIES), National Plumbing Code (NPC), Uniform Building Code (UBC), Underwriters Laboratories, Inc. (UL), American Association for Health, Physical

should be noted that these vary widely with regard to their rigor and enforcement. At the federal level, school facilities are subject to Environmental Protection Agency (EPA) regulations for hazards such as asbestos, radon, and lead; standards of the Occupational Safety and Health Administration (OSHA); and accessibility requirements under the Individuals with Disabilities Education Act (IDEA)[8] and the Americans with Disabilities Act (ADA).[9]

Although enforcement of these laws and regulations results in safer, healthier, and more physically accessible schools, it does not necessarily lead to modern, educationally appropriate facilities. Furthermore, although many aspects of the physical environment in new schools are legislated and regulated, not all standards are consistently enforced across states and localities. The result has been that existing schools remain an object of concern because numerous national reports have concluded that their infrastructure still is in a state of emergency. Although many safe, modern schools do exist, reports have argued that others are badly deteriorated, with many too old to safely function or too outdated to meet the demands of a modern education and equality of opportunity.

Although Alcott's description may be an artifact of his time, aspects of it linger today. Research on the quality of school environments has exposed shamefully substandard school facilities in the United States where unsafe and unhealthy classrooms resemble conditions in a poverty-stricken developing country.[10] In addition, research describes health hazards associated with air quality in portable classrooms, an alternative to new construction often used in response to mandated class size reduction or as a stopgap solution to growing student numbers.[11] These conditions, not unlike some of those Alcott described, are juxtaposed with new research linking student achievement and the physical environment.[12]

As awareness and sophistication of research into school infrastructure have grown, new understanding of the depth of need indicates that it is larger than previously

---

Education, and Recreation (AAHPER), American Association of School Administrators (AASA), American Institute of Electrical Engineers (AIEE), Association of Physical Plant Administrators (APPA), Association of School Business Officials (ASBO), American Society of Mechanical Engineers (ASME), American Society for Testing and Materials (ASTM), Council of Educational Facility Planners, International (CEFPI), National Board of Fire Underwriters (NBFU), and the National Bureau of Standards (NBS). In addition are state and local building and safety codes.

8 P.L. 94–142.

9 See, "Americans with Disabilities Act of 1990, as Amended," for the full text of the current law, U.S. Department of Justice, Civil Rights Division, www.ada.gov/pubs/adastatute08.htm.

10 See, for example, Jonathan Kozol, *Savage Inequalities: Children in America's Schools* (New York: Harper Perennial, 1992); Jonathan Kozol, *Shame of the Nation* (New York: Crown Publishers, 2005).

11 See, e.g., California Environmental Protection Agency, *Environmental Health Conditions in California's Portable Classrooms* (Sacramento: California Air Resources Board and California Department of Health Services, 2004), www.arb.ca.gov/research/indoor/pcs/leg_rpt/leg_rpt.htm; and, U.S. Environmental Protection Agency, "Portable Classrooms" (Washington, DC: IAQ Design Tools for Schools), www.epa.gov/iaq/schooldesign/portables.html.

12 See, Faith E. Crampton and David C. Thompson, "When Money Matters: School Infrastructure Funding and Student Achievement," *School Business Affairs* 77 (November 2011): 14–18.

believed—and is still growing.[13] Previous estimates of deferred maintenance alone in U.S. schools were estimated at $112 billion in 1995 by the U.S. Government Accountability Office (GAO) and $127 billion in 1999 by the U.S. Department of Education.[14] More recent research shows these needs remain unfunded; and newer data argue that if unmet needs are vast in only the context of general upkeep and repair, they are staggering in the context of a fuller definition of school infrastructure and equal educational opportunity. As outlined below, a comprehensive definition of school infrastructure is much more than deferred maintenance in that it also includes new construction, renovations, retrofitting, additions to existing facilities, and major improvements to grounds.

- *Deferred maintenance.* Refers to maintenance necessary to bring a school facility up to good condition, i.e., a condition where only routine maintenance is needed. If a facility is in such poor condition that it cannot be brought to good condition or if it would cost more than to construct a new facility, deferred maintenance can refer to replacement of an existing facility.
- *New construction.* May be a response to pupil overcrowding; to federal, state, or local mandates requiring additional facilities such as class size reduction measures, or to projected enrollment growth. Construction of a new facility includes the building(s); grounds (purchase, landscaping, and paving); and fixtures, major equipment, and furniture necessary to furnish it.
- *Renovation.* Includes renovations to an existing facility for health, safety, and accessibility for the disabled. Renovation may include work needed to accommodate mandated educational programs.
- *Retrofitting.* Applies to areas such as energy conservation (e.g., installation of insulation or energy-efficient windows) and technology readiness (e.g., electrical wiring, phone lines, and fiber optic cables).
- *Additions to existing facilities.* May be necessary to relieve overcrowding; to meet federal, state, or local mandates such as class size reduction; or to accommodate projected enrollment growth. Cost of additions usually includes fixtures, major equipment, and furniture necessary to furnish them.
- *Major improvements.* Refers to grounds, such as landscaping and paving.[15]

Results from the most recent comprehensive national study of school infrastructure found that states' funding needs totaled approximately $255 billion.[16] (See Table 9.1.)

---

13 See, generally, Faith E. Crampton and David C. Thompson, Eds., *Saving America's School Infrastructure* (Greenwich, CT: Information Age Publishing, 2003). See, also, a special issue of the *Journal of Educational Administration* (Spring 2009) titled "Building High Quality Schools."

14 U.S. Government Accountability Office, *School Facilities: Condition of America's Schools*; and Laurie Lewis, Kyle Snow, Elizabeth Faris, Becky Smerdon, Stephanie Cronen, and Jessica Kaplan, *Condition of America's Public School Facilities: 1999* (Washington, DC: U.S. Department of Education, National Center for Education Statistics, June 2000).

15 Faith E. Crampton, David C. Thompson, and Janice M. Hagey, "Creating and Sustaining School Capacity in the Twenty-First Century: Funding a Physical Environment Conducive to Student Learning," *Journal of Education Finance* 27 (Fall 2001): 633–652.

16 Crampton and Thompson, *School Infrastructure Funding Need.*

Given differences in enrollments as well as the condition and adequacy of existing facilities, funding need varies across states, ranging from $326 million in Vermont to $25.4 billion in California, with the average state funding need at $5.1 billion. It is therefore not surprising that the American Society of Civil Engineers, an organization that rates the quality of the nation's infrastructure, gave schools a grade of "D" in its most recent evaluation.[17]

Although it is easy to understand that the ultimate impact of failure to address infrastructure funding needs is deterioration of the learning environment, policymakers have found it challenging to address, in part due to the magnitude of funding need. In response, litigation has emerged as an aggressive, grassroots solution to force reluctant states to address inadequate and inequitable facilities and funding. Accordingly, Thompson and Crampton[18] noted:

> By most apparent indicators, efforts to blaze a trail of successful state-level school facility litigation have increased, as there has been a noticeable spike since 2001 in state supreme court-level school finance lawsuits containing substantial facility claims. Results have ranged from slowly evolving language in facility equity/adequacy holdings such as New York's gains above a basic constitutional requirement to provide enough light, space, heat, and air to permit children to learn,[19] to relatively aggressive requirements for equitable access to adequate facilities such as Arkansas' constitutional requirement for substantially equal facilities,[20] New Jersey's requirement of adequate facilities including 100% state financing in plaintiff districts,[21] Ohio's requirement that the state's educational system cannot result in indefensible facility deficiencies,[22] Texas' requirement that facilities cannot be judged apart from a system-wide context,[23] and Wyoming's requirement to measure adequate school facilities that must be provided at state expense.[24]

Plaintiffs in at least 38 states have cited funding for infrastructure in school finance lawsuits, with six focusing claims exclusively on inequitable and inadequate infrastructure funding: Alaska, Arizona, Colorado, Idaho, Louisiana, and New Mexico. And some success has been experienced by plaintiffs in a number of states.[25] In the most

---

17 American Society of Civil Engineers, "2013 Report Card for America's Infrastructure: Schools," www.infrastructurereportcard.org/a/#p/schools/overview.

18 David C. Thompson and Faith E. Crampton, "An Overview and Analysis of Selected School Finance and School Facilities Litigation," *West's Education Law Reporter* 243, no. 2 (June 11, 2009): 507–545.

19 *Campaign for Fiscal Equity, Inc., et al., Appellants, v. State of New York et al.*, 801 N.E.2d 326 (2003).

20 *Lake View School District No. 25 v. Huckabee*, 91 S.W.3d 472 (2002).

21 *Abbott v. Burke*, 790 A.2d 842 (2002).

22 *DeRolph v. State*, 754 N.E.2d 1184 (2002).

23 *Neeley et. al. v. West Orange-Cove School District et. al.*, 176 S.W.3d 746 (2005).

24 *State v. Campbell County School District*, 32 P.3d 325 (2001).

25 See, Crampton and Thompson, *School Infrastructure Funding Need*; Faith E. Crampton and David C. Thompson, "When the Legislative Process Fails: The Politics of Litigation in School Infrastructure Funding Equity," in *Money, Politics, and Law: Effects on Education Finance:*

TABLE 9.1 State-by-State Estimates of School Infrastructure Funding Need: 2008

State	Funding Need ($)	State	Funding Need ($)
Alabama	5,069,059,471	Montana	903,409,390
Alaska	775,715,820	Nebraska	2,779,311,486
Arizona	6,424,629,084	Nevada	2,463,711,114
Arkansas	4,504,230,180	New Hampshire	685,093,824
California	25,400,000,000	New Jersey	10,398,548,661
Colorado	4,717,014,029	New Mexico	2,008,136,116
Connecticut	2,571,117,670	New York	21,167,156,040
Delaware	530,312,223	North Carolina	9,819,859,212
Florida	8,881,365,640	North Dakota	427,883,841
Georgia	5,227,583,658	Ohio	9,320,000,000
Hawaii	3,365,700,000	Oklahoma	2,396,415,132
Idaho	1,090,149,588	Oregon	2,459,489,866
Illinois	8,200,000,000	Pennsylvania	9,259,270,785
Indiana	3,888,271,836	Rhode Island	696,885,594
Iowa	4,652,130,594	South Carolina	7,086,687,050
Kansas	4,562,816,736	South Dakota	522,751,086
Kentucky	1,015,791,056	Tennessee	3,583,000,000
Louisiana	7,293,509,670	Texas	12,575,827,059
Maine	658,548,867	Utah	3,101,211,906
Maryland	3,854,108,000	Vermont	325,741,824
Massachusetts	4,344,231,022	Virginia	8,536,780,554
Michigan	8,868,404,735	Washington	6,281,190,790
Minnesota	3,733,853,859	West Virginia	1,192,639,251
Mississippi	3,439,395,568	Wisconsin	4,379,994,205
Missouri	8,806,396,974	Wyoming	360,708,381
Total			$254,606,228,518

Source: Faith E. Crampton and David C. Thompson. *School Infrastructure Funding Need: A State-by-State Assessment and an Analysis of Recent Court Cases*. Washington, DC: American Federation of Teachers, 2008.

recent, case, *Kasayulie*,[26] the plaintiffs sought equitable funding for school facilities in remote, rural areas of Alaska. The case was settled in October 2011 with the state agreeing to spend $146 million for construction and renovation of schools in five Alaskan villages. That this lawsuit was originally filed 14 years ago adds a cautionary

---

Intersections and Conflicts in the Provision of Educational Opportunity, Yearbook of the American Education Finance Association, edited by Karen DeMoss and Kenneth K. Wong (Larchmont, NY: New York: Eye On Education, 2004), 69–88. See also, David C. Thompson and Faith E. Crampton, "School Finance Litigation: A Strategy to Address Inequities in School Infrastructure Funding," in *Saving America's School Infrastructure*, edited by Faith E. Crampton and David C. Thompson (Greenwich, CT: Information Age Publishing, 2003), 163–190.

26 *Kasayulie et al. v. State of Alaska*, Consent Decree and Settlement, 3AN-97–3782 CI, October 4, 2011.

note: While plaintiffs are increasingly seeking adequate and equitable funding for school infrastructure, litigation is often a long and expensive road to reach that goal.

Unless forced to do so by litigation, most states have not developed school infrastructure funding plans comparable to those for funding schools' operating costs. Table 9.2 reveals the patchwork approach most states have taken toward funding school infrastructure, with several states providing no funding whatsoever.

Although health, safety, and construction standards have greatly improved school environments, the magnitude of infrastructure funding needs; growth in deferred maintenance; reluctance of legislatures and Congress to include infrastructure as an important element of equal educational opportunity; and vast inequities in local fiscal capacity have all contributed to the state of school infrastructure in the U.S.; that is, one that does not uniformly offer every child a physical environment conducive to learning. As a result, many school districts lurch from one infrastructure-related crisis to another, often diverting instructional funds to pay for emergency repairs.

How Is School Infrastructure Funded?

The condition of public education's physical infrastructure is a cumulative image of how states have chosen to aid (or not aid) funding of school facilities.[27] As we will see, there is a sharp difference in how general education is aided compared to how facilities and related capital needs are funded. In contrast to the complex formulas developed to provide school districts with state funding for operating costs through basic aid, categorical aid, and weighting factors, funding of infrastructure in those states where it does exist is primitive in comparison.

One possible explanation for the lack of state aid for infrastructure may be reluctance of states to abandon the "tradition of local control." From the inception of state aid to local school districts dating from the common school movement in the 19th century, states have delegated the building and maintenance of facilities to local school districts. With that delegation, states permitted school districts to use local property taxes for infrastructure expenditures, although local voter approval was and is usually required. The dawn of the 20th century, however, brought many economic, education, demographic, legal, and societal changes that increased pressure on local tax bases. As the United States moved from an agrarian to an industrial society, there was rapid growth in the size and number of cities with their own infrastructure needs—e.g., roads and sanitation systems—that placed new demands on local tax bases. At the same time, a public education system that had been largely confined to elementary grades now expanded to include high schools, requiring increased expenditures for operations and

---

27 This section does not specifically address federal funding of school infrastructure, given its extremely limited role. At present, the only federal support is through "tax credit bonds" which do not provide school districts with direct funding, but rather reduce the cost of borrowing. See, "Stimulus Funding and Tax Credit Bonds for School Construction" (Washington, DC: National Clearinghouse for Educational Facilities, 2011), www.ncef.org/school-modernization/chart.pdf. See, also, Cassandria Dortch, "School Construction and Renovation: A Review of Federal Programs" (Washington, DC: Congressional Research Service, December 2013), www.fas.org/sgp/crs/misc/R41142.pdf.

TABLE 9.2 State School Infrastructure Funding Programs

State	General Aid Support	Project-Based Aid	Debt Service Grant	Loan	State Bond Guarantee	Other*	None
Alabama	X						
Alaska			U				
Arizona	X						
Arkansas			U				
California					X		
Colorado						X	
Connecticut		E					
Delaware		E					
Florida	X						
Georgia		A					
Hawaii		A					
Idaho						X	
Illinois							X
Indiana				X			
Iowa						X	
Kansas		E					
Kentucky		A	U				
Louisiana							X
Maine		A					
Maryland		AE			X		
Massachusetts		AE			X		
Michigan							X
Minnesota	X			X			
Mississippi	X						
Missouri	X						
Montana		E					
Nebraska							X
Nevada							X
New Hampshire		E					
New Jersey		E	E				
New Mexico		E					
New York		E					
North Carolina				X		X	
North Dakota							X
Ohio		AE					
Oklahoma							X
Oregon	X						

TABLE 9.2 *continued*

State	General Aid Support	Project-Based Aid	Debt Service Grant	Loan	State Bond Guarantee	Other*	None
Pennsylvania		A					
Rhode Island		E					
South Carolina		A					
South Dakota							X
Tennessee						X	
Texas	X		E		X		
Utah	X				X		
Vermont		A					
Virginia	X			X			
Washington		E					
West Virginia		AE					
Wisconsin							X
Wyoming		A					

Notes: For Debt Service Grants, U = Unequalized; E = Equalized. For Project Grants, A = Approved (i.e., must be approved by the state); E = Equalized.

*Other: California uses a competitive grant process. A portion of the Idaho lottery profits are distributed through the Idaho State Department of Education School District Building Fund. Iowa provides a flat grant per pupil from state sales tax revenues. North Carolina earmarks a portion of sales tax for school construction. Tennessee provides state aid using a square foot cost matrix for which it will reimburse school districts up to 50 percent.

Sources: Compiled from multiple sources: Deborah A. Verstegen, "A 50 State Survey of School Finance Policies," http://schoolfinancesdav.wordpress.com; and independent research by the authors.

infrastructure. Successive waves of immigration further swelled student enrollments and costs. Fourth, a number of states passed laws restricting child labor in factories, making it more likely they would attend public schools.[28] Fifth, as education's importance to society grew, more states passed compulsory education laws or expanded those already in existence, further increasing enrollments.

Although educational growth in the early 20th century was accompanied by economic growth that helped to accommodate increasing enrollments, the stock market crash in 1929 plunged the nation into the Great Depression of the 1930s, and education spending plummeted. In contrast, after World War II, the "baby boom" years necessitated the rapid building of numerous new schools, but the resulting buildings were often of poor quality. As a result, the poor quality of their construction contributed to a backlog of maintenance costs while the emergence of new education technologies made them, and even more solidly built older schools, obsolete.

---

28 U.S. Department of Labor, "Child Labor Laws and Enforcement," *Report on the Youth Labor Force* (Washington, DC: Bureau of Labor Statistics), www.bls.gov/opub/rylf/rylfhome.htm.

All of these problems were worsened by the reluctance of states to become involved in funding school facilities. There were a few exceptions, but these were generally narrowly targeted toward a specific goal. For example, in 1901 Alabama began to aid capital outlay—the purpose, though, was to help rural schools and did not imply a broader state duty to education. In 1903, Delaware and South Carolina began offering capital aid to schools for African-American children; and between 1898 and 1927 aid plans designed to incentivize school district consolidation were enacted in Arkansas, Delaware, Maine, Minnesota, Missouri, New York, Oklahoma, Pennsylvania, Rhode Island, Tennessee, and Wisconsin. The result of such selective aid schemes was that as late as World War II, only 12 states provided any type of aid to capital outlay and debt service for local schools.[29]

Over time, states have become more aware of school infrastructure concerns, especially as some courts have begun to link infrastructure needs to school finance fairness. As seen earlier in Table 9.2, 41 states now provide some type of financial support, be it direct or indirect, to school infrastructure—although not necessarily adequate, equitable, or uniform. As a point of comparison, it is estimated that states cover, on average, approximately 27% of state-local spending on school infrastructure,[30] compared to the average state share of 44.1% for operating costs.[31]

In sum, 41 states provide some level of direct aid for school district infrastructure costs, while nine provide none. Almost half of states provide some aid through project grants—which may or may not be equalized, and may or may not require state approval—while 10 do so through their general aid formula. States making less aggressive efforts turn to indirect aid mechanisms like loans or bond guarantees. As we will see below, the structure of state infrastructure aid to school districts bears some similarities to basic and categorical aid for operating expenditure, although there are also some significant differences.

Full State Funding

As the name implies, full state funding plans assign total responsibility to the state for the cost of building programs. Under these conditions, the state pays for school facility construction, and in return may expect to control many of the planning and construction decisions. For example, under a full state funding scheme, a school district may need to develop specifications promulgated by a state building authority and receive formal, agency approval before commencing construction, renovations, or additions to existing facilities. In addition, the district may be placed on a waiting list that reflects the authority's assessment of the urgency of the request in relationship to all other districts in the state. Only two states—Arizona and Hawaii—have full state funding. Because the state of Hawaii has only one school district, its school infrastructure aid is de facto

---

29 Thompson et al., *Fiscal Leadership for Schools*, 559.
30 21st Century School Fund, *Federal Spending on PK-12 School Facilities* (Washington, DC: November 2010) 4.
31 See Table 2.1 in Chapter 2.

full state funding. However, Arizona arrived at full state funding by way of school finance litigation.[32]

Full state funding of school infrastructure has the same advantages found in fully funded general aid formulas (see Chapter 3). Full state support conceptually represents the most equitable system, in that facilities are funded based on the wealth of the entire state rather than the individual district. The scope of identifying the full extent of needs of all school districts often results in the creation of a state department or agency whose sole or primary responsibility is school infrastructure funding. However, as attractive as full state funding of school infrastructure may be to school districts, some local communities may be wary of the trade-off of local autonomy for state aid.

Project-Based Aid

Project-based aid for school infrastructure is used in some form by 22 states. It may or may not be equalized, and it rarely covers the full cost of an infrastructure project, e.g., the cost of constructing a new school or renovating an existing facility. If it is not equalized, it resembles a flat grant.

When equalized, the amount of aid the school district receives is generally inversely related to its fiscal capacity, usually defined as property wealth per student. However, the state may cap aid per project based on its assessment of what a particular project should cost—or based upon limited state funds. In some cases, the state may allow the school district to raise additional funding to exceed the state cap, although this will distort the equity impact of the state aid. Equalization aid for school infrastructure bears some similarities to general aid formulas that also calculate funding relative to the district's ability to pay. However, equalization aid for infrastructure is particular to a certain building project and so, unlike general aid, is time-limited to the duration of the project. Project-based aid also bears some similarities to categorical aid in that it can be used only for a specific building project. However, as we learned earlier, some states do not equalize categorical aid.

Equalized project-based aid can also be compared to matching grants if the match set by the state is reflective of the district's ability to pay. On the other hand, if the state sets an arbitrary ratio, for example, 50/50, based upon political considerations that all districts be treated the "same," a matching grant is in fact disequalizing because it advantages property-wealthy school districts. In addition, the state will likely need to cap total aid, as its revenues are not limitless, and so the state would be well advised to develop criteria that determine eligibility and priority.

A variation on project-based aid is "debt service" aid where debt service is defined as the annual payment of principal and interest a school district makes on its long-term debt for school infrastructure. As Table 9.2 indicates, only a handful of states use debt service aid as either their only form of financial support for school infrastructure or an addition to other types of aid. Debt service aid somewhat resembles categorical aid in that it is targeted for a specific purpose. While school districts generally welcome any

---

32 *Roosevelt Elementary School District No. 66 v. Bishop*, 877 P.2d 806 (Ariz. 1994).

state aid for infrastructure, debt service aid generally requires the district to first make its annual debt payment out of existing funds and then seek whatever percentage reimbursement the state offers.

General Aid Support

Ten states build infrastructure aid into their general or basic aid programs. Separate from maintenance and operations, which have often been considered current operating expenses and thereby included in general aid formulas, aid to infrastructure has only recently been included as a component. Such programs may or may not distribute aid according to equalization principles for operating aid. The logic for inclusion of infrastructure funding as part of general aid lies with the belief that facilities are part of the total educational program of the district and therefore deserving of support.

State Loans and State Bond Guarantees

State loan programs and state bond guarantees represent indirect aid to school infrastructure. In all, nine states use state loan programs, and the majority of those use loans in addition to direct infrastructure aid. Only Indiana uses state loans as its sole support for school infrastructure. State loan programs may be helpful to districts with a less than optimal credit rating; here, the state's stronger credit rating may lower their cost of borrowing. However, one should keep in mind that some localities may have better credit ratings than the state; as such, a state loan would increase their interest costs. However, if the state loan program does not require local voter approval, the school district may find it preferable to risking voter rejection in a local bond referendum. Like a bond, a state loan must be repaid by the district, and local property tax revenues are usually the only source available.

A state bond guarantee can also lower a school district's borrowing costs for school infrastructure. Because the state guarantees to repay the local bond if the school district defaults, the district may be able to borrow funds at a lower cost (i.e., interest rate). Over the course of paying back, for example, a 20-year bond, this can amount to a substantial savings in interest costs to the district. Unlike a state loan, the state makes no upfront investment of its own funds with a bond guarantee. However, states have a risk exposure with both loan and bond guarantee programs if a district defaults. Five states use bond guarantees.

State School Building Authorities

A state school building authority (SBA) is not a type of aid, but rather a mechanism for distributing aid. However, it is worth mentioning here because it is a variation on the more traditional method of distributing infrastructure aid through a state department of education. Hence, an SBA is the exception rather than the rule with regard to state administration of school infrastructure funding.

Historically, an SBA has offered the advantage not only of distributing aid or making loans but also housing experts like architects and engineers whom school districts could access in the planning stages of an infrastructure project at low or no cost. Depending upon state law, an SBA may draw upon private investors, issue state bonds, or receive legislative appropriations to provide school infrastructure funding. In all cases, SBAs are subject to state law and regulation. More recently, SBAs have been used in the wake of court decisions demanding equitable and adequate funding for school infrastructure. In states like Arizona and Ohio, SBAs assess school infrastructure needs and associated cost; prioritize school infrastructure projects across the state; set criteria for new school buildings, e.g., square footage; and allocate funding based upon those criteria. Often school districts have little or no discretion to supplement the state funding. As such, SBAs have both advantages and disadvantages. On the positive side, they can offer districts expertise in planning and designing a school facility at little or no cost. This is helpful particularly for smaller districts that usually do not have a facilities department. Second, SBAs may offer aid or loans to districts without the requirement of local voter approval. On the other hand, SBAs may control the type of facility a district can build, leading to criticisms of "cookie cutter designs" that are not responsive to local needs or preferences.

Intermediate Summary

Although a number of state courts have mandated state aid to school infrastructure to remedy inequities, several states still provide no aid to school facilities, and many others offer limited amounts of aid. Among those states aiding school infrastructure costs, classification of aid schemes is challenging because states do not use comparable language, and the numerous hybrid funding plans are difficult to categorize. Taken conjointly, several types of aid programs exist, although it must be emphasized that almost no states support school infrastructure at the same level seen for general operating aid. As will be seen in the next section, school districts remain heavily impacted by infrastructure costs.

How Is the Local Cost Share Funded?

By every measure, the cost of school facilities is enormous. According to industry estimates, approximately $10.0 billion is projected to be spent on school construction in 2014.[33] Of this amount, $6.4 billion is estimated for new construction with $1.9 billion for additions and $1.7 billion for modernization. While this may seem to be a huge expenditure, it represents a decline of over $3 billion from 2013.

These figures, however, do not take into account school district debt on construction projects, which the U.S. Department of Education estimated was $18.8 billion in 2011 for interest alone.[34] Although state aid undoubtedly pays some portion of these long-

---

33 Paul Abramson, "School Renovations Led Increase in Spending: The 19th Annual School Construction Report," *School Planning and Management*, http://webspm.com/research/2014/02/annual-school-construction-report/asset.aspx?tc=assetpg.

34 U.S. Department of Education, *Digest of Education Statistics*, "Summary of Expenditures for Public Elementary and Secondary Education and other Related Programs, by Purpose: Selected Years, 1919–20 through 2010–11," Table 236.10, http://nces.ed.gov/programs/digest/d13/tables/dt13_236.10.asp.

term costs, the vast majority of school districts throughout the nation have had to finance a large share of infrastructure projects using revenue derived from local property taxes. Generally, the local share is paid from some combination of three funding sources: current revenues, sinking funds, and bonded indebtedness.

Current Revenues

In most states, local school districts generally must supplement state aid to meet their facility needs, and total responsibility for infrastructure costs rests entirely with the local district in no-aid states. Although several methods for raising local moneys exist, financing capital needs through current revenues is the oldest. As implied, local revenue is derived on an annual basis from property taxes levied during the current year. For example, if a district has an assessed valuation of $500 million and a statutorily permissible tax rate for capital outlay of four mills, the district can generate $2 million in current revenues for infrastructure purposes. Similarly, if a district has a valuation of only $7 million and the same maximum tax rate, current revenues for capital projects will raise only $28,000. If, in the same example, the state were to have no limit on tax rates in local districts, the poorer district would have to levy about 286 mills to generate the same revenue available to the wealthy district at four mills.

The benefits and limitations of local financing via current revenues are evident in the illustration above. The major advantage is that current revenue is a cash or "pay as you go" method that avoids interest costs. Additionally, districts are likely to be more cost conscious if revenue must be on deposit prior to expenditure. At the same time, serious drawbacks exist. The most important results from disparate property wealth across school districts in a state, in that high property-wealth districts can afford state-of-the-art school facilities while low-wealth districts will struggle to provide even minimally adequate ones.

Few school districts use the current revenue method because many local tax bases are insufficient. In addition, most states limit the maximum millage that can be levied for school district infrastructure projects. However, even if states allowed unlimited local tax leeway, it would be impossible to raise adequate funds in property-poor school districts. As a result, the usefulness of the current revenue approach is mostly confined to small projects.

Sinking Funds

A sinking fund is similar to a savings account where the school district accumulates funds until they are sufficient to pay cash for an infrastructure project. In this scenario, states allow school districts to levy general or special taxes to be placed in a reserve fund for a specified project or for undesignated purposes. Assuming an adequate tax base, sinking funds also have the ability to grow if the money is invested in interest-bearing accounts. For example, a tax levy of $1 million per year invested at 5% interest would amount to $5.8 million at the end of a five-year period.

A sinking fund has advantages for both school districts and taxpayers. A major benefit is that it encourages long-term planning for school infrastructure. Additionally, a sinking fund saves the school district money because no interest costs are incurred since no money is borrowed. However, sinking funds still depend upon the property wealth of the district. As a result, only wealthier districts generally have sufficient resources to set aside. Second, inflation will reduce the future value of a sinking fund; even a low inflation rate of 2% reduces the value of $1 to only 67 cents after 20 years. Third, accumulating large sums is not advisable, unless they are earmarked for specific projects, because voters who originally approved a tax levy might disfavor eventual uses of the sinking fund.

Bonded Indebtedness

Because neither current revenues nor sinking funds are usually feasible solutions to larger infrastructure projects, school districts frequently turn to bonded indebtedness. Bonding is a device by which districts are statutorily permitted to incur long-term debt for the purpose of acquiring fixed assets such as facilities. Although debt is generally prohibited under state law for school districts' current operations, it is generally allowed for infrastructure-related projects. Methods by which districts may incur bond debt depend on the laws of each state. In most states, school districts are authorized to bond for infrastructure needs subject to statutes on referenda and debt limitations. In other states, differences relate primarily to whether districts are fiscally independent or dependent, and on whether the state controls bonding through a central state authority.

Although bonding is a form of borrowing money, it is different from traditional private borrowing in several ways. When individuals or businesses want to borrow money for construction, they typically approach a lending institution to request a mortgage or its commercial equivalent—i.e., a debt instrument that uses the purchased property to secure the loan in case of default. In contrast, governmental units do not operate in this manner. Although bonds create a legal debt, the private paper is replaced by the bond mechanism, which has two key features. The first feature is that bonds are sold at open market and purchased by investors instead of a traditional lender. The second feature is that public properties purchased through bond sales cannot be foreclosed. Thus a bond sale for school facility purposes creates neither a mortgage nor collateral. Rather, the school district as a unit of local government pledges its full faith to secure the debt.

Bonding has many benefits. Investors see government bonds as attractive investments because the chance of default is low, and the interest paid is usually tax-exempt. Although government bond interest rates are generally lower than private market rates, bonds are attractive investments because the untaxed earnings may net the investor more income than higher yield investments after taxes—a win/win situation as schools pay lower interest rates and investors invest safely under favorable tax conditions. The only drawback to bonding for school districts is the added cost of interest the school district pays over the life of each bond issued, which for a new school facility is usually 20 years.

The process of bonding follows similar steps in all states. Most states require a local referendum (bond election) whenever a school district wants to pursue an infrastructure project that exceeds current revenues or cash reserves. A referendum is a request for voter approval of infrastructure debt by placing the question on the ballot at a general or special election. When voters approve a bond issue, they are agreeing to pay higher property taxes over the life of the bond to retire the debt or more specifically, to repay the bond buyers. To amortize the bond repayment schedule, the district levies taxes that are deposited to a special fund from which it makes semiannual or annual payments.

When a district decides to initiate a bond sale, a series of steps are involved. Determination of the infrastructure project and an estimate of its cost is usually the first step. Next, the district determines if it can afford to undertake the project. This step is critical because every state places debt limits on local units of government, including school districts. Generally, the debt limitation is expressed as a percentage of the assessed valuation of the school district. For example, if a district were to have an assessed valuation of $500 million with a 10% debt ceiling, total debt in terms of borrowed principal could not exceed $50 million. The third step is to schedule a bond election. State statutes are very specific in these matters. While the local district usually has little involvement in actually conducting an election, the district typically makes all decisions about election timing and carries sole responsibility for any campaigning to enhance the likelihood of voters approving the bond issue. If the referendum fails, the district must regroup to determine cause and decide whether to resubmit the question to voters. Generally, any new election is accompanied by escalated public relations and may include a scaled-down project at lesser cost. If the referendum is successful, the district can proceed to the fourth step of preparing the bond sale. Specialized legal counsel is required due to the complexity of bond laws, and financial counsel is required because the bond market is complex and competitive. After counsel have prepared for the bond issue, an official advertisement is issued to investors, usually through widely read financial publications and by bond prospectus.

Although the bonding process is normally completed by following these four steps, the infrastructure project is only beginning. The planned work must be performed, and the project actually extends beyond construction completion and first occupancy because the district has committed to long-term debt repayment. This requires revisiting the financial plan on an annual basis, levying taxes and depositing proceeds into special debt service funds in preparation for disbursement, and maintaining and protecting the new physical assets. As seen in earlier chapters on budgeting, accounting, and taxation, all of these processes are important to the successful operation of a school district. Facilities and bonding are areas of special care not only because so much money is at stake, but also because a school district's infrastructure makes it possible to carry out the instructional mission of schools.

INFRASTRUCTURE PLANNING AND FACILITY MAINTENANCE

Until now our discussion has centered on how schools raise money for infrastructure projects, primarily from the perspective of building new facilities, major remodeling and renovation, or acquisition and integration of technology—projects requiring large sums of money. Although big projects can involve current revenues either in the form of local dollars or state aid, there are two other facets to budgeting for infrastructure that must be discussed: facility planning, and maintenance and operations.

What Is the Role of Infrastructure Planning?

Although school districts engage in long-range planning in many areas, in some ways infrastructure planning predicts the success or failure of all other plans. An excellent curriculum built on the latest technology will be weakened if facilities are poorly designed or maintained. Likewise, the most highly skilled teachers will be frustrated if classrooms are cramped or unsuited to the content to be taught. For example, older buildings with inadequate technology infrastructure often cannot support the technology expected in today's classrooms and media centers. Similarly, older buildings with inadequate ventilation systems are unsafe for chemistry labs. Even new buildings may be problematic if overcrowded or built with insufficient attention to the learning environment. Although modern, safe facilities will not overcome ineffective teaching, planning for infrastructure is more than just architectural design—it is the integration of space with the instructional and support functions of a modern school system.

The value of infrastructure planning has long been recognized. Poor planning is costly through wasted money, lack of long-range flexibility, and underutilization of facilities. As a result, planning requires organization to oversee all aspects of facility planning and operations. Larger school districts often have an assistant superintendent who oversees all facility-related tasks. Usually this person has a staff who perform more specialized functions. In smaller districts, these duties may fall to the superintendent or business manager, with greater reliance on outsourcing for needed services. Although district size may drive how the school system organizes its planning activities, all districts need a staff person who is knowledgeable about both education and infrastructure management.

Alternatively, large districts may have an office of facility planning. This office has as its major task the ongoing study and analysis of facility needs according to five goals. The first goal is to prepare and maintain a comprehensive analysis of all facilities in the district. The second is to assure a well-designed physical environment to enhance teaching and learning. The third goal is to assure that all facilities remain useful over the life of each building because outmoded facilities hinder teaching and learning and are often costly to maintain. The fourth goal is to evaluate facilities for future educational programs in ways that assist decisions to reconstruct or retire buildings. The fifth goal is to preserve maximum flexibility in all buildings so that future generations are served. Facilities planning should thus reflect careful thought about the following:

- School-age population to be served
- Location and transportation of school-age population
- Programmatic offerings of the district and each school

- Long-range capital needs of the district
- Fiscal ability of taxpayers in the district
- Organizational structure of the school system
- Economic and demographic future of the district

The following areas make up planning for infrastructure: demographic planning, capital program planning, facility planning and programming, architectural planning, and construction planning. Because they are the elements districts use to justify many decisions about the total educational program, they deserve a brief discussion.

Demographic Planning

Demographic planning is the study of a district's profile including social, economic, and population issues. Demographics drive school infrastructure planning because the goal is to serve the needs of the school community.

Demographic planning varies greatly based on the unique characteristics of each school district. For example, districts with growing populations must anticipate housing patterns so that land can be bought ahead of rising market trends. Other districts engage in demographic planning to predict future facility needs in relation to stable or declining enrollments. A major task of demographic planning is to conduct accurate facility surveys that research the district's profile, analyze findings and propose alternative solutions, and recommend a plan of action. A comprehensive educational survey describes the community's characteristics and educational needs, determines pupil population characteristics, describes the educational program, appraises existing facilities in relation to needs, develops a master plan, assesses resources, and makes recommendations. Because it is comprehensive, the survey forms the basis for careful long-range infrastructure planning.

Description of community characteristics and educational needs is the starting point. The survey should analyze population characteristics, density, and changes over time. It should examine changes in land use, including zoning and changes that have occurred because of population trends. Analysis should examine traffic and assess development and land use under growth conditions to predict likely locations for new schools as well as continued viability of existing facilities. Other community characteristics, such as vocational opportunities, parental expectations, and public attitudes toward schools and taxes should be studied as well. Finally, one of the most important elements in demographic planning is enrollment projection, which was discussed in Chapter 5.

Capital Program Planning

Capital program planning is the anticipation of a district's capital needs in relation to its demographic profile. Its purpose is to analyze the district's financial characteristics and status to estimate the ability of the district to pay for current and future infrastructure needs.

The normal result of capital program planning is creation of a capital improvement plan (CIP) that projects all school district capital needs for the future, usually over a period of 5 to 20 years. The CIP prioritizes projects, primarily because resources are seldom sufficient to address all needs at one time, especially if current revenues are expected to provide a significant part of the money. For example, roof replacement on all buildings more than ten years old might be the highest priority. Another example might find the district trying to replace computers in all classrooms according to a priority schedule. More aggressive implementation of CIPs can occur if bonding is used. For example, a district might replace all roofs and HVAC (heating, ventilation, air-conditioning) systems in a single bond issue, or it might retrofit all buildings with wireless technology to support new school-based technology centers. When renovation, retrofitting, or new construction is contemplated, the CIP must provides an analysis of revenues over the full period of debt retirement. Finally, the CIP should be reviewed and updated as projects are completed and as needs and financial conditions change.

Facility Planning and Programming

The purpose of facility planning and programming is to identify the desires and constraints under which any educational facility will have to function. Generally, this activity involves consideration of the educational goals and objectives of the district and each individual school, and it also usually defines instructional and organizational plans. Stakeholders should be involved in facility planning and programming, including community and staff along with professional planners, such as architects. Overall goals should include the following:

- Is the facility structurally sound?
- Is it healthy and safe?
- Is it efficient to operate?
- Does it support the educational program?
- Is it attractive and comfortable?
- Is its location convenient for the users?
- Is its space optimally used?
- Is it the right size?
- Can it be modified?

If answers to any of these are negative, the district should undertake modifications.

In addition to the questions above, school districts are increasingly taking into consideration environmental issues in facility planning and programming, commonly referred to as "green" building and construction.[35] The U.S. Green Building Council offers a LEED (Leadership in Energy and Environmental Design) certification process that provides a framework for identifying and implementing practical and measurable

---

35 "Green" refers to methods and practices that reduce or avoid adverse environmental impacts. See, National Research Council, *Green Schools: Attributes for Health and Learning* (Washington, DC: Committee to Review and Assess the Health and Productivity Benefits of Green Schools, The National Academies Press, 2007).

green building design, construction, operations, and maintenance solutions.[36] Even with a strong commitment to green construction, school districts need to do a careful cost–benefit analysis of options.

Architectural Planning

All major facility projects require professional architectural planning. This has become especially true with regard to applicable statutory and regulatory requirements for health, safety, and accessibility. Additional considerations are energy efficiency and sensitivity to environmental concerns (or "green" practices). Consequently, architectural planning represents a fourth activity in school infrastructure planning.

Although architects or engineers are generally engaged to design new or reconstructed schools, a number of states now require school districts to use architectural services whenever an educational facility is modified. For example, the addition of an elevator to improve the accessibility of an existing school building may be subject to a number of state and local building and safety codes that might require the entire facility to be brought up to current building codes, increasing the cost of the project dramatically. Similarly, the removal of an interior wall in an older school building to create a larger space may expose asbestos insulation from the original construction, requiring a costly specialized removal or containment process in addition to closure of parts or all of the facility.

Selection of an architect is a critical element of facility planning. Most districts use the services of one architect for smaller projects, but engage in a design competition if larger projects, like new construction, are involved. Retrofitting and remodeling projects like installation of a new HVAC system or divider walls to reshape interior spaces are sometimes noncompetitive. Large projects such as renovation, expansion, or new construction typically require competition. Because competition is complex and costly, the process is usually reduced to asking architects to submit portfolios containing a description of their experience and qualifications, examples of their work, and rough cost estimates. The board, administrative staff, and consultants make a judgment based on such items as experience of the firm, budget, and overall reputation. As emphasized in earlier chapters, care must be taken to follow all statutory requirements in awarding contracts, including contracts for professional services.

Construction Planning

The value of architectural services is evident in two critical aspects of facility planning. The first aspect involves planning the project and working to develop project specifications. The role of architects is to work within the physical and fiscal realities of the district and to work with staff to be sure the facility will function well. The second aspect involves actual oversight of the project through completion. These two features are part of the architect's overall responsibility in construction planning. The legal liability and technical competence involved in these tasks make architectural services an absolute necessity.

---

36 U.S. Green Building Council, "LEED Green Building Certification System," www.usgbc.org/Docs/Archive/General/Docs3330.pdf.

Construction planning represents the fifth task in infrastructure planning by joining the architects, educational consultants, and school staff to design a facility project. Because architects are not educators, school districts generally need the services of a consultant to create educational specifications that communicate the district's vision to the architect. Educational specifications are first stated in general terms by school and district staff and communicated to the consultant. The consultant reviews the statements and examines existing facilities. Depending on the nature and size of the project, the consultant may work with a committee to define needs and expectations. The goal is for the consultant to use the district's broad vision to create a specific document that leads the architect to develop an appropriate design. For example, the educational specifications define the school program by classroom and by instructional facility, including requirements for all special areas, e.g., media center/library, cafeteria, auditorium, and areas for physical education, art, music, and vocational training. The importance of these activities is underscored by the Council for Educational Facility Planners International (CEFPI), which has described educational specifications as the blueprint for the future.

If new construction is required, activities may result in preliminary designs and drawings being presented to the school board. Once preliminary plans are approved, actual working drawings and specifications are developed. Plans must be examined to ensure that the design is integrated with curricular and instructional goals. Input from school site and instructional leaders is essential during the design phase to avoid inefficiency and waste.

When the design is complete, actual physical improvements begin. The major task of school and district officials during the work phase is to maintain close contact with the project. Lack of oversight could result in legal problems if it is later found that the district should have kept itself better informed of any problems. A second reason is that the district must state in writing any concerns about or changes to the project. A third reason is that payments for work will be made during the construction phase, and the district must be satisfied before any funds are released.

The work phase requires scheduled payments from the district's cash reserves or from bond proceeds. These payments satisfy material and labor claims. Architectural fees are usually a percentage of the project; in contrast, contractor fees are set by competitive bidding. When the project is finished, a percentage is typically held back pending final acceptance and proof that bills, payrolls, and mechanics' liens by all contractors, subcontractors, and vendors have been satisfied. Additionally, the board's attorney must assure that the district will have clear title.

The role of planning for infrastructure is broad and includes demographic plans, capital program plans, educational program plans, and architectural and construction plans, all of which apply to both alteration and expansion of facilities and to new construction. All infrastructure projects must be financed by legally permissible methods using cash or debt, and expert counsel ranging from legal and financial services to architectural and construction services must be used. The role of the school district is to acquire and coordinate these services—a role that demands sound educational and fiscal planning.

What Is the Role and Nature of Maintenance and Operations?

We have stressed the value of planning because the cost of physical infrastructure and the dependence of educational programs on facilities are enormous. As we noted earlier, a sound educational program is hindered by poor school facilities. As a result, an effective program of maintenance and operations (M&O) is critical in order to keep facilities and grounds in good condition and ready for use.

Organizing for M&O

The maintenance and operations function is often organized under a central office administrator with line authority over all physical plant activities and related staff. Organizational structure depends on school district size, with large districts employing dozens of employees. A medium-size school district might resemble the organizational chart in Figure 9.1, where both diversification of work and efficiency of scale are evident. As Figure 9.1 indicates, final responsibility rests with the school board, which delegates to the superintendent, who, in turn, delegates to a general director. As a result, facilities planning and operations and maintenance are joined, with a key person coordinating their performance.

Figure 9.1 develops a central maintenance division that provides services to all schools in the district. These services are often provided on an in-house basis if the district has decided it is more cost-efficient to employ permanent staff with specific skills, rather than to outsource some or all of these functions to private firms. Figure 9.1 illustrates a school district of approximately 16,000 students and provides an example wherein the district has decided that it has enough work to justify the cost of operating its own maintenance division. An assistant superintendent for facilities planning would oversee a general director, who, in turn, oversees a director of maintenance and operations. The director of maintenance and operations oversees a supervisor of maintenance and a supervisor of operations. As district size decreases, the organizational chart becomes simpler and less formal, even though the same tasks still need to be performed.

Organizing for maintenance and operations demands assessing facility needs on the basis of cleaning, repairing, and replacing the district's capital assets. The overarching organizational tasks therefore includes determining maintenance and conducting facility operations.

Determining Maintenance Needs

As a rule, maintenance of buildings requires skilled evaluation of all component systems. Component systems include footings, foundations, and basements; interior and exterior walls; roofs and flashings; doors, windows, and frames; floors and ceilings; mechanical systems; electrical systems; aesthetics, equipment, and furniture; grounds; and energy conservation. This list points out the need for skilled employees and specialized contracted maintenance. Foundations, footings, and basements should be regularly inspected by staff for visible problems, and regular evaluation by engineers or architects should be scheduled. Walls and roofs should be inspected regularly, with repairs like sealing cosmetic cracks and light masonry repointing done in-house. Mechanical and electrical systems should be inspected, with problems reported

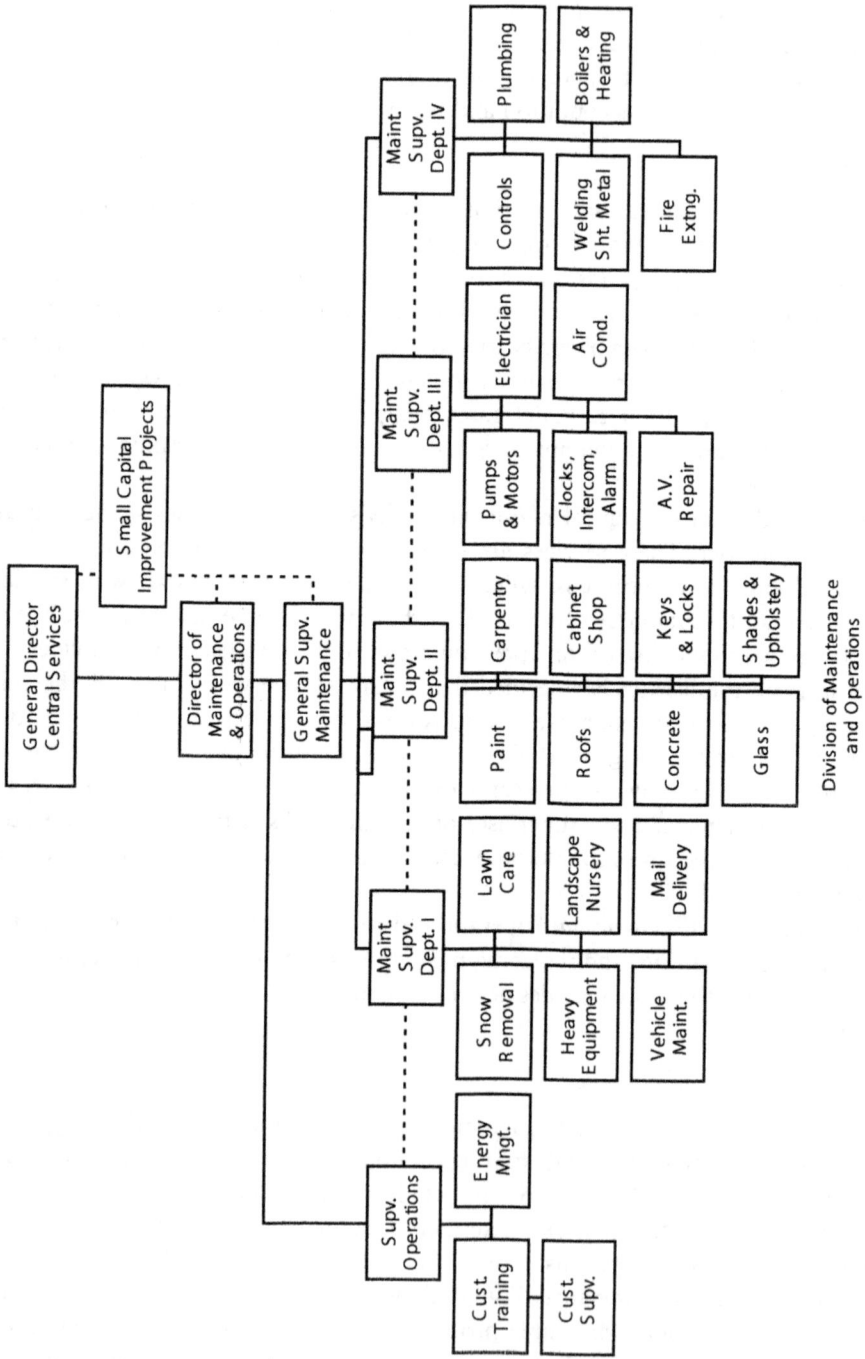

FIGURE 9.1 Sample Facilities Organizational Chart

General Director Central Services

Small Capital Improvement Projects

Director of Maintenance & Operations

General Supv. Maintenance

Supv. Operations
- Energy Mngt.
- Cust. Training
- Cust. Supv.

Maint. Supv. Dept. I
- Lawn Care
- Snow Removal
- Landscape Nursery
- Heavy Equipment
- Mail Delivery
- Vehicle Maint.

Maint. Supv. Dept. II
- Carpentry
- Paint
- Cabinet Shop
- Roofs
- Keys & Locks
- Concrete
- Shades & Upholstery
- Glass

Maint. Supv. Dept. III
- Pumps & Motors
- Electrician
- Clocks, Intercom, Alarm
- Air Cond.
- A.V. Repair

Maint. Supv. Dept. IV
- Controls
- Plumbing
- Welding Sht. Metal
- Boilers & Heating
- Fire Extng.

Division of Maintenance and Operations

promptly. Painting, refastening trim, cleaning traps, replacing washers in valves, adjusting doors and windows, and replacing shades and lighting can be done in-house. A maintenance plan should also address energy conservation, including a formal energy audit and energy-saving steps.

The goal of determining maintenance needs is to identify concerns and to prevent new problems. Once needs are known, the district must schedule and fund repair or replacement. As a general rule, districts should spend a minimum 4% to 6% of the general operating budget for maintenance. Much of the problem of poor facility conditions today stems from failure to follow a program of routine and preventive maintenance. In difficult financial times, schools and districts often cut back on routine maintenance or postpone preventive maintenance in order to protect educational programs and staffing levels. As discussed previously, this results in a backlog of deferred maintenance that will cost the school district more in the long run and could negatively affect the learning environment for students and staff.

Conducting Facility Operations

Although maintenance is key to the financial and instructional health of schools, smooth day-to-day operation of facilities is equally important to the safety and welfare of everyone at school. As we stated previously, the physical condition of facilities has an impact on learning: Dirty or poorly maintained schools send a message to staff, students, parents, and the community that education is not valued. Students attending well-maintained schools feel pride; staff morale is higher; and parental and community support for education is enhanced. Routine maintenance is essential, and its contribution to student success should not be undervalued.

The maintenance function comprises the tasks of keeping a school open for use. As a rule, the most important skill is organization. Maintenance staff must be organized for efficiency within the limits of cost, labor, and time. Every aspect of maintenance must be organized by task and timetable so that staff know what needs to be done, and when it must be accomplished. Generally, tasks can be broken down into routines of vacuuming, sweeping, mopping, dusting, cleaning glass, and emptying trash; steam-cleaning, buffing, or waxing floors; cleaning whiteboards or chalkboards; cleaning halls including walls, water fountains, and waste containers; and noting damage needing repair. Daily activities include both routine tasks and minor repairs, although component system evaluation by staff can occur on a monthly or quarterly basis. Minor repairs like fixing trim or changing lightbulbs can be scheduled on an as-needed basis, while other tasks such as painting should be done during nonschool times. Daily tasks should be performed on staggered schedules using a square-foot formula or by enrollment size of the school.

Although many additional activities not described here are needed to ensure a clean, safe, and healthy school, no aspect is more important than initial and ongoing training and development for custodial and maintenance staff. Training may result in overall improvements including higher standards of service, lower employee costs stemming from greater efficiencies, less waste, fewer hazards, less deterioration of school plant and equipment, more flexibility in shifting employees among buildings, and greater respect for custodial and maintenance workers on the part of the public. Facility operations and maintenance are critical to the good work of schools and depend on highly competent staff to create the best possible conditions for equal educational opportunity.

The Role of the School Leader in Maintenance and Operations

Site-level school leaders are ultimately responsible for the appearance and condition of their schools—as a consequence, they should become familiar with district maintenance and operations policies and procedures because it is their duty to ensure that the total school environment is conducive to student learning.[37]

Depending on school district size and the presence or absence of collective bargaining agreements, the responsibilities of school leaders for maintenance and operations can vary greatly. In smaller districts, they may be directly involved in hiring, supervising, and evaluating maintenance staffs. In larger districts where custodial staffs are more likely to be covered by a collective bargaining agreement, hiring, supervision, and evaluation may be centralized. Alternatively, in large school systems custodial and maintenance operations may be outsourced to one or more private contractors. In such cases, site leaders need to familiarize themselves with the content of collectively bargained agreements or outsourcing contracts. By doing so, they will avoid many problems and will be better prepared to engage all staff—both instructional and noninstructional—proactively in maintenance, repair, and operational issues. The overall goal is to create a school culture that values schools' physical condition and appearance as important factors in the learning environment.

Although the size, cost, and complexity of maintenance and operations—indeed, the entirety of infrastructure—causes primary responsibility to be located in the school district's central office, the opportunity to enhance the safety and security of school facilities and grounds through sound maintenance and operations occurs first at each school site, and the school leader plays a key role. Some measures are straightforward—e.g., requesting and maintaining sufficient exterior lighting of buildings, parking lots, and other areas including athletic fields is an effective low-cost deterrent to crime. Other maintenance issues fall to school site leaders such as ensuring that exterior and interior door locks are in good working order and cannot be easily bypassed. Likewise, if the school's grounds have shrubbery near doors and windows, the school leader should request that they be pruned in order to prevent their use as cover by vandals and criminals. Likewise, school leaders should insist on prompt repair of cracked or uneven sidewalks and parking lot potholes that place students and adults at risk of injury. Similarly, prompt removal of graffiti discourages gang activity and vandalism. In other words, risk management and maintenance/operations are district-wide and school-wide obligations, and close attention to these issues can greatly reduce barriers to the effectiveness and increase enjoyment of the learning environment.[38]

---

37 See Faith E. Crampton, David C. Thompson, and Randall S. Vesely, "The Forgotten Side of School Finance Equity: The Role of School Infrastructure Funding in Student Success," *NASSP Bulletin* 88 (September 2004): 29–56.

38 Some school districts have proactive policies in place for use by school site leaders. Additional assessment tools are available—see, e.g., Tod Schneider, Hill Walker, and Jeffrey Sprague, *Safe School Design: A Handbook for Educational Leaders* (Eugene, OR: ERIC Clearinghouse on Educational

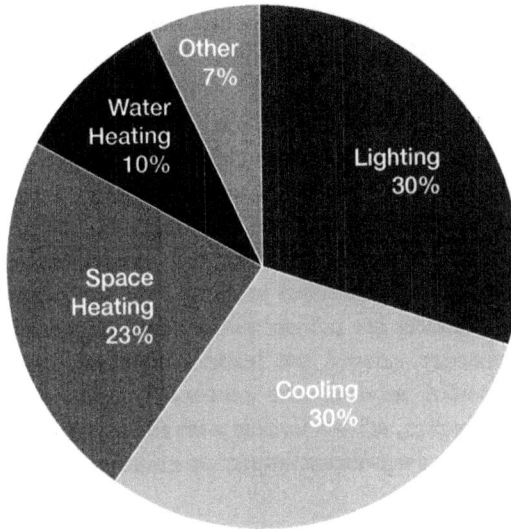

FIGURE 9.2 Typical School Energy Use Distribution

Source: U.S. Department of Energy. "EnergySmart School Tips." http://files.eric.ed.gov/fulltext/ED511654.pdf.

Increasingly, schools and districts are concerned about creating and maintaining environmentally friendly or sustainable facilities, inclusive of both indoor and outdoor spaces. Although many of these concerns are addressed at the district level, e.g., projects to retrofit schools with energy efficient doors and windows, there is much that school leaders and their staffs can do at the site level with regard to the "green" initiatives and by doing so not only set a good example for students, but also include them in these efforts, particularly because many students today have an intense interest in preserving and improving the environment.[39]

Energy efficiency is attractive to school and district leaders not only because it addresses environmental sustainability, but also because—pragmatically—it reduces utility costs. On average, over half (53%) of a school's energy costs are attributable to heating and cooling costs with an additional 30% for lighting and 10% for water heating (see Figure 9.2). Focusing on environmental impact and energy efficiency, the U.S. Department of Energy (DOE) has undertaken the "EnergySmart" initiative to provide schools with concrete suggestions to reduce energy use without compromising the quality of the teaching and learning environment.[40] Some "tips" are low or no cost and can be initiated by school leaders with the assistance of staff and students. Simple

Management, College of Education, University of Oregon, 2000), 40–41; and Jessie Shields Strickland and T. C. Chan, "Curbside Critique: A Technique to Maintain a Positive School Yard Image," *School Business Affairs* 68 (May 2002): 24–27.

39 Organizations, such as the Healthy Schools Campaign (www.healthyschoolscampaign.org) and Council for Educational Planners International (www.cefpi.org) offer a number of suggestions to engage students in such activities.

40 See, for example, U.S. Department of Energy, *EnergySmart Schools Tips: Retrofitting, Operating, and Maintaining Existing Buildings* (Washington, DC: Office of Energy Efficiency and Renewable Energy, Building Technologies Program), http://apps1.eere.energy.gov/buildings/publications/pdfs/energysmartschools/ess_quick-wins_fs.pdf.

steps like turning out lights in classrooms when not in use or turning off computers and peripherals at the end of the day not only reduce energy use but make staff and students more energy aware.

A similar approach can be taken at the site level with regard to "green cleaning." For example, the use and overuse of some cleaning chemicals contribute to poor air quality in schools. The Healthy Schools Campaign offers a number of inexpensive suggestions that can be implemented at the school level, such as recycling paper and plastic; conserving water; maintaining uncluttered classrooms and work spaces; and handling food and potential contaminants properly.[41] More comprehensive approaches that involve custodial practices are subject to the cautions mentioned previously; that is, before initiating changes, school site leaders must take into consideration, for example, whether custodial services and personnel supervision are centralized or outsourced. All in all, however, school leaders with the assistance of their site councils, staffs, and students can have a significant impact on environmental issues at the site level.

WRAP-UP

Budgeting for school infrastructure is highly complex, but as noted at the outset of this chapter, it is a false economy to underspend for facilities. The physical environment of schools is important for student learning and staff morale as well as parental and community support of local schools. Although this chapter has presented a number of broad issues that are often considered the domain of central administration, school leaders play a critical role in the maintenance and operations of their respective schools. Importantly, they set the tone that the built environment of the school, along with school grounds, is an essential component of student success.

POINT–COUNTERPOINT

POINT

With research telling us that school infrastructure plays a critical role in students' academic success, states have a responsibility to ensure that all children attend safe, clean, and modern schools. As such, states must take a lead role in funding school infrastructure to compensate for inequities in local fiscal capacity.

COUNTERPOINT

From the beginning of the common school movement, construction and maintenance of school facilities have been a local responsibility. The tradition of local control has allowed school districts to decide for themselves the kinds of facilities they want. Because greater state funding almost always leads to more state control, states should not take a lead funding role in order to respect local autonomy.

---

41 Healthy Schools Campaign, "The Quick + Easy Guide to Green Cleaning in Schools," http://greencleanschools.org/#num1.

- With which of these viewpoints are you most in agreement? Why?
- In your estimation, would your school district benefit from a larger or smaller state role in funding school infrastructure than is currently state law? How so, and why?

CASE STUDY

As the newly hired vice principal at a pre-K-8 school, you were brimming with enthusiasm at the thought of working closely with colleagues, parents, and students. You were especially eager to impress the principal, who had already earned your esteem by informing you that she saw you as an equal partner in leading the school, even though this was your first formal administrative position. She had indicated she wanted you to become involved immediately and that one of your many responsibilities was oversight of the day-to-day operations of the school, including maintenance of the building and grounds. You knew this was an important role because you had already noticed the cleanliness and attractiveness of the school and because the principal had repeatedly emphasized that the appearance and condition of the building were symbolically important to staff, students, and community. She had also noted that this was accomplished on a very limited budget. The principal had then introduced you to the head custodian, who had been with the school 20 years. When the principal left the two of you to get acquainted, the head custodian's pleasant demeanor immediately vanished. Wasting no time, he curtly informed you that he obviously knew his job well and that he would not welcome any interference in his maintenance of the building and grounds. You had thanked him for his candor and assured him that you wanted to work cooperatively, but inwardly you had a sinking feeling.

At the initial all-school meeting, the principal introduced you to the faculty and mentioned that one of your responsibilities was ensuring the smooth daily operation of the school. She encouraged faculty and staff to come to you with any maintenance or repair issues. The next day was the first day of classes, and early that morning three veteran teachers marched into your office to angrily report that their classroom windows would not open and that it would be impossible to teach or learn since the temperature was predicted to be very hot that day. Two of the teachers added that they had submitted work orders to fix the windows last spring before the end of the school year. Soon thereafter, a teaching assistant appeared in your doorway to report that a student restroom toilet was overflowing and that water and waste were seeping into the hallway. In character with your emerging day, the assistant added that this particular toilet had overflowed several times last year. At exactly that point, a distraught parent stormed into your office to complain that her asthmatic daughter had been once again been placed in one of the portable classrooms and had had an attack a few minutes ago. As she ended her story, she emphasized that she had made numerous complaints last year about how something was triggering her child's asthma and had requested that her daughter not be asked to travel between buildings—but, as she put it, her request obviously had been ignored.

Faced with multiple problems, you immediately contacted the head custodian and outlined the problems. "We'll get on them," he responded crisply, "but you'll need to pay overtime for me and my staff. We can't attend to emergencies and get our regular work done too."

Below is a set of questions. As you respond, consider your learning in this chapter and apply your knowledge to the situation:

- How will you address the head custodian's request for overtime? Explain your rationale.
- In hindsight, is there anything you could have done prior to the first day of school to prevent these problems (or similar ones) from occurring?
- As you look toward the rest of the school year, how will you ensure the smooth day-to-day operations of the school?

PORTFOLIO EXERCISES

- Research how school infrastructure is financed in your state. This may include obtaining state department of education documents or examining relevant statutes. If your state uses an aid formula to assist in debt service, determine the type of aid, the size of the allocation, how districts qualify for aid, and the impact of the formula on your district. If your state does not provide aid to facilities, determine whether any surrounding states do.

- Interview your director of facility planning (or the central office administrator with this responsibility) to determine how current infrastructure projects are funded in your school district. Identify how much debt your district currently carries for school infrastructure, the nature of the debt, and the amortization schedule.

- Obtain a copy of your district's capital improvement plan. Interview your director of facility planning to determine how planning for school infrastructure occurs in your district. Ask how your district assesses its short, intermediate, and long-term needs. Determine the total cost of the capital improvement plan and its impact on local taxes.

- Interview the appropriate central office person with regard to daily and scheduled maintenance and operations. Learn how these functions are organized at the district level and the amount and percentage of the school district's annual operating budget devoted to M&O. Ask about the role of site-based leaders, like principals, in school maintenance and operations.

- Does your school use "green" cleaning methods? If so, how do these compare to the recommendations in this chapter? If not, how could your school start to incorporate them?

WEB RESOURCES

The Center for Green Schools, www.centerforgreenschools.org

Council of Educational Facilities Planners International, www.cefpi.org

Healthy Schools Campaign, www.healthyschoolscampaign.org

National Center for the Twenty-First Century Schoolhouse, edweb.sdsu.edu/schoolhouse

National Clearinghouse for Educational Facilities, www.ncef.org

U.S. Department of Education, "Green Ribbon Schools," www2.ed.gov/programs/green-ribbon-schools/index.html

U.S. Environmental Protection Agency, "Healthy School Environments," www.epa.gov/schools

U.S. Environmental Protection Agency, "Creating Healthy Indoor Environments in Schools," www.epa.gov/iaq/schools

INTERACTIVE WEB RESOURCE

American Society of Civil Engineers, "School Infrastructure Funding Needs by State," www.infrastructurereportcard.org/a/#e/school-funding-needed

RECOMMENDED READING

Bello, Mustapha A., and Vivian Loftness. "Addressing Inadequate Investment in School Facility Maintenance." School of Architecture Paper 50. Pittsburgh, PA: Carnegie Mellon University Research Showcase, 2010.

Council of Educational Planners International. *Safe Schools: A Best Practices Guide*. Washington, DC, Spring 2013. http://media.cefpi.org/SafeSchoolsGuide.pdf.

Crampton, Faith E., and David C. Thompson, Eds. *Saving America's School Infrastructure*. Volume II in the series "Research in Education Fiscal Policy and Practice: Local, National, and Global Perspectives." Greenwich, CT: Information Age Publishing, 2003.

Earthman, Glen L. *Planning Educational Facilities: What Educators Need to Know*, 3rd ed. Lanham, MD: Rowman & Littlefield, 2009.

Healthy Schools Campaign. "The Quick + Easy Guide to Green Cleaning in Schools." http://greencleanschools.org/#num1.

Kozol, Jonathan. *Savage Inequalities: Children in America's Schools*. New York: Harper Perennial, 1992.

National Clearinghouse for Educational Facilities. "Mitigating Hazards in School Facilities." Washington, DC, 2008. www.ncef.org/pubs/mitigating_hazards.pdf.

National Research Council. *Green Schools: Attributes for Health and Learning*. Committee to Review and Assess the Health and Productivity Benefits of Green Schools. Washington, DC: National Academies Press, 2007.

Thompson, David C., and Faith E. Crampton. "An Overview and Analysis of Selected School Finance and School Facilities Litigation." *Education Law Reporter* 243 2 (June 11, 2009): 507–545.

U.S. Department of Education. *Planning Guide for Maintaining School Facilities* (Washington, DC: School Facilities Maintenance Task Force, National Center for Education Statistics, 2003), http://nces.ed.gov/pubs2003/2003347.pdf.

U.S. Department of Energy. *EnergySmart Schools Tips: Retrofitting, Operating, and Maintaining Existing Buildings*. Washington, DC: Office of Energy Efficiency and Renewable Energy, Building Technologies Program, http://apps1.eere.energy.gov/buildings/publications/pdfs/energysmartschools/ess_quick-wins_fs.pdf.

CHAPTER 10

Budgeting for Transportation and Food Service

THE CHALLENGES

Safe, reliable transportation to and from school is a basic need for students and families throughout the country.

The Civil Rights Project at UCLA[1]

When students are hungry and distracted, they're not learning.

Arne Duncan, Secretary, U.S. Department of Education[2]

CHAPTER DRIVERS

Please reflect upon the following questions as you read this chapter:

- What are the definition, role, and scope of auxiliary services?
- What are the origins and purposes of school transportation systems?
- How is school transportation funded?
- How does the law relate to school transportation funding?
- What other school transportation issues are relevant to budgeting?
- What are the origins and purposes of food service systems?
- How is food service funded?
- What other food service issues are relevant to budgeting?

---

1 UCLA Civil Rights Project, "Transportation," http://civilrightsproject.ucla.edu/legal-developments/court-decisions/resources-on-u.s.-supreme-court-voluntary-school-desegregation-rulings/crp-transportation-fact-sheet-2009.pdf.

2 National Education Association, "Survey: Three out of Five Teachers See Hunger in the Classroom," www.neahin.org/about/news/survey-three-out-of-five.html.

SETTING THE STAGE

As we draw closer to the end of our study of how public schools are funded, we also must devote time to examining the area of auxiliary or support services. Our goal is twofold. First, there is a tendency in society to see the work of schools as almost entirely instructional, which can lead to other areas of school district operations being undervalued when, in fact, they should be highly prized for their role in providing equal educational opportunity. Our second goal follows closely, in that a book examining the many aspects of schools and money would be incomplete if it failed to address transportation and food services because schools would be negatively impacted absent these essential operations. In sum, every child has a right to equal educational opportunity, and so should be able to get to and from school without hardship, and attend classes free of hunger through the provision of healthy, nutritious meals. Equal opportunity is mocked when schools are physically inaccessible or when children are malnourished.

We open our discussion by defining the role and scope of auxiliary services. Our interest then turns to the origins and purposes of student transportation systems, along with a discussion of the intersection of law with the transportation function. We round out the transportation section with an examination of how transportation is funded in the 50 states, concluding with a consideration of other relevant transportation issues such as bus purchasing, bus maintenance, and safety. In similar fashion, we turn next to food service systems, examining the issues and funding methods used throughout the nation. Of importance to this discussion is consideration of the organization and fiscal management of food services, inasmuch as food service—unlike most school district operations—is designated a revenue-neutral enterprise, i.e., self-supporting, and subject to strict federal regulations. In sum, our discussion in this chapter considers a key element of students' educational experience through the exploration and appreciation of thethe role of auxiliary services in the teaching and learning mission of schools.

The Role of Auxiliary Services

Although auxiliary services can be more broadly defined, we use the term here to refer to selected noninstructional support services, usually funded under segregated fund accounting systems. This definition typically limits auxiliary services to the areas of pupil transportation and school food services. These two auxiliary operations are complex regardless of school district size. For example, urban districts may use a large fleet of buses to transport thousands of pupils over relatively short distances while rural districts with much smaller enrollments often operate many buses to transport students much longer distances in sparsely populated areas. Regardless of enrollment or geography, school districts face similar types of operating costs: staffing; bus safety; vehicle maintenance and replacement; and liability insurance. Similarly, food services often must employ a range of staff to plan and operate a program that includes breakfast, lunch, afterschool snacks, and summer meal programs; free and reduced-price meals for low income children; commodity support programs that lower the cost of meals and bolster agricultural markets; federal and state subsidies; and extensive federal oversight and regulation. Given the scope and cost of pupil transportation and food services, with annual expenditures of $21.8 billion and $20.0 billion, respectively, in 2010,[3] it is clear that each of these represents a major cost for schools. Thus, the role of auxiliary services is substantial and demands efficient organization and close management because these essential noninstructional support services contribute meaningfully to the educational mission of schools.

THE TRANSPORTATION FUNCTION

Pupil transportation is one of the most visible services provided by school systems. Bright yellow school buses arrive in front of the homes of more than 25 million schoolchildren in the United States each morning,[4] and the bus is often the last school contact of the day. The transportation function is even larger, however, ferrying students on field trips and to athletic and academic events, so that recent data indicate an approximate total of 9 billion student rides per year.[5] Pupil transportation is indeed a major cost factor in many school district budgets. In addition, schools as a whole are viewed more favorably by parents and the public when the transportation function operates smoothly. When buses are late or a child is dropped off at the wrong location, everything about schools may become suspect in the eyes of the community. As a consequence, transportation is one of the most critical noninstructional activities of any school system.

What Are the Origins and Purpose?

Widespread transporting of students to and from school largely developed as a result of school district consolidation dating from the early 20th century. Although assumed to have arisen primarily as a result of the invention of motor vehicles, school transportation and state financial support have been in existence since 1869 when Massachusetts became the first state to spend public funds for pupil transportation. While the Massachusetts law was the first of its kind, pupil transportation grew rapidly with the enactment of compulsory attendance laws and school and district consolidation, as well as the advent of motor vehicles. School district consolidation alone led to major changes in the role of transportation, with the number of school districts decreasing dramatically from 117,108 in 1940 to 13,588 in 2011.[6]

---

3 U.S. Department of Education, *Digest of Education Statistics 2012*, Table 208, "Total Expenditures for Public Elementary and Secondary Education, by Function and State or Jurisdiction, 2009–10," http://nces.ed.gov/programs/digest/d12/tables/dt12_208.asp.

4 Ibid., Table 206, "Students Transported at Public Expense and Current Expenditures for Transportation," http://nces.ed.gov/programs/digest/d12/tables/dt12_206.asp.

5 *School Transportation News* (September 2011), www.stnonline.com.

6 U.S. Department of Education, *Digest of Education Statistics 2012*, Table 98, "Number of Public School Districts and Private Elementary and Secondary Schools: Selected Years 1869–70 through 2010–11," http://nces.ed.gov/programs/digest/d12/tables/dt12_098.asp.

Unlike some aspects of fiscal support for schools, U.S. taxpayers have seemed willing to spend for transporting students from the earliest days. Support was likely due to a common recognition that what individuals could do only poorly could be done far more efficiently by an entire community. Early on, a spurring factor was geographic isolation in a largely agricultural nation, a demographic that has changed substantially over time. The size and scope of pupil transportation has also been affected by federal laws, such as the 1975 enactment of P.L. 94–142, The Education of All Handicapped Children Act, a landmark law that mandated equal opportunity for special education students, including not only instructional programs but also transportation. A number of court rulings following *Brown v. Board of Education* and the enactment of the Civil Rights Act of 1964 mandated busing to achieve racial integration.[7] More recently, year-round schools, charter schools, private schools, and intradistrict and interdistrict school choice have enlarged the scope and cost of pupil transportation services. As a result of the sheer magnitude of transportation systems along with regulation for student safety, dramatic fluctuations in fuel prices, environmental concerns and alternative "green" fuels,[8] and rising insurance costs for operation and liability, the transportation function has experienced enormous changes in size, complexity, and importance since its humble origins.

While the purpose of pupil transportation is simple, its full application is more complex. No student has equal educational opportunity if schooling is inaccessible due to lack of transportation, and states and local districts have long worked to make schools available to students who live beyond reasonable distances. Providing such service has evolved into a multibillion dollar industry ranging from employment of bus drivers to purchasing insurance against a set of myriad risks. These costs are greatly affected by issues of efficiency and accountability—concepts that are themselves made more complicated by competing public goals. For example, parents often have one set of expectations for a transportation system while the state and school district might operate from a different perspective. Similarly, pupil transportation may require new facilities, and shifts of populations in a community may create new transportation demands. Additionally, each state, as well as each school district, has unique needs that may impact transportation system designs. For instance, no two states or school districts are identical on variables such as population density, number of pupils to be transported, topography, climate, road conditions, and length of routes—factors which affect the number and size of buses placed on routes. To make such matters even more challenging, there are many other decisions that fall to the local level, such as whether a school district should operate its own bus system or outsource the transportation function to a private, for-profit company. Local decisions are also affected by the design and funding of state aid formulas.

---

7 For a history of busing used as means to achieve racial integration of schools, see *Integrating Suburban Schools*, by Adai Tefera, Erica Frankenberg, Genevieve Siegel-Hawley, and Gina Chiricigno (Los Angeles, CA: The Civil Rights Project at UCLA, 2011), 7–16.

8 See, for example, "Alt-Fuel School Bus Options Are Growing," by Kelly Aguinaldo, *School Bus Fleet*, May 22, 2014, www.schoolbusfleet.com/Channel/Green-School-Bus/Articles/2014/05/Alt-fuel-school-bus-options-are-growing.aspx.

Because the design, operation, and implementation of a pupil transportation system is so complex, districts often devote a salary line to a transportation director who is charged with setting and implementing bus management policies; developing and administering the transportation budget; recruiting, screening, and hiring staff; providing staff training programs; and coordinating maintenance services. Also, the transportation director has responsibility for planning bus routes for regular and special education students as well as cocurricular activities and field trips.

The director of transportation services must have a range of talents and specific skills. The relevant knowledge base includes ability to efficiently organize a transportation fleet; effective human relations skills in working through human resource problems; and the ability to maintain positive relations with parents and the community. Additionally, the transportation director must be skilled in decision making in order to lead people and manage problems effectively. The director must have expertise in technology-assisted route development, route-planning software, budgeting, and labor laws, as well as competence related to legal requirements such as employee drug testing and handling of hazardous materials. Because of potential liability involved in all aspects of the transportation function, the director must demand strict accountability because the transportation director, in cooperation with administrative supervisors, is ultimately responsible for all transportation issues.

Although many people are involved in carrying out the total transportation function, the transportation director is the first-line person responsible for overseeing operations and ensuring district transportation goals are met. These goals and accompanying policies, procedures, and responsibilities should be placed into a comprehensive transportation manual that is written in a style accessible to a layperson. All transportation regulations, as well as employee evaluation policies, should be included in the manual. Recruitment plans, job descriptions, training information, and the requirements for each job should be included, and special emphasis should be given to bus safety, driver training, pupil discipline, energy conservation, disability issues, public relations, bus routes, and bus schedules. Some school districts also place some or all of the information one would find in the manual on their website as an information source for staff, parents, and the community.[9] While these elaborate procedures and responsibilities seem only distantly akin to the origins of transporting children at taxpayer expense, the basic purpose has not changed; that is, making education available to every child on an equal basis still remains the first goal.

What Is Transportation Law?

While all transportation issues are complex, none is more serious than the area of transportation law. Many court cases have focused on liability in transporting students, and a large body of case law has centered on the issue of authorization to provide

---

9 Brittany-Marie Swanson, "Tips for Enhancing Your Transportation Website," *School Bus Fleet* (September 13, 2011), www.schoolbusfleet.com/Channel/Management-Training/Articles/2011/09/Tips-for-Enhancing-Your-Transportation-Website.aspx.

transportation at public expense.[10] Several cases have addressed the use of public funds to transport private school students,[11] and other cases have addressed who can be transported,[12] as well as whether districts have authority to deny transportation.[13] Of course, transportation for desegregation has been heavily litigated and continues to be of court interest.[14] While it is not the purpose of a school finance textbook to review the law's relationship to school transportation, a brief overview underscores its potential impact on the budget process.

Access to education via transportation services has been the focus of lawsuits at the U.S. Supreme Court level on many occasions. In a case seemingly unrelated to transportation, the U.S. Supreme Court ruled in *Cochran v. Louisiana State Board of Education* in 1930 that public funds could be used to buy textbooks for children attending private schools because it applied a test that became known as the child-benefit theory.[15] According to *Cochran*, courts could relax the church–state entanglement prohibition in the U.S. Constitution by deciding whether the child is the prime beneficiary of a public expenditure involving private schools.[16] If children received the benefit, the Court reasoned, the expenditure would not violate separation of church and state if other care was taken. *Cochran* became the basis for a 1947 ruling affecting transportation in *Everson v. Board of Education* when the Court ruled that reimbursing bus fare to parochial and private school children was permissible in that public and private interests were not crossed with the establishment of religion by applying the child-benefit theory to busing.[17] The Court observed that transportation is like police,

---

10 See, e.g., *Raymond v. Paradise Unified School Dist.*, 31 Cal. Rptr. 847 (Cal. 1963); and *Woodland Hills School Dist. v. Pennsylvania Dept. of Educ.*, 516 A.2d 875 (Pa. 1986).

11 See, e.g., *Board of Educ. v. Antone*, 384 P.2d 911 (Okla. 1963); and *Cumberland School Comm. v. Harnois*, 499 A.2d 752 (R.I. 1985).

12 See, e.g., *Madison County Board of Educ. v. Brantham*, 168 So.2d 515 (Miss. 1964); and *People ex rel. Schuldt v. Schimanski*, 266 N.E.2d 409 (Ill. 1971).

13 See, e.g., *Shaffer v. Board of School Dir.*, 522 F. Supp. 1138 (Pa. 1981); *Kansas v. Board of Educ.*, 647 P.2d 329 (Kan. 1982).

14 See, e.g., *U.S. v. Jefferson County Board of Educ.*, 372 F.2d 836 (11th Cir. 1967); *Swann v. Charlotte-Mecklenburg Board of Educ.*, 312 F. Supp. 503 (N.C.1970), aff'd, 402 U.S. 43 (1971); *Monroe v. Jackson-Madison County Sch. Sys. Bd. of Educ.*, No. 72–1327, United States District Court for the Western District of Tennessee, Western Division, 2007 U.S. Dist. Lexis 39789. (Decided May 18, 2007); *Parents Involved in Community Schools v. Seattle School Dist. No. 1*, Nos. 05–908 and 05–915, Supreme Court of The United States, 2007 U.S. Lexis 8670, December 4, 2006, decided together with No. 05–915, *Meredith, Custodial Parent And Next Friend Of McDonald v. Jefferson County Bd. of Ed et al.*, on certiorari to the United States Court of Appeals for the Sixth Circuit (June 28, 2007).

15 281 U.S. 370, 50 S. Ct. 335 (1930).

16 The First Amendment to the U.S. Constitution reads: "Congress shall make no law respecting an establishment of religion, or prohibiting the free exercise thereof; or abridging the freedom of speech, or of the press; or the right of the people peaceably to assemble, and to petition the Government for redress." This has been interpreted to mean that "entanglement" of church and state could follow from involving public funds and private schools, and resulted in the so-called "Lemon test" of *Lemon v. Kurtzman* (403 U.S. 602, 91 S. Ct. 2105 [1971] rehg. denied), which applies a tripartite test to determine if a law has the effect of (a) advancing the cause of religion, (b) resulting in excessive entanglement, or (c) has a secular purpose. Opponents of "parochiaid" object on the grounds of these three prongs of the *Lemon* test.

17 330 U.S. 1, 67 S. Ct. 504 (1947), rehg. denied.

fire, and other protections available to churches and other private organizations, saying that to deny a benefit would make the state an adversary of the church. Yet, despite the Court's long-ago rulings in *Cochran* and *Everson,* issues of commingling public funds with private and religious interests have returned many times for further judicial rulings.[18]

The arena of transportation law continues to be unsettled, as illustrated by a more recent case involving questions of violating equal opportunity when children must pay bus fees to get to school. This issue was taken up by the U.S. Supreme Court in *Kadrmas v. Dickinson Public Schools.*[19] Underlying the dispute was an attempt by the state of North Dakota to encourage school consolidation, which included financial incentives for districts that voluntarily participated. A school district chose not to consolidate and simultaneously decided to begin charging fees for bus service. Plaintiff parents brought suit, claiming a constitutional right to a free public education. The Supreme Court ruled for the defendant state, holding that the fee was rational and that equal protection was unharmed. The Court held that the state's financial problems were a rational basis for instituting fees, that transportation services need not be provided at all, and that purely economic legislation must be upheld unless it is patently arbitrary. The Court left several issues unsettled, such as whether education is a constitutional right, but it settled generally that schools may charge user fees. In an unfolding world, the right to a free public education presently includes allowing charges for transportation—a practice permitted in some states despite protests by state court litigants who assert that transportation is part of a free system of public schools.[20]

A large body of other transportation litigation also financially impacts schools, particularly since transportation is an activity fraught with potential liability. Although pupil transportation is in general very safe, bus-related accidents and injuries do occur. The risk element is heightened for school districts because they serve as a common carrier rather than a private carrier and consequently have the utmost duty to ensure student safety. As a generalization, districts accept many forms of liability when transporting pupils. Liability is controlled by various state tort concepts and is further affected by individual states' statutes regarding pupil transportation. As we will discuss in greater detail later in Chapter 11, a tort claim may arise when a school district or an employee is charged with negligence. To establish negligence, someone must have been injured, and it must be shown that a reasonable person similarly situated could have foreseen and prevented the injury. When school employees control and operate the transportation function, opportunity is present for an injured party to allege negligence and to attempt a liability claim against the school district's resources.

---

18 The net effect of *Everson* was to allow each state to opt whether to offer transportation services to nonpublic school students. As expected, states have not issued identical rulings, e.g., denying transportation as in *Luetkemeyer v. Kaufmann,* 364 F.Supp. 376 (W.D.Mo. 1973), aff'd, 419 U.S. 888, 95 S.Ct. 167 (1974) and permitting transportation as in *Pequea Valley School Dist. v. Commonwealth of Pennsylvania, Dept. of Educ.* 397 A.2d 1154 (Pa. 1979), appeal dismissed 443 U.S. 901, 99 S.Ct. 3091 (1979).

19 487 U.S. 450, 108 S. Ct. 2481 (1988).

20 See, e.g., *Sutton v. Cadillac Area Pub.Schs.,* 323 N.W.2d 583 (Mich. Ct.App. 1982); *Salazar v. Eastin,* 890 P.2d 43 (Cal. 1995).

For example, the transportation director is usually the person who sets bus stops—if an accident occurs, liability may arise if hazards were ignored.

Although exhaustive legal analysis is beyond the scope of this chapter, it is important to emphasize that liability suits raising transportation questions have had varying results. For example, in *Vogt v. Johnson* a 7-year-old child waiting for a school bus at the designated stop tried to cross the highway and was killed.[21] The Minnesota Supreme Court ruled that the driver of the bus, acting as agent of the district, was not liable at the time of the accident because custodial responsibility for the child had not yet arisen and because no amount of precaution on the part of the district would have prevented the accident. Significantly, while some cases have upheld this logic, there have been other cases to the contrary, as in the Oklahoma decision in *Brooks v. Woods* which stands in sharp contrast.[22] In *Brooks,* the district was held negligent due to the location of a school bus stop and the subsequent resulting injury to a student. The bus stop had been established adjacent to a five-lane highway with a 45-mile-per-hour speed limit, and the scheduled arrival of the bus fell directly within rush hour traffic. While waiting for the bus, a child was hurt. Key to the ruling was that the child was known by the school to have physical and cognitive disabilities. The appeals court ruled that the district's duty to exercise responsible care extends to any activity of bus transportation that rests outside the control of parents.

No exhaustive set of guidelines can be created for every situation a school district and its employees may face. However, in a negligence case the defendant must show that all actions were those of a reasonable and prudent person under the circumstances. A few more cases illustrate how such liability may turn. In *Mitchell*, a North Carolina school district was held liable when a child fell on an icy sidewalk and was crushed under the bus wheels.[23] Testimony revealed that the bus was not in its usual loading spot and that adequate supervision was lacking. In the New York case of *Cross*, a bus left the road after failing to negotiate a curve.[24] Testimony revealed that the driver had said that he was sleepy and had asked students to talk to him. In addition, he was seen rubbing his eyes and yawning. Other transportation liability cases also exist involving violence, drugs, and unruly activity. Questions of governmental immunity under individual states' laws may apply, as in the Texas case of *King* where a girl was struck by a car as she crossed the road after being dropped at a school bus stop.[25] According to the bus driver, the girl and her friends routinely walked along the drop-point side of the road for some distance after exiting the bus, and consequently the driver regularly left the location rather than waiting several minutes for the girls to eventually cross the road. The court held for the defendant school district, ruling that since several minutes had lapsed between the time of bus stop departure and the time of accident that the state's statutory immunity against tort claims applied; and that any waiver of immunity

---

21 153 N.W.2d 247 (Minn. 1967).
22 640 P.2d 1000 (Okla. Ct. App. 1981).
23 161 S.E.2d 645 (N.C. 1968).
24 371 N.Y.S.2d 179 (N.Y. App. Div. 1975).
25 *King v. Manor Indep. Sch. Dist.*, No. 03–02–00473-CV, Court of Appeals of Texas, Third District, Austin, Tex. App. Lexis 6346 (2003).

would have required conditions similar to those in a sister case of *Hitchcock* where the state's immunity was waived given that the child was struck immediately upon exiting the school bus.[26]

Because the specifics of each case, requirements of individual state law, and applicability of standard of care based on age of the child are controlling, exhaustive discussion is not feasible. What matters is that school districts can be held negligent in the arena of pupil transportation. In such cases, evidence has shown that the potential for injury was foreseeable and that actions by the board or its agent did not meet the minimum standard of care. As we will see later in Chapter 11, failure to protect students may be the causal factor leading to injury, and districts and personnel may be held liable. Under these conditions, the transportation function and the law are constant companions.

How Is Transportation Funded?

Growth in school transportation systems in the United States since the beginning of the 20th century has resulted in vast increases in the number of children carried in school vehicles at public expense. Costs are likely even higher than noted at the outset of this chapter in that no single agency fully tracks transportation costs in schools that fall outside uniform state reporting for instructional programs, such as transportation for cocurricular activities and field trips.

Most states provide some form of aid to local school districts for pupil transportation purposes, with the exceptions of Arkansas, Indiana, Louisiana, and Rhode Island (see Table 10.1). Like other forms of state aid, transportation aid varies widely in amount and distribution method. Almost half of states use some type of reimbursement formula, be it equalized, capped (allowable), or full reimbursement. Nine states include transportation aid as a component of their general aid formula while eight states allocate state aid based upon pupil density. The remaining four states distribute aid based upon a flat amount per pupil transported.

Table 10.2 presents an example of transportation aid distributed on a per-pupil basis. In Wisconsin, state transportation aid is distributed essentially as a flat grant, which on its face might appear inequitable. However, from the table we see that the per-pupil amount is adjusted upward depending upon the distance a student must be transported, such that during the regular school year, per-pupil aid ranges from $15 to $275. As long as these amounts represent reasonable estimations of the actual cost of transporting a student, the formula embodies some degree of fairness. However, some might argue that it does not adjust for geographical differences in cost, such as those in urban vs. rural areas.

In every state, the transportation formula and its funding are an outcome of the legislative process and governor approval. As such, even though those involved may express a strong belief in the importance of student transportation, the reality is only three states (Delaware, Hawaii, and Wyoming) fully fund district transportation costs.

---

26 *Hitchcock v. Garvin*, 738 S.W.2d 34 Tex. App. Dallas (1987).

TABLE 10.1 State Transportation Aid Formulas: 2011

State	In Funding Formula	Density Formula	Equalized Reimbursement	Full Cost Reimbursement	Allowable Reimbursement	Per-Pupil Formula	None
Alabama					X		
Alaska						X	
Arizona		X					
Arkansas							X
California					X		
Colorado		X					
Connecticut			X				
Delaware				X			
Florida	X						
Georgia					X		
Hawaii				X			
Idaho					X		
Illinois					X		
Indiana							X
Iowa	X						
Kansas		X					
Kentucky		X					
Louisiana							X
Maine		X					
Maryland					X		
Massachusetts					X		
Michigan	X						
Minnesota	X						
Mississippi		X					
Missouri					X		
Montana					X		
Nebraska					X		
Nevada					X		
New Hampshire	X						
New Jersey						X	
New Mexico					X		
New York			X				
North Carolina					X		
North Dakota					X		
Ohio					X		
Oklahoma							

TABLE 10.1 *continued*

State	In Funding Formula	Density Formula	Equalized Reimbursement	Full Cost Reimbursement	Allowable Reimbursement	Per-Pupil Formula	None
Oregon	X		X				
Pennsylvania			X				
Rhode Island							X
South Carolina					X		
South Dakota	X						
Tennessee	X						
Texas		X					
Utah					X		
Vermont						X	
Virginia		X					
Washington						X	
West Virginia	X						
Wisconsin						X	
Wyoming				X			
Total	9	8	4	3	17	5	4

Source: Compiled from multiple sources: "A Quick Glance at School Finance: A 50 State Survey of School Finance Policies (2011)," by Deborah A. Verstegen, http://schoolfinancesdav.wordpress.com; and independent research by the authors.

TABLE 10.2 Sample Transportation Aid Formula

Distance in Miles	Regular School Year	Summer School
Less than 2 miles (hazardous area)	$15 per pupil	none
Over 2 up to 5 miles	$35 per pupil	$4 per pupil
Over 5 up to 8 miles	$55 per pupil	$6 per pupil
Over 8 up to 12 miles	$110 per pupil	$6 per pupil
Over 12 miles	$275 per pupil	$6 per pupil

Source: Wisconsin Department of Public Instruction. Pupil Transportation Aid, 2013–2014. http://sfs.dpi.wi.gov/sfs_pupiltran1.

Because the amount of state transportation aid a school district receives is based on its audited records, aid qualification requires careful and thorough record-keeping. In addition, most states regularly audit school districts for transportation overpayment. Conversely, districts do not want to shortchange themselves, for example, by lax record-keeping that undercounts the number of students using transportation or actual number of miles traveled on bus routes. Such records generally include the following:

- Area maps and bus route information
- Address and destination of students claimed for aid

- List of students using more than one kind of transportation (e.g., vocational or special education)
- List of nonpublic school students and school choice students transported, if claimed
- Evidence of bus seating capacity for each student claimed
- Evidence of bridge or road condemnation or construction if the most direct route from home to school is inaccessible
- Evidence of mileage driven on all routes by all buses
- Basis and work paper showing calculation for pro-rated costs
- Summary and original documents for all pupil transportation for regular routes, special and vocational education, and other eligible transportation
- Claims for payments in lieu of pupil transportation showing dates, mileage, rates, and total payments
- Evidence of insurance costs for vehicles
- Evidence of price of buses and depreciation history
- List of leased or lease-purchase buses, and dates of lease

Note that state laws differ with regard to requiring school district to provide transportation for private school students as well as for students who attend choice schools, such as charter and voucher schools, in addition to intradistrict and interdistrict school choice programs, sometimes referred to as "open enrollment."

Without accurate records, reimbursement problems arise. Problems range from denial of state aid to liability for malfeasance, fraud, or even negligence if questions about fiscal impropriety are raised. In addition, the state may withhold aid until sufficient documentation is provided or demand reimbursement for aid improperly paid to the district.

What Other Issues Are Relevant?

Several other important transportation considerations need to be addressed before leaving this topic. These are: owning vs. outsourcing; the use of technology in transportation operations; elements of bus purchasing; and planning for maintenance and safety.

Owning vs. Outsourcing

With school district budgets ever more constrained, outsourcing may appear to be an attractive approach to control costs.[27] However, the benefits and disadvantages of district ownership of the transportation fleet versus outsourcing deserve careful consideration. First, there may be logic to outsourcing bus services for districts with cash flow problems because outsourcing avoids the substantial upfront investment of resources usually required to purchase a bus fleet, along with costs for ongoing maintenance and

---

27 It is estimated that somewhere between 11% and 20% of school districts outsource transportation. See, Michael Fickes, "Make Outsourcing Work," *School Planning and Management* (July 2011), peterli.com/spm/resources/articles/archive.php?article_id=3061.

periodic bus replacement. At a beginning cost of $85,000 for a typical 65-passenger school bus,[28] purchasing a bus fleet is a major upfront investment for any school district. Furthermore, state transportation aid may not cover bus purchases, placing the financial burden on local taxpayers. Second, labor is a major cost component of pupil transportation, from bus drivers and mechanics to administrative staff. Here school districts may save money by outsourcing if the contractor pays lower wages and provides fewer benefits to its employees than the district normally would provide for similar workers. Third, particularly for smaller districts, a contractor whose sole business is pupil transportation may, through greater experience and expertise, be more efficient and hence offer the same service for a lower cost than the district can on its own.

Counterarguments include school district and community concerns about how to maintain ongoing, quality service by a private contractor in order to ensure the safety of students and avoid public relations debacles, e.g., a bus accident caused by an unqualified driver that results in student injury. Second, districts lose the ability to screen potential transportation employees not only for driving records but also for prior convictions for crimes against children. Finally, a private contractor may not be as flexible or cost-effective when it comes to one-time or infrequent transportation needs, such as field trips or afterschool activities. At the same time, school districts are not relieved of liability issues associated with pupil transportation when they outsource, and so they still need to maintain adequate liability insurance. All of these issues underscore the need for careful legal and financial analysis as part of the decision process when a district is considering outsourcing transportation services.

A final note of caution is in order. If outsourcing is chosen, school districts need to engage professional legal advice, e.g., to specify that the contractor is an independent agent and will comply with all relevant federal and state statutes, rules, and regulations along with district transportation policies and procedures. Also, the contractor must provide proof of appropriate insurance for property damage and bodily and personal injury, even though the district is well-advised to continue to carry liability insurance.

Technology and Transportation Services

As technology has advanced and become more affordable, many school districts, even smaller ones, have embraced technology-assisted route development and route-planning software. These time-saving technology tools maximize routing efficiency primarily by finding the shortest routes. For most districts, these systems can reduce labor, maintenance, and fuel costs significantly.[29] Some programs also include GPS tracking so that individual buses can be tracked in real time by supervisors, ensuring that drivers are following their prescribed routes. When two-way communication is added, a driver in distress can contact a supervisor immediately for assistance, e.g., in the event a bus breaks down. In turn, school district officials know the exact location of the disabled

---

28 Florida Department of Education, *Price and Ordering Guide for School Buses, 2013–2014*, www.fldoe.org/transportation/pdf/1314PricingOrderingGuide.pdf.

29 Jim Romeo, "The Wheels on the Bus Go Round and Round," *School Planning and Management* (September 2011), http://peterli.com/spm/resources/articles/archive.php?article_id=3108.

bus, expediting assistance. Although this feature may not necessarily improve efficiency, it significantly enhances safety for both driver and passengers.

In addition to technology-assisted routing, technology can facilitate the creation of fleet maintenance databases. Software programs incorporate garage operations, vehicle replacement, mechanical repair and maintenance, and fuel consumption records into databases that can be manipulated to analyze cost efficiencies, e.g., expenditures on preventive maintenance vs. emergency repairs. Additionally, the number and type of repairs for each vehicle; age and condition; operating cost per mile; and cost per individual vehicle repair can be tracked and analyzed. Item and total costs are accounted for and used to inform decisions about continued maintenance or disposal. For example, a district might find that maintenance costs for a particular bus were $500 in the first year compared to $5,000 in its fifth year of operation. This information can be joined with other costs, such as labor and vehicle down-time, to determine the most cost-efficient junctures for purchase of replacement vehicles. In addition, these types of databases often facilitate generation of state-mandated transportation reports. The benefit is sizable, in that records can be quickly gathered, formatted, and analyzed, saving many staff hours compared to manual data gathering and calculation.

Purchasing Buses

Our discussion about owning, outsourcing, and using cost–benefit analysis is particularly relevant with regard to bus purchases. As noted previously, the price of a typical, full size (65-person capacity) school bus starts at $85,000, making this is a big ticket purchase for any school district. Costs quickly increase in increments of several thousands of dollars for each of the following options: a wheelchair lift, seatbelts, or airconditioning.[30] In addition, the district may need to purchase one or more smaller, customized buses to supplement its fleet. The planning and execution of such large expenditures requires care and attention to detail to avoid even more problems at vehicle delivery time that could arise from failure to write thorough and detailed bid specifications or from failure to follow state-specific purchasing laws.

Choice of fuel also affects the initial purchase price of buses. Although it is estimated that 95% of school buses continue to use diesel fuel, there is growing interest in alternative fuels that save money and the environment.[31] The most popular of these is biodiesel, a blended fuel,[32] followed by CNG (compressed natural gas), and propane. The newest entrants are hybrid and electric plug-in buses although they are not yet widely used.

Bus purchases are normally handled at the district level, using state-mandated competitive bidding specifications to detail the desired vehicle features. The central purpose of competitive bidding is to secure the lowest price for a bus that meets a detailed set of specifications, often referred to as the lowest reasonable or responsible

---

30 Florida Department of Education, *Price and Ordering Guide for School Buses.*

31 Ryan Gray, "Alternative Fuels," *School Transportation News,* February 12, 2013, www.stnonline.com/resources/clean-school-bus/alternative-fuels.

32 For more information on biodiesel fuels, see the U.S. Environmental Protection Agency, "Biofuels and the Environment," www.epa.gov/ncea/biofuels.

bid. Competitive bidding also provides a level playing field in that the purchaser, be it state or school district, cannot give a particular vendor an advantage over others. As a rule, most states' bid laws set a threshold purchase price, e.g., $10,000, above which competitive bids must be sought. These laws are usually very specific with regard to how the notice of bids must be published; how bids will be opened; how the lowest responsible bid will be determined; and how errors in bids will be handled. Such laws build important accountability and efficiency safeguards into purchases that involve large amounts of taxpayer dollars. In a few states, bus purchases are centralized so that a state agency prepares the bid specifications, awards the bids, and provides buses to school districts. This is not typical, however, meaning that experienced school district personnel, usually found in the school district's business office, are required.

Finally, a few words about the options of leasing or a lease-purchase are in order. Although long-term leasing of buses is less common than purchasing a new or even used bus, some districts may find it financially advantageous. However, there are often state laws and regulations that pertain to leasing and lease-purchase, and these may include competitive bidding of the contract. Here too school districts need to do a careful cost–benefit analysis before making a final decision and seek legal counsel related to leasing and lease-purchase contracts.

Safety and Maintenance

The importance of competitive bidding laws, rising bus costs, energy efficiency, concern for the environment, and liability issues has increased the amount of time school districts devote to issues of safety and maintenance of school vehicles. Parents are naturally concerned that the school buses their children ride be safe, even though, according to the National Highway Traffic and Safety Administration (NHTSA), school buses are exceedingly safe when compared to other motor vehicles in terms of accidents, injuries, and fatalities.[33] Federal law, primarily through the NHTSA, mandates certain safety features for school buses. Based upon agency regulations that took effect in 1977, school buses are now designed to protect passengers from injury during a crash by "compart-mentalization," which consists of "strong, closely spaced seats, that have energy-absorbing seatbacks."[34] Currently, NHTSA requirements for lap/shoulder belts, also referred to as three-point lap/shoulder occupant restraint systems, pertain only to newly manufactured small school buses (under 10,000 pounds vehicle weight) which carry only 20% of students nationwide. Although NHTSA has maintained for decades that its research has shown that lap/shoulder restraints are ineffective in larger school buses, there is still a certain amount of controversy surrounding their stance. For example, in the late 1990s, the agency acknowledged that their compartmentalization regulations did not provide adequate protection to students involved in side collisions. As a result, in 2008, the agency expanded requirements for newly manufactured, large school buses, raising the height of seat backs from 20 to 24 inches. In addition, NHTSA has found that compartmentalization is not as effective for pre-K students as it is for older, larger

---

33 NHTSA, "School Buses," www.nhtsa.gov/School-Buses.

34 NHTSA, "Seatbelts on School Buses," www.nhtsa.gov/Vehicle+Safety/Seat+Belts/Seat+Belts+on+School+Buses+---+May+2006.

students and has recommended, but not required, child seats with restraints. NHTSA regulations do not prevent states from taking additional safety measures on their own. In 2012, five states—California, Florida, New Jersey, New York, Texas—required some type of safety belt on school buses.[35]

While safe equipment is an essential aspect of a good transportation system, it must be emphasized that vehicle maintenance and ongoing staff training are critical to any discussion of funding pupil transportation services. Obviously, good drivers cannot offset bad buses, nor can new equipment offset bad drivers. Consequently, issues of liability underscore the relationship among safety, maintenance, and personnel so that equipment maintenance and staff training become invaluable safety aids to saving lives and prolonging bus life. Safety requires drivers to ascertain that loading and unloading zones are free from moving traffic and that students have adequate time to cross streets. Bus safety information also needs to be distributed to parents and community members, preferably using several types of media. Maintenance includes drivers' daily vehicle inspections, including a walk-around to detect fluid leaks, tire problems, and faulty lights, flashers, or stop arms. The transportation director should establish a regular maintenance schedule that includes routine maintenance, like oil changes and brake inspections, as well as maintenance to ensure safety and equipment life. Bluntly put, good maintenance practices save lives and money by reducing accidents due to faulty equipment and by extending the working lives of buses, but obviously all these precautions come at a cost, making transportation a significant demand on the budget.

THE FOOD SERVICE FUNCTION

Like transportation, the food service function plays a critical role in effective and efficient operation of schools by providing a vital support system for the instructional process. It takes knowledge and skill to successfully plan and operate a system that meets the nutritional needs of children, and—as stated at the outset to this chapter—it makes no sense to argue for equal educational opportunity if children come to school hungry. As a result, a brief review of the food service function is needed in order to understand how it operates, how meal prices are set under federal, state, and local participation, and how revenues and expenditures in food service budgets are balanced.

What Are the General Issues?

The importance of the school food service function cannot be overemphasized because the role of nutrition in academic success is fundamental.[36] Data from earlier sections

35 Anne Teigen, "School Bus Safety," *Transportation Review* (Denver, CO and Washington, DC: National Conference of State Legislatures, August 2010); Crystal Cook and Douglas Shinkle, "School Bus Safety," *Transportation Review* (Denver, CO and Washington, DC: National Conference of State Legislatures, July 2012), www.ncsl.org/documents/transportation/Schoolbus_tranrev0810.pdf.

36 Barbara H. Fiese, Craig Gundersen, Brenda Koester, and LaTesha Washington, "Household Food Insecurity: Serious Concerns for Child Development," *Social Policy Report* 25, no. 3 (Ann Arbor, MI: Society for Research in Child Development, 2011).

of this book suggest that schools face tremendous challenges, some beginning in the home, that serve as formidable barriers to effective teaching and learning. Most striking among those barriers is evidence that poverty affects a large percentage of schoolchildren today, in highly predictable ways. The data show that many children come to school from impoverished homes, with an astonishing 45% (32.3 million) of U.S. children living in families classified as low income.[37] For children in most ethnic minority groups, the percentages are even higher: Black, 66%; Hispanic, 64%; and Native American, 64%. These percentages stand in stark comparison to the percentages for White and Asian-American children in low income families, each at 32%, although even these percentages are disturbingly high.

These and other data linking improved academic performance to nutrition have long sparked interest at federal, state, and local levels. Debate over the appropriate role for government has raged for decades, with the federal government supporting health and nutrition in various ways ranging from cash aid to surplus commodity distributions. The role of food services in schools has increased substantially over time, with many schools now serving both breakfast and lunch in large part because many children are undernourished. While food service cannot solve all of the challenges facing public education, it can be a positive force by making school a better learning environment for children.

How Is Food Service Funded?

Food service programs in schools have a long history of federal, state, and local support with the federal government playing a dominant role.[38] All these sources make up the revenue side of food service operations.

Federal Support

The federal government's involvement in the provision and funding of school food services grew out of the dire economic conditions of the Great Depression of the 1930s when farmers were receiving very low prices for their crops, if they could sell them at all. As a result, surplus food commodities grew as great masses of the unemployed and their families went hungry. In 1935, the federal government intervened, enacting the Agricultural Adjustment Act (Public Law 74–320), a law that not only assisted farmers,[39] but also resulted in the authorization of the U.S. Department of Agriculture

37 Yang Jiang, Mercedes Ekono, and Curtis Skinner, "Basic Facts about Low Income Children: Children under 18 Years 2012" (New York: National Center for Children in Poverty), www.nccp.org/publications/pub_1089.html. The authors define low income as less than two times the federal poverty level. They point to previous research that asserts families need an income of at least this level to meet basic needs.

38 For an excellent summary of early food service programs in U.S. schools dating back to the 19th century, see Gordon W. Gunderson, *The National School Lunch: Background and Development*, www.fns.usda.gov/nslp/history.

39 The Agricultural Adjustment Act supported farmers in two major ways. First, it authorized the President to impose quotas when imports interfered with agricultural adjustment programs. It also appropriated 30% of federal customs receipts to expand agricultural exports and domestic usage

(USDA) to distribute surplus food commodities to public and nonprofit schools. At the same time, as part of the "New Deal," federal legislation to address unemployment, the WPA (Works Project Administration) provided jobs for the unemployed on public works projects, including school lunch programs. By 1941, WPA school lunch programs were operating in every state as well as Washington, DC, and Puerto Rico.[40]

In 1946, the National School Lunch Act (Public Law 79–396) firmly established the role of the federal government in school food services through distribution of grants to states for food as well as facilities and kitchen equipment for nonprofit school lunch programs. A few years later, in 1954, Congress passed the School Milk Program Act (Public Law 83–597), providing federal funds to schools to purchase milk as part of their food services program. Then, in 1966, federal support expanded beyond school lunches, with the School Breakfast Program which began as a two-year federal pilot project targeted to "nutritionally needy" students as authorized in the Child Nutrition Act (Public Law 69–642).[41] The school breakfast program was subsequently written into federal law in 1975 through amendments to the Child Nutrition Act (Public Law 94–105). Less well known is the federal Summer Food Service Program which was created in 1968 as a three-year pilot project to provide meals to low income students over the summer when school is not in session.[42] It was later expanded and formalized through several pieces of federal legislation to its present format. In 1998, the Child Nutrition Reauthorization Act of 1998 (Public Law 105–336) expanded the National School Lunch Program to include snacks to students involved in certain after-school activities.[43]

Entering the 21st century, we have seen a greater emphasis on healthy, nutritional food choices for children across the nation. As part of that movement, the Fresh Fruits and Vegetable Program was enacted as part of the Farm Security and Rural Investment Act of 2002 (PL 170–171). Although this initially was a pilot program in four states and an Indian reservation, subsequent legislation expanded it to all 50 states, the District of Columbia, Guam, Puerto Rico, and the Virgin Islands.[44] The most recent federal legislation, the Healthy, Hunger-Free Kids Act of 2010 (Public Law 111–296), encompasses most of the school nutrition programs mentioned previously.[45] The Act also contains several provisions designed to improve access to and quality of foods served in school meal and afterschool snack programs, as follows:

---

of surplus commodities. See, Geoffrey S. Becker, "Farm Commodity Legislation: 1933–98," *CRS Report for Congress* (Washington, DC: Congressional Research Services, 1999).

40 Gunderson, *The National School Lunch: Background and Development.*

41 U.S. Department of Agriculture, "School Breakfast Program History," www.fns.usda.gov/sbp/program-history.

42 U.S. Department of Agriculture, "Summer School Food Service Program History," www.fns.usda.gov/sfsp/program-history.

43 U.S. Department of Agriculture, "Afterschool Snacks," www.fns.usda.gov/school-meals/afterschool-snacks-faqs.

44 U.S. Department of Agriculture, "Fresh Fruits and Vegetables Program History," www.fns.usda.gov/ffvp/program-history.

45 U.S. Department of Agriculture, "Healthy Hunger Free Kids Act," www.fns.usda.gov/school-meals/healthy-hunger-free-kids-act.

- Upgrades nutritional standards for school meals by increasing the federal reimbursement rate for school lunches by 6 cents for districts that comply with federal nutrition standards, the first real reimbursement rate increase in over 30 years.
- Improves the nutritional quality of all food in schools by providing the USDA with the authority to set nutritional standards for all foods sold in schools, including vending machines, "à la carte" lunch lines, and school stores.
- Increases the number of eligible children enrolled in the school meals programs by using Medicaid data to directly certify children who meet income requirements without requiring individual applications, connecting approximately 115,000 new students to the school meals program.
- Enhances universal meal access for eligible children in high poverty communities by eliminating paper applications and using census data to determine school-wide income eligibility.
- Provides more meals for at-risk children nationwide by allowing Child and Adult Care Food Program (CACFP) providers in all 50 states and the District of Columbia to be reimbursed for providing meals to at-risk children after school, paving the way for an additional 21 million meals to children annually.
- Empowers parents by requiring schools to make information more readily available about the nutritional quality of school meals, as well as the results of any audits.
- Improves the quality of foods supplied to schools by building on and further advancing the work the USDA has been doing to improve the nutritional quality of the commodities that schools get from USDA for use in their lunch and breakfast programs.[46]

Although many think first, and sometimes only, of the U.S. Department of Education with regard to federal involvement in pre-K–12 education, this section makes clear the longstanding leadership role of the U.S. Department of Agriculture (USDA) as it relates to school food services. To give a sense of the scope of the USDA's involvement, consider that over 7 billion meals, consisting of 5.2 billion lunches and 2.1 billion breakfasts, were served to school children through the National School Lunch and School Breakfast programs in 2013, an investment of $15.74 billion in federal funding.[47]

State Support

Individual states' contribution to school food service funding is difficult to summarize since each state is free to control its level of involvement or to choose no involvement at all. Although most states have chosen to receive federal school food aid, no uniform method of state funding has followed. Any review of current state law reveals a wide range in food service program participation, with the major feature being relatively little

---

46 U.S. Department of Agriculture, "Secretary Vilsack Statement on Passage of the Healthy Hunger-Free Kids Act" (Newsroom, December 2, 2010), www.fns.usda.gov/pressrelease/2010/063210.

47 U.S. Department of Agriculture, Food and Nutrition Service Overview, "Summary of Annual Data FY2009–2013," www.fns.usda.gov/pd/overview.

uniformity in approach or level of support. Without doubt, the most meaningful observation about the states' role in school food programs is that state funding is typically quite small compared to the federal contribution and especially small when compared to the proportion of total spending for school food services that occurs in the United States. However, states can play an important role in the administration of federal school meal programs.[48]

The Local Role

The goal of a district's school food services program is to be self-supporting in that the prices set for meals in combination with federal aid provide the full cost of the program. However, a USDA study found that, on average, school districts provide 18% of the school food services budget.[49] When a district funds a portion of the food services budget, it has two potential revenue sources. First, it may shift local tax revenue from other budgeted areas—a decision that can prove controversial if, for example, parents protest this takes needed funds from instructional programs. Second, the district may raise the prices for meals served to students who do not qualify for free or reduced-price meals, and for adults. However, raising prices too much may decrease participation, and as participation drops, per-meal cost rises which in turn can necessitate further price increases, creating a vicious circle. Labor and food costs consume, on average, 90% of a typical food services budget,[50] meaning that districts are vulnerable to fluctuations in costs associated with these two budget categories. In addition, districts must factor in longer-term capital costs for facilities and kitchen equipment. To further complicate matters, all of these budget items are subject to geographic cost variations.[51]

What Other Issues Are Relevant?

While entire books exist on managing food service operations, three additional topics merit examination here: federal compliance, organizing for food service, and financial management.

Federal Compliance

Because the federal government supplies a substantial portion of a school district food services program's revenue, it comes as no surprise that these funds come with a number of regulations. Following are descriptions of USDA nutritional guidelines for the school lunch, breakfast, and afterschool snack programs along with reimbursement rates.

---

48 National Governors Association, "State Strategies to Help Schools Make the Most of their National School Lunch Program," *Issue Brief* (Washington, DC: NGA Center for Best Practices, January 11, 2010), 1.

49 U.S. Department of Agriculture, "School Lunch and Breakfast Cost Study II: Summary of Findings" (Washington, DC: Food and Nutrition Service, Office of Research, Nutrition, and Analysis, April 2008).

50 Ibid.

51 Michael Ollinger, Katherine Ralston, and Joanne Guthrie, *School Food Service Costs: Location Matters*, Economic Research Report 117 (Washington, DC: U.S. Department of Agriculture, Economic Research Service, May 2011).

Table 10.3 presents federal nutritional guidelines for the school lunch and breakfast programs based upon weekly (5-day) consumption. These vary somewhat with the age of students, with older students being provided with more fruits, vegetables, grains, and protein. The overall goal is to provide all students with well-balanced, nutritious meals within a range of calories appropriate for their ages. The nutritional guidelines for the afterschool snack program are simpler. A daily afterschool snack is required to contain at least two different components of the following: a serving of fluid milk; a serving of meat or meat alternate; a serving of vegetables or fruits or full strength vegetable or fruit juice; or a serving of whole grain or enriched bread or cereal.[52]

For the 2013–2014 school year, federal reimbursement per lunch was $2.93 (free lunch eligible); $2.53 (reduced-price lunch eligible); and $0.28 (paid lunch).[53] For the breakfast program, reimbursement per breakfast was $1.58 (free breakfast eligible); $1.28 (reduced-price eligible); and $0.28 (paid breakfast).[54] For the afterschool snack program, reimbursement per snack was $0.80 (free snack eligible); $0.40 (reduced-price eligible); and $0.07 (paid snack).[55] Eligibility for free or reduced-price meals (breakfast, lunch, or afterschool snacks) is determined by the USDA as follows: "Children from families with incomes at or below 130% of the poverty level are eligible for free meals. Those with incomes between 130% and 185% of the poverty level are eligible for reduced-price meals, for which students can be charged no more than 40 cents."[56] Specifically, for the 2013–2014 school year, 130% of the poverty level was calculated at $30,615 for a family of four, while 185% was $43,568.[57]

It is apparent from the information in this section that schools and districts need to be vigilant and detail-oriented to ensure that the meals provided meet federal guidelines in order to be reimbursed at the rates described. However, even after taking into consideration the availability of federally subsidized commodities, maintaining a self-supporting food services program financially can be challenging.

Organizing for Food Service

The growing complexity and sophistication of school food service programs has led to cost analyses of how districts can better manage programs and expenses. Organizing has centered on types of management systems best suited to a district's needs, along

---

52 U.S. Department of Agriculture, "The School-Based Afterschool Snack Program," www.fns. usda.gov/sites/default/files/AfterschoolFactSheet.pdf.

53 U.S. Department of Agriculture, "National School Lunch Program," www.fns.usda.gov/sites/default/files/NSLPFactSheet.pdf.

54 U.S. Department of Agriculture, "The School Breakfast Program," www.fns.usda.gov/sites/default/files/SBPfactsheet.pdf. Note also: "Schools may qualify for higher 'severe need' reimbursements if 40% or more of their lunches are served free or at a reduced price in the second preceding year. Severe need payments are up to 30 cents higher than the normal reimbursements for free and reduced-price breakfasts. About 77% of the breakfasts served in the School Breakfast Program receive severe need payments."

55 U.S. Department of Agriculture, "The School-Based Afterschool Snack Program."

56 U.S. Department of Agriculture, "National School Lunch Program."

57 Ibid.

TABLE 10.3 Federal Nutritional Guidelines for School Lunch and Breakfast Programs

Meal Pattern	Breakfast Meal Pattern			Lunch Meal Pattern		
	Grades K–5	Grades 6–8	Grades 9–12	Grades K–5	Grades 6–8	Grades 9–12
Amount of Food per Week (Minimum per Day)						
Fruits (cups)	5 (1)	5 (1)	5 (1)	2½ (½)	2½ (½)	5 (1)
Vegetables (cups)	0	0	0	33/4 (¾)	33/4 (¾)	5 (1)
Dark green	0	0	0	½	½	½
Red/Orange	0	0	0	¾	¾	1¼
Beans/Peas (Legumes)	0	0	0	½	½	½
Starchy	0	0	0	½	½	½
Other	0	0	0	½	½	¾
Additional Veg to Reach Total	0	0	0	1	1	1½
Grains (oz. equivalent)	7–10 (1)	8–10 (1)	9–10 (1)	8–9 (1)	8–10 (1)	10–12 (2)
Meats/Meat Alternates (oz. equivalent)	0	0	0	8–10 (1)	9–10 (1)	10–12 (2)
Fluid milk (cups)	5 (1)	5 (1)	5 (1)	5 (1)	5 (1)	5 (1)
Other Specifications: Daily Amount Based on the Average for a 5-day Week						
Min–max calories (kcal)	350–500	400–550	450–600	550–650	600–700	750–850
Saturated fat (% of total calories)	< 10	< 10	< 10	< 10	< 10	< 10
Sodium (mg)	< 430	< 470	< 500	< 640	< 710	< 740
Trans fat	Nutrition label or manufacturer specifications must indicate zero grams of trans fat per serving.					

Source: U.S. Department of Agriculture. "Final Rule Nutrition Standards in the National School Lunch and School Breakfast Programs: January 2012." www.fns.usda.gov/sites/default/files/dietaryspecs.pdf.

Note: Numbers in parentheses represent number of servings.

with effective management of food service budgets. This has primarily resulted in choosing between outsourcing food services to a for-profit company or using in-house operations which may be either centralized or decentralized in nature.

Outsourcing

Districts may choose to outsource all or a portion of the food services function.[58,59] For example, some districts outsource the entire operation, including hiring and training of employees, while others outsource only purchasing. Still others limit outsourcing to a

---

58 Kate Beem, "Hot Potato in the School Cafeteria," *The School Administrator* (September 2004), www.aasa.org/SchoolAdministratorArticle.aspx?id=14122.

59 To place our discussion in context, industry sources estimate that between 12% and 15% of school districts outsource their food service. See, Fickes, "Make Outsourcing Work."

consulting role. For school districts, the outsourcing decision generally centers around efficiency or cost-effectiveness, but such decisions are not without pro's and con's. Several potential benefits are listed below:

- Full service outsourcing may provide cost savings because contractors pay lower wages and provide fewer benefits to their employees than the school district does.
- Full service outsourcing can relieve school districts of the time involved in day-to-day management of food services and can reduce the burden of record-keeping.
- Greater expertise of for-profit companies that specialize in food purchasing can yield cost savings, higher quality, and more food choices.
- For-profit companies may have food professionals with expertise in menu planning that yield more, and more appetizing, selections which, in turn, increase participation and hence lower the cost per meal.
- For-profit companies may have professional marketing expertise that can be tapped to increase participation. Increased participation reduces per-meal cost, resulting in cost savings.
- An expert consultant from a for-profit firm may enable a struggling food service program to successfully address financial and operational challenges while keeping the program district-based.

Critics respond that hiring a well-qualified, in-house professional food services director offers many of the same benefits offered by contractors at a lower cost because school districts do not need to and cannot, by federal law, make a profit from food services.[60] Small school districts might consider sharing one full-time director. Second, privatization of food service employees can prove to be controversial in a community, for example, if district employees are fired and replaced with a for-profit company's employees—even though cost savings would be realized. Even when contractors retain some or all district employees, they may convert full-time positions to part-time positions in order to reduce costs and maximize profits, leaving former full-time district employees no longer eligible for benefits. In this scenario, school boards and community members may raise concerns about increased turnover and the quality of food service personnel who have daily contact with children. Other concerns include:

- Districts may not have the expertise necessary to draft a specific and detailed request for proposals (RFP) that ensures that engaging a for-profit firm will result in the cost savings envisioned while complying with numerous and complex federal regulations.
- Outsourcing does not relieve the district of its responsibility (and liability) to audit the food service program for compliance with USDA guidelines.
- School–community relations may be negatively affected when an outside firm displaces local employees or is perceived as less caring and committed to the school children served by the food services program.

---

60 Ibid.

In-house Operations

Districts that provide the food service function in-house generally use one of four meal production systems: (1) On-site kitchens only; (2) base or central kitchen only; (3) mostly on-site kitchens; and (4) mostly satellite kitchens.[61] On-site kitchens are based in a school where district employees prepare and serve all of the food in their respective school, whereas a central kitchen is generally not located in a school but provides meals to one or more school sites. In contrast, a base kitchen is located in a school where it prepares food for other schools in addition to its own. Finally, a satellite school kitchen receives some or all of the food served in the school from a base kitchen or a central kitchen. Although one might be tempted to assume that the greater economies of scale are achieved with a central or base kitchen, a research report by the U.S. Department of Agriculture found no significant difference in cost among the four meal production systems.[62] However, individual school districts would do well to conduct their own careful cost analysis to determine which approach is most cost-effective in their particular situation. In addition, even though use of a central or base kitchens may offer cost savings over school site kitchens, critics point out that effectiveness may be hurt because site control is lower and because rigidity, over-standardization, and non-responsiveness may follow in a large centralized operation. As always, districts need to be aware of community perceptions and preferences. For example, even in tight budget times, parents and community members might prefer to forego cost savings so that each school has its own kitchen to tailor meals to its particular student body.

Financial Management

Finally, no discussion of the food service function in schools is complete without consideration of the complexity of budgeting. Food service budgeting can be over-whelming due to the number of school sites, food programs, and federal requirements. Generally, the food service manager, in cooperation with the district's budget director, establishes receipts and disbursements for each school site as part of the budget process and provides key leadership in setting meal prices. This process requires an extensive knowledge base, exceptional organizational skills, and a research capacity that includes the ability to analyze historical data and forecast revenues and expenditures. Complexity further arises in that each school site must be evaluated for the impact of changes in enrollments and participation levels; costs of food, labor, and supplies; capital costs; menus; and meal prices. This is detail-oriented work that may be complicated by daily collection of cash at the school site.

The goal of food service management is accuracy of records and reliability of predictions. The process calls for budget items to be reduced to subcategories, and finally to monthly projections. Potential trouble spots can be identified in this manner, and plans can be made for the entire year. As with every budget in the school district,

---

61 Susan Bartlett, Frederic Glantz, and Christopher Logan, "Executive Summary," *School Lunch and Breakfast Cost Study II*, Nutrition Assistance Report Program Series (Washington, DC: U.S. Department of Agriculture, Office of Research, Nutrition and Analysis 2008), www.fns.usda.gov/ora/menu/published/CNP/FILES/MealCostStudyExecSum.pdf.

62 Ibid., v.

monthly food service projections are assembled into an annual budget wherein revenue and expenditure should balance. The food service budget then becomes an integral part of the overall school district budget, exactly like budgets for other support services. Our discussion of local choices re-enters at this point, since actual program cost minus federal and state aid yields the cost per meal that must be charged or—alternatively—locally supplemented. For example, Figure 10.1 presents a spreadsheet of food service revenues

	TOTAL ANNUAL MEALS	FEDERAL		STATE		DISTRICT LOCAL		TOTAL 7-1-03 to 6-30-04
		RATE	Reimbursement	RATE	Reimbursement	PRICE	REVENUE	
LUNCHES								
Paid Elem	64,000	.4152	$26,573	.0450	$2,880	2.49	$159,360	$188,813
Jr. High	35,000	.4152	$14,532	.0450	$1,575	2.79	$97,650	$113,757
Sr. High	33,000	.4152	$13,702	.0450	$1,485	2.95	$97,350	$112,537
Free	20,000	2.5852	$51,704	.0450	$900			$57,404
Reduced	12,000	2.1852	$26,222	.0450	$540	0.40	$4,800	$31,562
Adult	5,000					3.49	$17,450	$17,450
TOTAL	169,000		$132,733		$7,380		$376,610	$516,723
BREAKFAST								
Paid Elem	6,000	.2400	$1,440				$0	$1,440
Jr. High	3,500	.2400	$840				$0	$840
Sr. High	2,000	.2400	$480				$0	$480
Free	1,800	1.3100	$2,358					$2,358
Reduced	900	1.0100	$909			0.30	$270	$1,179
Adult							$0	$0
TOTAL	14,200		$6,027				$270	$6,297
SNACKS								
Paid Elem	64,000	.0600	$3,840				$0	$3,840
Jr. High		.0600	$0				$0	$0
Sr. High		.0600	$0				$0	$0
Free	20,000	.6500	$13,000					$13,000
Reduced	12,000	.3200	$3,840			0.15	$1,800	$5,640
Adult							$0	$0
TOTAL	96,000		$20,680				$1,800	$22,480
KINDERGARTEN								
MILK								
Paid		.1450	$0				$0	$0
Free-Average Dealer Cost			$0					$0
TOTAL	0		$0				$0	$0
OTHER CASH								
Sales/Income								$0
12 Months Total Income			$159,440		$7,380		$378,680	$545,500

FIGURE 10.1 Sample Food Service Revenue Calculation

for Fiscal Year 2014 for a hypothetical school district. For example, this district served 64,000 paid elementary meals, for which it received 41.52¢ federal reimbursement and 4.5¢ state aid. According to the spreadsheet, the district charged $2.49 per elementary meal for students who did not qualify for free or reduced-price meals and adult staff based on actual cost. If, when preparing next year's budget, it is believed that costs will go up, the district will have to decide whether to: (a) raise prices; (b) use local tax dollars to supplement the food service fund; or (c) seek new efficiencies such as analyzing outsourced versus in-house services.

WRAP-UP

Our discussion in this chapter underscores the vital contribution of auxiliary services to student learning. Equal opportunity does not exist if children cannot get to school or if they come hungry. Though seldom in the educational spotlight, transportation and food service represent significant expenditures and significant liability. The result of our exploration is to once again observe the intricately interrelated parts of a complete educational system where each piece makes a critical contribution and cannot be slighted without harm to students.

POINT–COUNTERPOINT

POINT

Schools today have been asked to take on many costly responsibilities that formerly belonged to parents, churches, or charities. Diverting limited instructional funds to subsidize school meals, particularly breakfast and afterschool snacks, is a questionable use of limited resources, particularly when so many schools are facing budget reductions, laying off teachers, and increasing class sizes.

COUNTERPOINT

With record numbers of school-aged children living in poverty and even many middle-class families struggling to make ends meet, it is unrealistic to think that families are widely derelict in their duty. The only way to raise test scores is to care for the whole child, starting with adequate nutrition.

- Which of these views best represents your beliefs and experiences? Explain.
- How do your district and school food services "measure up" on student nutrition? Could your district and school better promote students' healthy eating within and outside the school? If so, what suggestions would you offer?
- Examine your school district's budget (and school-level budget if available). Is the food services program self-supporting? If not, discuss with your district's director of food services the financial challenges the program faces and what might be done to make it self-supporting.

CASE STUDY

As business manager of your geographically large suburban school district, you have seen transportation costs and problems increase sharply over the last four years. Chief among your concerns have been skyrocketing fuel prices, local pressure to address environmental concerns aimed mostly at the district's large diesel fleet, and safety concerns following a recent bus crash. In fact, the superintendent was quoted recently in the local press, stating that the district intended to make significant investment in these matters and that he was certain long-term benefits and savings would accrue from these new expenditures. While no details were given in the press, you later learned that his goal was to reduce bus route travel time and costs through routing efficiencies, cheaper vehicle operation, and new technologies to help with safety concerns. When you met with him later about these ideas, he indicated that he expected you to prepare an analysis of options and costs that would meet with board and community approval.

Back in your office, you reflected on your efforts over the last four years. You had already worked on these problems, but faced significant challenges, e.g., a lack of fuel storage tanks had prevented bulk purchasing that would help hedge against rising prices, budget limitations made replacement purchases of aging, inefficient buses too costly, and other efforts, such as installing video cameras on the district's school buses, were met with opposition by some school board members and parents as too intrusive and possibly violating children's privacy. As you pondered the situation, you realized that the good news was the superintendent had indicated openness to sizable expenditure in search of long-term solutions—the problem, though, was that you needed to identify and price solutions that might work in your situation.

As you strategized, a plan began to emerge. You had recently attended a national conference on transportation and had visited vendor displays featuring innovations in route management and tracking, safety and security, and fuel cost and operational savings. You recalled that you had seen software designed to optimally match smaller buses to routes in order to use less fuel; the use of global positioning systems (GPS) to track bus real-time locations and stops and to remotely monitor vehicle performance; the use of alternative fuels to save money and reduce emissions; and ways to retrofit existing vehicles for fuel efficiency and reduced emissions. You also recalled advances in safety and security such as heat-sensing devices to improve pedestrian safety around school buses. It might work, you thought—the key was how much would it cost to engage these efficiencies and savings.

Below is a set of questions. As you respond, consider your learning in this chapter and apply your knowledge and experiences to the situation.

- In your estimation, which options being considered by the business manager deserve the highest priority? Why?
- Consider the potential costs and benefits associated with each of the proposed options and classify each along two dimensions: high, medium, or low cost; and high, medium, or low benefit.
- What cost efficiencies and security measures have been taken in your own school district? How much time and money has been invested in these concerns? How successful have these initiatives been in addressing cost, safety, and security issues?
- Do you believe most school staff members will agree that money spent in search of these improvements is worthwhile, even if at the expense of instruction? Why or why not?

PORTFOLIO EXERCISES

- Identify how transportation is funded in your state. Analyze the state funding formula to determine how many dollars are available and the relative emphasis on transportation in your state. Determine how much state transportation funding your school district receives annually. Learn how the unaided portion of the transportation budget is met in your local district.

- Discuss with your school district's transportation director how transportation services are structured in your district. Include issues related to decisions about owning versus outsourcing, purchasing, bid laws, maintenance and safety, and driver training. Learn how transportation routing is carried out in your district.

- Determine whether your school or district has a transportation website. If so, using what you have learned in this chapter, review the website and assess its strengths and weaknesses as a resource for staff, parents, students, and the community. If there are weaknesses, suggest ways that these might be addressed.

- Identify how food service is funded in your state. Determine the mix of federal, state, and local aid to food service in your school district. Learn how meal prices are set and the philosophy that drives your school district's contribution to the food service fund.

- Meet with your district's food service director to learn how the district has structured this operation. Include issues such as compliance with federal and state requirements, local decisions about in-house vs. outsourced services, and satelliting vs. the use of central kitchens. Discuss the responsibilities of the food service director, the basis for approved menus, and other aspects of financial management.

- Determine whether your school or district has a food services website. If so, using what you have learned in this chapter, review the website and assess its strengths and weaknesses as a resource for staff, parents, students, and the community. If there are any weaknesses, suggest ways that these might be addressed.

WEB RESOURCES

Transportation

National Association for Pupil Transportation, www.napt.org

National Association of State Directors of Pupil Transportation, www.nasdpts.org/index.html

National Highway Traffic Safety Administration, "School Buses," www.nhtsa.gov/School-Buses

National School Transportation Association, www.yellowbuses.org

School Food Services

Healthy Schools Campaign, www.healthyschoolscampaign.org

Food Research and Action Center, www.frac.org

School Nutrition Association, www.asfsa.org

U.S. Department of Agriculture, Food and Nutrition Service, www.fns.usda.gov/fns

INTERACTIVE WEB RESOURCES

Use the National Center for Children in Poverty's 50-State Demographics Wizard to create custom tables of national- and state-level statistics about low income or poor children. Choose areas of interest, such as parental education, parental employment, marital status, and race/ethnicity—among many other variables: www.nccp.org/tools/demographics.

State Anti-Bullying Laws and Policies: http://www.stopbullying.gov/laws.

RECOMMENDED READING

Aguinaldo, Kelly. "Alt-Fuel School Bus Options Are Growing." *School Bus Fleet*, May 22, 2014, www.schoolbusfleet.com/Channel/Green-School-Bus/Articles/2014/05/Alt-fuel-school-bus-options-are-growing.aspx.

Blush, Linda F., and Michael J. Martin."Connecting the Dots: Keys to a Successful Special-Needs Transportation Program." *School Business Affairs* 76 (November 2010): 22–24.

Cook, Crystal, and Douglas Shinkle. "School Bus Safety." *Transportation Review*, July 2012. Denver, CO and Washington, DC: National Conference of State Legislatures. www.ncsl.org/documents/transportation/Schoolbus_tranrev0810.pdf.

Gray, Ryan."Alternative Fuels." *School Transportation News*, February 12, 2013. www.stnonline.com/resources/clean-school-bus/alternative-fuels.

Gunderson, Gordon W. *The National School Lunch Background and Development.* Washington, DC: U.S. Department of Agriculture, n.d., www.fns.usda.gov/nslp/history.

National Learning Corporation. *School Transportation Coordinator.* New York, 2005.

Sackin, Barry D. "School Food Service: Outsource or Self-Op?" *Journal of Child Nutrition and Management* 1 (Spring 2006). docs.schoolnutrition.org/newsroom/jcnm/06spring/sackin/index.asp.

Schirm, Allen, and Nancy Kirkendall, Eds. *Developing and Evaluating Methods for Using American Community Survey Data to Support School Meals Programs.* Interim Report. Washington, DC: National Research Council, National Academies Press, 2010. www.nap.edu/catalog.php?record_id=12917.

Swanson, Brittany-Marie. "Tips for Enhancing Your Transportation Website." *School Bus Fleet*, September 13, 2011. www.schoolbusfleet.com/Channel/Management-Training/Articles/2011/09/Tips-for-Enhancing-Your-Transportation-Website.aspx.

UCLA Civil Rights Project. "Transportation." n.d. http://civilrightsproject.ucla.edu/legal-developments/court-decisions/resources-on-u.s.-supreme-court-voluntary-school-desegregation-rulings/crp-transportation-fact-sheet-2009.pdf.

U.S. Department of Agriculture. "Summer Food Service Program Frequently Asked Questions." www.fns.usda.gov/cnd/Summer/FAQs.htm.

U.S. Government Accountability Office. *Meal Counting and Claiming by Food Service Management Companies in the School Meal Programs.* Washington, DC, 2009.

U.S. Government Accountability Office. *School Meal Programs: Experiences of the States and Districts that Eliminated Reduced-Price Fees.* Washington, DC, 2009.

CHAPTER 11

Legal Liability and Risk Management

THE CHALLENGE

School violence is not just a modern phenomenon; surprisingly, it has a history of more than 200 years in the United States. Periodic, high-profile events, such as school shootings, temporarily raise public awareness and concern, but memories fade, and investment in addressing school safety has typically been short lived and more rhetorical than purposeful. Policy makers and stakeholders from diverse domains and perspectives have too often emphasized punishment over prevention and security measures over learning principles in efforts to foster safe and orderly schools.

Mayer and Cornell (2011)[1]

CHAPTER DRIVERS

Please reflect upon the following questions as you read this chapter:

- What is the relationship of schools to the law?
- How do schools derive legal authority?
- What is the origin and nature of legal liability?
- What is immunity, and how does it apply to schools?
- What is tort liability?
- What other kinds of liability arise in schools?
- What do legal liability and risk management mean in the context of school funding today?

---

1 Matthew J. Mayer and Dewey G. Cornell, "How Safe Are Our Schools?" *Educational Researcher* 39 (October 2011): 16–28.

MODERN REALITIES

We would be remiss in this book if we failed to take a realistic view of legal liability and risk management in schools. Education, whether offered in a traditional public school or a public charter school, is subject to legal liability and the resultant risk management. Applicable state statutes largely govern liability and risk management in public schools. Regarding issues of liability and risk management, one must first consider the broadest perspective by considering the relationship of law to public schools, including how schools are granted authority and how liability issues enter into play. Next, this chapter examines how immunity and liability affect common school interests, such as civil rights, defamation, educational malpractice, and contractual liability. Finally, the chapter closes by considering how legal liability and risk management affect the decisions and actions of education stakeholders. This chapter provides a fitting conclusion to Part II of this text by warning that liability represents a significant threat to a school district's financial assets.

THE LAW AND SCHOOLS

Association of the law with public schools is older than the nation itself. Earlier it was noted that the American colonies enacted laws, such as the Ye Old Deluder Satan Act of 1647 in the Massachusetts colony, requiring establishment of schools, and that the nation's first compulsory education law was enacted in that same state in 1852. Such laws were obviously designed to force compliance, and it stands to reason that some people did not obey and were likely held accountable under the law. States enact laws in order to force certain individuals to conform to societal expectations for the betterment of the individual, while also authorizing improvement of the social order and for other regulatory purposes.

The relationship of law to schools today far exceeds the first colonial laws. Schools must be especially concerned with the legal rights of children, equal access to educational programs, special programs for the economically disadvantaged, fair funding, and a host of other issues relating to constitutional and statutory protections. Legal rights extend to employment, with complex laws governing the rights of employees and employers so that schools are often engaged in legal procedures and outcomes. Also, as noted in Chapter 4, state statutes tightly control the fiscal affairs of school districts. The concept of legal liability overarches all transactions and relationships in schools: it is fundamental to say that school districts and every person associated with schools may be jointly and severally liable for wrongful acts and omissions.

The law and schools thus have a two-part relationship. One part of the relationship focuses on regulation for organizational purposes, while the other focuses on liability for wrongful acts or omissions. Much of this text relates to the regulatory aspect of statutes because most chapters are deeply rooted in legal prescription for carrying out the educational mission. This chapter focuses on the risks and costs of liability, because the law and schools have established a close partnership with profound budget implications.

The Derivation of School Authority

Schools enjoy significant authority and control over matters that are purely educational in scope, design, and function. However, one must understand that such authority is both broadly derived and at the same time limited. Thus, it is important to identify the sources and limitations of schools' legal authority in order to gain a foundational understanding of the relationship between schools and the law.

Schools derive legal authority from both constitutional and statutory roots. These sources are complex and interrelated. An overarching view notes that school authority originates in the United States Constitution, the U.S. Congress, the federal judiciary, the constitutions of the individual states, state statutes, state courts, and state boards of education. Each source has had a significant influence on the educational enterprise, so much so that the very existence of the local school district, its board of education, and its educational mission are derived from the combination of these powerful forces.

United States Constitution

Involvement of the federal government in education is both peripheral and influential. Starting with early federal interest through land grants to newly formed states to be used for educational purposes, federal involvement in schools has grown to be a significant force. The federal path has been indirect because the U.S. Constitution is a document of limited powers, meaning Congress cannot assume powers without specific authorization in the Constitution. As noted earlier, the Constitution is silent regarding a federal education role. In the absence of authority, Congress has had to find other ways to affect education because only a Constitutional amendment could establish a direct federal role in schools. In the context of this chapter, the U.S. Constitution both grants authority and creates liability for schools by endowing certain rights to citizens relating to education, while leaving direct responsibility for education to the states.

Congress

Given only limited constitutional powers, Congress itself has had to become the vehicle for federal involvement in schools. Although having no direct education role, Congress has found a path through the general welfare clause of the Constitution,[2] which Congress utilizes to pass many laws affecting schools by interpreting general welfare benevolently and broadly. Through the years, Congress and various federal agencies have issued grants worth billions of dollars in aid to hundreds of programs in elementary and secondary schools and higher education. In related actions, Congress has found other ways to indirectly drive education policy by tying seemingly unrelated federal

---

2 The preamble states: "WE THE PEOPLE of the United States, in Order to form a more perfect Union, establish Justice, insure domestic Tranquility, provide for the common defense, promote the general Welfare, and secure the Blessings of Liberty to ourselves and our Posterity, do ordain and establish this Constitution for the United States of America." Article 1, Section 8 of the Constitution states: "The Congress shall have the Power to lay and collect Taxes, Duties, Imposts and Excises, to pay the Debts and provide for the common defense and general welfare of the United States . . ."

moneys to education in order to pressure states to follow federal education policy. For example, Congress has often tied federal revenue sharing for such projects as highways to congressional educational interests by threatening withdrawal of highway funds if states do not adopt federal education goals. Likewise, federal laws affecting special education and civil rights powerfully impact schools, as do other laws such as the No Child Left Behind Act[3] and its subsequent reauthorization. In the context of this chapter, Congress both grants authority to schools and creates liability by passing laws supporting certain educational initiatives that result in both benefit and liability.

Federal Judiciary

A significant source of authority in schools also rests with the federal courts. In a complex hierarchical legal system, federal rulings may take precedence over state courts, as in the familiar appeal to the U.S. Supreme Court as the court of last resort. In essence, federal courts hold great sway over education by applying federal constitutional requirements to schools. Racial integration, special and compensatory education, and countless other educational programs are examples of the result of federal courts' interest in education issues. Congressional involvement at this level is felt, too, as Congress exerts enormous control over education through the courts by virtue of its role in approving federal judges whom Congress hopes will take a supportive view of federal interests, including federal goals for education. Similarly, Congress is responsible for writing most of the laws tested in federal courts. The upshot is that although the federal government cannot assume a direct role in education, its influence has been significant by its interpretation of the general welfare clause. In the context of this chapter, federal courts both grant authority and create liability for schools.

State Constitutions

The same authority that prevents a strong federal role in education conversely grants full power over schools to the individual states. The constitutional conventions of each state almost invariably mentioned education, writing into the earliest charters an active role for states. Indeed, school finance litigation today always turns first to the states' constitutional framers' intent to test whether states are meeting their constitutional obligations. The language of a state constitution's references to education can be a powerful influence regarding educational policy, granting sweeping power to the state or significantly limiting it. In essence, states have plenary power over schools, subject only to higher federal protections such as Fourteenth Amendment due process. In fact, all sources of law at the state level regarding education derive from an individual state's constitutional authorization to its legislature. In the context of this chapter, state constitutions both grant authority and create liability for schools by requiring legislatures to devise enabling educational statutes, which in turn result in both authority and liability.

---

3 PL 107–110.

Every state has a state constitutional mandate to provide some form of public elementary and secondary education for the people of the state. Each state constitution is different and can only be interpreted within state courts and ultimately the applicable state supreme court as to the obligation that the state legislature has to fund and offer public education. Each state constitution is different although many state constitutions have virtually the same education clauses. In some instances the founders of the state merely copied the language from another state constitution. In some instances while the words were the same, the constitutional minutes clearly reflect different interpretations. As one Supreme Court justice has noted, state constitutions are the "laboratories of democracy" in that they may differ significantly from the U.S. Constitution as long as they are not in conflict.[4]

State Legislatures

Short of constitutional proscription, a state legislature has authority to write and pass any legislation it chooses affecting schools, subject only to the duties and constraints interpreted by courts based on the applicable constitution. Although those duties and constraints are formidable, given federal and state education laws and constitutional requirements for educational equity, state legislatures have plenary control over schools. For example, nothing in federal or state constitutions typically forbids a legislature from creating or abolishing a state department of education, consolidating or reorganizing school districts, increasing or decreasing state financial support for education, or a host of other far-reaching reforms.[5] The source of such power and restrictions rests in each state's constitution and in its relationship to the courts, which interpret the constitutionality of legislative actions. In essence, states control the statutes governing schools and may create or abolish educational structures at will, limited only by the constitutionality of their actions.

State Judiciary

The system of checks and balances in U.S. government calls for separation of the executive, legislative, and judicial branches. State courts frequently have been asked to test the limits of state legislative power, thereby creating one of the very few checks on legislative prerogative. In the context of this chapter, state courts therefore guard the legality of state acts under the state constitution, making state courts a source of authority and the evaluator of liability in schools.

State Boards of Education

Although state legislatures have full power over schools, nearly all states have delegated responsibility for conducting education to a state board of education. State boards are

---

4 Justice Louis Brandeis opined that a "state may, if its citizens choose, serve as a laboratory; and try novel social and economic experiments without risk to the rest of the country." *New State Ice Co. v. Liebmann*, 285 U.S.262 (1932).

5 One should note that in certain instances, the office of state school superintendent, state board of education and/or school districts may be found in state constitutional language wherein the power of the legislature is much more circumscribed.

arms of the state, usually created in statute and subject to the legislative will. Alternatively, state boards may be constitutional creations, but usually are still under legislative control. As such, schools are legislatively based, with authority passed to lower administrative units. In the context of this chapter, state boards both grant authority and create liability for schools by virtue of the rules and regulations they promulgate and administer.

Local Authority to Act

At the bottom of the hierarchy are local boards of education, to which states have delegated daily operation of schools. In nearly all states, school districts are not mentioned in the state constitution. As such, local school districts are subject to state control and may be organized as determined by the legislature and state board. In essence, local districts exist at the pleasure of some higher unit of government and are subject to all laws and regulations—in effect, school districts are ordered to actually carry out the state's educational duties. In the context of this chapter, local school boards function in a constitutionally limited context of state and federal laws under the watchful eye of a state legislature and state board of education—an environment that passes significant responsibility and liability to the actual delivery of public education.

THE ORIGIN OF LIABILITY

The concept of liability is deeply rooted in this nation's history. Many excellent sources detail development of American jurisprudence, all such sources beginning with the nation's inheritance from English law. Among those imported precepts are the key elements of sovereign immunity and tort law. Although many other aspects of law, including criminal law, at times apply to public schools, issues involving torts and immunity arise most often and may place public and personal financial resources in jeopardy.

Sovereign Immunity

Sovereign immunity refers to a precept from English law that literally argued, "the King can do no wrong." The importance of this concept is immediately apparent because law is often based on following certain logic to an obvious conclusion. If, then, courts accepted that the king could do no wrong and that a king is the head of state, then the state could do no wrong. The ramification is obvious—government is immune in its acts or omissions, a concept not greatly at odds with other sovereign views such as the divine right of kings.

Although Americans today might ponder sovereign immunity and ask how anyone ever tolerated such raw power, it is the case that sovereign immunity was unquestioningly transported into colonial law. The impact of English law on government was seen quickly in the new nation, as the 1812 Massachusetts case of *Mower* held that the state was not liable for its acts.[6] Sovereign immunity in *Mower* and subsequent cases was based on four distinct viewpoints. One viewpoint argued that the government has limited resources so that proliferation of lawsuits stemming from a ruling, even for limited liability, would be detrimental to the public treasury. A second view held that government must be free from fear of liability because any act of law does not carry equal benefit for each citizen. A third view held that government is the people, especially in a democracy, such that it follows that suit against government is a suit against oneself. A fourth view also held that committing an illegal act is never within the authority of government, so that a wrongful act exceeds any legal authority. This logic also became integral to many U.S. Supreme Court decisions, with the Court noting as early as 1869 that "[e]very government has an inherent right to protect itself against suits" and that "the principle is fundamental and applies to every sovereign power."[7] Presently, sovereign immunity is a concept entirely defined by state statute, particularly for public schools. Thus, each state defines the concept along a continuum from a complete lack of sovereign immunity to a few states with virtually complete sovereign immunity. Some states have limited sovereign immunity in the sense that there are severe financial limits to such claims. The concept of complete state sovereign immunity has survived nearly unquestioned in this nation until only recently.

Erosion of sovereign immunity was especially aided by two related events. The first event was congressional enactment in 1946 of the Federal Tort Claims Act[8] establishing liability for acts by the federal government. In passing the act, Congress agreed that absolute sovereign immunity was no longer viable federal policy, thereby permitting claims where previously no recourse had existed. Only employees acting within their discretionary functions permitted certain claims as the Act actually established only limited liability and preserved immunity for intentional torts and errors of omission. The second event followed as states enacted similar laws, again providing at least some recourse against potential abuses of government. The result of these two events led naturally to numerous suits in equity and made possible claims against the financial assets of federal, state, and local governments.

Although federal and state case law is vast when tracing the assault on sovereign immunity, *Molitor* illustrates the fundamental logic underlying all such claims.[9] In this 1959 case, the state supreme court of Illinois traced the origins of sovereign immunity and its adoption into state law via *Waltham*[10] and *Kinnare*.[11] Sovereign immunity had been established in Illinois for towns and counties in *Waltham* and had been extended to school districts in *Kinnare*, wherein it was held that a school board was not liable for the death of a laborer who fell from a rooftop, even though the school district had not provided safety measures such as scaffolding. Many years later, *Molitor* reversed

---

6 *Mower v. The Inhabitants of Leicester*, 9 Mass. 247 (1812).
7 *Nichols v. United States*, 74 U.S. 122 (1869).
8 See, 28 U.S.C. § 2874; 28 U.S.C. § 1346.
9 *Molitor v. Kaneland Comm. Unit Dist.*, 18 I11.2d 11, 163 N.E.2d 89 (Ill. 1959).
10 *Town of Waltham v. Kemper*, 55 Ill. 346 (1870).
11 *Kinnare v. City of Chicago*, 171 Ill. 332, 49 N.E. 536 (1898).

on the immunity ruling, as the court held a school district liable for injury to a student when a school bus hit a culvert and exploded. The court rejected the traditional argument that permitting liability required wrongful use of public funds to settle claims and further held that depletion of the state treasury was no longer a good defense. The Illinois court quoted a New Mexico case, taking that view as its own:

> The whole doctrine of governmental immunity from liability for tort rests on a rotten foundation. It is almost incredible that in this modern age of comparative sociological enlightenment, and in a republic, the medieval absolutism supposed to be implicit in the maxim "the King can do no wrong" should exempt the various branches of government from liability for their torts.[12]

Through a long and tortuous history, the concept of governmental liability has taken on new importance. Federal, state, and local governments may now be liable under certain conditions, and employees face the same risk because acting in official capacity is no longer an automatic defense. Of particular importance are the established exceptions to sovereign immunity, as it is decided that liability may apply to proprietary acts, nuisances, and Eleventh Amendment issues, along with other exposure relating to constitutional infringements. In sum, the cracks in immunity defenses have opened all units of government, including schools and school officials, to liability exposure, wherein the outcome of a liability claim will depend on statute and facts and venue—conditions requiring careful management to minimize the financial impact of successful claims. Again, claims under federal law are significantly different than those controlled by state statutes. School districts may be liable for claims under certain federal claims but not under state statutes. In some instances, schools may be liable under both federal and state claims.

Proprietary Acts Exception

Many states as well as courts have established major exceptions to the concept of sovereign immunity. One of the more widely accepted exceptions to immunity involves proprietary acts. This exception occurs as a court determines whether the act at trial was governmental or proprietary in nature. The distinction rests in the definition of a governmental function as exercise of police power or a constitutional, legislative, administrative, or judicial power conferred upon federal, state, or local government and its agents—in contrast, proprietary acts are outside the primary scope of the governmental unit itself, i.e., a school district.

In the context of schools, the difference comes by distinguishing educational activities from other school-sponsored events not central to the educational mission. For example, athletic events outside school time or other voluntary events may invoke a different liability threshold than class field trips. Rulings on such distinctions are inconsistent, however, even given similar circumstances. For example, a spectator in *Sawaya* was injured when a bleacher railing failed at a game where two school districts

---

12 *Barker v. City of Santa Fe*, 47 N.M. 85, 136 P.2d at 482.

had rented a football stadium from a third school district.[13] The state supreme court of Arizona held the third district liable, finding the event to be proprietary. In contrast, in the identical case of *Richards*, a Michigan court found no liability, holding that the district did not intend to make a profit from the event and was merely providing an educational activity.[14] The controlling feature seems to be how individual state courts, within controlling state statutory language, have ruled regarding immunity, as illustrated by a Michigan court in *Ross* which stated, "When a governmental agency engages in mandated or authorized activities, it is immune from tort liability unless the activity is proprietary in nature."[15] In contrast, a Texas court wrote in *Stout*, "Since a school district is purely a governmental agency ... it performs no proprietary functions separate from governmental functions."[16] Liability for proprietary acts is therefore subject to interpretation of state legislative intent in abrogating immunity and further subject to state courts' attitude toward governmental immunity and liability.

Nuisance Exception

A more familiar immunity exception rests in nuisances. A nuisance allows a condition that injures or endangers health, safety, or welfare. When a nuisance claim arises, it is nearly always in the context that the nuisance was knowable and that there was no attempt or only inadequate effort to prevent an injury. Probably the most common nuisance claim relates to attractive nuisances, which require higher levels of care because the nuisance may be expected to create problems. In the context of schools, a classic example is seen in the Michigan case of *Hendricks* where the court held that a school district had not created or maintained a nuisance when it piled snow on a playground, resulting in a climbing injury to a child.[17] The court stated that to establish a claim of intentional nuisance against a governmental agency, a plaintiff must show that there is a genuine nuisance condition and that the agency intended to create a hazard. Importantly, though, case law is replete with challenges reaching an opposite conclusion.

While nuisance liability is unpredictable in that establishing liability depends on specific laws and jurisdictions and the unique facts of each case, the concept of nuisance represents another instance in which exception to governmental immunity has been successful in the modern context. Clearly, in the case of schools, a finding for liability relies heavily on the standard of care required for the particular age of injured persons—and as a matter of prudence, it is also clear that prevention is advisable to safeguard against liability.

Eleventh Amendment Exception

A special situation relates to a third area in which governmental immunity has been at least partially overturned. The Eleventh Amendment to the U.S. Constitution in 1795 provided that

---

13 *Sawaya v. Tucson High Sch. Dist.*, 78 Ariz. 389, 281 P.2d 105 (1955).
14 *Richards v. School Dist. of City of Birmingham*, 348 Mich. 490, 83 N.W.2d 643 (1957).
15 *Ross v. Consumers Power Co.*, 420 Mich. 567, 363 N.W.2d 641 (1984).
16 *Stout v. Grand Prairie Sch. Dist.*, 733 S.W.2d at 296 (Tex. App. 1987).
17 *Hendricks v. Southfield Public Schools*, 178 Mich. App. 672, 444 N.W.2d 143 (1989).

the judicial power of the United States shall not be construed to extend to any suit in law or equity, commenced or prosecuted against one of the United States by citizens of another State, or by citizens or subjects of any foreign state.[18]

The Eleventh Amendment was a response to two lawsuits in 1791 and 1792, in which claims against states were brought in Maryland and Georgia. In *Vanstophorst*, foreign residents had brought suit against the state of Maryland for recovery of bad debts.[19] In *Chisholm*, residents of South Carolina had sought a judgment against the state of Georgia.[20] The potential for federal liability spurred passage of the Eleventh Amendment to deny recourse under applicable constitutional protections.

The Eleventh Amendment closed off an opportunity for litigants. This basis of immunity was successful for years, as the U.S. Supreme Court ruled repeatedly that the intent of the amendment was express, including barring suit against a state by citizens of another state and prohibiting citizens from bringing federal suit against their own states. Schools have enjoyed Eleventh Amendment immunity as well under the assumption that the state was implicated to such an extent that liability would extend to schools as arms of the state.

Limits regarding immunity under the Eleventh Amendment, however, have been established. In some instances, states have voluntarily waived any right to Eleventh Amendment immunity. Usually, waiver is available only when the state legislature explicitly permits and sets forth its intent to allow suit against itself, as in *Edelman*.[21] Congress has additionally and purposely limited other Eleventh Amendment immunity, as in the Individuals with Disabilities Education Act (IDEA),[22] where Congress specifically denied immunity to states from federal suits for violations of IDEA. Similarly, because Congress has granted itself power to write legislation invoking penalties for successful equal protection claims, Eleventh Amendment immunity is unavailable when such a violation occurs. A final limitation is important for schools because Eleventh Amendment immunity may depend on whether courts view schools as a direct arm of the state. This distinction was made in *Mt. Healthy* as the U.S. Supreme Court held local school districts in a similar light to city and county governments, rather than in the traditional context of seeing schools as an arm or extension of the state.[23] In this case, liability was present because the Court saw schools as political subdivisions of the state due to the taxing power and autonomy of the school district.

In the overall context of sovereign immunity, governmental agencies still enjoy significant protection from liability, but exceptions and changing attitudes have severely limited what was once absolute immunity. Federal statutory limits regarding immunity have been an important catalyst for increased liability, especially in context of the

---

18 U.S. Constitution, Amendment XI.
19 *Vanstophorst v. Maryland*, 2 U.S. (2 Dall.) 401 (1791).
20 *Chisholm v. Georgia*, 2 U.S. (2 Dall.) 419 (1792).
21 *Edelman v. Jordan*, 415 U.S. 651, 94 S. Ct. 1347 (1974).
22 PL 108–466.
23 *Mt. Healthy City Sch. Dist. Bd. of Educ. v. Dole*, 429 U.S. 274, 97 S. Ct. 568 (1977).

Federal Tort Claims Act and the Eleventh Amendment. Enactment of state tort claims acts likewise has meaningfully limited immunity defenses. Doctrinal modifications by courts distinguishing proprietary acts and nuisances have given further footholds to claimants. The result of a complicated historical erosion is that neither absolute immunity nor absolute liability is the unquestioned eventuality today in most states, so that school districts and officials must regard liability—and its potential claim against school districts and potentially personal resources—as an ever-present companion.

Tort Liability

With no assurance of immunity, dependent upon controlling state statutes, all units of government now have potential liability for a wide variety of acts and omissions. As a result, a huge body of statute and case law exists concerning a variety of issues regarding liability.

Most governmental liability arises from the law of torts. A tort is a wrongful act other than a breach of contract for which relief may be obtained in the form of damages or an injunction. A tort is a civil claim governed by applicable state statutes. A claim for tort liability is thus broad, taking in a great many wrongs affecting nearly every aspect of human existence. Torts may arise from defamation, civil rights, negligence, and a variety of other issues. Although the scope of claims is great, most torts fall into one of three categories: *intentional* torts, torts involving *negligence*, and *strict liability* torts. The law of torts applies to schools as governmental agencies, and individual personal liability may be a concern as well. For the purposes of this text, intentional torts and negligence are most relevant to schools.

Intentional Torts

An intentional tort is defined as a wrong by someone who intends to do something the law has declared wrong. Such torts involve intent or malice, although malice may be simple indifference. Most such cases in schools probably do not involve true intent or malice, but there are many opportunities for intentional tort claims wherein it is alleged that some act crossed the line of intent and was accompanied by reasonable expectation of harm.

One of the frequent intentional tort claims in schools relates to corporal punishment, as school personnel are sometimes charged with having crossed the intent line. Such cases usually allege assault and battery. Assault is any threat to inflict injury which, when coupled with a display of force, would give a victim reason to fear bodily harm. Battery is usually filed in such cases too, as it is defined as the touching threatened by assault. While as a rule courts have been unwilling to outlaw corporal punishment and the U.S. Supreme Court clearly said in *Ingraham* that there is no violation of the Eighth Amendment's prohibition against cruel and unusual punishment,[24] there is a vast record of intentional tort claims against schools regarding this issue. These claims should give rise to considerable caution on the part of school personnel from both moral and

---

24 *Ingraham v. Wright*, 430 U.S. 651, 97 S. Ct. 1401 (1977).

legal perspectives. For example, cases have involved students who were beaten severely enough to produce medical trauma, as in *Ingraham*, which resulted in a hematoma, or as in *Mathis*,[25] which claimed post-traumatic stress disorder, and other acts such as a teacher kicking a disobedient student.[26] While these cases did not find schools liable, other cases have found oppositely. For example, a teacher was convicted of assault and battery for having broken a student's arm by shaking and dropping him to the floor.[27] Likewise, a teacher was liable for breaking a pupil's collarbone upon throwing him into a wall.[28] Liability was also found when a third-grader was held upside down by her ankles while the principal struck her with a paddle.[29] Similarly, liability was found when a physical education teacher allowed a student to drown, thinking the child was joking and sending students into the water instead of rescuing the child himself.[30] While these cases seem outrageous, the existence of these issues indicates that common sense does not characterize everyone who works in schools. Intentional torts make up a large part of liability case law, and it is certain that schools will continue to face such claims. Obviously, there is a real possibility that wrongful acts in schools may also end up in criminal court—again, a concept not entirely foreign to schools.

Negligence

Another frequent tort action in schools is a negligence claim. Negligence is defined as conduct falling below a legally established standard of care, resulting in harm. Teachers, as well as building principals, are generally thought of as highly skilled professionals given their education, training, and certification. In examining such claims, liability depends on the facts regarding breach of duty, proximate cause, and actual harm.

Duty refers to proof that the actor had a responsibility to the injured party. A duty can arise from statute or what a reasonable person would have done in like and similar circumstances. Inadequate supervision is probably the most common allegation for breach of duty in schools, followed by claims involving lack of proper instruction and failure to maintain a safe environment. The standard most often applied is the "reasonable person" test, whereby a defendant's actions are compared to the prudence and skill that would be applied by a reasonable person in the same or similar circumstance. For the purposes of this chapter the focus is how this issue relates to school-based liability; the added dimension of superior skill or knowledge is key, so that the reasonableness test takes on the crucial characteristic of the behavior of a professional under the same or similar circumstance. Proximate cause relates to whether the action, or inaction, in fact caused the injury because there is no liability if there is

---

25 *Mathis v. Berrien County Sch. Dist.*, 378 S.E.2d 505 (Ga. App. 1989).

26 *Thompson v. Iberville Parish Sch. Bd.*, 372 So.2d 642 (La. Ct. App. 1979), writ denied, 374 So.2d 650 (La. 1979).

27 *Frank v. Orleans Parish Sch. Bd.*, 195 So.2d 451 (La. Ct. App. 1967).

28 *Sansone v. Bechtel*, 429 A.2d 820 (Conn. 1980).

29 *Garcia v. Miera*, 817 F.2d 650 (10th Circ. 1987).

30 *Thompson v. Bagley*, 2005 Ohio 1921, 2005 WL 940872 Ohio Ct. App. (2005).

no unbroken chain of events leading to the defendant. Further, the negligence must be substantial; that is, negligence, while easily claimed, must meet a threshold of impact.

The issue of negligence in schools arises from a duty to protect students from foreseeable harm. Schools have a duty to protect children in terms of their health, safety, and welfare. Under the *in loco parentis*[31] doctrine, this duty is broad, as illustrated by *Garcia*, where a five-year-old boy was sexually molested when he was sent to the bathroom alone in violation of the school's written guidelines.[32] The court found that the assault was preventable by proper supervision, which was defined as the degree of supervision a *parent* of ordinary prudence would take in comparable circumstance. Although the court agreed that a school cannot foresee and take precautions against sudden spontaneous acts by other students and that the school had no history of similar incidents, liability still applied based on the school's knowledge of danger to unattended students—knowledge implied via the school's written security policies and via the principal's testimony admitting the risks to unescorted students in hallways and restrooms. Similarly, the U.S. Supreme Court spoke in *Davis* to the duty of educators to guard against student violence and harassment.[33] The victim was a fifth-grade girl who had been sexually harassed by another student. She reported the events to teachers, but the school still took no action. Charges were filed, with the defendant admitting to sexual battery, whereupon the victim's mother sued the board of education and school leaders for damages under Title IX of the Education Amendments of 1972.[34] The court found for plaintiffs, stating that educators are on notice that they may be liable for their failure to protect students from the tortious acts of third parties. The court further noted that state courts routinely uphold claims alleging that schools have been negligent in failing to protect students from their peers—notably, the court cited cases from as early as 1953 in longstanding support for its ruling.

Case law is by no means unanimous, however, in focusing liability on schools at the state level, in part due to the question of immunity.[35] State rulings favoring immunity have led to suits in federal court, asserting that schools have a federal constitutional duty to protect students from danger.[36] These causes of action are known as civil rights torts, or a section 1983 claim, an action allowing plaintiffs to seek compensatory and punitive damages when liability can be successfully established.[37]

The liability issues at stake can be illustrated in several cases. In *Leffal*, an 18-year-old student was killed by random gunfire in a school parking lot after a school dance.[38] The issue was whether the student's constitutional rights were violated by the decision of the school district to sponsor the dance even after being asked by local police

---

31 Translated as "in place of a parent."

32 *Garcia v. City of New York*, 646 N.Y.S.2d 508 (App. Div. 1996).

33 *Davis v. Monroe County Bd. of Educ.*, 119 S. Ct. 1661 (1999).

34 20 U.S.C. § 1681–1688.

35 See, e.g., *Chesshir v. Sharp*, 19 S.W.3d 502 Tex. App.—Amarillo (2000) where state statutory immunity protected a teacher when a five-year-old boy splattered hot grease on his face from a hot frying pan in the classroom.

36 See, e.g., *Graham v. Independent Sch. Dist.*, 22 F.3d 991 10th Cir. (1994).

37 42 U.S.C. § 1983.

38 *Leffal v. Dallas Indep. Sch. Dist.*, 28 F.3d 521 5th Cir. (1994).

to stop sponsoring such events until adequate security could be provided. Only two unarmed guards were assigned to the dance and they were unable to prevent the violence. Notwithstanding the school's prior knowledge of danger, the court noted that although students were required to attend school, they were not required to attend dances so that the school's failure to protect against violence did not violate the Constitution. The court noted that the standard under §1983 is a "deliberate indifference" standard where the plaintiff must show that (1) an unusually serious risk of harm existed, (2) the defendant had actual knowledge of, or was willfully blind to, the elevated risk, and (3) the defendant failed to take obvious steps to address the risk.[39] Similar results followed in *Rudd* when a student warned his teachers that another student had brought a gun to school.[40] Officials failed to find the weapon despite a thorough search, whereupon later in the day the suspect pulled out the gun and killed another student on his school bus. The state supreme court held that the school district was not liable under the Arkansas Civil Rights Act and further enjoyed immunity from tort liability.

The difficult nature of liability claims is illustrated by the fact that courts have exercised considerable caution when limiting broad constitutional freedoms in the name of safety. In 1999, the U.S. Supreme Court noted that the maintenance of discipline in schools requires that students be restrained from assaulting one another, abusing drugs and alcohol, and engaging in criminal actions.[41] But a heavy burden is still present for school officials when deciding to potentially infringe on constitutional rights. The controlling authority has continued to be *New Jersey v. TLO*,[42] where the Supreme Court provided a two-part test for reasonableness in school searches for contraband, including weapons. The court held in *TLO* first that a search must be justified at its inception and second that it must be permissible in scope so as not to excessively intrude in light of the age and gender of the student and the nature of the infraction.[43] The *TLO* standard calls for school authorities to only have a reasonable suspicion as opposed to the higher criminal standard of probable cause. The principles set out in *TLO* were affirmed by the U.S. Supreme Court in *Safford*, where the court found a middle school's strip search of a 13-year-old girl suspected of bringing ibuprofen to school in violation of the school district's zero tolerance drug policy was unreasonable.[44] Today, courts are confronted with school violence and examination of issues of freedom of expression. For example, courts have examined First Amendment protections in cases of threats of violence. Although "fighting words" and threats presenting a clear and present danger historically have not enjoyed First Amendment protection, courts have taken into consideration whether such statements made in school settings are believable. A variety of issues have been brought before the courts attempting to clarify the rights of students

---

39 *Leffal* 28 F.3d at 531.

40 *Rudd v. Pulaski County Special Sch. Dist.*, 20 S.W.3d 310 Ark. (2000).

41 *Davis v. Monroe County Bd. of Educ.*

42 *New Jersey v. TLO*, 469 U.S. 325 (1985).

43 See, e.g., *Vernonia School Dist. v. Acton*, 515 U.S. 646 (1995); see also *Smith v. McGlothlin*, 119 F.3d 766 9th Cir. (1997).

44 *Safford Unified Sch. Dist. v. Redding*, 531 F. 3d 1071, affirmed in part, reversed in part, and remanded.

within the realm of free speech. At least one court has written that threats by students are limited to those statements that convey "a gravity of purpose and likelihood of execution."[45] On the other hand, the U.S. Supreme Court has upheld the expulsion of a student displaying a "BONG HiTS 4 JESUS" sign at a public event while being released from school.[46]

The cases presented within this chapter illustrate that liability is a serious issue for school districts and staff. The data alone are enough to stir anxieties and to leave school leaders without a clear roadmap on how to deal with keeping schools both safe and free. One line of court cases leads to the view that schools may restrict student behavior in the name of safety without fear of liability, while another line of cases warns that courts will not be sympathetic to trampling of constitutional freedoms. In actuality, middle-ground perspectives provide the best course of action. First, there is a strong duty to exercise the reasonable person rule, consistently applying it to all issues ranging from freedom of speech to search and seizure under reasonable suspicion of safety concerns. Second, school leaders should not fear liability for having acted affirmatively, inasmuch as they might otherwise be held liable for failing to exercise appropriate care. Third, courts generally do not hold educators liable for injuries resulting from spontaneous acts of violence if these acts were unforeseeable—as a rule; this includes injuries caused by nonstudent assailants. However, school leaders are expected to be watchful, as a significant duty exists when the assailant is a student: since courts will consider a student's prior conduct, evidence of previous antisocial behavior suggests that the student's future violent acts may have been predictable. Fourth, there is a significant responsibility for preparedness, including evidence of sound risk management training. The reasoning of courts in student suicide cases may be applied analogously to all these issues and particularly to school violence; that is, without adequate training school employees may underestimate threats of violence. In essence, training in risk prevention may soon become a standard of care for educators.

The discussion in this section clearly indicates a strong potential for negligence claims against school districts and persons in their official and individual capacities. Whether the person was operating in his or her official capacity often tends to center upon a case-by-case factual basis. Of particular concern is that damages may apply if negligence is established. Damages may be compensatory or punitive, depending on whether they are awarded as compensation for actual loss or as punishment for negligence. Compensation may include medical bills and loss of earnings, and may also be given for injuries such as emotional distress or pain and suffering. Other monetary judgments may be assessed too, including exemplary damages meant to make an example of negligent behavior in order to reduce its likelihood of recurrence. For school districts and staff, the issue is clear: liability represents a significant potential claim against financial assets—either by personal vulnerability or by having to budget school district moneys in anticipation of potential liability claims.

---

45 *Lovell v. Poway Unified Sch. Dist.*, 847 F.Supp. at 784 S.D. Cal. (1994).
46 *Morse v. Frederick*, 551 U.S. 393 (2007).

Civil Rights

Of all the areas of potential liability faced by school districts, none has garnered more media attention than civil rights litigation. Stemming from the Civil Rights Act of 1875[47] and extending today to embrace a vast body of constitutional and statutory protections against all forms of discrimination, civil rights have come to represent a constant liability concern for schools.

Civil rights cases have been litigated in the nation almost since its birth. The Civil Rights Act of 1875, however, opened a new era by seeking to prevent both lawful and unlawful racial discrimination following the Civil War. Because federal law is controlling on states, it was reasonable to turn first to federal courts in an attempt to more broadly construe liability beyond simply strict racial discrimination. The Civil Rights Act of 1875 was consequently the legal premise underlying much subsequent litigation, including *Brown v. Board of Education* in 1954,[48] which marked the end of "separate but equal" educational provision in the United States. The basic concept of liability under this federal act was thereby extended to include personal liability of public officials who violate the federal constitutional or statutory civil rights of another individual. This law, usually referred to in relevant part as Section 1983, denied immunity from liability:

> Every person who, under color of any statute, ordinance, regulation, custom, or usage, of any State or Territory, subjects, or causes to be subjected, any citizen of the United States or other person within the jurisdiction thereof to the deprivation of any rights, privileges, or immunities secured by the Constitution and laws, shall be liable to the party injured in an action at law, set in equity, or other proper proceeding for redress.[49]

Given such strong language, the struggle over civil rights became even more intense and has had especial importance for schools. Recognizing that every governmental and private action could be closely scrutinized for intent and effect, school officials are required to be vigilant in making certain that their acts are honorable and above reproach. The fundamental question of liability for acts of school officials was reviewed in *Wood v. Strickland*, which examined school board members' liability risk.[50] Although the U.S. Supreme Court has generally held for officials' immunity when acting in good faith, the court noted in *Wood* that board members are not immune under §1983 if they knew or reasonably should have known that an action taken within a sphere of official responsibility would violate constitutional rights, or if an action intended a deprivation of constitutional rights. As a consequence, *Wood* set a new standard of "qualified good faith" immunity, wherein liability may arise under three specific conditions. First, board members are legally bound to make decisions within current

---

47 18 Stat. 335–337
48 347 U.S. 483 (1954).
49 42 U.S.C. §1983.
50 *Wood v. Strickland*, 420 U.S. 308 (1975).

law. Second, ignorance of the law is no excuse. Third, immunity is forfeited if it can be shown that the violator intended harm or if those actions originated in vindictiveness or spite.

A significant burden was thus placed on schools by §1983—a weighty and expansive burden due to the vast range of possible wrongs. The range of liability now takes in a panorama of possible grievances, with governmental units—including schools—required to clearly state and meticulously observe compliance with nondiscrimination. Yet despite the weightiness of §1983 and related law, a judgment for plaintiffs is not an automatic outcome of a civil rights allegation. Liability usually revolves around a standard of indifference—for example, if a school official acts callously toward the rights of an individual, liability may arise in both official and individual capacities and can be very costly because §1983 provides that actual and compensatory damages as well as attorney fees may be assigned to the defendant. Civil rights liability has therefore generated a justifiably high level of anxiety. For example, in *Kinsey* a superintendent was awarded $250,000 for mental anguish and loss to his reputation when he was fired after supporting certain candidates in a school board election.[51] Likewise, punitive damages have been awarded, as in *Fishman* when a school district fired a teacher over First Amendment free speech claims.[52] These awards were not especially large, particularly in the context of recent litigation involving such issues as sexual harassment or special education; rather, the cases cited herein are purposely chosen to represent the *less* flamboyant claims arising under civil rights. As a result, many civil rights claims are settled out of court without regard to fault because the cost of defense may be higher than the cost of settlement—a cost that diminishes the school district's resources in either event.

Defamation

Still another liability concern relates to defamation. In most instances affecting schools, defamation attaches to faculty and students, with claims most often relating to student records. Schools and individuals, within their scope of employment, accumulate and report data regarding staff and students, a trend that has only increased with accountability and performance-based school reforms. For example, administrators and boards of education must evaluate teachers and are at times required to dismiss staff. Likewise, the whole educational process consists of gathering and analyzing data regarding students and preserving it in perpetuity. While these are among the fundamental duties of schools, they are ripe opportunities for liability if improperly carried out.

Defamation may be libel, in which case harm is done to another person in writing. Defamation also may be slander, in which case the harm is done verbally. In either case, defamation may be *per se* or *per quod*. Defamation *per se* is words requiring no proof

---

51 *Kinsey v. Saldo Indep. Sch. Dist.*, 916 F.2d 273 5th Cir. (1990), reh. en banc, 925 F.2d 118 5th Cir. (1991).

52 *Fishman v. Clancy*, 763 F.2d 485 1st Cir. (1985).

of harm beyond their clear meaning. Defamation *per quod* requires an examination of facts. Either form is an actionable tort that may invoke liability and for which the only defenses are privilege and good faith. In all cases, schools and staffs are vulnerable to defamation claims given such a record-intensive environment. Many states specifically protect school administrators in giving references regarding employees from any claim. However, this again is predicated on the defense that the individual who gave the review believed the statements were true, acted in good faith, and was acting within the scope of their employment.

The defenses of privilege and good faith allow schools to conduct the business of preparing and distributing information about pupils and staff. Although these are the only defenses against defamation, they are not inconsequential in that they make it possible to prepare student transcripts and teacher employment records. Care is required, however, because the gravity of permanent records has resulted in only a qualified immunity privilege that holds these records to a higher standard than is true in most other instances. In particular, a defense of privilege in schools is more difficult than for other public officials—for example, justices and state officers have absolute privilege as long as they act officially, and that same privilege extends to anyone involved in judicial or legislative acts such as testimony. In contrast, schools have only a qualified privilege in that they are protected only when carrying out duties common to such organizations and provided that they are acting in good faith. Qualified privilege is further restricted, in many states, in that even truthful statements lacking good intent, or statements thought to be true, are actionable. Countless examples of this limitation abound, as in an oft-quoted case when a teacher described a student as "ruined by tobacco and whiskey."[53] To be safe, statements must be made in good faith and may not go further than to state the facts.

Schools may also readily encounter defamation issues when making statements concerning teachers' fitness to teach and in performance evaluations, although courts are slow to act except in clear factual instances. As noted in *Malia*,[54] qualified immunity is the rule except when it is clearly shown that comments were motivated by personal malice or animosity, or when the evidence against privilege and good faith is overwhelming. A similar opportunity for problems arises in permanent or anecdotal student records, particularly given accessibility under the Family Rights and Privacy Act (FERPA) passed by Congress in 1974.[55] This act stipulated which records must be available to parents and students and laid out rules regarding which parts of school information are public or confidential. Under FERPA, student records may not be released without written consent of the parent; pupil records must be open to parents of children under 18 and to the child once age 18 is reached; a record must be kept of anyone examining school records; contents of files may be challenged; and public directory information must be identified in advance of publication. As a consequence, school records maintenance may leave a trail leading to a successful defamation claim,

---

53 *Dawkins v. Billingsley*, 172 P. 69 (1918).

54 *Malia v. Monchak*, 543 A.2d 184 (Pa. Commwlth.Ct. 1988).

55 20 U.S.C. § 1232. (The complete title is Family Educational Rights and Privacy Act, generally referred to as FERPA.)

with liability attaching for schools and individuals. As always, avoiding liability requires sound policies based on competent legal advice.

Educational Malpractice

Another liability concern for schools is the matter of educational malpractice. Although broad-based in its potential implications, the general issue is the relationship between student achievement and quality of instruction—an issue undoubtedly destined to become more important as accountability pressures on schools increase. The issue is not new; since the 1970s schools have feared that malpractice claims would eventually gain traction.

Educational malpractice seeks to apply tort law to students' academic failure. Malpractice might be seen as an intentional tort or as negligence. Claims have been hard to prove, however, as an intentional tort would need to show that a school maliciously sought to impede a child's progress. A claim for negligence has been more common. Early malpractice cases raised the question of whether students have the right to a particular achievement level under compulsory attendance laws, while more recent cases have asked whether schools have been negligent in diagnosing educational needs. The leading case continues to date back to 1976 in *Peter W.*[56] wherein the plaintiff tested the claim that a student receiving a high school diploma under a California statute requiring graduates to be able to read at the eighth grade level had been the victim of malpractice because his reading level never surpassed fifth grade. The student alleged negligence and argued that his parents were not informed about his deficiencies. The lower court dismissed and was upheld on appeal. The appeals court discussed at length the duty requirement, finding no duty on which to base an action due to inability to articulate a workable standard of care, noting that teaching involves many different and conflicting theories of how and what a child should be taught. The primary basis for the court's logic, however, lay in public policy considerations given the burdensome litigation that would be generated by a successful lawsuit. As the court noted, holding schools accountable for all academic functions would expose them to tort claims—real or imagined—by countless numbers of disaffected students and parents. A similar view was taken by a New York court of appeals in a case brought by a learning-disabled student who argued that he could not cope with filling out simple job applications. In dismissing the $5 million negligence suit, the appeals court in *Donohue* also cited public policy, noting that solutions would require judicial monitoring of day-to-day implementation of educational policy.[57]

Recent cases have generally followed this trend. In *Ross*, a high school basketball star was recruited to a university that promised support for academic deficiencies.[58] The student sued for negligence and breach of contract based on malpractice and negligent admission. A federal district court dismissed, and on appeal the court stated that malpractice claims have been widely rejected, largely due to lack of a satisfactory

---

56 *Peter W. v. San Francisco Unif. Sch. Dist.*, 60 C.A.3d 814, 131 Cal. Rptr. 854 (1976).
57 *Donohue v. Copiague Union Free Sch. Dist.*, 47 N.Y.2d 440, 418 N.Y.L.Q.2d 375 (1979).
58 *Ross v. Creighton Univ.*, 957 F.2d 410 (7th Cir. 1992).

standard by which to evaluate and due to the potential torrent of malpractice litigation. Other courts have noted the pervasive difficulties that could arise in managing a successful malpractice claim given the impreciseness of measuring damages and further pointing out that parents are not helpless bystanders because they have recourse through local school districts and state education agencies.[59] But notwithstanding, malpractice will continue to be an area of watchfulness, especially in light of No Child Left Behind and other accountability standards that are increasingly attracting public scrutiny, along with equal access issues.

Contracts

Finally, but not surprisingly, school districts should be concerned for liability involving contracts. School districts in all states are authorized to enter into contracts for hiring staff, buying supplies and equipment, and carrying out facility projects. School districts are thus liable for contractual performance, including breach of contract. Liability by either party to a contract usually relates to bad faith or failure to observe one or more of the basic elements of contracts. To be valid, a contract must have mutual consent, including offer and acceptance; have consideration in the form of inducement to enter into the contract; must be entered into by competent parties; must serve a lawful purpose; and must conform to any other requirements of law. Most contracts in school districts do not present problems, but some special cases involve a greater risk of liability.

Most contractual problems involving school districts arise around authority to enter into a contract, and such problems are defined by the state-specific nature of contract law. As a rule, only boards of education may enter into contracts for the school district, although agency is often granted to administrators to initiate contracts on behalf of a board of education. Contracts by agents still must be ratified by the board of education, and many of the challenges involving contracts have centered on whether a contract is enforceable when a board of education wishes to nullify a contract by agency. Various rulings may be found. For example, in *Community Projects*, the court held that only a board of education had contractual power and that an agreement to purchase goods signed by a principal was invalid.[60] An opposite finding came in *Hebert* as a court held that because the board had ultimate power to contract and had given power to a principal over extracurricular activities that led to a contract, it had granted an implied power to contract.[61] The key to contractual authority lies in the concept of ministerial duties versus discretionary duties of boards of education. Ministerial duties are those duties of a board of education that it may choose not to perform for itself—for example, supervision of playgrounds and curriculum management. Discretionary duties are those other duties that the board of education has elected to carry out itself, such as evaluating the superintendent or approving the school district budget and the amount of local taxes. While ministerial duties may be delegated, discretionary duties

---

59 See, e.g., *Christensen v. Southern Normal School*, 790 S.2d 252 Ala. (2001).
60 *Community Projects for Students v. Wilder*, 298 S.E.2d 434, 435 N.C. App. (1982).
61 *Hebert v. Livingston Parish Sch. Bd.*, 438 So.2d 1141 La. App. (1983).

cannot. Contracts by board of education agents (e.g., administrators) are controlled within this distinction, in that expenditure is a discretionary power and may not be delegated. Notwithstanding, boards of education often appoint an agent to deal with contracts, therein creating a level of risk by appointing someone who does not have legal authority to actually make a contract. Under these conditions, a school district is not legally bound if it refuses to ratify the contract; conversely, though, the board of education may choose to ratify an invalid contract.

Under these conditions, disputes concerning recovery arise if one party claims the other party has breached a contract. The likely scenario is that at least one party to a contract, acting in the belief that a valid contract existed, provided products or services, while the other party failed to pay the bill. Recovery may involve damages or return of actual products. The two issues of greatest concern in such situations are whether there is an express or an implied contract and whether it can be shown that the contract itself was invalid for any reason. An express contract is one in which the duties and rights are expressly agreed upon by all parties. An implied contract is one in which at least one party has acted to read a contract into the actions of both parties, even though there was no express agreement. The difference is not trivial. In the case of an implied contract, the appropriate court must consider the value of goods or services so that a fair value can be established because—if recovery were permitted—recovery is limited to the reasonable value of goods or services. In the case of an express contract, however, recovery is controlled by the value expressly agreed to without concern for whether the amount is reasonable. In the latter instance, it is particularly prudent to avoid contracts that are unreasonable, as courts will generally bind both parties to an improvident contract if the contract were determined to be both valid and express.

In some instances, however, the contract itself may be invalid. As discussed earlier, an invalid contract is one that fails to conform to all required elements. For example, no contract could exist if mutual acceptance were lacking or if one party was legally incompetent, including lack of authority to enter into contracts or when the contract's purpose is outside the law. Similarly, lack of consideration voids a contract, as gifts or free services do not meet the consideration test. Further, contracts may be invalid due to failure to follow a prescribed form. For example, a contract required to be in writing, but made orally, is invalid. These instances create particular problems under recovery claims in that services or products may have already been rendered and consumed before the dispute is known, making an equitable claim more difficult by asking a court to either relax the statutory requirement or to allow uncompensated benefit to one party. While each case is unique, the general rule has been that if all other elements of a contract were satisfied and if the school district had express authority to contract, then it would be liable under implied contract so long as the form or requirements of the contract did not violate other statutory provisions. To some extent, the outcome depends on the court's attitude toward the question of whether equity or strict statutory application is more important when dealing with issues of public policy.

Case law involving contract recovery is legion. One of the areas of frequent dispute involves additional work by one party beyond the expectations of the other party. This situation often arises in construction projects. For example, the court held against a school district in *Flower City* where a contractor who was hired to remove asbestos from a school also cleaned up and repaired fire damage, whereon the school district refused to pay for extra services.[62] In contrast, the court ruled for the board of education in *Owners Realty* when a contractor performed additional work while removing asbestos.[63] The court reasoned that no other recourse was available in that the written contract barred claims for additional compensation. Absent such specifics or in tandem, however, courts also consider broader principles. In general, if it were found that cause exists for a claim against a public body, the first issue is whether the goods are returnable or if they have been consumed—if the goods can be returned, courts usually permit physical recovery. The second issue is whether an implied contract will be found if it were determined that no express contract existed. The third issue is equity; that is, boards of education may not abuse their power in voiding contracts, and vendors may not raid the public treasury by misusing contract law.

Contract law is complex. Yet common sense is easily applied. First, school districts do have contractual authority. Second, the required elements of contracts apply, and boards of education are expected to protect the public treasury through economy and compliance. Third, contract law may differ across the states, making it important to know specific state statutory requirements. Fourth, boards of education may appoint agents, but they may not delegate their discretionary duties, and contracts and expenditure of funds are discretionary duties. Fifth, courts tend to guard the treasury at the expense of outside parties. Sixth, boards of education may not abuse their preferential treatment by taking advantage of the law's protectiveness toward the public treasury. Seventh, contracts are unassailable if in proper form. Under these conditions, schools and school leaders can avoid serious contractual problems.

WRAP-UP

The relationship between public schools and the law in the United States has been in place for centuries, with signs of ever-increasing entanglement. Educational policy and process are topics that stir public interest, and the contemporary desire to do battle in court has accelerated what was already an adversarial relationship defined by many groups taking an interest in and responsibility for the educational enterprise. It is not surprising, then, that all actions in schools, including personnel matters, civil rights, application of educational policy, and constitutional responsibility for education, have been tested in the courts.

As noted at the outset, this chapter does not try to exhaustively review every area of risk and liability that schools may encounter. However, it is not necessary to be an attorney in order to obey the law and to understand that the paramount duty of school

---

62 *Flower City Insulations v. Board of Educ.*, 594 N.Y.S.2d 473 N.Y. App. Div. (1993).
63 *Owners Realty Management v. Board of Educ. of New York*, 596 N.Y.S.2d 416 N.Y. App. Div. (1993).

personnel is to assess and minimize risks and to act as a reasonable person would act under the same conditions given the same level of skill and knowledge presumed to the position in order to protect the safety, health, and welfare of children. School personnel are skilled professionals as a result of their training and experience. This charge strongly asserts that local school districts and individual schools should enact formal risk management plans as the first line of defense, wherein legal risks are systematically predicted and reduced through well-constructed policies, procedures, and practices. Only then should risk management turn to ensuring against liability and loss; that is, insurance serves as the indispensable second line of defense by protecting against unforeseen risk, but school districts should not substitute insurance for methodical risk prevention. In sum, planning for risk and liability is an act of budget stewardship—an act calling for managing the inevitable risks every school district faces.

POINT–COUNTERPOINT

POINT

Schools today have taken on many characteristics of prisons, with fences, metal detectors, guards, and remote monitoring devices that rob children of their carefree years. The ominous cloud of potential rights violations has greatly aided miscreants' free rein in schools by obstructing officials who attempt to deal with unacceptable behavior.

COUNTERPOINT

While schools today must be cautious in dealing with potential liability, the problem is overblown because most schools are effective sites of learning that prepare students for productive lives. Although the media may demonize schools as prisons where the inmates are in control, effective school leaders have sufficient power to manage the learning environment, as evidenced by the success most schools enjoy.

- Which of these viewpoints best represents your beliefs and experiences? Explain.
- What security measures exist in your school? Why were these measures enacted? How effective have these measures been? Are there areas that could be improved? If so, how?
- How can schools reduce liability risks without taking on more prison-like characteristics?

CASE STUDY

As the assistant principal in charge of student discipline at your high school, you are not surprised at the school administrative team meeting to hear the principal address concerns about student conduct. As in most high schools, staying on top of an energetic bunch of teenagers is always a challenge, but recent events have put student conduct strongly on the radar screen. In the last few weeks several boys have reported instances of bullying in locker rooms and hallways, and several girls have indicated they are seriously considering filing sexual harassment charges against other pupils for inappropriate text messages. In addition, there have been fights and vandalism at school-sponsored night activities, and the local media reports of school news seem to be taking on the tone of a police log. Judging from news stories, these events have attracted the attention of both the superintendent and the school board, who are worried that the types and numbers of incidents have escalated from typical daily discipline issues to a serious matter with potential legal liability for the district, which not only would be bad publicity but also could be costly.

At the school administrative team meeting, the principal indicates that the school board will soon ask all high schools in the district to undertake a self-assessment on management of student discipline and the security and safety of students and staff during the school day and at cocurricular events. Indeed, the superintendent has already instructed principals to initiate assessments that would result in individualized building-based risk management plans.

Since your primary job assignment deals with discipline issues, you fully expect to play a big part in these events. True to form, the principal asks you to head a task force to develop a building-level, comprehensive risk management plan. While the principal leaves it to you to determine committee structure and scope of the management plan, she makes it clear that the end product should be guided by best practices and should carefully assess current conditions, assess current and prospective needs, and offer actionable recommendations for site-level improvements. You know you have a big task ahead and will need to do significant research and enlist a dedicated, creative committee.

- What questions need answers before you engage other persons in this process?
- Where will you turn for information on best practices?
- What are the elements of risk assessment and risk management that should be applied to this situation?
- Whom will you ask to serve on the site committee? Why?

PORTFOLIO EXERCISES

- Conduct a search of major newspapers in your state for articles involving schools, lawsuits, and liability—you may need to search several years. Using your learning from this chapter, analyze the allegations and make a judgment on the merits of the claims.

- Contact the superintendent's office or the business director in your school district and discuss how the district approaches risk management from a philosophical and operational perspective. Ask whether the district has a written risk management plan. Obtain a copy and review what the district believes is important and the preventive measures described.

- Talk to your principal about what your school does to assess risk and to protect against liability. Probe the scope of risk management and liability as understood by your principal and the general issues that are relevant on a daily basis in your school.

WEB RESOURCES

American Tort Reform Association, www.atra.org

Association of School Business Officials International, www.asbointl.org

Education Commission of the States, www.ecs.org

Education Law Association, www.educationlaw.org

National School Boards Association, www.nsba.org

Risk Management Association, www.rmahq.org

Risk Management Society, www.rims.org

Public Risk Management Association, www.primacentral.org

Public School Risk Institute, www.schoolrisk.org

School Leaders Risk Management Association, www.slrma.org

StopBullying.gov, www.stopbullying.gov

RECOMMENDED READING

Conn, Kathleen. *Bullying and Harassment: A Legal Guide for Educators, Association for Supervision and Curriculum Development.* Alexandria, Virginia, 2004.

DeAngelis, Karen J., Brian O. Brent, and Danielle Ianni. "The Hidden Cost of School Security." *Journal of Education Finance* 36, 3 (Winter, 2011): 312–337.

Frelsand, Kelly, and Janet L. Horton. *Documentation System for Teacher Improvement or Termination.* Cleveland, OH: Education Law Association, 2007.

Frieden, Thomas R., Linda C. Degutis, and W. Rodney Hammond. *Measuring Bullying Victimization, Perpetration, and Bystander Experiences: A Compendium of Assessment Tools.* Atlanta, GA: Centers for Disease Control and Prevention, National Center for Injury Prevention and Control, 2011. www.stopbullying.gov/references/index.html.

Johnson, Cheryl P., and Steve Levering. "Today's School Risk Manager." *School Business Affairs* 75 (June 2009): 12–13.

Mayer, Matthew J., and Dewey G. Cornell. "How Safe Are Our Schools?" *Educational Researcher* 39 (October 2011): 16–28.

Rossow, Lawrence F., and Laurel Logan-Fain. *Law of Teacher Evaluation.* Cleveland, OH: Education Law Association, 2013.

PART

III

A View of
the Future

CHAPTER 12

Site-Based Leadership

THE CHALLENGE

> Leadership not only matters: it is second only to teaching among school-related factors in its impact on student learning.
>
> Leithwood, Louis, Anderson, and Wahlstrom (2004)[1]

CHAPTER DRIVERS

Please reflect upon the following questions as you read this chapter:

- What is the strategic concept involved in site-based leadership?
- What are the roles of principals, central office staff, school site councils and others in site-based leadership?
- How do issues of organization, areas of legitimate control, and data access affect site-based leadership?
- What budget issues are involved in site-based leadership?
- How does this entire book come together around site-based leadership?

---

1 Kenneth Leithwood, Karen Seashore Louis, Stephen Anderson, and Kyla Wahlstrom, *Review of Research: How Leadership Influences Student Learning* (Minneapolis: Center for Applied Research and Educational Improvement, University of Minnesota, 2004).

PULLING IT TOGETHER

Throughout this textbook, site-based leadership has been mentioned frequently. At times our treatment of the concept has been direct, but most often it has only hinted at the growing importance of school-based leadership. A companion purpose, though, has been to integrate site-based leadership into our entire discussion. As we near the end of our introduction to school finance and resource management, we address site-based leadership head-on and explain more fully why it is so important. As a result, we use site-based leadership in this chapter to pull together the many parts of this book.

We begin by first reviewing the strategic concept underlying site-based leadership in order to establish an operational framework. We then turn to the roles of principals, teacher leaders, central office staff, school site councils, and others in a site-based environment. These participant roles lead to discussion about membership, organization, areas of legitimate control, and information access—critical aspects if site-based governance is to have an impact on student learning. With concepts and roles in place, we arrive at the crux of this chapter by examining the financial implications of shared leadership, including decision making about general site costs, personnel, instruction, infrastructure, student activities, and accountability, i.e., the key topics from earlier chapters are revisited in the context of site-based leadership. In sum, this chapter pulls together all that we have explored in this book and couches it in the context of tomorrow's constituent-based educational organization. In many ways, this chapter is the point of the entire book—the application of money by knowledgeable people who stand on the firing line of schools.

THE SITE CONCEPT

Variously named as site-based management, school-based management, or even simply decentralized decision making, site-based leadership has enjoyed high visibility on policy agendas in the United States for more than two decades. Although some form of site-based leadership has existed in schools for many years, school reform and accountability, beginning in the 1980s, resulted in a broader understanding that instructional and resource decisions should be located closer to where teaching and learning actually take place—the individual school site. The fiercely competitive context in which public education now finds itself also has lent a hand to popularizing the site-based concept, as school choice initiatives—like charter schools, virtual schools, interdistrict choice (open enrollment), and vouchers—have forced states and local school districts to scrutinize their instructional and budgetary attitudes and practices. In addition, policymakers were spurred in the 1990s to reconsider school-based leadership because court decisions on school funding in Kentucky and New Jersey profoundly affected the educational status quo. In the case of Kentucky, the *Rose* decision forced redesign of the entire educational system to include strong school-based management, sparking similar legislation in several other states.[2] In the case of New

---

2 *Rose v. Council for Better Education*, 790 S.W.2d 186 (Ky. 1989).

Jersey, the state education funding system was overturned in multiple iterations of *Abbott*, requiring the state to equalize funding between the wealthiest and poorest school districts, and requiring districts to reallocate funding to individual schools in ways that would make each school site accountable.[3]

The site-based trend, arguably begun in modern form by *Rose*, has spread widely. According to the Education Commission of the States (ECS), school districts engage site-based management to some extent in virtually every state, and 37 states have statutes related to site-based decision making. ECS further noted that 17 states mandated site-based management statewide in some form and three states mandated it in specific districts.[4] Legislative interest continues today, as 66 bills on the topic of school-based management were signed into law between 2000 and 2014.[5] While laws among the states vary widely in scope, the net effect is that site-based leadership, including some degree of resource control at the school level, is entrenched and growing.

At the root of the site-based concept is the premise that individual schools should be given responsibility for curriculum, staffing, and budget decisions. Individual schools should be allocated a budget to carry out their educational programs, and each school must be held accountable, setting goals and conducting performance assessments with genuine consequences for success or failure. The premise rests on the concept that decisions made closest to where students are located are more effective than those made at levels that are more removed from the daily operation of schools. Although actual practice has varied, all site-based designs have sought to delegate money and authority to the school site in order to involve parents, teachers, and community members in meaningful decision making. Under these circumstances, school site leaders are faced with developing new skills because responsibility for learner outcomes is a very serious matter.

FRAMEWORK FOR IMPLEMENTATION

The concept of site-based leadership includes fostering an improved school culture that, in turn, leads to more effective decisions related to student achievement.[6] Implementation is complex, however, and requires a framework that carefully accounts for

---

3 *Abbott v. Burke* (M-1293–09) May 24, 2011. Also referred to as Abbott XXI.

4 Jennifer Dounay, "Site-Based Decisionmaking: State-level Policies," *ECS State Notes* (Denver, CO: Education Commission of the States, 2005), www.ecs.org/clearinghouse/61/13/6113.htm.

5 Education Commission of the States, "Recent State Policies/Activities: Governance—Site-Based Management," www.ecs.org/ecs/ecscat.nsf/WebTopicView?OpenView&count=-1&RestrictToCategory =Governance—Site-Based+Management.

6 It is important to note that there is no solid body of research evidence linking site-based leadership to improved student achievement. See, for example, "School-Based Management and Student Performance," *ERIC Digest*, no. 62 (Eugene, OR: ERIC Clearinghouse on Educational Management, 1991); Lori Jo Oswald, "School-Based Management," *ERIC Digest*, no. 99 (Eugene, OR: ERIC Clearinghouse on Educational Management, July 1995). Some have argued that these disappointing results are due to researchers' use of inconsistent or unclear definitions of the concept, or conversely that schools under study did not fully implement the site-based model as intended.

strategic readiness, the legitimate role of stakeholders, and effective utilization of newly acquired budget authority—concepts traditionally unfamiliar to individual school sites, but which form the backbone of site-based leadership.

What Is the Strategic Concept?

The most difficult task in implementing site-based leadership is creating a basis and culture for dramatic change. The literature on organizational theory clearly indicates that meaningful and lasting change must be brought about planfully. Although it is beyond the scope of this text to develop strategies for change, adopting site-based leadership requires careful preparation based on planning at the district and school levels about how change will be introduced and carried out. For example, an autocratic top-down imposition of site-based leadership is likely to be resented and, hence, ineffective. Likewise, a common error is to simply turn decisions over to school site councils without adequate groundwork in philosophy and operational skills. Because site-based leadership does not mean abdicating central authority to individual schools, the first part of a framework for implementation is a well-designed plan that accounts for the following three critical aspects of delegating power:

- Assessing the history and data on readiness of the individual school site
- Developing strategies for implementation based on assessment findings
- Creating accountability, timelines, and costs for implementing site-based leadership

Assessment

Site-based plans can be elaborate. Avoiding problems demands careful assessment strategies on two levels, and both levels should be completed before beginning the process of delegating decision making to the school site. The first level consists of organizing a site-based leadership plan for each school, understanding the historical justification for current practices, assessing the likelihood of success once site-based leadership is enacted, and making an informed choice at each school about how extensively to adopt site-based leadership. The second level consists of determining how the site-based plan will look at both district and individual school levels. In sum, assessment is the careful evaluation of the likelihood for success of site-based leadership in individual schools.

Implementation

Implementation begins directly after assessing readiness for site-based leadership. Site council members should be drawn from administrators, teachers, students, and parents, as well as the community members representing key stakeholders. To be effective, the site council should be inclusive, representing the diversity of the community. Also, site

---

However, even without a solid link to student achievement, the concepts of participatory decision making and parental and community involvement inherent in this leadership model offer many educational benefits as described in this chapter.

council members need orientation and training on their role and responsibilities. The eventual make-up of individual school site councils should be an outgrowth of the planning process. In sum, implementation is the act of building on assessment of readiness in preparation for the accountability structures that support site-based leadership.

Accountability

The newly formed school site council will need to devote much time and energy to developing an overall site-based leadership plan tailored to their specific school. Parameters of each site-based plan must be determined, timelines must be set, and accountability strategies must be agreed upon. The goal of these activities is not only to structure how site-based leadership and decision making will occur, but also how to reach agreement on the mission, goals, and appropriate responsibility of the council. The council will also benefit from access to the school district's legal counsel during this stage. As a first step toward developing accountability measures, the council must clearly articulate the following for their particular school:

- Beliefs
- Mission
- Climate
- Objectives
- Policy
- Preliminary planning document
- Collective bargaining and legal issues

Beliefs articulated in the school site leadership plan must be based on sound educational research, theory, and best practice. These statements should be simple and declarative, communicating a positive message of wide involvement. Belief statements should be generated by council members and merged in a cooperative process. For example, the following teacher beliefs are taken from districts using site-based leadership to build positive school-based culture:

Teachers in this building believe:

- students learn basic skills as a consequence of how teachers teach;
- expecting students to be successful will make it happen;
- success is more important than failure;
- sharing ideas increases student performance;
- in working together to coordinate programs within teams and across grades;
- in a positive attitude toward change;
- the student is at the center of the educational process.

A similar process should be used for developing mission statements at the school site level. Mission statements should be simple and clear. It is important that the focus be on the direct educational experiences of every student because mission statements declare actionable intent. Examples of mission statements include the following:

- This school will graduate students who will become productive, responsible citizens.
- This school will teach students to think as individuals and to think critically.

Mission statements are supported by goals and objectives. Goals and objectives provide greater specificity and yield measurable outcomes. Several states have enacted performance-based achievement plans that can serve as models. Goals and objectives might be stated in terms of student knowledge, dispositions, and performance. For example, the following statements could be adopted by a school site:

- Students will know where and how to access materials for conducting science investigations (knowledge).
- Students will show enthusiasm for science (disposition).
- Students will be able to locate resources and apply them to a problem (outcome).

Successful site-based leadership also depends on consensus for a positive school climate. Climate is complex and includes the following components:

- There is a stimulating, supportive environment.
- There are positive expectations for staff.
- There is constant feedback—positive and negative—that is always constructive.
- There is a feeling of family.
- Open communication is the rule and not the exception.
- Achievement and growth of students and staff are the reasons for the school to exist.
- There is closeness among parents, community, staff, and the principal.

The outcome of agreement on beliefs, mission, goals and objectives, and climate lead to formulation of site-based leadership policy and the implementation phase. These concepts go far toward establishing accountability for outcomes. Belief statements should be adopted as policy, and implementation is the process of carrying out these aims. A guiding document should result from these activities. It should set out everything discussed thus far, with additional caution that it should not infringe on collective bargaining agreements or other legal issues. To that end, all plans should be reviewed by the school district's legal counsel.

Implementing site-based leadership must be inclusive of the principal, site council, staff, parents, and community members who are charged with important, relevant, and substantive issues for which they will be held accountable. These issues comprise the ongoing work at each school once implementation is complete. Site-based leadership participants can reasonably be expected to work with the following:

- Instruction
- Student achievement and growth
- Student socialization
- Critical thinking skills
- Innovation

- Attendance
- Budgets
- Completion or graduation

What Is the Role of the Principal?

Success in implementing a site-based leadership plan is in large part a function of how well roles are carried out. A clear understanding of powers and limitations is essential to cooperative and productive relationships. As indicated in the epigraph to this chapter, research points convincingly to the critical role of principals in successful school-based reforms, if for no other reason than because a lead person must provide the rallying point and a procedural knowledge base. School principals are perfectly situated for such leadership by virtue of legal and positional authority. As a result, site-based designs cannot work unless principals understand and value shared decision making.

Site-based leadership requires principals to take the lead, delegating decisions to appropriate levels. This is harder than it sounds because the very first leadership act is to surrender the control of functions formerly housed in the principal's office or at a higher level. Schools successfully engaging in site-based leadership have strong principals who are unthreatened by control issues. In fact, these persons are typically stronger professionals because they must work harder and more effectively than their more traditional colleagues in order to achieve broad-based consensus. A key concept, however, is that delegation of authority must be realistic. Site council members should not be asked to make inappropriate decisions or to engage in work beyond their expertise. The balance is delicate because resentment follows when the work of site teams is viewed as trivial or as abdicating administrative responsibility. The principal fundamentally takes the role of leader, counselor, supporter, and encourager of the site council. Within this framework, delegation is not abdication of power, as the principal must support site council decisions to ensure their effective implementation.

The flip side of delegation is accountability because site-based leadership raises the performance standard for each person. Demands for accountability are increasing, and the primary rationale of policymakers in mandating a shared decision-making model is to increase school effectiveness. Discussion earlier in this chapter raised the issue of measurable outcomes, and the school site is where this accountability is envisioned and acted on most effectively. The role of the principal is to model accountability, individually and as a member of the site council.

Successful site-based designs are driven by strong principal leadership. As titular and functional head of the school, it is the principal who can most effectively initiate and guide school growth. The principal is the central link between the district, the individual school, and the community, and is further the position-holder with the legal and moral authority to effectuate change. This does not lessen the contribution of the site council or school staff; rather, it underscores how all effective organizations rely on a proactive leader to mobilize others.

What Is the Role of the Central Office?

A common misperception is that decentralization reduces the role and importance of central administration. Although relationships are changed, the central office becomes even more important because all school site powers flow from central office actions that enable and support site leadership. The issue of central support is critical because this level has delegated many decisions to individual school sites, including the power to make budget decisions. At the same time, central office administrators are accountable to the school board, where ultimate legal authority to approve budgets and hence expenditures rests.

Because the role of principals is critical to site-based plans, principals are paralyzed without the support of the central office and the board of education. The central office must educate principals and site council members about decentralization, making the role of central administration vital to implementing site leadership. Starting at the board level and working down through all central office ranks, organizational and financial structures must be created and publicly supported in order to send a message of genuine support. The central office must take the lead in delegating decision making to the school site level and must take a leadership role in educating site council members about sources of power, authority, revenue, expenditures, and curriculum. When central office administrators move from a position of control to one of support, site councils are genuinely empowered. The literature suggests four kinds of knowledge and skills that central office administrators and staff must develop when restructuring for school site leadership:

- Interpersonal and team skills for working together effectively
- Technical knowledge and skills for providing services
- Breadth skills for engaging in multiple tasks, especially the tasks decentralized to the site council as a result of a flattened organizational structure
- Business knowledge and skills for managing the financial aspects of the school site

What Is the Role of the Site Council?

The philosophical and operational shifts following from site-based leadership are significant. Issues of legitimate control, access to data, and budgeting join to form a very different environment as site councils begin to govern the operation of schools. In short, site councils assume many tasks formerly reserved to administrators and have the potential to have a powerful impact on the basic organizational design, including site costs, personnel, and student activities. These concepts form the remainder of this chapter.

Organization

Although states legislating site-based leadership have frequently mandated key organizational and membership issues, the general intent is that site councils should be organized around the goals of the individual school. Concern for readiness of site councils to assume their responsibilities is such that states often require an information and training phase, lasting in some cases as long as a year. The driving force behind organizing should be singular—realistic expectations and clear direction from the district. Stated simply, can the site-based leadership plan be accomplished? At the outset, organizational questions should be raised, among which the most important are the following:

- How is membership on the site council determined?
- What matters should the site council consider?
- Who has formal decision-making authority?

These questions set the tone for all site council decisions. Generally, site councils are empowered to address funding, instruction, and assessment of programs at their individual schools, but, importantly, the degree of specificity with which these roles are articulated by the central office has the potential for great benefit or misunderstanding.

Membership

Although both organizational and membership structures are often mandated, experience indicates that certain site council designs work better. Groups that are too large, too small, or nonrepresentative of the community have a hard time making decisions and gaining external support. The success of councils varies from school to school based on a host of issues, with data showing increased likelihood for smooth operation when the following structures are in place:

- The most manageable group size is approximately 10–12.
- Composition of the council should reflect the intent of strategic objectives and preliminary planning goals.
- The council should consist of the principal, lead teachers, support staff, parents, and community members.
- Members should have a broad perspective on public schools.
- The council must avoid individual platforms and agendas.

The organizational design should establish the principal as leader of the site council. This requires the principal to be a visionary, facilitator, organizer, motivator, resource for information and procedure, and risk-taker. Again, realistic expectations should rule—that is, principals must assess their own strengths and weaknesses and help the group understand its own. Assessment should ask, at a minimum, the following questions:

- Is the principal willing to delegate responsibility to others?
- Does the principal manage time well?
- Is the principal receptive to new ideas?
- Is the principal confident in the role as leader?
- Does the principal work well with groups?
- Does the principal have confidence in the ability of site council members?

Along with assessing the principal's readiness, membership on the site council means that professional staff also must be prepared to lead. Teachers need skills in two areas to make meaningful contributions: the instructional domain and the managerial domain. Questions to be addressed include the following:

- Do teachers see the value of site-based leadership?
- Are teachers' perceptions of site-based leadership accurate?
- Are teachers willing to accept decisions of the site council?
- Do teachers believe they should be involved in management?

Membership on the council must also include parents and community members. There should be a balance in representation from these two groups. Although all viewpoints are valued, there must be evidence of ability to work effectively in groups. Each of the questions asked about principal and teacher readiness can be applied to parents and community members as well:

- Do parents and community members see the value of site-based leadership?
- Are parents' and community members' perceptions of site-based leadership accurate?
- Are parents and community members ready to commit the requisite time?
- Do parents and community members accept that some areas are legally off-limits in the school environment?
- Do parents and community members have the necessary interest in management?

Once site council members have been selected on the basis of knowledge and disposition, the site council will need to meet regularly. The principal should chair the group, at least for the first year. Initial meetings should focus on reaching consensus among members on organization and process. It is important for the principal to allow everyone a voice in the decision-making process. The principal should lead the discussion concerning beliefs, vision, mission, and policies of the council. The initial process should focus on working collaboratively before trying to resolve any actual problems of the school.

Legitimate Control

Identifying the proper boundaries of site council control is crucial. Otherwise, frustration and overreaching can occur. Also, legal problems may arise if the council strays into constitutional, statutory, or other protected areas such as negotiated contract provisions. Most likely, the school site council will concern itself primarily with instruction and budget issues, at least in the early stages, making it important for all members to be well informed and willing to share power.

Working with instructional issues requires deep knowledge on the part of all site council members. They must broadly understand the instructional program at both school and district levels, and they must understand state curriculum requirements as well. The council will need access to data, with great care taken not to violate privacy laws. Very important is training regarding the implications of each decision the council makes—for example, improper access to data may violate the Family Educational Rights and Privacy Act (FERPA), such as the identification of individual students.[7] However, site councils generally need access to a wide range of data, by grade levels and programs, as follows:

- Enrollment data
- Attendance data
- Student achievement data
- Promotion and retention data
- Discipline counts, issues, and dispositions
- Dropout data
- Elementary, middle, and high school program offerings
- Special education, vocational, and early childhood data
- Library and resource data
- Student demographic data such as eligibility for free and reduced-price meals
- Other data, such as technology use in the school, accreditation, and curriculum information

These data are useful when analyzing district and school site structure; constituent satisfaction; internal and external comparisons for benchmarking purposes; and work environments. The data are integrated in many ways, in that they affect decisions about mission, goals, objectives, and programs while simultaneously providing feedback to help make strategic adjustments. For example, data might be used to determine that the school needs to adopt a new goal of improving attendance. Student assessment data, when combined with budget data, might be used in deciding whether or not to hire an additional teacher to reduce class size. Conversely, the council might use the same data to decide to use the money freed up from a retiring teacher to hire additional classroom aides instead of filling the teaching vacancy.

Legitimate control is an area that requires clear definition at both district and school site levels before site councils are actually empowered. Control is bounded by the reality of all chapters in this text, in that all genuine power rests in the ability to control and direct staff and money. Token councils spark deep resentment, and overreaching councils create equally complex problems. In sum, appropriately empowering site councils is an act of genuine leadership.

What Are the Budget Issues?

There would be no reason to discuss site-based structures in this text if it were not for the relationship between school-based leadership and school-based budgets. The power of site-based budgeting is secured when it is realized that budget, staffing, and curriculum are the cornerstones of educational productivity. In fact, everything that

---

7 20 U.S.C. §1232g; 34 CFR Part 99. See also, "Family Educational Rights and Privacy Act" (Washington, DC: U.S. Department of Education), http://www2.ed.gov/policy/gen/guid/fpco/ferpa/index.html.

matters in schools is wrapped up in these issues, as fully 80% to 85% of a district's budget is devoted to personnel and instruction—indeed, 100% when support services are understood in the context of instruction. The relationship of site-based leadership to the budget is therefore one of empowering site councils to increase student achievement through a spending plan. As a rule, the budget issues relevant to individual school sites are basic knowledge relating to overall context and site knowledge relating to general site costs, staffing issues, instruction, facilities, and student activities.

Basic Knowledge

The primary budget responsibility of a site council is for costs associated with the individual school site. However, the council needs a general understanding of overall budget structure in the district as a contextual foundation. The site council should examine overall budget issues before attempting to work with individual site budgets.

The entire site council needs to broadly understand revenue sources, the formula by which school districts receive funding, the school site budget, and various cost categories—i.e., the subjects that make up this textbook! Without basic knowledge, the site council will be unable to make effective decisions about instruction, staffing, supplies, infrastructure, maintenance, and a host of other budget-related issues. Specifically, the site council must develop an appreciation for the entire fiscal picture of the school district and for individual site costs in terms of the following:

- Sources of revenue to the district and methods of taxation
- State revenue sources
- Local revenue sources
- State aid formula(s)
- State accounting and reporting requirements

Early meetings of the site council should focus on acquiring this knowledge. Discussions should also describe funding for special education, transportation, food services, and other programs—all in context of the relationship between programs and revenue within the constraints of available fiscal resources. The goal is to have all site council members understand the flow of money to the district and to individual schools, while conceptually connecting funding to mission, goals, and objectives.

Site Knowledge

Because the site council will spend significant time on budget matters, it is important for members to see that some costs are beyond the control of individual schools (indirect costs) while other costs are within control (direct costs). A useful way of viewing indirect and direct costs is to see all costs that are not site-specific as indirect costs, and all costs specific to instruction and annual operations as direct costs. For example, bonding for new facilities is an indirect cost because bonding is beyond the scope of a school site council. A related concept is fixed costs. Fixed costs are those that do not change despite fluctuations in a given level of activity. Fixed costs may be direct or indirect, but they tend to be overhead costs regardless of the educational programs that go on within

TABLE 12.1 Classification of School and District Costs

Budget Item	Cost	
	Direct, Indirect, Marginal	Variable vs. Fixed
School staff compensation	Direct	Variable
School administration costs	Direct	Variable
Capital outlay (infrastructure)	Indirect	Fixed
Social services	Direct	Variable
Maintenance: daily, custodial	Indirect	Fixed
Central office employee compensation	Indirect	Fixed
Transportation	Indirect	Variable
Food services	Indirect	Variable
Purchasing	Direct	Variable
Maintenance of facility: repair, upkeep	Indirect	Variable
Utility costs	Direct	Variable
Learning programs	Marginal	Variable
Student activities	Direct	Variable

an individual school. Variable costs are the opposite of fixed costs; that is, they are expenses that vary in tandem with level of service. Finally, marginal costs are those that change if the school adds a level of service. Site councils have little control over fixed and some indirect costs, but they have greater control over direct, variable, and marginal costs, depending on how the school district has organized its site-based funding plan. The concept is important because it signals the boundaries of site councils. Examples of how various costs might be viewed in a given school district are shown in Table 12.1.

The classification scheme is based on certain professional judgments that would change substantially if site-based leadership were conceptualized differently in the target district. For example, the classification scheme assumes that at some point in time district cost–benefit analysis showed efficiencies that justified district-wide oversight of maintenance and transportation programs while personnel decisions are placed under the control of the individual site. Under a different scenario, personnel decisions would remain at the district level, for example, because of collective bargaining agreement language. Likewise, the site council could be given a small transportation budget for field trips and student activities, while day to day transportation functions remained at the district level.

The issue of control is illustrated by utility costs, such as heating, cooling, and lighting in the school building. One view is to place these costs at the district level as uncontrolled overhead costs. A different approach is to rebate back to the school any unspent utility funds as a bonus for energy efficiency and conservation. Energy efficiency then becomes of direct interest to the council and injects a measure of control where none would otherwise be present. In this scenario, the site council might develop an energy monitoring system. The same line of thinking might be applied to school facilities, with the site council analyzing the condition of the facility with primary concern for its instructional adequacy. In this example, the site council should make the district aware of ongoing infrastructure needs as well as maintenance and repair concerns.

Basic and site knowledge takes in a broad scope of legitimate control, and the effectiveness of site-based leadership should be judged by how well the site council holds itself accountable for both knowledge and results. Councils should be trained to give thoughtful answers to the following questions:

- What are our schools becoming?
- What should our schools be doing?
- What are our schools capable of doing?
- What is the effect of money on schools?
- What happens when our schools get more or less money?
- How does school money get tracked?
- What is a fair aid formula, and how does our state funding system compare to to others in terms of equity and adequacy?
- How should we organize for budgeting in our district?
- How is each school in our district funded?
- How do we recruit, select, reward, and retain staff?
- How does due process affect the site council?
- What are instructional budgets?
- What is the role of student activities?
- What is the role of school infrastructure, maintenance, and operations?
- What is accountability?
- Does the site council understand liability?
- Does the school district have a risk management plan?
- What is the school district budget process?
- How do we determine staffing needs?
- What are our compensation policies?
- What is instructional planning?
- How do we budget for instruction?
- What are activity funds?
- How are transportation and food services organized and funded in our district?

Revisiting a Sample School District

From the list above it is clear that school site councils should have significant input into a broad range of budget issues. For example, it is reasonable for each site council to decide how to allocate teaching and nonteaching staff to meet the school's mission, goals, and objectives. One site council might eliminate a vice principal position in exchange for an additional teacher to reduce class size, while another might choose larger classes in exchange for providing an aide in each classroom. A third might hire a guidance counselor to help at-risk students. Similarly, the site council might choose to implement new curricula at the expense of student activities, or it might opt for new cocurricular programs that are carefully justified on the basis of contributing to student outcomes.

The sample school district in Chapter 7 was modeled on this concept. As we created the scenario, we raised a series of questions that now provide both review and a solid rationale for site-based leadership. At the outset, we asked the following questions that should be raised regardless of school district organization. Site councils will find these particularly relevant:

- Who has responsibility for establishing the overall level of expenditure in a school district and school building?
- Who has responsibility for establishing expenditures for each major program or organizational unit?
- Who has responsibility for selection of specific resources within the allotted dollar amounts for each program?
- Who has responsibility for curriculum selection?
- Who has responsibility for initiation of new instructional programs or elimination of current programs?
- Who establishes capital outlay budgets and decides how facilities and equipment are allocated?
- Who has responsibility for establishing salaries and benefits?
- Who hires personnel?
- Who decides which items and amounts will be cut if needed?

These are the structural and operative issues facing school site councils, going to the heart of how budget, staffing, and curriculum are planned and executed. The sample district in Figure 7.6 (see Chapter 7) goes directly to these issues. Our sample school district chose to track instructional budgets using detailed accounting codes to permit accumulation of data by program; decentralize budget tasks; retain some central coordination at the board and director levels; allocate uniform amounts per pupil for instructional program purposes; retain transportation services centrally; allocate discretionary transportation budgets to schools; decentralize some aspects of infrastructure and equipment purchasing; and link expenditures to expected learning outcomes. In effect, Chapter 7 described a model school district that has acted to locate program and budget authority at the school site level while retaining district coordination and control of indirect costs like maintenance and construction for efficiency reasons. School sites, however, are authorized to determine how programs operate—in this particular example, site-based decision making led to a program allocation of approximately $892,000 to local school buildings. Accountability is a central feature of the hypothetical budget, as the fund accounting structure was designed to produce program and expenditure analysis, with all expenditures justified by expected outcomes.

Although considerably more complex than traditional ways of managing schools, site-based leadership funding designs have the potential to better integrate district and school goals into a coherent plan that serves the unique needs of each school site. Our questions earlier in Chapter 7 captured the principles and spirit of site-based leadership, in that a good site plan should have ready answers to the following queries:

- What is the district's overall mission?
- What are the district's goal statements?
- What is my school's overall mission?
- What are my school's goal statements?
- What were the results of the district's environmental scan?
- What were the results of my school's environmental scan?
- Does my school's educational plan reflect these needs?
- How can the site council spend its budget to address these needs?

FINAL COMMENTS

Several comments apply as we end this chapter on site-based leadership. First, the chapter does not blindly advocate site-based leadership. The scope of site-based leadership necessarily varies by school district and even across schools in the same district. At the same time, site-based leadership is not a means by which a local school board can shed its legal and financial responsibility; nor does it allow superintendents to avoid legitimate responsibility for decision making. Rather, site-based leadership is a concept that can improve the efficiency and effectiveness of direct services to students.

As a result, site-based leadership has key elements that should be required of all schools in the modern context. Simply put, why should any legitimate stakeholder be denied a role in the operation of schools? Further, why should any school district seek to retain centralized power when it will likely create resentment among stakeholders, erode public support, and potentially harm student learning? In today's complex social, political, and economic environment, schools and districts cannot afford to exclude stakeholders. The only remaining issue is to what extent site-based leadership should be enacted locally—a decision with powerful consequences because staffing, curriculum, and budgets are the cornerstones of educational productivity and equality of educational opportunity.

POINT–COUNTERPOINT

POINT

The advent of site councils has been of great benefit to schools by opening the doors to parents and the community. These individuals have useful insights into how schools are perceived and misperceived. Their participation in curriculum and budget matters is particularly helpful, as they often have creative program and funding ideas and become strong advocates for the school.

COUNTERPOINT

While the concept behind site councils is laudable, the practical application too often comes up short. Many site councils end up being rightly criticized for elitism, cronyism, favoritism, micromanaging, and basic ineffectiveness relating to their lack of expertise in the conduct of schooling.

- Which of these two opposing views best represents your beliefs about or experiences with site councils and the larger issues underlying their existence?
- If your school district has site councils, how are principals, teachers, and others involved in site council activities? Are their roles similar to or different from those described in this chapter? Describe the similarities or differences.
- If your school district has site councils, how effective are they in your estimation? Explain. How could their functioning be improved?

CASE STUDY

As a newly hired middle school principal, you were aware that your school district has a strong commitment to site-based management. In your hiring interview, you had learned that the state had enacted extensive site-based management requirements for public schools. As the superintendent fleshed out the broad details of the law and the basics of your school district's site-based structure, you gathered a definite sense that site councils were very actively involved in the life of schools in this district. The superintendent indicated that your effectiveness in working with your school's site council would be important to your overall success because the district took democratic leadership principles very seriously.

Shortly after the school year began, you held your first middle school site council meeting. You had met the council members earlier because the hiring process had also included an interview with them. The first council meeting of the year went very well, and you were pleased with how the site council chair had organized and conducted the meeting, engaging members in developing the year's work agenda. At that meeting, the council had agreed to review both the language arts and biological sciences curricula, as well as launching a drive to secure funding for a football weight training facility.

Approximately a week later, the site council chair dropped by your office to chat about the agenda. With the next regular meeting only a few weeks away, he indicated you needed some background in order to understand the dynamics of the site council. As he talked, you became concerned about the information he presented, including his description of the council's perception of the principal's role. He mentioned that several site council members were furious after hearing from a parent that one of the science faculty members had "scoffed" at creationism in her classes. He added that the same council members were also intent on reviewing the language arts curriculum for "inappropriate books." From what you could gather, some site council members believed their role was to approve curriculum content. As the meeting ended, you were uncertain about the chair's position on these matters, but you were certain that you faced a potentially difficult year. On his way out the door, the chair had added that the site council had secured a donor who had agreed to provide $200,000 in matching funds for the proposed athletic weight room.

Below is a set of questions. As you respond, consider your learning throughout this entire book and apply your knowledge and experiences to the situation:

- What is your reaction to the information presented by the site council chair?
- What are the fundamental issues in this case study that concern you? Why?
- How will you approach working with the site council—both in terms of the immediate situation and over the school year?

PORTFOLIO EXERCISES

- Write a reflection on how leadership is carried out in your school district. Who holds power and in what areas? If your reflection identifies evidence of site-based leadership, analyze how this is structured: What are its strengths and weaknesses?

- If your state or school district uses school site councils, research how councils came to exist, their purpose, scope of authority, and responsibilities. Examine relevant state statutes and local school board policies. Interview a principal about the duties of the site council and its operation. Ask others about their perceptions of the site council's effectiveness, e.g., teachers, administrators, and other staff.

- Volunteer to serve on a school site council. Alternatively, ask permission to attend and observe site council meetings.

WEB RESOURCES

American Association of School Administrators, www.aasa.org
American Federation of Teachers, www.aft.org
Association of School Business Officials International, www.asbointl.org
Council of Chief State School Officers, www.ccsso.org

National Association of Elementary School Principals, www.naesp.org

National Association of Secondary School Principals, www.nassp.org

National Center for Education Statistics, U.S. Department of Education, www.nces.ed.gov

National Education Association, www.nea.org

National School Boards Association, www.nsba.org

RECOMMENDED READING

Coleman, Andrew. "Toward a Blended Model of Leadership for School-Based Collaboration." *Educational Management, Administration, and Leadership* 39, no.3 (2011): 296–316.

Crampton, Faith E., and Randall S. Vesely. "Resource Allocation Issues for Educational Leaders." In *Handbook for Excellence in School Leadership*, 4th ed. Edited by Stuart C. Smith and Philip K. Piele, 401–427. Thousand Oaks, CA: Corwin Press, 2006.

Duffy, Frances M. *Power, Politics, and Ethics in School Districts: Dynamic Leadership for Systemic Change*. Lanham, MD: Rowman and Littlefield, 2005.

Education Commission of the States. "Recent State Policies/Activities: Governance—Site-Based Management." www.ecs.org/ecs/ecscat.nsf/WebTopicView?OpenView&count=-1&Restrict ToCategory=Governance—Site-Based+Management.

Epstein, Noel, Ed. *Who's in Charge Here: The Tangled Web of School Governance and Policy*. Washington, DC: Brookings Institution Press, 2004.

Kedro, James M. *Aligning Resources for Student Outcomes: School-Based Steps to Success*. Lanham, MD: Rowman and Littlefield, 2004.

Leithwood, Kenneth, Karen Seashore Louis, Stephen Anderson, and Kyla Wahlstrom. *Review of Research: How Leadership Influences Student Learning*. Minneapolis: Center for Applied Research and Educational Improvement, University of Minnesota, 2004.

Ouchi, William G. "Power to the Principals: Decentralization in Three Large School Districts." *Organization Science* 17(March/April 2006): 298–307.

REL West. *School-Based Budgeting and Management*. San Francisco, CA: WestEd, August 2009.

Walker, Elaine W. "The Politics of School-Based Management: Understanding the Process of Devolving Authority in Urban School Districts." *Education Policy Analysis Archives* 10 (August 4, 2002). epaa.asu.edu/epaa/v10n33.html.

World Bank. *What Is School-Based Management?* Washington, DC: World Bank Education, Human Development Network, November 2007.

World Bank. *What Do We Know about School-Based Management?* Washington, DC: World Bank Education, Human Development Network, November 2007.

CHAPTER 13

The Future of School Funding

THE CHALLENGE

Whatever it is that money may be thought to contribute to the education of children, that commodity is something highly prized by those who enjoy the greatest measure of it. If money is inadequate to improve education, the residents of poor districts should at least have an equal opportunity to be disappointed by its failure.

Coons, Clune, and Sugarman (1970)[1]

CHAPTER DRIVERS

Please reflect upon the following questions as you read this chapter:

- What are the lessons that you have drawn from this book?
- What are the future issues in school funding?

THE BIG PICTURE

The overarching goal of this textbook has been to provide aspiring and practicing school leaders with a broad contextual overview of money and schools. Funding for education is a complex topic, even though we have tried to make it as straightforward as possible. Although we introduced relevant concepts at considerable depth, we know that we have merely provided a foundation for the expertise that comes only with extended study

---

1 John E. Coons, William H. Clune III, and Stephen D. Sugarman, *Private Wealth and Public Education* (Cambridge, MA: The Belknap Press of Harvard University Press, 1970), 30.

and professional experience. Yet, it is precisely that point which makes this book relevant for our audiences. By seeing the big picture of school money, education leaders are better prepared to be effective decision makers in their schools and districts.

As we close this book, we invite readers to reflect on lessons learned and think about the future. Reflection anchors our understanding of how the many pieces of school funding fit together, and an eye to the future prepares us to deal with changes that continue to dominate the educational landscape. As traditional roles shift and as lines of authority, power, and influence become increasingly blurred, the future holds both promise and peril.

WHAT ARE THE ISSUES?

A fundamental theme throughout this book is that schools are facing a crisis of unequaled proportion that encompasses a complex mosaic of factors. Schools and society are changing rapidly, with profound implications for the future. On the surface, the problem seems simple in that equal educational opportunity must be provided to every child, but in reality the problem is vexing because resolving it requires agreement on diverse goals and substantial new investment of resources or dramatic reallocation of existing funds—with the latter having unknown and unforeseeable consequences for school funding, students, and society. Central to such decisions are the aims of schooling and the role of equity, adequacy, efficiency, and accountability. In addition, all of these issues are affected by larger concerns like the fiscal health of the economy and the ongoing debate as to the extent that provision of equal educational opportunity depends on money. The future of school funding will be framed by these debates, and without the full engagement of all education stakeholders—administrators, school boards, teachers, parents, and community members—it could be bleak.

Lessons from This Book

The social, political, and economic context of education discussed in Chapter 1 provided a sobering lesson. In the United States, schools are a source of both cynicism and optimism. Critics of public education point out that U.S. students continue to lag behind peers in developed, as well as some developing, nations on measures of academic achievement on international tests. At the same time, Americans overall continue to the view education as an engine for economic mobility and prosperity, even though recent research evidences that economic mobility is now lower in the United States than in many other developed countries,[2] and disparities in income in the United States between the rich and the poor have reached historic highs, even as the middle class shrinks. A central lesson of this chapter is that equality of educational opportunity costs money

---

2 Raj Chetty, Nathaniel Hendren, Patrick Kline, Emmanuel Saez, and Nicholas Turner, "Is the United States Still a Land of Opportunity? Recent Trends in Intergenerational Mobility," NBER working paper series, Working Paper 19844 (Cambridge, MA: National Bureau of Economic Research, January 2014), www.equality-of-opportunity.org.

while at the same time finite resources dictate that education leaders often have to make hard choices.

Chapter 2 transitions to education policymaking, exploring the role of education as both an economic and social good. Education can be viewed as an investment in human capital, and research time and again has supported this investment because of the returns to the individual and society. This chapter also chronicled the history of school governance in the United States, making evident that today's education system is rooted in the history and richness of U.S. democracy. Part of that history is also the evolution of local, state, and federal systems of taxation, from which public education draws fiscal support. The final portion of the chapter traces the quest for adequate and equitable school funding through federal and state courts, noting that the quest continues. The struggle over values in education was again apparent in this chapter, as disagreements over the worth of education and who should pay for schools continue to play out in the education policy arena.

In Chapter 3, we discussed basic funding sources and structures. We noted that while taxes have never been popular, over time extensive federal, state, and local tax systems have nonetheless developed, from which schools derive their revenues. We explored the revenue structures at each of these levels and their relative contributions to education funding. Although the federal share of public education revenues is not insignificant, it plays a minor role with states and local school districts shouldering around 90%. We noted that each state's school funding system was the product of its unique political, social, and economic history. The lessons learned from this chapter were twofold. First, taxes are the product of political environments where education competes with other worthy public services for limited resources. Second, although state aid formulas have the potential to provide equity and adequacy in school funding at the district level, some states have been more successful than others in achieving this goal. Additionally, school finance litigation has often provided the impetus for states to move closer to those goals.

Chapter 4 opened Part II, "Operationalizing School Money," by moving from a broad policy perspective into a more detailed analysis of budgeting in schools by examining fiscal accountability and professionalism. This chapter encouraged an appreciation of the public trust placed in education leaders as fiscal stewards, emphasizing the fiduciary responsibilities of school administrators and staff and identifying how school revenues and expenditures are structured. Admittedly, these are challenging topics to present in brief form, but the overarching message was that school leaders need at least a basic knowledge of the types of money received by schools, how money can be spent, and how public funds are guarded against error, misuse, and fraud.

Chapter 5 focused on budget planning. The first part of the chapter discussed ways to organize for budgeting, including common approaches to budgeting, while the second half explored budget construction. Implicit were two key arguments. First, the central purpose of budgeting is to implement equal educational opportunity by converting dollars into programmatic priorities. Second, budgets should be viewed as the principal planning system by which political and legal approval is secured for providing education to children; that is, budgets are more than an accounting tool. Rather, they are a tool for making informed educational decisions.

We next turned to analyzing the major cost determinants of budgets. In Chapter 6, we looked at the relationship of school money to the personnel function, which represents a major portion of school budgets. Pragmatic concerns, such as determining staff needs, recruitment, and selection were addressed along with compensation and costing out salary proposals. Importantly, negotiations, due process, and alternative reward systems were also considered. With personnel-related expenses consuming on average 80% of a school budget, this chapter made clear that it is critical for school leaders to be knowledgeable about personnel budgets.

Chapter 7 moved to the heart of school budgeting by exploring instructional costs. This chapter focused on organizational options, including site-based management, as well as instructional budget concepts and elements. Much time was devoted to looking at district and school-based budgeting, including an introduction to the role of site-based leadership. Two key lessons emerged. First, budgeting for instruction is the most important activity in schools because it enables teaching and learning to occur. Second, instructional budgets should reflect the mission and goals of the district and individual school.

Chapter 8 turned to budgeting for student activities, an area whose importance in schools should not be underestimated. These activities are integral to students becoming well-rounded individuals. For school leaders, who often have oversight of student activity funds, many opportunities and pitfalls exist in managing this important dimension of school life. This chapter focused on identifying the many activity fund accounts in a typical school district, distinguishing between student and district activity funds, and on appropriate handling of money associated with activity funds at the individual school level. Nonactivity funds, like petty cash, were also discussed with cautions to school leaders to develop rigorous and consistent disbursement and accounting procedures.

Chapter 9 focused on budgeting for school infrastructure. First, the chapter established that the physical environment of schools is a critical factor in student success. At the same time, it is severely underfunded. Few federal resources are available. State aid varies tremendously, with some states providing no aid at all. In sum, the quality of school infrastructure is largely a matter of school district wealth, except in states that have experienced successful litigation. The chapter then presented the methods available to school districts to finance major school infrastructure projects, as well as the planning process. Finally, effective maintenance and operations practices to support a school district's infrastructure by keeping it in a condition that supports teaching and learning were surveyed.

In Chapter 10, transportation and food service were presented as essential programs that support the educational process. While the instructional mission of schools rightly receives great attention, it is also true that equality of educational opportunity is obstructed when children are hungry or deprived of the means by which to attend school. Transportation costs vary dramatically by type of district depending upon its size and student population. Overall, school districts depend upon state and local revenues to fund transportation. On the other hand, federal funding provides the bulk of revenue for school meals, but it is tightly regulated. However, the federal government funds free and reduced-price meals for students in poverty—a major contribution to equal education opportunity. For school leaders, both transportation and food service require prudent fiscal management as well as attention to statutory and regulatory requirements.

In Chapter 11, our journey moved to legal liability and risk management in school settings. The purpose of the chapter was to inform school leaders of broad liability principles and to encourage careful planning for risk management. Central to the chapter was the concept that educational leaders need to understand the sources of authority enjoyed by schools; the nature and limits of immunity; the problems encountered when laws and rights are violated; and the loss of discretionary revenue resulting from liability-related issues. The overriding lesson was caution in all matters because the law and schools are constant companions.

Chapter 12 revisited the topic of site-based leadership, taking highlights from each previous chapter to create a unified picture. A theme of this textbook has been that school leaders, along with staff, parents, and community members must be empowered to participate in budgetary decisions and equipped with the skills to effect positive change through fiscal resource allocation. To meet that goal, the chapter provided a detailed framework for implementing site-based leadership, beginning with the district level decision of which decisions and responsibilities to delegate, followed by creation of an implementation plan, and selection and training of a diverse and inclusive school site council, comprised of the principal, staff, parents, and community members.

The Future of School Funding

The unsettled and evolving nature of society and schools promises a full slate of issues and challenges into the foreseeable future. Major public debate is longstanding on these, although the intensity is increasing. The list is familiar—the politics of money; the impact of the economy on schools; the enhancement of equity, adequacy, accountability, and efficiency in school funding; and the social and economic consequences of school choice. Although these issues appear in previous chapters, a final look with an eye to the future of school funding provides appropriate closure to this book.

The Politics of Money

Democracy and capitalism, at times, seems an odd pairing with inevitable tensions, for example, between profit and the public good. Without a counterweight, unbridled capitalism results in a simple equation of money equals power—including the power to purchase privilege and influence.

The United States has long committed to individual initiative and personal freedom. The strength of these often conflicting national goals has experienced ebb and flow, as a collective social conscience has predominated at times, and the free market has triumphed at others. Indeed, we learned early in this book that the current public school system was created in the mid-19th century as the "common schools" movement to ensure that the poor and immigrants had access to a basic education. Many of the current social programs we take for granted today were born out of the poverty and human suffering of the Great Depression in the 1930s while others arose from the social and political activism of the 1960s. Trickle-down economics and government downsizing during the 1980s and early 1990s represented the opposite side of the coin. Then, the first decade of the new millennium brought unprecedented global economic challenges and the worst economic recession since the 1930s.

Many factors go into the politics of money, but it is an undeniable reality that public school funding is dependent on the conscience and good will of individuals and government, often with conflicting priorities. Scarcity and self-interest have been in evidence for the last few decades, beginning with tax relief initiatives such as Proposition 13 in California in 1978 that gutted funding for public schools and extending to more recent efforts at the state and federal levels to eliminate or scale back social programs that historically have provided an economic safety net for our most vulnerable citizens. The roaring economy of the 1990s did little to offset this trend. Instead, many states returned revenue surpluses to individuals and provided tax breaks to the private sector. Similarly, the sweeping education reforms of the federal No Child Left Behind Act (NCLB) placed new demands on schools for accountability as measured by high stakes testing, imposing sanctions on states and school districts whose schools failed to make "adequate yearly progress," up to and including requiring the provision of school choice options for students in affected schools. Although some new federal funding accompanied NCLB, many states and school districts protested it was insufficient and amounted, in large part, to an unfunded mandate. The combination of these events with current economic conditions and ongoing demands for efficiency and accountability by fiscal conservatives does not inspire optimism that public schools will receive much in the way of increased funding in the near future.

The Economy

The politics of money are interwoven with the condition of the economy. School funding is inextricably tied to the health of the economy at local, state, federal, and global levels. Despite historic growth in school revenue over time, the impact of the economy on schools can be dramatic, as seen in many states where in recent years taxpayer attitudes and shifting economic fortunes have led to severe state-imposed funding cuts to public education. As background, the economic boom of the 1970s was followed with losses for schools during tight budgets of the 1980s, and the mindset of reductionism carried into the prosperous 1990s as Congress and individual states continued to scale back funding despite a strong economy and record surpluses. Then, the aftermath 2007–2009 economic recession had dire consequences for schools, with economic instability following some states into the present—a condition made worse in some cases by state structural deficits, some of which resulted from the short-sighted tax breaks in the boom years of the 1990s. Clearly, the state of the economy drives not only tax revenues but also public and political attitudes about spending on education.

Equity, Adequacy, Efficiency, and Accountability

The concepts of equity, adequacy, accountability, and efficiency reflect longstanding but sometimes conflicting social, fiscal, and political goals in the United States, with the result being that our form of government reflects a perpetual tension between social conscience and individual freedom. The tension is apparent in a nation that is still uncomfortable with its history of social inequality, trying at times to aggressively use government to remedy past injustice and at other times ignoring its unsavory past. Desegregation of schools in the 1950s; the War on Poverty of the 1960s; the bitter legal battles in the 1970s over school funding; the rise of racial quotas and preferences in the workforce in the 1980s; and then weakening of affirmative action. The same period has been characterized by calls for accountability and efficiency, as school reform has swept the country following reports of dismal achievement, and as advocates of fiscal austerity have harshly criticized government expenditure on public education as well as a broad range of social services, often referred to as the social safety net. The legacy of such conflict finds school districts starved for adequate resources.

The result has been a conflicted society, sometimes with perplexing outcomes. For example, the last 40 years produced U.S. Supreme Court decisions barring entanglement of church and state in schools, only to see those rulings overturned or weakened in recent years for example, by allowing taxpayer-funded vouchers for students attending private, religious schools. Likewise, protracted litigation upheld racial preferences in college admissions, with those decisions also assaulted with sizable success in very recent years. School funding litigation has followed the same uncertain path of victories and reversals, and the psychology of change and unrest has provided fertile ground for critics decrying the lack of student achievement in public schools and leading many states to enact stringent standards, including financial sanctions against low-achieving schools. As increasingly extreme ideological and advocacy groups have rallied around one or more of these values, divisive political and social strife and gridlock have resulted—often to the detriment of children. A lessening of these forces in the near future seems unlikely. Schools are often caught in the middle because they cannot fully satisfy one constituency without offending another.

School Choice

An outgrowth of issues raised here has been the expansion of school choice. School choice takes many forms, such as interdistrict and intradistrict[3] choice—forms of public school choice that have quietly existed for many decades in a number of states.[4] In 1991, a new form of public school choice emerged with the creation of charter schools by statute in Minnesota.[5] By 2012, 42 states and the District of Columbia also had charter school laws.[6] The original vision of charter schools was as incubators of educational innovation that, once proven effective in this microcosm, could be disseminated more broadly to traditional public schools. In reality, charter schools have served many purposes, in large part due to differences in state statutes. In 2012, charter schools enrolled 2.1 million students, equivalent to 4.2% of all public school students.[7]

---

3 Intradistrict school choice today also includes magnet schools, although magnet schools originally emerged in the 1960s to encourage voluntary desegregation.

4 Interdistrict and intradistrict public school choice are also often referred to as "open enrollment."

5 Grace Kena, Susan Aud, Frank Johnson, Xiaolei Wang, Jijun Zhang, Amy Rathbun, Sidney Wilkinson-Flicker, and Paul Kristapovich, *The Condition of Education 2014* (Washington, DC: U.S. Department of Education, National Center for Education Statistics, 2014), 38. http://nces.ed.gov/pubs2014/2014083.pdf.

6 Ibid.

7 Ibid., 38–39.

The most controversial form of school choice remains private school choice in the form of vouchers that give public tax money to private and religious schools. Unlike supporters of other forms of school choice, voucher advocates are comprised largely of individuals and groups from opposite ends of the socioeconomic spectrum; for example, some poor urban parents of color have supported vouchers as a lifeboat that will save their children from what they perceive to be the sinking ship of failed urban public schools. At the opposite end of that spectrum are wealthy white conservatives who see public schools as a failed monopoly; they believe that in a capitalistic society the "market" always works better and more cheaply than government. Other core advocates of vouchers have been Christian conservatives and others who prefer a faith-based education for their children. All of these groups share an interest in the politics of money. If money were no object, poor urban parents would move to more affluent communities with high achieving, state of the art schools. Wealthy white conservatives who support vouchers believe that dismantling what they view as an inefficient government monopoly would reduce the cost of education, improve education for poorly served students, and provide tax relief for individual taxpayers. Those with preferences for a faith-based education often take the position that their tax dollars have already paid for schools, and so having to pay tuition to send their children to a private, religious school constitutes "double taxation."

More radical forms of school choice, like vouchers, have become a flashpoint in the politics of schools and incorporated elements of equity, adequacy, accountability, and efficiency into a context that bears heavily on future funding for public schools. Research in this area must be viewed with caution as it is sometimes biased by personal ideology, conservative and liberal, rather than an objective analyses of solid data. To further complicate matters, federal and state courts have not been unanimous in their views of voucher plans.[8] As always, the language of federal and state constitutions, as well as state law, powerfully affects the outcome of such litigation. For example, the U.S. Supreme Court upheld the Cleveland voucher program in 2002,[9] while the Florida Supreme Court struck down a statewide voucher program in 2006.[10] Less controversial forms of private school choice, such as tax credits and tax deductions for private school tuition, used in a handful of states, have for the most part survived court scrutiny.[11] However, these plans have been subject to the criticism that they primarily benefit middle and upper income families because parents usually must pay their child's tuition upfront and then wait several months to file for the tax credit or tax deduction. For many low income parents, this is an insurmountable barrier. Furthermore, the poorest of families may not be required to file a tax return and hence are unlikely to benefit from tuition tax credits.

---

8 Lenford C. Sutton and Richard A. King, "School Vouchers in a Climate of Political Change," *Journal of Education Finance* 36 (Winter 2011): 244–267.

9 *Zelman v. Simmons-Harris*, 536 U.S. 639 (2002).

10 *Bush v. Holmes*, 919 So. 2d 392 (Fla. 2006).

11 Luis A. Huerta and Chad d'Entremont, "Education Tax Credits in a Post-*Zelman* Era: Legal, Political and Policy Alternatives to Vouchers?" (New York: Center for the Study of Privatization in Education, Teachers College-Columbia, 2006), www.ncspe.org/publications_files/test_2.pdf.

There is no evidence to suggest any of the forms of educational choice discussed here will fade away. In fact, new forms of educational choice continue to emerge, like virtual or "cyber" schools, some of which have been established through existing charter school or open enrollment laws.[12] In addition, private virtual schools are readily available. Thus far, virtual schools have had broad appeal to parents who previously home-schooled their children. However, funding related to virtual schools has become contentious in some states and has even led to litigation, as in Pennsylvania and Wisconsin. A frequent source of dispute is that the state aid received by virtual schools is equal to that received by schools housed in actual buildings requiring maintenance and upkeep, while virtual schools do not incur similar expenses. Further, the addition of previously home-schooled students to public school rolls via virtual schools represents a new and largely unforeseen expense to many state school aid systems.

It is likely that the various forms of public and private school choice will remain for the forseeable future. The upshot is that elementary and secondary education is becoming a consumer marketplace, with public schools being forced to join in the competition for enrollment-driven funding with private religious and nonsectarian schools as well as for-profit entities.

A FINAL WORD

The purpose of this chapter was to present a realistic assessment of the challenges facing the funding of public education. For over 150 years, public education has been a cornerstone of economic opportunity and upward mobility in the United States. However, the nation is at a crossroads. With rising social and economic inequality, those on both ends of the political spectrum, conservative and liberal, have raised questions about the continued investment of tax revenues in a public education system that continues to trail other developed countries in academic achievement. Not only is public education enmeshed in a complex social, economic, and political environment, it also finds itself squarely in the middle of a bitter partisan divide with regard to the role of government. There are no simple solutions.

Education needs great leaders who understand the relationship between money and equal educational opportunity, and who possess the knowledge and expertise to deploy those resources for the benefit of all children. Schools need leaders who promote the success of all students by understanding, responding to, and influencing the larger political, social, economic, legal, and cultural context in which education is embedded. In other words, money and leadership matter.

---

12 Justin C. Ortagus, Luke J. Stedrak, and R. Craig Wood, "The Funding of Virtual Schools in Public Elementary and Secondary Education," *Educational Considerations* 39 (Spring 2012): 44–54.

POINT–COUNTERPOINT

POINT

A substantial body of research demonstrates that students in poverty, as well as other students commonly defined as at risk of academic failure, need greater resources to be academically successful. It is clearly a matter of equity and equality of educational opportunity that states provide the additional funding for these students. If these children are not successful, i.e., drop out of school, they become a lifetime tax burden on the rest of society given their greater unemployability and use of social services and the criminal justice system.

COUNTERPOINT

The federal government already provides significant funding for poor students as well as others categorized as "at-risk," e.g., funding for special education and English language learners as well as free and reduced-price breakfast and lunch. In addition, almost every state also provides some extra funding for these students. With all these "special" aids, it is the average student who is shortchanged by being placed in larger classes with little individual attention. The real problem is that schools and school districts are not using their funding efficiently.

- Given your experience and the readings in this text, which position seems more accurate? Why?
- In your view, can schools provide equal educational opportunity to all students and still be efficient? Explain.

CASE STUDY

At the start of your second year as an urban school superintendent, you were shocked to read this morning's local headline, "Parental Satisfaction with Local Schools at All Time Low." A nationally known conservative policy think-tank had conducted a survey of parents in your school district, unbeknownst to you and the school board, and had released the highly critical report to the media. One of the major areas of discontent, according to the news account, was what parents perceived as arbitrary assignment of their children to schools. If the media had accurately reported parental attitudes, parents were demanding not only to choose their children's school but also to have a wider array of choices, like specialty schools, alternative schools, and even virtual schools.

While you would not have welcomed the news at any point, you were especially concerned about the timing of negative press. The headline had hit just as you were in the midst of your contract renewal with the board, and the combination of these factors was unsettling because this was your first contract renewal, and you knew there were tensions within the board about your performance. For example, this year's student test scores, while showing some improvement, were not as high as hoped for, and, as a result, several schools in the district were facing state and federal sanctions—unwelcome news that had already received unflattering local media coverage. To make matters worse, the state legislature was now considering a bill to permit vouchers in all urban school districts in the state, which you feared could skim off the best and brightest students (along with their engaged parents) and their attendant funding, leaving your district to educate an increasingly high-cost and challenging student body.

Immediately upon arriving at your office this morning, you called an emergency administrative cabinet meeting. You announced that you were creating a task force to draft a decisive response to the study, with the charge to develop low or no-cost options that would satisfy parental demands. You indicated that that the task force would need to find ways around the financial barriers most urban school districts, including yours, typically face—e.g., a budget able to cover only the bare necessities of instruction and a long list of problems like much needed maintenance and repairs. As you summed up the charge, you emphasized the need for thinking outside the box by saying that the district needs to consider some significant restructuring to meet these demands because reallocating resources was the primary way out of this situation.

Because the headlines and your contract negotiations were hitting simultaneously, you announced that you would personally chair the task force and that you would select about a dozen individuals to serve with you. As you closed the meeting, you indicated that some members of your administrative cabinet would be appointed to the task force and that a rigorous meeting schedule would follow because you expected to form a response in three months or less. Back in your office, you wondered about the risk inherent to your actions, but under the circumstances you knew you needed to be seen as a proactive problem-solver.

Following is a set of questions. As you respond, consider your learning throughout this book and apply your new knowledge to the situation.

- Whom will you select to join you on this task force? Explain your rationale.
- Brainstorm the options you might present in your final report. Detail the costs, if any, of each option as well as the potential educational benefits.
- In addition to the task force, are there other responses or initiatives the school district might undertake to empower parents?
- Are there any assumptions or beliefs in this case study that give you cause for concern? If so, why?

PORTFOLIO EXERCISES

- Identify three major educational issues at national or state levels and provide your rationale for selecting them. Discuss how funding is associated with each and indicate whether you believe (based on your readings here and other research) that sufficient funding is available. Discuss how greater funding might be secured. Be as specific as possible, e.g., would additional funding come from local, state, or federal levels, grants, private funding, or some combination?

- Prepare a report on education policy issues in your state such as the political environment for school funding, the condition of the state economy, the impact of school choice, and demands for equity, adequacy, efficiency, and accountability. Use resources such as news articles and publications of local or state policy think tanks and stakeholder groups like teacher unions, taxpayer associations, and community organizations.

WEB RESOURCES

American Legislative Exchange Council, www.alec.org

Brown Center on Education Policy at the Brookings Institution, www.brookings.edu/brown.aspx

The Cato Institute, www.cato.org

Center on Budget and Policy Priorities, www.cbpp.org

Center on Education Policy, www.cep-dc.org

Council of the Great City Schools, www.cgcs.org

Council of State Governments, www.csg.org

Economic Policy Institute, www.epi.org

Education Commission of the States, www.ecs.org

Education Next, www.educationnext.org

Education Policy Analysis Archives, www.epaa.asu.edu

Heritage Foundation, www.heritage.org

Manhattan Institute for Policy Research, www.manhattan-institute.org

National Center for the Study of Privatization in Education, www.ncspe.org

National Conference of State Legislatures, www.ncsl.org

National Governors Association, www.nga.org

The Program on Education Policy and Governance at Harvard University, www.ksg.harvard.edu/pepg

The Urban Institute, www.urban.org

U.S. Government Accountability Office, www.gao.gov

RECOMMENDED READING

American Federation of Teachers. *Do Charter Schools Measure Up? The Charter School Experiment after 10 Years.*Washington, DC: July 2002. http://criticaltep.files.wordpress.com/2010/01/charterreport02.pdf.

Anyon, Jean. *Radical Possibilities: Public Policy, Urban Education, and the New Social Movement.* New York: Routledge, 2005.

Callahan, Raymond. *Education and the Cult of Efficiency: A Study of the Social Forces that Have Shaped the Administration of Public Schools.* Chicago: University of Chicago Press, 1962.

Crampton, Faith E., Ed. "Education Finance Issues of National Importance in the 21st Century." A special issue of *Educational Considerations* 36 (Fall 2000). http://coe.ksu.edu/ed considerations/download/EdConsF00toc.pdf.

Friedman, Milton. "The Role of Government in Education." In *Economics and the Public Interest,* edited by Robert A. Solo, 123–144. New Brunswick, NJ: Rutgers University Press, 1955.

Glass, Gene V. "The Realities of K-12 Virtual Education." Boulder, CO and Tempe, AZ: Education and the Public Interest Center, Education Policy Research Unit, 2009. http://nepc.colorado.edu/files/PB-Glass-VIRTUAL.pdf.

Grubb, W. Norton. *The Money Myth: School Resources, Outcomes, and Equity.* New York: Russell Sage Foundation, 2009.

Huerta, Luis A., and Chad d'Entremont. "Education Tax Credits in a Post-*Zelman* Era: Legal, Political and Policy Alternatives to Vouchers?" New York: Center for the Study of Privatization in Education, Teachers College–Columbia, 2006. www.ncspe.org/publications_files/test_2.pdf.

Levin, Henry M., and Patrick J. McEwan, Eds. *Cost-Effectiveness and Educational Policy.* Annual Yearbook of the American Education Finance Association (Larchmont, NY: Eye on Education, 2002).

Nelson, F. Howard, Bella Rosenberg, and Nancy Van Meter. *Charter School Achievement on the 2003 National Assessment of Educational Progress.* Washington, DC: American Federation of Teachers, 2004. http://nepc.colorado.edu/files/EPRU-0408–63-OWI%5B1%5D.pdf.

Ortagus, Justin C., Luke J. Stedrak, and R. Craig Wood. "The Funding of Virtual Schools in Public Elementary and Secondary Education." *Educational Considerations* 39 (Spring, 2012): 44–54.

Ravitch, Diane. *The Death and Life of the Great American School System: How Testing and Choice Are Undermining Education.* New York: Basic Books, 2010.

Ravitch, Diane. *Reign of Error: The Hoax of the Privatization Movement and the Danger to America's Public Schools.* New York: Alfred A. Knopf, 2013.

Sutton, Lenford C., and Richard A. King. "School Vouchers in a Climate of Political Change." *Journal of Education Finance* 36 (Winter, 2011): 244–267.

Wise, Arthur E. *Rich Schools, Poor Schools: The Promise of Equal Educational Opportunity.* Chicago: University of Chicago Press, 1968.

Index